© Author and the Publisher
Published by: Ω Irene Publishing
Sparsnäs 1010
66891 Ed
Sweden
irene.publishing@gmail.com
www.irenepublishing.com
First Edition 2015

Cover photo: Teddy bears in parachutes
landing in Belarus in support for
human rights July 2012. Photo reprinted
with permission from Studio Total.

ISBN 978-91-88061-01-0

Humorous Political Stunts
Nonviolent Public Challenges to Power

UNIVERSITY OF WOLLONGONG

Humorous Political Stunts

Nonviolent Public Challenges to Power

A thesis submitted in fulfilment of the
requirements for the award of the degree

Doctor of Philosophy (PhD)
from

UNIVERSITY OF WOLLONGONG,
AUSTRALIA

by

Majken Jul Sørensen, MA

School of Humanities and Social Inquiry

Approved November 2014

Thesis Certification

I, Majken Jul Sørensen, declare that this thesis, submitted in fulfilment of the requirements for the award of Doctor of Philosophy, in the School of Humanities and Social Inquiry, University of Wollongong, Australia, is wholly my own work unless otherwise referenced or acknowledged. The document has not been submitted for qualifications at any other academic institution.

Majken Jul Sørensen

28 August 2014

Publications in support of this thesis

Sørensen, Majken Jul. "Humor as a Serious Strategy of Nonviolent Resistance to Oppression." *Peace & Change* 33, no. 2 (2008): 167-90.

Sørensen, Majken Jul. "Humorous Political Stunts: Speaking 'Truth' to Power?". *European Journal of Humour Research* 1, no. 2 (2013).

Sørensen, Majken Jul, and Brian Martin. "The Dilemma Action: Analysis of an Activist Technique." *Peace & Change* 39 no. 1 (2014): 73-100.

Sørensen, Majken Jul "Radical Clowning - Challenging Militarism through Play and Otherness" *HUMOR: International Journal of Humor Research (in press)*.

A small part of the text in chapters 3,4,6 and 7 is a slightly modified version of some of the text that appeared in these articles.

For Howard Clark

Abbreviated table of contents

Contents

Chapter 4: Radical clowning as humorous political activism 260

List of abbreviations and organisations

CIRCA: *See* Clandestine Insurgent Rebel Clown Army.

Clandestine Insurgent Rebel Clown Army: Clown group originating in Britain that has inspired many activist groups.

The Chaser team: Australian comedy team, responsible for the APEC stunt in Sydney in 2007 among many other things.

FMK: Folkereisning Mot Krig, Norwegian pacifist peace organisation originating in 1937.

FMV: Försvarets materielverk (Swedish Defence Materiel Administration), operates NEAT/Vidsel Test Range.

John Howard Ladies' Auxiliary Fan Club: Australian group originating in 2004 to challenge Australia's conservative prime minister from 1996 to 2007, John Howard.

Kampanjen Mot Verneplikt: (The Campaign Against Conscription) Scandinavian network originating in 1981, primarily concerned with the conditions of total resisters.

KMV: *See* Kampanjen Mot Verneplikt.

Netwerk Vlaanderen: Belgian network concerned with responsible banking. Organised the ACE bank stunt and the demining action against AXA bank.

NEAT: *See* Vidsel Test Range.

Ofog: Swedish anti-militarist network originating in 2002. The name roughly translates into "mischief".

Orange Alternative: Polish organisation active in the 1980's, among many happenings responsible for bringing elves to life on Children's day in 1987.

Otpor: Serbian network originating in 1998, responsible for the Dinar za Smenu action among many other stunts.

1

S.I.N: Samvittighetsfanger I Norge (Prisoners of Conscience in Norway). Loose network that cooperated with Kampanjen Mot Verneplikt.

Solvognen: Danish experimental theatre group which organised the Santa action in Copenhagen 1974.

Studio Total: Swedish PR company which organised the dropping of teddy bears over Belarus in 2012.

Vidsel Test Range: Europe's largest overland military test site, located in the north of Sweden. Administered by the Swedish Defence Materiel Administration (FMV). Formerly known as NEAT, North European Aerospace Test range.

Voina: Russian art collective, responsible for painting a giant penis on Liteiny Bridge in St. Petersburg in 2010.

Yes Men: US activist group specialising in "identity correction" and responsible for impersonating representatives of Dow Chemicals and the World Trade Organisation among many other stunts.

Note on translations

All translations of quotes, article titles, concepts etc. originally appearing in Danish, Swedish and Norwegian are done by me.

Abstract

Humour and seriousness are frequently posed as opposites both in academia and everyday language. However, some nonviolent actions are both humorous and serious and living proof that the dichotomy misses an important type of humour. These *humorous political stunts* publicly challenge dominant discourses and powerful institutions and people in five distinct ways. 1. *Supportive stunts* are framed as ostensible attempts to help, celebrate and protect from harm. 2. *Corrective stunts* present an alternative version of dominant discourses by hijacking the identity or message of people, companies and institutions. 3. *Naïve stunts* disguise their critique behind a pretended innocence, and 4. *absurd stunts* defy all claims to truth and rationality. In 5. *provocative stunts* the pranksters transcend power by appearing not to care about the consequences of infuriating the powerful. The particular dynamics of these five strategies are explored through 15 short examples covering everything from struggles against neoliberalism and controversial bank investments to dictatorships. A *theatre metaphor* further illustrates how humorous political stunts can be analysed.

The nuances about relations of power and humour uncovered by this typology illustrate why it is inadequate to discuss whether humour should be considered subversive or a vent for frustration as has been debated within humour studies for decades. Instead the interesting question is *what role* humour can play in facilitating resistance, since political humour is so diverse and takes place in such different contexts that it is misleading to evaluate its impact as if it is all the same. Two in-depth case studies are the basis for the further exploration of humour and nonviolent action. Inspired by participatory action research methodology, the study has utilised archival material, media reports, interviews, workshops, and participant observation to document and analyse the use of humour by the groups Ofog and KMV.

3

Ofog is a Swedish anti-militarist network working on issues related to the arms industry, military recruitment and military test sites. Ofog activists have found the use of humour to be a positive way to reach out to media, passers-by and potential new activists. Even more important is humorous political stunts' contribution to the *discursive guerrilla war* waged by activists. Power does not just manifest itself in brutal repression and exploitation, but also in dominant discourses about what is true, right and just. In this struggle, humorous incongruity can deconstruct patterns of domination through the use of exposure, exaggeration, parody and irony among many other techniques.

Kampanjen Mot Verneplikt, KMV, was a Scandinavian campaign against conscription active in the 1980s. Here the focus is the work for improving the conditions for Norwegian total resisters who refused both military and alternative service. KMV pursued different strategies in its work, one of which was to create a spectacle around court hearings and imprisonments, including several humorous political stunts. Together with the legal work of filing charges against the state for violation of their human rights, KMV's spectacular actions were crucial in changing the law on conscientious objection.

The phenomenon of humorous political stunts is discussed in relation to Vinthagen's theory of nonviolent action and its four dimensions. Just like other nonviolent actions, some stunts are strong in one dimension while others mainly work in another. Almost all the stunts temporarily contribute to breaking power and many also include a dialogue facilitation element. The absurd and naïve stunts have demonstrated a particular ability to be part of utopian enactment and normative regulation, since Santas, clowns and similar figures speak to people's imagination and hopes for a more just and peaceful world.

Analysing humorous political stunts can give both academics and activists insights into what type of stunt is most likely to empha-

sise a certain aspect of a humorous nonviolent action in relation
to various audiences. It will also bring a deeper understanding of
the nature and dynamics of power, resistance and humour.

Acknowledgements

Many people have supported me in the process of writing this thesis. Brian Martin has been the most supportive and encouraging supervisor one can imagine, and his gentle guidance has cheered me on in moments of doubt. Brian has always made time for talking about any questions I have had, and participating in his amazing writing programme meant that I had developed good writing habits already before I became a PhD student.

Without the 3 year *International Postgraduate Tuition Award* and *University Postgraduate Award* from the University of Wollongong, I would never have been able to carry out this research. I have also received two grants from the Faculty of Arts fund for Higher Degree Research conference and research support in 2011 and 2012. When I have been in Wollongong, many colleagues have helped me feel at home and given useful feedback, especially during the meetings in the writing group and at the Bingi and Gong gatherings. Some of you I got to know better than others. Ian Miles became my first friend, helped out with all sorts of practical matters and was never afraid to question the usefulness of humour when I ran over with enthusiasm early in the research project. Sharon Beder, Richard Gosden, Jason MacLeod, Jody Warren, Brendan Riddick and Mary Scott all followed my research project during several years. Many of you opened your homes to me with great hospitality.

In Sweden, the Resistance Studies group at the University of Gothenburg welcomed me at their seminars in spite of the lack of official affiliation and also organised for me to present and discuss my thesis at a public seminar in August 2014. Brian Palmer, Véronique Dudouet and Håkan Thörn all kindly agreed to read and comment on the manuscript at this event.

Martin Smedjeback, Daniel Ritter and Henrik Frykberg have spent numerous hours commenting on drafts and suggested many useful changes and additions. Stellan Vinthagen has been my mentor when it comes to the study of nonviolent resistance since he was my teacher in 2002, and shared valuable insights from the mysterious workings of the world of academia during the following decade. There are no words to express how much this has meant to me. Stellan has commented on both early drafts and the nearly finished manuscript, always with very constructive suggestions for improvement.

During a relaxing summer visit, Janne Flyghed promised to read the whole manuscript, and more than a year later six hundred pages overloaded his mailbox. Janne's support and critical questions were both an important reassurance and led to considerable improvement. He joined the chorus of "shorter, shorter" that others had started earlier, something which actually convinced me to chop out more than 100 pages which will become a later project.

My deep felt gratitude goes to all the activists who have dared to experiment with humour in a world of persistent seriousness, and especially to those who were willing to be interviewed and participate in workshops and so enthusiastically shared their experiences and reflections with me. Because I promised them anonymity they cannot be named, but you know who you are. In Ofog, you all contributed to make me feel welcome and find a place to belong and laugh together. Although some of you will probably disagree with some of my conclusions on the actions we did together I feel confident it will not disrupt our friendships and common journey for a better world.

Cecilie Fonnesbech advised me on some translation challenges; Tormod Otter Johansen helped out with how best to translate and explain legal concepts. Tormod, Anna Johansen and Malene Raben Jørgensen opened their homes to me when I was staying overnight in Gothenburg and Copenhagen.

I dedicate this work to my dear friend Howard Clark who was such a great inspiration as an activist and researcher and passed away suddenly in 2013. With his great sense of humour, Howard loved the subject of this thesis, but unfortunately never got to read it. Although any mistakes in the text are my responsibility, they would probably not have been there if Howard had not left us so unexpectedly and way too early.

Finally, my partner and life companion Jørgen Johansen deserves more thanks than can be expressed in words – for always loving me, supporting me and believing in my capacity to become a good researcher.

Introduction

What happens when nonviolent political activists use humour to challenge those they consider more powerful than themselves? What does it mean to the activists, and what types of responses do the use of humour generate from opponents, media, police, bystanders and other activists?

These questions first started to interest me in 2003 when a Serbian activist told me about his experience with using humour to oppose the rule of the Serbian dictator Slobodan Milošević. According to the young man who had been active in a group called Otpor, humour had been an effective way to make Otpor different from other opposition groups and attract new young activists. Humour also lowered levels of fear and created situations it was difficult for the regime to find an adequate response to.

My primary focus is how subordinate and marginalised political groups use humour to expose, ridicule and influence those they consider more powerful than themselves, both in dictatorships and in democracies. It is explorative research that raises more questions than it answers.

There is an inherent contradiction in trying to use the rational mode of communication to analyse expressions made in the humorous mode. In the discourse of science and research ambiguity is usually treated as an undesired anomaly, but in the humorous political stunts which are my main unit of analysis, the ambiguities are a necessity. In addition, humour is fragile and loses much of its edge and special flavour as soon as one starts to analyse it and tear it apart. Anyone who has ever tried to explain a joke will know what I mean.

When I have mentioned the theme of this thesis, I have been met with two types of reactions. So called "ordinary people" and political activists have generally reacted with enthusiasm and

9

believed political humour to be a useful tool. I have enjoyed the privilege that my research area turned out to be a good topic for dinner conversations, including with people I met for the first time. Most of these "ordinary people" share the view that is prevalent in many societies – that humour is something positive and valuable in human interaction. They have no doubt that humour can have an effect on politics and rarely question the more troublesome sides of humour. However, in the literature on humour, it has for decades been a persistent claim that humour cannot "really" have an impact on relations of power, and that it is "just" a way of letting off steam. This discrepancy between an everyday understanding and part of the scholarly work on humour indicates that here is an interesting research question that deserves more attention. In addition, such different views are not just interesting from a theoretical point of view, but can have implications for the decisions activists struggling for a better world make about which methods to use.

The data I have relied on indicate that the positions of unbridled optimism and strong scepticism are both inadequate, and that the reality of real world activism is complex. It is not straightforward to use humour in order to achieve political change and it can be extremely difficult to convey the message that activists want to send to the intended audiences. The sceptic's idea that humour cannot really change anything might look simple, but begs a whole set of questions about what "real change" is, and how one is to know when it has happened. It assumes the existence of a neutral position from which to judge an outcome. This idea about "real change" usually also implies a comparison with other types of political dissent, which the sceptic considers more genuine. What this ideal type of resistance ought to look like is not clear to me, so I do not know if by "real resistance" they mean conventional, rational protest or a violent struggle. The only thing that is obvious is that dichotomous views on power and resistance cannot accommodate the complexities needed to understand what happens when marginalised political activists use humour within campaigns of nonviolent resistance.

Thesis outline and guiding questions

I have approached the theme of humour, political activism and relations of power from various angles and with a range of different methods. I consider it quite naïve to expect humour alone to be able to dismantle powerful institutions and discourses, so the question is not whether humour can change relations of power. Instead, the question that has guided my research has been:

What role can humour play in facilitating resistance to dominant discourses and powerful institutions and people?

In order to approach this question, it was logical to start with investigating:

1. What does existing research on nonviolence, power, humour and political protest say about the role of humour in resistance to dominant discourses and powerful institutions and people?

This is the subject of chapter 1, which begins by outlining theories of nonviolence, identifying the two different but overlapping traditions of principled and pragmatic approaches to nonviolence. It continues with an introduction to societal theories on humour, and in particular the humour that is used to express protest and dissent. Central concepts such as power, resistance, nonviolence and humour are defined here.

Chapter 2 explains how the examples and cases in Chapter 3-6 were selected and how the research strategy was designed. The methods of semi-structured interviewing, participant observation and document analysis that I have used are also explained. The chapter places the thesis within an emancipatory approach to research, taking its point of departure in standpoint theory and participatory action research oriented strategies.

Chapter 3 introduces the phenomenon of *humorous political stunts*, a concept I have developed to distinguish public humorous performances that challenge relations of power from other types of political humour. Taking all the findings from existing research on nonviolence, power, humour and political protest into consideration requires one to abandon thinking that implies that humour is "one thing" and instead take its complexities into account and ask:

2. What different types of humorous political stunts exist?

In chapter 3, 15 examples of humorous political stunts serve to show the diversity of the phenomenon and develop an original typology of five different types of stunts called *supportive, corrective, naïve, absurd* and *provocative*. The defining characteristic of this contribution is the way the stunt relates to the truths and rationalities upheld by people in positions of power.

In order to explore the phenomenon of humorous political stunts in more detail, I have been guided by another two questions:

3. What role can humorous political stunts play in facilitating outreach, mobilisation, and a culture of resistance?

4. What does the use of humour mean to those who perform humorous political stunts?

These questions are primarily addressed in the two case studies in chapter 4-6.

Chapter 4 is about clowning, one particular version of the absurd stunt that a number of activists have used. The chapter is based on interviews with people from the anti-militarist network Ofog in Sweden and the findings suggest that clowning opens up space and communicates nonviolent values.

Chapter 5 is an in-depth case study of how Ofog uses and perceives outward directed humour. It is based on 2½ years of research inspired by participatory action research methodology that I did together with the network. Experiences from a number of humorous political stunts confronting military recruitment, military test sites and arms production are discussed in relation to the model presented in Chapter 3. The chapter also discusses ethical aspects of using humour.

Chapter 6 is an historical case study of the Scandinavian *Kampanjen Mot Verneplikt* (KMV), which means "Campaign Against Conscription". Throughout the 1980s the group challenged militarism by refusing both military and substitute service, when a growing number of young men chose to become so-called *total resisters*. In Norway the consequence of total resistance was 16 months in prison. One of the campaign's strategies was to use spectacular and sometimes humorous actions in order to challenge this law. The chapter traces how humorous and non-humorous elements in the campaign complemented each other and finally resulted in a law change in 1990. Since humour was only one factor among several others, humour is not the only focus in this chapter. I also investigate in detail the legal work KMV did and the particular circumstances surrounding the law change.

For the two case studies on Ofog and KMV I have chosen to make a thorough documentation of the humour used by the two groups. Not all the details are necessary in order to present my arguments about humorous political stunts but I consider it important to contribute to documenting their experiences, since these two groups have not had any part of their history written elsewhere.

Chapter 7 both addresses the overall question of what role humour can play in facilitating resistance to dominant discourses and powerful institutions and people, and one specific question related to this:

5. How do the different forms of humorous political stunts affect the logic of a nonviolent action?

This question is approached by identifying how the five types of humorous political stunts relate to the four dimensions of non-violence called *dialogue facilitation, power breaking, utopian enactment* and *normative regulations*. The existing data show that the humorous political stunt has its strength in its possibility to break monopolies of power, for instance when it contributes to what I call the *discursive guerrilla war* about who is to define what is true, right and just. In certain cases humorous political stunts can also contribute to dialogue and serve as an utopian enactment and regulate norms.

Dreaming about a better world

Some humorous political stunts appeal to reason and logic after having taken a detour, but many appeal more to emotions and the multiple meanings and truths that exist simultaneously in the world. Stephen Duncombe in his book *Dream* calls for progressives to make more use of imagination and speak to people's fantasies when they do politics.[1] Humorous political stunts are one answer to this. Duncombe argues that Enlightenment was once a progressive dream, but in democracies progressives now need bigger dreams that can speak to people's longing for drama and spectacle if they want to seriously challenge the dominant world order. Appealing to reason, logic, restraint and moderation the way many social movements working on issues like climate change and global justice do today is doomed to fail. Duncombe writes that "truth and power belong to those who tell the better story".[2] His book illustrates vividly how desires and dreams are

---

[1] Stephen Duncombe, *Dream: Re-Imagining Progressive Politics in an Age of Fantasy* (New York: New Press, 2007).
[2] Duncombe, *Dream: Re-Imagining Progressive Politics in an Age of Fantasy*: p. 8.

manufactured and constructed, not a self-evident constant that can be taken for granted.

Duncombe does not consider himself a postmodern provocateur claiming there is no truth. On the contrary he is very firmly grounded in the reality of an unjust world order that causes early death and suffering for many. However, it does not matter that this is the truth, and that that this truth is available for people to know, if they don't care or don't want to believe it. The consequence is that if progressives want to reach the hearts and minds of people, truth and reason are not enough: they need to speak to the imagination as well. Duncombe suggests looking to places like Las Vegas and popular video games and analysing what is so attractive about them. What type of desires do they promise to fulfil, and what spectacles can progressives offer instead that appeal to the same desires? Duncombe is very critical of the dreams sold in Las Vegas and violent video games, but suggests that progressives have to let go of their fear of the spectacle and find ways to make their own participatory spectacles that can make people dream. Duncombe almost echoes peace researcher Elise Boulding in her book *Cultures of Peace*[3] when he suggests that "without dreams we will never be able to imagine the new world we want to build."[4] With stories of the Reclaim the Street movement and Billionaires for Bush, stunts and carnival within the same tradition as the humorous political stunts presented here, he also points towards a possibility, a potential for these types of stunts to become bigger. What they offer, like Las Vegas and video games, is a possibility to participate, to be active, to be involved. And as Duncombe finishes his introduction: "To embrace dreams as part of a winning strategy for progressive

---

[3] Elise Boulding, *Cultures of Peace: The Hidden Side of History*, (Syracuse, NY: Syracuse University Press, 2000).
[4] Duncombe, *Dream: Re-Imagining Progressive Politics in an Age of Fantasy*: p. 25.

politics may be just a dream itself, but really, at this point, what do we have to lose?"[5]

---

[5] Duncombe, *Dream: Re-Imagining Progressive Politics in an Age of Fantasy*: p. 27.

Chapter 1: Nonviolence, humour and relations of power

Introduction

Two different academic traditions are brought together to provide the background for this thesis. Within peace studies, nonviolence is a field which investigates alternatives to violence in the struggle for social change. To illustrate the dynamics of nonviolent struggle I present two very different approaches. Mohandas K. Gandhi, leader of the Indian struggle against the British colonial power, personifies the idea of nonviolence as a way of life, an idea nonviolent scholar Gene Sharp argues against. His academic writing concentrates on explaining nonviolence as a technique which is available as an effective tool for everyone and where moral principles are irrelevant. The introduction to literature on nonviolence is concluded with the theory of Stellan Vinthagen which combines ideas from Gandhi and Sharp with modern sociology to provide new insights on nonviolent resistance.

The other academic tradition relevant to discussing humour as a method of challenging power relations is humour studies. This is also a multidisciplinary field that has caught the interest of psychologists, sociologists and a number of other disciplines. I primarily focus on the social aspects of humour. After a brief introduction to the various ways of understanding humour's role in society and the sociology of humour developed in the incongruity tradition, I suggest that part of the traditional definition of humour is problematic when it comes to political humour, since it treats the humorous and the serious as opposites.

The major part of the literature review in this chapter focuses on the research done on humour, protest and social conflicts. It covers a wide range of approaches including traditional folly and humour used against occupations and employers. Along the way I evaluate and comment on a number of the works presented.

Literature on nonviolence

Nonviolent resistance to injustice has been carried out for centuries without any academic analysis. Literature on the subject is a combination of practitioners' own descriptions of what they have done and others' descriptions and analysis. Recently it has become part of the academic discipline of peace studies. Much literature on the subject consists of case descriptions of particular struggles combined with some theory or strategic discussion, like *Nonviolent Social Movements: a Geographical Perspective* edited by Stephen Zunes, Lester R. Kurtz, and Sarah Beth Asher,[6] *Unarmed against Hitler: Civilian Resistance in Europe, 1939-1943 by Jacques Semelin,*[7] *A Force More Powerful* by Peter Ackerman and Jack Du-vall,[8] *Strategic Nonviolent Conflict* by Peter Ackerman and Christopher Kruegler,[9] *Waging Nonviolent Struggle* by Gene Sharp with Joshua Paulson,[10] and Sharon E. Nepstad's *Nonviolent revolutions.*[11] Sometimes other terms are used for the same or very similar phenomena, such as "people power", or "civil resistance"

---

[6] Stephen Zunes, Lester R. Kurtz, and Sarah Beth Asher, *Nonviolent Social Movements: A Geographical Perspective* (Malden, MA: Blackwell, 1999).

[7] Jacques Semelin, Unarmed against Hitler: Civilian Resistance in Europe, 1939-1943. (Westport, CT: Praeger, 1993).

[8] Peter Ackerman and Jack DuVall, *A Force More Powerful: A Century of Nonviolent Conflict* (New York: St. Martin's Press, 2000).

[9] Peter Ackerman and Christopher Kruegler, *Strategic Nonviolent Conflict: The Dynamics of People Power in the Twentieth Century* (Westport, CT: Praeger, 1994).

[10] Gene Sharp, *Waging Nonviolent Struggle, 20th Century Practice and 21th Century Potential* (Boston: Porter Sargent, 2005).

[11] Sharon Erickson Nepstad, *Nonviolent Revolutions: Civil Resistance in the Late 20th Century* (Oxford: Oxford University Press, 2011).

in *People Power* edited by Howard Clark[12] and *Civil Resistance and Power Politics* edited by Adam Roberts and Timothy Garton Ash.[13] In his book *Unarmed Insurrections: People Power Movements in Nondemocracies* Kurt Schock combines nonviolent theory with social movement theory.[14] In a recent study, Erica Chenoweth and Maria Stephan have convincingly shown how nonviolent campaigning is more effective than armed struggle in achieving its goals.[15] They have compared 323 violent and nonviolent campaigns between 1900 and 2006, and found that nonviolent campaigns were "nearly twice as likely to achieve full or partial success as their violent counterparts".[16] They have deliberately looked specifically at three types of resistance where "common sense" says that violence will be more effective than nonviolence – anti-regime, anti-occupation and secession. Nevertheless, even in these hard cases, nonviolent campaigns are more likely to achieve their goals. Chenoweth and Stephan's main explanations for the relative success of nonviolent resistance are that it generally is more participatory than violent insurrections, and therefore better can build broad movements where everyone can participate. Nonviolence also increases the chance that security forces will defect.

The Indian independence movement and the US civil rights movement are two of the most documented and analysed

---

[12] Howard Clark, ed. *People Power: Unarmed Resistance and Global Solidarity* (London: Pluto Press, 2009). See also April Carter, *People Power and Political Change: Key Issues and Concepts* (Abingdon, UK: Routledge, 2012).
[13] Adam Roberts and Timothy Garton Ash, eds., *Civil Resistance and Power Politics: The Experience of Non-Violent Action from Gandhi to the Present* (Oxford: Oxford University Press, 2009).
[14] Kurt Schock, *Unarmed Insurrections: People Power Movements in Nondemocracies* (Minneapolis, MN: University of Minnesota Press, 2005).
[15] Erica Chenoweth and Maria J. Stephan, *Why Civil Resistance Works: The Strategic Logic of Nonviolent Conflict* (New York: Columbia University Press, 2011).
[16] Chenoweth and Stephan, *Why Civil Resistance Works:* p. 7.

nonviolent struggles, but numerous other examples of campaigns and actions all around the world exist. For a while, various terms such as "civil defence", "social defence" and "civilian based defence" were used to describe defence against invasion and occupation where nonviolence played a major role.

Defining violence and nonviolence

Many definitions of violence exist, I find the definition developed by peace researcher Johan Galtung useful. He distinguishes between *direct*, *structural* and *cultural violence*. *Direct violence* is the intentional harm or threat of harm of other human beings. This can be killings or other physical attacks. When I use the term *violence* alone, this is the type of violence I refer to. *Structural violence* is when an unjust system harms people, for instance if they die early because of lack of food, clean water, and sanitation. Frequently I will refer to structural violence as *injustice*.[17] *Cultural violence* is the belief systems which make it possible to uphold the unjust structures or legitimise direct and structural violence.[18]

When it comes to nonviolence I find Stellan Vinthagen's definition useful. He defines a nonviolent action as an attempt to overcome violence and repression without using any violence yourself.[19] This definition has two aspects, which he calls *against-violence* and *without-violence*. To take action without using violence

---

[17] This distinction between direct and structural violence was first made by Johan Galtung, "Violence, Peace, and Peace Research," *Journal of Peace Research* 6, no. 3 (1969).

[18] Johan Galtung, *Peace by Peaceful Means: Peace and Conflict, Development and Civilization* (London Sage Publications, 1996).

[19] Stellan Vinthagen, *Ickevåldsaktion: En Social Praktik Av Motstånd Och Konstruktion* (Göteborg: Institutionen för freds- och utvecklingsforskning (PADRIGU) Göteborgs universitet, 2005), PhD thesis. p. 26.

(without-violence) does not by itself make it nonviolence. People can sit outside their parliament and enjoy the sun. That is an everyday event that has nothing to do with nonviolence even if it happens without violence. But if they sit there and make it visible that this is a protest against the government's use of violence, for example the wars it is waging, then it is a nonviolent action. They do it without using violence, in order to confront someone else's violence (against-violence). Nonviolent actions can take many different forms; some well-known examples are strikes, boycotts and acts of civil disobedience. Nonviolent actions have been used in struggles as diverse as antimilitarism, civil rights and environmental protection as well as against dictatorships and foreign occupations. Although some authors consider the two terms *nonviolence* and *nonviolent action* to imply a different ideological or philosophical approach[20], I use all the forms of the word *nonviolence* interchangeably.

Many misunderstandings of what nonviolent action is exist.[21] For one thing, it is a common mistake to associate nonviolence with passivity and avoidance of conflict. But with Vinthagen's definition, nonviolent action is about confronting various forms of violence. Frequently nonviolent methods are used to escalate conflicts in order to make violence and repression visible to others and force them to take a stand. Martin Luther King Jr., the leader of the civil rights movement in the United States, wrote in his famous "Letter from a Birmingham jail" as a response to his critiques:

> ... You may well ask, "Why direct action? Why sit-ins, marches and so forth? Isn't negotiation a better path? You

---

[20] Gene Sharp, *Sharp's Dictionary of Power and Struggle: Language of Civil Resistance in Conflicts* (New York: Oxford University Press, 2012).
[21] For an excellent discussion of the misunderstandings regarding nonviolence from a social science perspective, see Kurt Schock, "Nonviolent Action and Its Misconceptions: Insights for Social Scientists," *PS: Political Science & Politics* 36, no. 4 (2003).

are quite right in calling for negotiation. Indeed, this is the very purpose of direct action. Nonviolent direct action seeks to create such a crisis and foster such a tension that a community which has constantly refused to negotiate is forced to confront the issue. It seeks so to dramatize the issue that it can no longer be ignored. My citing the creation of tension as part of the work on the nonviolent-resister may sound rather shocking. But I confess that I am not afraid of the word "tension". I have earnestly opposed violent tension, but there is a type of constructive, nonviolent tension which is necessary for growth.[22]

For some people it sounds like a contradiction to work for a nonviolent world by escalating conflict. But the confusion only happens when one confuses *conflict* with *violence*.

Another common misunderstanding about nonviolent action is to think that no one gets hurt or dies in a nonviolent struggle. However, nonviolence only means that at least one side refrains from using violence, and it is not a requirement that other sides do the same. Many people have been killed and hurt during nonviolent struggles for social change.

Gandhi: Nonviolence as a way of life

Nonviolence can be divided into two main categories – those who treat it as a technique in a struggle for change, sometimes referred to as *pragmatic nonviolence*, and those who consider it a lifestyle involving one's whole life, called *principled nonviolence*.[23]

---

[22] Martin Luther King Jr., quoted in David P. Barash, *Approaches to Peace: A Reader in Peace Studies*, 2nd ed. (New York: Oxford University Press, 2010). p. 172.

[23] See for instance Judith Stiehm, "Nonviolence Is Two," *Sociological Inquiry* 38, no. 1 (1968); Brian Martin, "Researching Nonviolent Action: Past Themes and Future Possibilities," *Peace & Change* 30, no. 2 (2005). Stiehm is an early example of making this distinction, although she used the term "conscientious nonviolence" rather than "principled".

However, this should be understood as a spectrum with two opposite poles rather than distinct categories. The divide is artificial and many writers and practitioners do not fit neatly into one end of the spectrum. Nevertheless it is a useful analytical distinction for presenting the whole spectrum of thinking on nonviolence based on the Weberian ideal types. In the next section, the theories of scholar Gene Sharp will introduce the idea of nonviolence as a technique. Regarding nonviolence as a way of life, Mohandas Karamchand Gandhi will show the way. More than anyone else, he made the concept of nonviolent struggle for change available to the world when he led the struggle for an independent India against the British colonial power, and he personifies the idea of nonviolence as a way of life.

Gandhi, often referred to as *Mahatma* Gandhi, (an honorary title he himself did not approve of) wrote extensively about nonviolence in the form of letters and articles.[24] He did not himself write a coherent theoretical framework of nonviolent action, but wrote throughout his life about what he called his "experiments with truth."[25] By studying how he practiced his method and the texts he wrote, many scholars have systematised his ideas. The most systematic attempt of developing a coherent norm system was done in Norwegian by Johan Galtung and Arne Næss.[26] The

---

Sometimes what I call *pragmatic nonviolence* is called *strategic nonviolence,* but the problem with this label is that it implies that *principled nonviolence* is not strategic.

[24] His collected work consists of 100 volumes. See Gandhi, *The Collected Works of Mahatma Gandhi,* 6th rev. ed., 100 vols. (New Delhi: Publications Division, Ministry of Information and Broadcasting, Govt. of India, 2000).

[25] This is also the title of his autobiography. Mohandas Karamchand Gandhi, *The Story of My Experiments with Truth* (Ahmedabad: Navajivan Publishing House, 1927).

[26] Johan Galtung and Arne Næss, *Gandhis Politiske Etikk,* 3. utg. ed. (Oslo: Pax, 1994).

amount of literature on Gandhi is enormous, and still growing.[27] In this short introduction I will rely on the way Vinthagen has described Gandhi's practical philosophy.[28] This is a thorough work based on his study of Gandhi's own writings and more than enough to cover the core ideas necessary here.

---

[27] The annotated bibliography is more than 1000 pages long. See Ananda M. Pandiri, *A Comprehensive, Annotated Bibliography on Mahatma Gandhi* (Ahmedabad: Navajivan Publishing House, 2002).
[28] Vinthagen, *Ickevåldsaktion*.

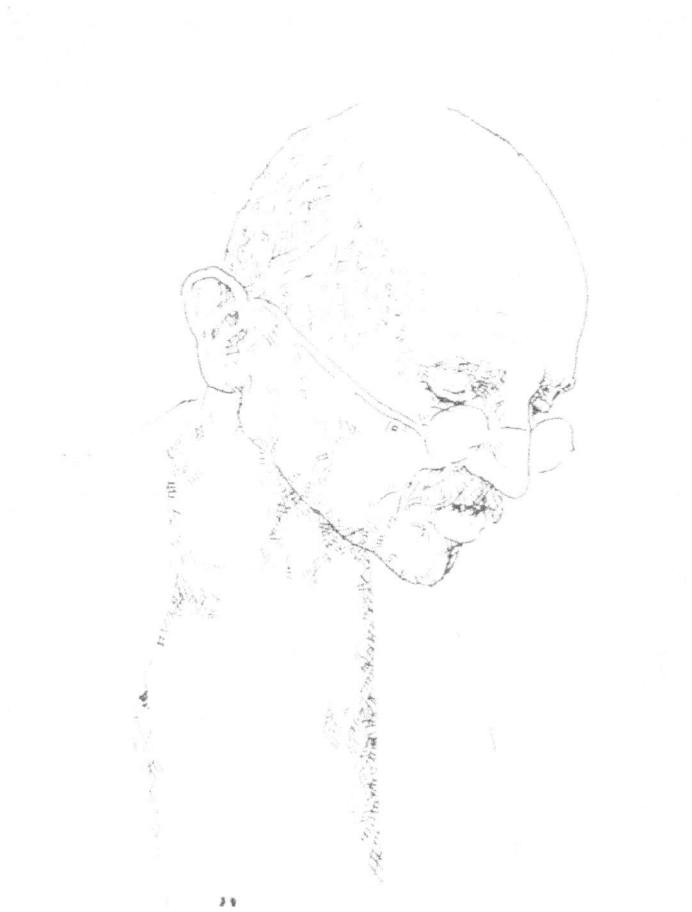

Illustration 1. Mohandas Karamchand Gandhi. Drawing by Siri Mette Henriksen

Gandhi was a very religious person, and in order to understand his whole philosophy, one also has to consider his spiritual sides and the meaning he attached to them. However, it is possible to understand his practical use of nonviolence and the logic in the method without dwelling on his religious writing. Since I am concerned with the role of humour within the practical application of nonviolent action, I will only describe the minimum which is required to understand nonviolence as a way of life.

The central concept in Gandhi's writing is *satyagraha* which is often taken to mean *nonviolent struggle*. However, his ideas about nonviolent struggle reach much further than what many other writers mean when they use this term, which is the reason I will use satyagraha when referring specifically to Gandhi's philosophy. Satyagraha comes from Sanskrit and loosely translates as *soul force* or *truth force*. For Gandhi, satyagraha consist of three parts: 1. Truth (*satya*), 2.nonviolence (*ahimsa*) and 3. self-suffering (*tapasaya*). All three are closely related and combined they are the basis of satyagraha. Truth is closely connected to God, and only God knows the whole and full Truth (with capital T). All people should strive to know Truth, but will only ever find what they believe to be truth (with lower case t). However, it is their obligation to fight for this truth, but remaining humble towards the possibility that they are wrong. Acknowledging the possibility that people can be mistaken leads Gandhi to nonviolence, ahimsa. If one person in her fight for her truth kills someone else, she has denied that person the possibility to be right and the possibility that she herself is wrong. If it later turns out that she is wrong and the dead person was right, it is not possible to apologise and revive the person. This possibility remains open if she struggles for her truth with nonviolent means. Should that happen, she and the people she struggles against have together gotten one step closer to Truth.[29] It is not necessary to be religious in order to acknowledge that no one knows the whole and full truth.

---

[29] Vinthagen, *Ickevåldsaktion*. pp. 60-62.

The means to reach towards Truth is to strive for ahimsa, which means *nonviolence* or *love*. According to Vinthagen, ahimsa is a collective non-egoistic self-realisation (not to be confused with western ideas about individual self-realisation). The collective aspect is that one person's suffering is connected to other people, and the collective self-realisation is concerned with diminishing the amount of suffering and violence in the world. For Gandhi, it is not possible to reach the truth as long as other people suffer. Therefore, ahimsa is about much more than avoiding the use of violence oneself: it also includes opposing the violence of others. This part of Gandhian thought is central in Vinthagen's definition of nonviolence. The total absence of violence is an unachievable goal, but what is realistic is an eternal striving towards reducing violence. In the struggle against violence, suffering is inevitable, which leads to the third aspect of satyagraha, self-suffering, *tapasya*. The idea of self-suffering is foreign to many, but has nothing to do with masochism. I will return to this when I show how Vinthagen uses the concept.

Gandhi did not distinguish between the means and the ends of a goal; each depends on the other. He is supposed to have said that "If you take care of the means, the ends will take care of themselves", but there is no source for this quote. Nevertheless, it summarises his ideas about nonviolence nicely. If people use nonviolence (ahimsa) to reach their goals, the result will be marked by that approach.

Another aspect of Gandhi's thought which I will return to later is the idea of "constructive work". Parallel with the struggle against violence and injustice, those struggling for nonviolent social change should also work to build the world they want to see. Gandhi's campaigns during the Indian independence struggle were almost always *for* something, and not just against it. This is an aspect of nonviolence which is lacking in the technical approach to nonviolent action which Sharp represents.

Sharp: A pioneer for a pragmatic approach to nonviolent action

In the 1950's US scholar Gene Sharp set out to prove that nonviolence was not just an option for committed pacifists who based their choice on strong moral principles, like Gandhi had done, but an effective strategy which everyone could use in their struggles for freedom and justice. Although he of course based his work on what others had done previously, he was the first to develop systematic, academic thinking about nonviolence. His book *The Politics of Nonviolent Action*[30] is a groundbreaking analysis of nonviolence. Although forceful critiques of his ideas have been published, it is unquestionable that his contribution to the study of nonviolence has been unique and far reaching.

Sharp's analysis starts with the concept of power. He insists that power does not come in a certain amount where more power to one person automatically means less power to someone else. To agree with his approach to nonviolence, one has to accept that governments, police and courts are only powerful as long as people obey and let them get their way. This is called a consent theory of power. Since power is a relationship, people always have the possibility to withdraw their consent to being governed by someone else. The basic idea is that when people stop obeying laws and orders, those usually considered "powerful" become "powerless".

Many factors influence elites and authorities' ability to remain in control – e.g. material and human resources, personal authority and charisma as well as the sanctions they can impose. But in order to stay in power, they always depend on obedience. Even if they can invoke prison or death penalty on those who are

---

[30]Gene Sharp, *The Politics of Nonviolent Action* (Boston: Porter Sargent, 1973).

28

disobedient, every person in a position of authority is always depending on a certain number of obedient citizens to carry out the sanctions, such as police officers, soldiers, prison guards and executioners, to mention just a few. The day these functionaries decide to withdraw their obedience, the elites fall to the ground. However, since the daily news provides abundant evidence of brutal repression, violence and injustice, a central question is: Why do people obey? Of course fear of sanctions plays a role, Sharp says, but that is not the whole answer. Habit, self-interest or the idea that obedience is a moral obligation also kick in. In addition, potentially disobedient persons might lack the self-confidence and belief in their own ability to achieve change. However, obedience is not eternal and inevitable, even in dictatorships where it has persisted for decades. The giving and receiving of orders always occur in an interaction between two or more persons.[31] In Sharp's opinion, each individual always has a choice to disobey,[32] a point of his theory which has received some criticism. In Vinthagen's theory, this aspect of disobedience has been modified to some degree.

In his introduction to nonviolence as a technique, Sharp writes: "In political terms nonviolent action is based on a very simple postulate: people do not always do what they are told to do, and sometimes they do things which have been forbidden to them."[33] Thus, nonviolent action can both occur when people avoid doing what they usually do or have been requested to do, or they can do something they normally do not do, or which is specifically forbidden.[34] If people's ordinary behaviour is important in order authorities to uphold their position, "acts of omission" can have a huge effect – for example if the police

---

[31] Sharp, *The Politics of Nonviolent Action.* p. 16.

[32] Sharp, *The Politics of Nonviolent Action.* p. 26.

[33] Sharp, *The Politics of Nonviolent Action.* p. 63.

[34] Sharp, *The Politics of Nonviolent Action.* p. 68.

refuse to arrest protesters, or soldiers desert or mutiny. Less dramatic "acts of omission" are tax refusal or strikes. Actions which people are not expected to do or are directly forbidden can be organising a boycott or a demonstration, or it can be illegal actions involving civil disobedience, a theme I will return to in chapter 5 about Ofog.

Sharp described 198 different methods of nonviolent action giving numerous historical examples of their use. However, this number is rather artificial since only creativity limits the possibilities. His three broader categories are a more operational concept for analysis:

1. Methods of protest and persuasion
2. Methods of noncooperation
3. Methods of nonviolent intervention

Well known methods of protest and persuasion include demonstrations, petitions and letter writing campaigns. Two traditional methods of noncooperation are the strike and the boycott. Examples of methods of nonviolent intervention are the sit-ins which the civil rights movement did in segregated restaurants in the southern states in the US in the 1960's or the establishment of a parallel education system which the Kosovo Albanians did in the 1990's.

According to Sharp, people striving for nonviolent social change can achieve their goals in four different ways:

1. Conversion: The opponent ends up viewing the issue completely differently, and is convinced that the nonviolent activists are right.
2. Accommodation: The opponent accommodates the demands of the nonviolent activists, for example because she sees that she cannot win, but without changing her point of view fundamentally.

3. Nonviolent coercion: Things change without the consent of the opponent. He loses control of the situation when he no longer has access to the resources he once had, for example when police and army refuse to shoot nonviolent activists.

4. Disintegration: In rare cases the opponent simply disintegrates and falls apart after prolonged nonviolent coercion, and there is no longer anyone to negotiate with.[35]

For some nonviolent activists it is a goal to convert the opponent and make her agree that the nonviolent activists are right. This is a quite high demand and it is seldom that a complete conversion happens. Sharp thinks that it is mainly religious nonviolent activists who work with this goal in mind. Many of Gandhi's actions had the goal to change the hearts of the British, and he thought that the self-suffering played an important part in this. However, social distance between the nonviolent activists and those they want to convert can make it difficult to touch someone's heart and convert her. No matter how much they are willing to suffer it does not matter if those who witness the suffering do not consider them human. In the case of India, Thomas Weber has shown how the self-suffering of the Indian independence activists did not work directly on the police ordered out to beat them up, but indirectly on so-called third parties. His case study of the salt raids at Dharasana in 1930 shows that the refusal to fight back did not touch the police or the British authorities at all. Those who were converted by the suffering were the general public in the US who read the journalist Webb Miller's moving report of the events. When it came to the police responsible for the beating, Miller observed how the

---

[35] Sharp developed the first three categories in Sharp, *The Politics of Nonviolent Action*. For disintegration, see Sharp, *Waging Nonviolent Struggle, 20th Century Practice and 21th Century Potential*: pp. 46-47.

refusal to offer any resistance when attacked made the aggressors even more furious.[36]

I consider it important to think of the *opponent* not as a single individual, but an organisation or other unit whose members share a common goal. Apart from this particular goal their interests usually differ a lot. A state, a company or an organisation is seldom an integrated whole, and although leaders may try to speak with one voice when communicating with others, individuals within the unit can vary a lot in their approaches to a nonviolent movement (and vice versa of course). Even when leaders are not converted, other supporters of the opponent, such as police or military personnel, may be. Anyone aiming to convert someone must avoid humiliating their opponent, and the activists will have to signal that a conversion will not harm the converted. In order to touch the heart of the opponent in this way, it does not matter how many activists participate. It is their dedication which counts.

When an opponent accommodates to the demands of the nonviolent activists, but without actually changing his mind, Sharp thinks the opponent considers the nonviolent activists an irritation rather than a threat. He might also consider the costs of continued struggle more damaging than giving in to some of the activists' demands. If there is a chance of withdrawing with honour intact he will do that.

The third way the activists can achieve their goals are through nonviolent coercion. The opponent has not changed her mind in any way, and she is prepared to keep on fighting as previously. She will not negotiate or withdraw. But still she cannot win, because the nonviolent activists have cut off her access to central

---

[36] Thomas Weber, "'The Marchers Simply Walked Forward until Struck Down': Nonviolent Suffering and Conversion," *Peace & Change* 18, no. 3 (1993).

resources for the struggle. Maybe some of her former allies have been converted, or they see which way the wind blows and prefer to change side while there is still time. Nonviolent coercion is well-known from strikes or threats to strike. When it comes to nonviolent coercion, numbers count. If a large number of people are disobedient, it is harder for the opponent to continue as before. However, even more important than the number is the position of the disobedient. Key disobedient people make a bigger difference than the general public. Those who are armed on behalf of the state, such as police and military, are important, but the system also depends on courts, key industry and infrastructure.

A central concept in Sharp's theory is *political jiu-jitsu*, which he uses to describe what happens when an opponent's supporters abandon him because he is perceived to overreact to the nonviolent confrontation. The term is derived from the Asian sport jiu-jitsu, where the fighters try to use the opponents' own weight and force in order to win. When a nonviolent movement is met with violent repression, the same effect can happen. When the opponent is seen to misuse his force, previous supporters might leave him and he loses his position in the end. It can be difficult to convince supporters and bystanders that violent repression is necessary against someone who remains nonviolent. Sharp describes the phenomenon this way:

> Cruelties and brutalities committed against the clearly nonviolent are likely to disturb many people and to fill some with outrage. Even milder violent repression appears less justified against nonviolent people than when employed against violent resisters. This reaction to repression is especially likely when the opponent's policies themselves are hard to justify. Thus, wider public opinion may turn against the opponent, members of his own group may

33

dissent, and more or less passive members of the general grievance group may shift to firm opposition.[37]

The dynamic of political jiu-jitsu shows why it is important for those who choose nonviolence to remain nonviolent, including when faced with repression. Even a tiny bit of violence is likely to change the dynamic. The opponent can be expected to focus on the violence, no matter how little and how justified it may appear in some eyes, and this violence is likely to be the excuse for using all the force at his disposal. If those who want change use violence, they will shift the game to an arena where the opponents have the upper hand thanks to his access to the use of force.

Brian Martin has further developed the concept of political jiu-jitsu in his work on the dynamics of backfire.[38] Martin reveals how violent repression sometimes backfires, not only in cases of nonviolent resistance. Many factors influence this dynamic, it is not enough for an injustice to happen. People also need to know about it, and the perpetrators of injustices that have a potential to backfire do everything possible to avoid such reactions. Martin describes five techniques perpetrators use to minimize outrage, such as cover up their actions and discredit the victims.

Sharp's theory has received much critique, especially the way he insists that power is based on consent. Kate McGuinness presented a theoretical feminist critique of this consent theory, claiming that Sharp did not have much to offer feminists resisting patriarchy.[39] Martin shows how the core of Sharp's theory is very actor oriented, thus making the forces that prevent people

---

[37] Sharp, *The Politics of Nonviolent Action*. p. 657
[38] Brian Martin, *Justice Ignited: The Dynamics of Backfire* (Lanham, MD: Rowman & Littlefield, 2007).
[39] Kate McGuinness, "Gene Sharp's Theory of Power: A Feminist Critique of Consent," *Journal of Peace Research* 30, no. 1 (1993).

from taking nonviolent action secondary. Another aspect which is not covered by Sharp's theory is the complexity of many cases of domination, for instance when someone is both subordinate but nevertheless occasionally benefit from the system. Martin sums up his critique:

> The point is that Sharp's picture focuses first and foremost on the ruler-subject dichotomy and on consent and its withdrawal, whereas a detailed analysis of the structures of power can only enter as an afterthought or as a general context for the consent picture.[40]

Vinthagen: Four dimensions of nonviolence

Stellan Vinthagen's conceptual exploration of nonviolent action, developed in his thesis *Ickevåldsaktion: En social praktik av motstånd och konstruktion* (Nonviolent action – A Social Practice of Resistance and Construction) combines Gandhi's and Sharp's insights on nonviolence with modern sociological theories developed by Jürgen Habermas, Erving Goffman, Pierre Bourdieu and Michel Foucault.[41] With this combination, he takes nonviolent theory a major step further in understanding it to be a "multi-dimensional rationality". Nonviolence is a combination of resistance and construction, expressed through four aspects which he calls *dialogue facilitation, power breaking, utopian enactment*, and *normative regulation*. Together they explain the unique rationality of nonviolent action as a tool for change, using insights from contemporary sociology to explain the rationality of nonviolence in a way which takes critique of Gandhi and Sharp seriously.

---

[40] Brian Martin, "Gene Sharp's Theory of Power," *Journal of Peace Research* 26, no. 2 (1989): p. 217.
[41] The thesis is so far only available in Swedish: Vinthagen, *Ickevåldsaktion*. Forthcoming in a shorter version in English, as Stellan Vinthagen, *A Theory of Nonviolent Action: How Civil Resistance Works* (London: ZED Books, Forthcoming 2014).

Dialogue facilitation

The choice of nonviolent action, as opposed to a violent alternative, means that nonviolent activists can be seen to engage in a kind of dialogue. In Gandhian terms, dialogue means that they are prepared to work towards a common Truth with their opponent. Vinthagen uses Habermas' thoughts on the *ideal speech situation* to develop this further. He shows how Habermas' concept of the ideal speech situation has many things in common with Gandhi's concept of satyagraha. In the ideal speech situation, the participants in the communication mean what they say and they treat each other's statements with mutual trust. The communication is undisturbed by power relations, and there is time enough to hear all people's opinions and explore what they mean. All people with a stake in the issue under consideration participate on equal terms and all have access to relevant information. Finally, everyone is ready to change their point of view based on convincing arguments by someone else. In practice, such an ideal speech situation will never occur, but is the utopia one should strive towards. In this situation, rational arguments are allowed to rule and the best argument wins, not the person who is most resourceful or best at manipulating. The ability to change one's opinion when confronted with good arguments is also a central aspect of Gandhi's philosophy, something he did himself on several occasions. In Gandhi's opinion it is a "blessing" to have an opponent, because the conversation with her helps everyone involved to reach a little closer towards Truth. In nonviolent actions, one acknowledges the possibility that one's opponent might be right, at the same time as one holds on to one's own truth until better arguments have been put forward.

Power breaking

The second aspect of Vinthagen's theory is the way nonviolence is used to break existing relations of power. Although dialogue should be free from power according to the utopia of the ideal speech situation, this is not the reality on the ground. Everyone working to change status quo is met with power in many different forms and thwarted by vested interests. The way Vinthagen describes power breaking is also a critique of Sharp's idea of power. Although they both agree that power happens in the interaction between people and is not something that exists in itself outside of the relationship, Vinthagen thinks that Sharp's view of power is too simplistic. Although individuals have a possibility to change their behaviour, this is not something they just do. Deciding to resist is not just an individual choice open to anyone who are oppressed. Using the theories of Michel Foucault and Pierre Bourdieu, Vinthagen shows that power and resistance are complex processes and not just a question of making the right choice. The research of both Foucault and Bourdieu shows that no one is outside of power and free to decide to resist. Through their upbringing, people become subordinated to power, and the power is so much part of them that they do not think about it – people just continue to act as they have always done. Obedience and submission are so infiltrated in everyone's life that they become part of their bodies, what Bourdieu calls *habitus*. For Vinthagen, power is something which people give away, often unconsciously and out of habit and conventional thinking. They are obedient because they have always been that, and "one has to follow the rules." Power should not be confused with money, property, high status or other things people associate with power. These manifestations can be tools for exercising power, but they are not power in themselves.[42]

In some of their writings, Foucault and Bourdieu almost make it sound as if resistance is not possible because power is everywhere. Vinthagen does not follow them in this. He thinks that people are at least to some degree free individuals who can make

---

[42] Vinthagen, *Ickevåldsaktion.* p. 258.

decisions about what is best for them.[43] But people, including nonviolent organisers, have to acknowledge and understand the systems of submission in order to be able to empower and liberate themselves. They need to fight actively and systematically against their internalised submission.

Even if nonviolent actions are a way of facilitating a dialogue with the opponent, the dialogue is influenced by the existing power relations. Although nonviolent actions should encourage dialogue and be open towards the opponent's good arguments, (in the cases where this is a person or an organisation) at the same time they should actively resist existing relations of power. This is of course a challenge, since those who benefit from the status quo seldom have reason to engage in dialogue until they are forced to do so. They frequently resist this dialogue on equal terms with all possible means, including devaluing the activists as persons and their motives, reframing what the action is about and using all official and unofficial sanctions at their disposal.

Utopian enactment

The third aspect of Vinthagen's theory of nonviolent action deals with how nonviolent actions can be a way of acting as if the societies the activists work towards already exist. This he calls *utopian enactment*. The activist should both believe and behave as if even the most brutal opponent at some point will be willing to change. The nonviolent action should make visible that the utopian situation is possible in principle, at least for a short moment while the action is being carried out.

Good nonviolent actions help people deal with hatred and enemy perceptions and undermine the idea that violence is normal. At the same time as the activists fight injustice, they

---

[43] Vinthagen, *Ickevåldsaktion*. p. 261.

should – to the degree it is possible – build the society they long for, just as in Gandhi's constructive work.

The problem with Habermas' ideal speech situation is not just existing power relations, but also emotions which will affect communication. Negative emotions of hatred, grief and sadness can lead to perceptions that some people are worth less than others, deserve to die or be harmed and longing for revenge for real or perceived past injustice. Facts like these influence communication from both the nonviolent activist and her opponent. Gandhi speaks about how activists should "touch the opponent's heart" to reach him or her, and that rational argumentation is not enough. He saw the self-suffering, tapasya, as one way of doing this. The ability to suffer can show the opponent the humanity of the nonviolent activist. The idea of suffering is closely connected to Indian philosophy of religion, but in Vinthagen's interpretation of the concept, self-suffering is different. He sees it as a risk of death or harm which the nonviolent activists accept as part of the struggle. Willingness to run risks is common among soldiers fighting in wars, and is nothing unique for nonviolent activists. It is not a *wish* to suffer or die, but means that one is prepared for it, or even counts on it, in the struggle for one's cause.

Vinthagen uses a drama model developed by Erving Goffman to show how nonviolent actions undermine the perception that violence is normal and for a short while dramatise what the society that the activists strive for could look like. An example from the civil rights movement in the US which Vinthagen himself uses can illustrate what he means: In May 1959, when segregation was still enforced in the southern states, a group of 10 African Americans went to Biloxi Beach in Mississipi to swim and have fun with family and friends. But this was a "white only" beach, and while the African Americans sang and walked with their picnics and swimming towels they were arrested. This way, they dramatised the injustice being done to them, and what justice would look like. The civil rights movement was good at

Illustration 2. Lunch counter sit-in in Richmond February 22, 1960 at the Thalhimer's Department Store. African American students sit orderly and ask to be served at a white only counter. Photo reprinted under GNU Free documentation license.

enacting injustices like this, where African Americans peacefully and with great dignity asked to be served in lunch restaurants for white people, or as Rosa Parks, refused to move from the seat where whites had priority on the bus. These activists were of course aware that they ran a risk of being beaten up by white people in favour of segregation or arrested by the police. But at the same time they made a live drama which showed what a more just society would look like, where going to the beach, buying lunch or taking the bus is nothing else than ordinary everyday life and not a confrontation.

Normative regulation

The fourth and last aspect of Vinthagen's theory is that in non-violent actions, the activists work towards making nonviolence the norm, something he calls normative regulation. In most societies people learn that violence is normal, at least in some situations. This "knowledge" about violence is internalised the same way as power, resulting in the perception that violence is normal even if they disapprove of it. Nonviolent activists try in different ways to "unlearn" this perception and make nonviolence the new norm. For Gandhi, the constructive programme was an important part of this education to make nonviolence central in all aspects of life. In western nonviolent movements, it is mainly through nonviolence training before big nonviolent actions that different organisations have tried to teach participants new ways of reacting. Only a small minority have taken up the idea of living in communities that emphasise nonviolence as a way of life.

Many nonviolent training methods were developed or refined during the civil rights struggle in the US. They aim to prepare the participants for what will happen during the action and make new and more desirable reactions a natural first choice. When the African Americans went into a restaurant for whites, it was important that all participants stayed calm and dignified if they were physically or verbally attacked. It should not be possible in any way to frame them as aggressive. Many people learn while growing up that it is acceptable to shout or hit back at an attacker, but the civil rights activists (as well as many other activists) had to unlearn this behaviour. Role plays are one method in this preparation, where the aim is to make dignified responses to attack and abuse a part of the body's natural reaction. The question is of course to what degree previous lessons can be unlearned and new behaviour internalised. Can this be done during a weekend course before a major nonviolent action? The nonviolent discipline in many actions with thousands of participants shows that this can be done when it comes to the action itself, but is the change so thorough that the new behaviour becomes part of a new way of life? Gandhi would probably have been sceptical of the idea that a weekend course can change well established ways of reacting much. He saw life in the communities, *ashrams*, as a daily training where nonviolent activists should live their life as a service to society and the constructive programme. For an individual to experience profound change it is often necessary to create new social relations and to be in an environment where the majority really does experience nonviolence as the norm.

Attitudes to humour in research on nonviolence

Both of the two traditions of nonviolence introduced above have shown very little interest in humour. In her PhD thesis Janjira Sombutpoonsiri gives an execellent overview of the different attitudes towards humour.[44] Those who are closest to perceiving nonviolence as a principled way of life usually dismiss humour as a legitimate method in a conflict because it can humiliate and ridicule and in the long run be counterproductive to peaceful conflict resolution.[45] However, Gandhi said that "if I had no sense of humour, I should long ago have commited suicide"[46], so this broad generalisation should be taken with a grain of salt.

Among the pragmatic approaches where nonviolence is seen as an effective method in a political struggle rather than a moral obligation, the attitude to humour is a little more positive. In his 198 methods of nonviolent resistance, Sharp also includes one which is called "Humorous skits and pranks," (number 35) where he uses examples from Eastern Europe, but he does not

[44] Janjira Sombutpoonsiri, "The Use of Humour as a Vehicle for Nonviolent Struggle: Serbia's 1996-7 Protests and the *Otpor* (Resistance) Movement" (PhD Thesis, La Trobe University, 2012).
[45] Sombutpoonsiri, "The Use of Humour as a Vehicle for Nonviolent Struggle," pp. 7-8.
[46] Mohandas Karamchand Gandhi, *All Men Are Brothers*, 1st Indian ed. (Ahmedabad: Navajivan Publishing House, 1960). p. 218.

elaborate any further on the issue.[47] Sombutpoonsiri traces a similar lack of interest for humour and even scepticism towards its effectiveness among other scholars from the proponents of pragmatic nonviolence. Humour does not seem to be found worthy of serious attention.[48]

With this introduction to the core ideas about nonviolence and their attitude to humour, it is time to turn to theories of humour and in particular the relevant research on protest and social change.

Humour research

Humour research is a multi-disciplinary field, and many different authors have written about the subject over the centuries. Psychology is the area which has produced the largest amount of academic research, but humour has also been studied from the perspective of rhetoricians, linguists, sociologists, theorists of literature, philosophers, communication theorists, and anthropologists. In his book *Blind Men and Elephants*[49], Arthur Asa Berger illustrates how each of these disciplines has contributed to explaining humour, but like in the poem to which his book title refers, each of them only sees part of the subject in question, and therefore they are not able to explain the whole of it.

There is no theory of humour with which everyone agrees. A common way of categorising theories is into three schools[50] each

---

[47] Sharp, *The Politics of Nonviolent Action*: p. 148.
[48] Sombutpoonsiri, "The Use of Humour as a Vehicle for Nonviolent Struggle," p. 10.
[49] Arthur Asa Berger, *Blind Men and Elephants: Perspectives on Humor* (New Brunswick, NJ: Transaction, 1995).
[50] This is a common way of categorising the different theories, done e.g by Linda E. Francis, "Laughter, the Best Mediation: Humor as Emotion Management in Interaction," *Symbolic Interaction* 17, no. 2 (1994); John C. Meyer, "Humor as a Double-Edged Sword: Four

with its own underlying assumptions of what humour is and how it should be explained.

1.   *Relief theory* focuses on how humour can reduce tensions, and how it is used to express forbidden ideas and deal with taboo topics. Sigmund Freud is the person most closely associated with this approach to humour.

2.   *Superiority theory* claims that humour is a way of showing who is superior, and even when we laugh at ourselves, we laugh at a part of us which is inferior. 16th century philosopher Thomas Hobbes put forward this theory. In modern times, Charles R. Gruner is the only humour theorist who claims that all humour is based on aggression, and a dichotomy of winning-losing.

3.   *Incongruity theory* is concerned with the cognitive perception of what is funny, and is the most widespread way of explaining humour today. This theory says that in order for us to perceive something as funny, there has to be an incongruity or ambiguity which forces us to think in more than one dimension at the same time.

Although some theorists see their own theory as a way of explaining *all* humour, each of these three perspectives contributes something meaningful to the understanding of humour, but no single one provides the full explanation. Humour is not one thing, but a label which has relations to both cognitive processes, emotions within the individual, interpersonal relations in small groups as well as broader social relations in our societies. As

---

Functions of Humor in Communication," *Communication Theory* 10, no. 3 (2000); Michael Billig, *Laughter and Ridicule: Towards a Social Critique of Laughter* (London: Sage, 2005); Simon Critchley, *On Humour* (London: Routledge, 2002).

sociologist Jerry Palmer has suggested, it seems unrealistic to demand that one theory should explain all this.[51]

Incongruity theory explains the cognitive process that needs to be present in order to generate humour. Relief theory is one way of explaining why an individual chooses to use humour in a certain situation, or laugh at a particular joke. Superiority theory can explain some forms of aggressive humour.

Since this thesis is about the use of humour as a method of social activism, the humour I present here is constructed to be part of a social conflict. It is kicking upwards to criticise particular people in power or systems of power – for example dictators, elected politicians considered to take themselves too seriously, dominant "isms" of any kind, or a company profiting from environmental exploitation or human suffering. Therefore it should be no surprise that it includes many examples of humour which some people would call aggressive – that is, humour which criticises, humiliates, ridicules or in some way aims at "speaking truth to power". Nevertheless I want to emphasise that I do not consider this a contribution to Gruner's theory about humour's universal aggressiveness.[52]

It is not the purpose here to discuss all the literature on humour, and I will only look in depth at the theories and literature which are relevant for the theme of humorous political activism which aims to challenge power relationships. This means that I will focus on sociological theories of humour and what has been written about political humour or humour related to social conflict.

---

[51] Jerry Palmer, *Taking Humour Seriously* (London: Routledge, 1994). p. 5.
[52] Charles R. Gruner, *The Game of Humor: A Comprehensive Theory of Why We Laugh* (New Brunswick, NJ: Transaction Publishers, 1997).

Defining humour

Humour is special way of communicating. In itself, it is neither good nor bad. It can be used to hurt other people, and it can be used to make them happy, just like other methods or mediums for communication. In his article "Humor as a Double-Edged Sword: Four Functions of Humor in Communication", John C. Meyer calls this ability to both unite and divide "the paradox of humour".[53] Michael Billig has identified three other paradoxes of humour. It is both universal and particular, meaning that all cultures have a sense of something that is funny, but not everyone finds the same things funny. [54] In addition, the impulse to laugh appears to be biological.[55] Another paradox that Billig has identified is similar to Meyer's paradox: Humour is both inclusive and exclusive. Finally, there is the third paradox regarding humour's ability to be mysterious and resist rational analysis at the same time as it *is* possible to understand and analyse it.[56]

My focus is on political humour which aims to criticise power. Most of the examples I provide are from grassroots organisations who "kick upwards" and criticise abuse, self-righteousness and dominant truths and world views. That humour can be used in this way does not exclude the fact that it is frequently used to ridicule minorities and humiliate those at the bottom of society as well.[57]

Psychologist Rod Martin, in his introductory book on humour and psychology, uses this definition with four components:

---

[53] Meyer, "Humor as a Double-Edged Sword: Four Functions of Humor in Communication," p. 323.
[54] Billig, *Laughter and Ridicule: Towards a Social Critique of Laughter.* p. 176.
[55] Rod A. Martin, *The Psychology of Humor: An Integrative Approach* (Burlington, MA: Elsevier Academic Press, 2007). pp. 2-3.
[56] Billig, *Laughter and Ridicule: Towards a Social Critique of Laughter.* p. 176.
[57] Critchley, *On Humour.*

1.   Humour has a social aspect, which is associated with play. When using humour, people operate in a different mode than when they talk seriously.

2.   Secondly, there is a cognitive-perceptual component of humour. This is the mental process which needs to happen in order for people to perceive something as funny.

3.   Humour also has an emotional aspect. People do not just react to something funny intellectually, it also creates a good feeling. English does not really have a word to describe this feeling, but Martin calls it *mirth*.

4.   Finally, the emotion of mirth is frequently expressed through laughter. Laughter is a signal that this is play and not serious.[58]

This is a useful operational definition, but the way the humorous is contrasted with seriousness makes this an inadequate way of defining some political humour which has a serious intent. Although political humour operates within a play frame and generates laughter and amusement this should not be confused with not being serious.

One interview with an Ofog activist in particular caused me to question Martin's (and most other humour researcher's) choice of words. Lisa and I had just talked about a humorous nonviolent action that activists in Ofog had carried out, and Lisa had expressed concern about the problems with combining the ironic with the serious when it became obvious how problematic the term serious is in this context:

> Majken: But [how do you mean], when you talk about serious and non-serious, because I think that something like Reality AB [the action] is very serious…?

---

[58] Martin, *The Psychology of Humor: An Integrative Approach*: chapter one.

Lisa: yes, yes, serious was maybe the wrong choice [of word], ehh, serious as in non-ironic, that is what I mean

Majken: yes, yes, grave and… (hesitant)

Lisa: yeeees (hesitant)

Majken: The other is also grave, no, it is very difficult with the words (both laugh)

Lisa: Yes, grave and serious

Majken: Yes, I think I understand what you mean

When I first listened to this interview I felt very embarrassed that I did not manage to express myself more clearly, but then realised that humour research had not provided me with a language to have this kind of conversation. The core of the problem was that both everyday language and humour research use a terminology that is not adequate for talking about humour that has a very serious intent.

I am not the first to notice this contradiction, since it is implicitly addressed in a book title like *Taking humour seriously*, [59] and briefly mentioned as a side comment by scholars writing about political humour.[60] Linda Hutcheon in her book about irony writes that "even humorous ironies can be deadly serious.[61] However, the implication for humour studies as such has not been discussed. I

[59] Palmer, *Taking Humour Seriously*.
[60] Villy Tsakona and Diana Elena Popa, "Humour in Politics and the Politics of Humour: An Introduction," in *Studies in Political Humour: In between Political Critique and Public Entertainment*, ed. Villy Tsakona and Diana Elena Popa (Amsterdam ; Philadelphia: John Benjamins Pub. Company, 2011) Suzana B. Rodrigues and David L. Collinson, "'Having Fun'? Humour as Resistance in Brazil," *Organization Studies* 16, no. 5 (1995): p. 755.
[61] Linda Hutcheon, *Irony's Edge: The Theory and Politics of Irony* (London: Routledge, 1995). p. 26.

suggest that if the term "seriously" is replaced by "rational argument", Martin's definition is still valid.

Sociological theory on humour

The sociologists of humour have hardly paid any attention to political humour and its relations with power. The focus has been on developing broader sociologies of humour and humour's place in everyday life and interaction. Marvin Koller described the different social functions of humour, including social correction and provoking thought.[62] Michael Mulkay made an important contribution to the study of humour when he suggested that the humorous mode or discourse operates in a way which is very different from the serious mode or discourse we engage in most of the time.[63]

In the serious mode, we do our best to avoid misunderstandings, incongruity and double meanings. We assume that there exists a "real" world, and that other people potentially can see the world more or less the same way as us. When we discover that someone perceives that reality in a way which is different to our own understanding, we look for explanations for the discrepancies.

In contrast, says Mulkay, we have the humorous mode, which requires us to think in a different way. It is based on incongruity and duality, and we can only grasp humour when we switch to the humorous mode of understanding the world, where inconsistency and ambiguity are part of the rules. As I mentioned when discussing definitions of humour, I agree with this differentiation between a humorous and a non-humorous mode of communication. However, I think it is inappropriate to call the other mode *serious*, since this indicates that humour cannot be

---

[62] Marvin R. Koller, Humor and Society: Explorations in the Sociology of Humor (Houston: Cap and Gown Press, 1988).
[63] Michael J. Mulkay, *On Humour: Its Nature and Its Place in Modern Society* (Cambridge: Polity Press, 1988).

serious. Instead I will refer to the non-humorous mode as *rational*. I do not disagree with the basic idea that Mulkay presents, since it is the incongruities in the humorous mode which appear to be essential to him, I just point out that the word "serious" is misleading.

Within the same tradition of incongruity, Peter Berger has written about how humour requires us to think in more than one dimension at the same time[64], and Jerry Palmer has brought our attention to the fact that humour has to be negotiated, to be permitted, in order to be able to happen. Every theory of humour also needs to take into consideration that humorous intent is not enough for humour to succeed. Humour is fragile and can easily fail. This does not mean that the butt of the joke or prank has to agree that something is funny, but either the situation demands or the audience agrees that this was humorous.[65] He points to the fact that there is a huge difference between laboratory experiments with psychology students and a stand-up comedy show in real life. Every comedian knows that a show has to be "built up", and the joke which is a success towards the end can't be told until the audience is warmed up.[66]

In his writing about humorous incongruity, Palmer works with a concept he calls *the logic of the absurd*, which consists of two parts. In order for an incongruity to be funny, it has to appear suddenly in order to surprise us. At the same time the cognitive process of perceiving something as both implausible and slightly plausible at the same time has to happen.[67] Palmer thinks that a combination

[64] Peter L. Berger, *Redeeming Laughter: The Comic Dimension of Human Experience* (New York: Walter de Gruyter, 1997).
[65] Palmer, *Taking Humour Seriously*.
[66] Palmer, *Taking Humour Seriously*: p. 4.
[67] Palmer uses this joke to discuss the concept: "Doctor, come at once! Our baby swallowed a fountain pen". "I'll be right over. What are you doing in the meantime?" "Using a pencil." (page 95). People only laugh

of an incongruity as well as an adequate level of arousal is required to produce humour. If the arousal is too high, we will experience a feeling of threat and anxiety rather than mirth.[68] Elliott Oring has used the term *appropriate incongruity* to express similar thoughts.[69] The development of incongruity theory within psychology is long and complicated, but the details are not relevant here.[70]

When we go to a comedy show, the situation immediately makes us understand that something is intended to be funny, but in everyday interaction, it is a constant negotiation about what constitutes humour and what does not.[71] There is no automatic relationship between intention and what others perceive. Shared humour depends on shared context and knowledge of the cues that make a situation humorous as well as emotional resonance.[72] However, something can be negotiated as humour, even if the

---

at this situation if they understand it as a joke, where the narrative development involves the creation of a sudden incongruity. In this case, says Palmer, people consider the parents' reaction highly implausible, and at the same time it is possible to consider it just a little bit plausible, since the doctor's question of what they are doing in the meantime is phrased so ambiguously that it can be understood in more than one way. However, had this been a real situation, it is more likely that the parents had said that they did not know what to do. Palmer also discusses what cues make people understand that this is a joke, because they would not laugh at this story if it had been told "cold" as a true story (they would have been concerned about the baby's safety).

[68] Palmer, *Taking Humour Seriously*: p. 100.

[69] Elliott Oring, *Engaging Humor* (Urbana, IL: University of Illinois Press, 2003). chapter 1.

[70] Readers interested the background can start by reading Martin, *The Psychology of Humor: An Integrative Approach*; Oring, *Engaging Humor*; Palmer, *Taking Humour Seriously*. Here are many references to psychologists who started the investigations of incongruity.

[71] Palmer, *Taking Humour Seriously*: p. 111.

[72] Palmer, *Taking Humour Seriously*: p. 150.

butt of it disagrees and sees this as non-humorous, an important point which I will return to later. When something which is intended as humour is perceived differently, Palmer thinks there can be many different explanations. He points to reasons such as the skills of the performer or the use of mediums we now consider old-fashioned, like silent movies. In addition, intended humour can be considered offensive either because of the structure of the humour, the relationships between the parties involved or the nature of the occasion.[73]

Murray S. Davis also places himself firmly in the incongruity tradition,[74] and argues that nothing is incongruous in itself, only in relation to something else, when there is something which does not fit in.[75] Along the same lines as Oring and Palmer, Davis argues that the incongruity has to be moderate in order to be considered funny.[76] Davis' contribution to the sociology of humour is a thorough description of all the different ways humour can be generated when one unit of a social system is replaced with something incongruent. This way, humour draws our attention to the essential parts of social systems and what it means to be human.[77]

---

[73] Palmer, *Taking Humour Seriously*: p. 164.

[74] Murray S. Davis, *What's So Funny?: The Comic Conception of Culture and Society* (Chigaco: University of Chicago Press, 1993). p. 12.

[75] Davis, *What's So Funny?: The Comic Conception of Culture and Society*: p. 13.

[76] Davis, *What's So Funny?: The Comic Conception of Culture and Society*: p. 15.

[77] Davis considers incongruity and ambiguity to be two different ways of constructing humour, and both require that we take out part of a system and replace it with an incongruent part. *Incongruity* is when we see a problem which is internal in the system, something does not really fit in. *Ambiguity*, on the other hand, is when we encounter external similarities, so that something fits into more than one system at the same time. Davis himself continues that it can be hard to separate the

Summing up the sociologies of humour, it is obvious that the incongruity tradition has been a common point of reference for sociologists. Political humour has not played a major role in any of these works which aim to categorise and explain how humour works in society. An exception to this, which is the focus of the next section, is the category of political jokes.

A sociological article that deserves mentioning in this section as well is "Romance, Irony, and Solidarity" by Ronald Jacobs and Philip Smith. They have looked at the relationship between irony and civil society, and are mainly concerned about improving theory of civil society. They are critical of existing theory of civil society because culture, emotions and identity have been neglected in this metanarrative and a consequence is

> a latently mechanistic conception of human action; a failure to consider identity as multiple, contradictory, hybrid, or public; and an inability to explain how democratic institutions and procedures sometimes promote social out-outcomes that are neither just nor moral.[78]

In order to have discourses within civil society that promote "healthy' political cultures"[79], Jacobs and Smith argue that the genres of romance and irony should be brought into public life and not delegated to the sphere of the private. Combined these two genres provide a discourse that makes room for the four attributes they consider essential for a descriptive/normative theory of civil society – inter-subjectivity, solidarity, reflexivity, and tolerance. Romance and irony each have virtues and vices which supplement each other. Among the positive sides of irony, Jacobs and Smith point towards irony's potential to disrupt

---

two in practice, and I will not apply this distinction. Davis, *What's So Funny?: The Comic Conception of Culture and Society*: p. 24.
[78] Ronald N. Jacobs and Philip Smith, "Romance, Irony, and Solidarity," *Sociological Theory* 15, no. 1 (1997): p. 61.
[79] Jacobs and Smith, "Romance, Irony, and Solidarity," p. 61.

power and encourage reflexive processes in civil society.[80] However, they also warn against irony's risk of being trapped in
fatalism and becoming disengaged from civil society if it just
creates ironic distance without providing alternatives.[81]

A similar argumentation is used by Robert Hariman in his article
"Political Parody and Public Culture"[82] where he argues that
parody is essential for a democratic public culture. According to
him "genres such as parody play a particularly crucial role in
keeping democratic speech a multiplicity of discourses."[83] The
reason is that as soon as something has been "doubled" through
parody, it can no longer pretend to be an uncontested truth.[84]

Several contributions to humour studies have focused on the
different functions of humour in relation to social interaction.[85]
However, their categorisations are not adequate to (or meant to)
understand political humour which challenges power relations.

---

[80] Jacobs and Smith, "Romance, Irony, and Solidarity," p. 71.
[81] Jacobs and Smith, "Romance, Irony, and Solidarity," p. 73.
[82] Robert Hariman, "Political Parody and Public Culture," *Quarterly Journal of Speech* 94, no. 3 (2008).
[83] Hariman, "Political Parody and Public Culture," p. 260.
[84] Adam Krause argues for the same connection between comedy, creativity and democratic thinking, although he suggest to distinguish between progressive humour and regressive humour (which is for instance racist and reinforcing stereotypes.) Adam Krause, *The Revolution Will Be Hilarious* (Porsgrunn, Norway: New Compass Press, 2013).
[85] Francis, "Laughter, the Best Mediation: Humor as Emotion Management in Interaction."; Meyer, "Humor as a Double-Edged Sword: Four Functions of Humor in Communication."; Craig Zelizer, "Laughing Our Way to Peace or War: Humour and Peacebuilding," *Journal of Conflictology* 1, no. 2 (2010).

Humour, politics, protest and social conflict

The amount of academic literature about political humour is enormous. Frequently it is approached as a certain type of genre (like satire, parodies or cartoons) presented in a certain medium (such as TV or the Internet).[86] Others have analysed political humour from a historical perspective,[87] politicians' use of humour,[88] or tried to create artificial experiments about the use of humour in equal and unequal power relations.[89]

Humour as an expression of social protest has a long history, but it is debated as to whether it works as a safety valve, allowing a dissatisfied population to let off steam now and then, or if it actually contribute to resistance. In this section, I begin with presenting research on political jokes and traditional folly as an

---

[86] See for instance Lijun Tang and Syamantak Bhattacharya, "Power and Resistance: A Case Study of Satire on the Internet," *Sociological Research Online* 16, no. 2 (2011). Hariman, "Political Parody and Public Culture." Jay D. Hmielowski, R. Lance Holbert, and Jayeon Lee, "Predicting the Consumption of Political TV Satire: Affinity for Political Humor, the Daily Show, and the Colbert Report," *Communication Monographs* 78, no. 1 (2011). Conal Condren, "Between Social Constraint and the Public Sphere: On Misreading Early-Modern Political Satire," *Contemporary Political Theory* 1(2002). Conal Condren, "Satire and Definition," *Humor: International Journal of Humor Research* 25, no. 4 (2012). Condren discusses the problems with defining satire and the limitations with considering it a literary genre.

[87] Martina Kessel and Patrick Merziger, *The Politics of Humour: Laughter, Inclusion, and Exclusion in the Twentieth Century* (Toronto: University of Toronto Press, 2012); Arthur Power Dudden, "The Record of Political Humor," *American Quarterly* 37, no. 1 (1985).

[88] See chapters two to five in Villy Tsakona and Diana Elena Popa, *Studies in Political Humour: In between Political Critique and Public Entertainment* (Amsterdam: John Benjamins, 2011).

[89] Norah E. Banas John A. Rodriguez DarielaLiu Shr-JieAbra Gordon Dunbar, "Humor Use in Power-Differentiated Interactions," *Humor: International Journal of Humor Research* 25, no. 4 (2012).

expression of protest, and continue with various case studies on humour as a form of protest against occupations and dictatorships. Both gender studies and organisational theory have also provided insights into humour's influence on power relations. The small body of literature which focuses specifically on humour as nonviolent resistance is presented before I round off with humour's relationship with other types of creative activism such as culture jamming, pranks and tactical carnival.

Political jokes

Jokes have been a relatively popular source for studying humour, both in psychology and when it comes to social aspects of humour. Because they come as a ready "package", jokes are short and do not require much explanation compared to everyday conversational humour. Jokes also differ from the comedy we watch on TV. Although professional comedians often use jokes, it is an even more packaged product. The public humorous stunts and performances which I will present are also very different from jokes.

One of those who has written most extensively on jokes from a sociological point of view and their relation to society is Christie Davis. Among other things he has studied jokes about stupidity and political jokes in the former Soviet Union.

In his book *Jokes and their Relation to Society* Davies explores how jokes about stupidity and the canny have developed from being about other localities (the next village, a certain region) to being about other ethnicities.[90] He illustrates how the butts of the jokes are not the very foreign, but those that are slightly different, like a distorted image of yourself in a strange mirror. Jokes about a certain group do not indicate that this group is a victim of hate,

---

[90] Christie Davies, *Jokes and Their Relation to Society* (Berlin: Mouton de Gruyter, 1998).

and they are not a sign of social conflict. As an example, he mentions that jokes about Poles and Irish people's stupidity in the US do not mean that they are the ones who are most marginalised. He quotes two English boys who are interviewed about jokes about the Irish, who says "We have nothing against the Irish; my father and his father are Irish. They are just *supposed to be stupid.*"[91] Davies argues that the reason people enjoy stupidity jokes is their own fear of the modern world, which is so complicated that people usually cannot explain how the machines they use every day work. This uneasiness leads people to joke about those whom they imagine cannot understand even the simplest things.[92]

In the former Soviet Union and Eastern Europe under Soviet dominance before the fall of the Berlin wall and the nonviolent revolutions in many of these countries, jokes about stupidity were not directed towards minorities, but towards the most powerful people in society, the party members, planners, bureaucrats and police. This way, jokes about stupidity became political jokes, in societies where the rulers did not just want to rule, but expected people to celebrate them and attempted to control all aspects of social and private life. However, Davies thinks that it is still the same mechanisms that guide these jokes. Behind the iron curtain they just took a slightly different turn.[93]

Davies is very hesitant in calling these jokes a protest. He understands them to be a sign of dissatisfaction and they showed that the communist systems were unstable, but they were not a sign of active resistance. He disagrees with those who have proposed that the more repressive a regime is, the more political humour directed against it one will find. There were more jokes about the

---

[91] McCosh 1979 p. 117, quoted in Davies, *Jokes and Their Relation to Society*: p. 24. Emphasis in original.
[92] Davies, *Jokes and Their Relation to Society*: p. 28.
[93] Davies, *Jokes and Their Relation to Society*: p. 78.

communist regimes after 1956 when control and repression were relaxed a bit compared to the previous decades. But neither does Davies support those who have put forward the opposite idea, that political jokes prevent resistance because they become a vent for frustration. He simply says that political jokes are a sign of the system's instability, but that they do not help or prevent active resistance.[94]

Gregor Benton, is his chapter "The Origins of the Political Joke"[95] about political jokes in the Soviet Union under dictatorship, insists that the political joke is not a form of resistance, and that a smart repressive regime permits jokes about it as "a clever insurance against more serious challenges to the system."[96] Without providing any documentation for his claim, he finishes his chapter with a very strong statement that claims that political jokes cannot change anything:

> But the political joke will change nothing. It is the relentless enemy of greed, injustice, cruelty and oppression – but it could never do without them. It is not a form of active resistance. It reflects no political programme. It will mobilise no one. Like the Jewish joke in its time, it is important for keeping society sane and stable. It cushions the blows of cruel governments and creates sweet illusions of revenge. It has the virtue of momentarily freeing the lives of millions from the tensions and frustrations to which even the best organised political opposition can promise only

---

[94] Christie Davies, "Humour and Protest: Jokes under Communism," *International Review of Social History* 52, no. S15 (2007).
[95] Gregor Benton, "The Origins of the Political Joke," in *Humour in Society: Resistance and Control*, ed. Chris Powell and George E. C. Paton (New York: St. Martin's Press, 1988).
[96] Benton, "The Origins of the Political Joke," p. 41.

long-term solutions, but its impact is a fleeting as the laughter it produces.[97]

Alexander Rose is another academic writer who looks at political jokes. In "When Politics is a Laughing Matter"[98] he explores the differences between jokes in democracies and jokes under authoritarian rule. He finds that in a democracy the focus is on individual politicians and their personal shortcomings, but not their politics. In authoritarian regimes, there is more focus on exposing the difference between the visions and realities of the politics.

Egon Larsen's book *Wit as a Weapon: The Political Joke in History*[99] is a collection of political humour which includes many examples of jokes as well as descriptions of some satirical journals and cabarets from around the world. The title suggests that the author thinks humour has an ability to influence people, but the book does not include any analysis of this or explain what sort of harm can be done with this "weapon".

"Wit and Politics: An essay on Laughter and Power"[100] by Hans Speier as well as Don L. F. Nilsen's "The Social Functions of Political Humor "[101] should also be mentioned in this section about jokes, since their data consist almost exclusively of jokes, supplemented by some witty remarks. Nilsen is categorising the political jokes according to the social function they serve when told by politicians or political commentators. The categories include disarming critics, making a point, or exposing chauvin-

---

[97] Benton, "The Origins of the Political Joke."p. 54.
[98] Alexander Rose, "When Politics Is a Laughing Matter," *Policy Review*, no. January (2002).
[99] Egon Larsen, *Wit as a Weapon: The Political Joke in History* (London: F. Muller, 1980).
[100] Hans Speier, "Wit and Politics: An Essay on Power and Laughter," *American Journal of Sociology* 103, no. 5 (1998).
[101] Don L. F. Nilsen, "The Social Functions of Political Humor," *Journal of Popular Culture* 24, no. 3 (1990).

ism, ineptitude, oppression, pretentiousness and relieving tension. Speier also divides his material into categories such as "The diversionary and soothing jokes", "The healing joke", "The cynical political joke" and so on. Speier reflects on the role of humour in relation to politics and power, and sees it as just another way of struggling for power, along with flattery, bribery and violence. He points out how certain jokes and techniques appear to be timeless and can travel huge distances. Speier thinks that there are more jokes from "above" at the expense of the downtrodden than from below that kick upwards, but does not document this claim.[102] This idea of humour's potential for reinforcing social hierarchies appears now and then[103] with a reference to two studies in two psychiatric wards where the high ranked staff initiated joking more often than lower ranked staff during staff meetings.[104] However, the data for these studies are from formal meetings, not recordings of what happens when the high ranked staff are not present. Coser even specifically mentions that the findings might have been different in more informal settings. In a similar way, Speier has no access to humour which is kicking upwards in the data he uses, since humour from "below" is not documented in the same way as speeches and biographies of statesmen. The discussion about numbers is quite irrelevant since it is unlikely to reach any conclusion, but I will provide many examples of political humour from below, although none will be in the form of jokes.

---

[102] Speier, "Wit and Politics: An Essay on Power and Laughter," p. 1353.
[103] See for instance Palmer, *Taking Humour Seriously*; Martin, *The Psychology of Humor: An Integrative Approach*.
[104] Rose Laub Coser, "Laughter among Colleagues," *Psychiatry: Journal of the Biology and the Pathology of Interpersonal Relations* 23, no. 1 (1960); J. Sayre, "The Use of Aberrant Medical Humor by Psychiatric Unit Staff," *Issues in Mental Health Nursing* 22, no. 7 (2001).

Traditional folly

One of the most cited works on carnival and traditional folly is Mikhail Bakhtin's *Rabelais and His World*,[105] which he wrote in the late 1930s during Stalin's rule. The book is a thesis about the French Renaissance writer Rabelais, whom Bakthin believes it is only possible to understand when the context of medieval carnival is taken into consideration. To Bakhtin, carnival is a liberation from the prevailing truths and order,[106] and the grotesque in art and literature (such as in Rabelais) is only possible to understand in the spirit of carnival. The book has been interpreted as a critique of the repression in the Soviet Union and was not published until 1965. Although still widely cited and acclaimed, Bakhtin's claims about carnival have also been strongly contested.[107]

Another author who writes about traditional folly but from a very different perspective is Anton Zijderveld who focuses on medieval and early modern Europe in his book *Reality in a Looking-Glass*.[108] Zijderveld thinks that traditional folly was diverse. Some of it was conservative in preserving traditions and enforcing social norms, but other aspects were critical of all norms and rules. More than anything else, traditional folly was ambiguous.[109]

The fools were outcasts and pariahs of society, but popular because of the entertainment they provided. Folly was often the

---

[105] M. M. Bakhtin, *Rabelais and His World*, trans. Helene Iswolsky (Bloomington, IN: Indiana University Press, 1984 [1965]).
[106] Bakhtin, *Rabelais and His World*: p. 10.
[107] See for instance Condren, "Between Social Constraint and the Public Sphere: On Misreading Early-Modern Political Satire." Simon Dentith, *Bakhtinian Thought: An Introductory Reader* (London: Routledge, 1995). p. 74.
[108] Anton C. Zijderveld, *Reality in a Looking-Glass: Rationality through an Analysis of Traditional Folly* (London: Routledge & Kegan Paul, 1982).
[109] Zijderveld, *Reality in a Looking-Glass: Rationality through an Analysis of Traditional Folly*: p. 4.

expression of a pagan past, covered by a thin layer of Christianity. It could be a disguise for critique but most entertainers were ready to ridicule everything and everyone and did not have a political agenda. Church leadership and double standards were good material for entertainment, and much unrest was released through folly. Nevertheless, Zijderveld thinks that most of the fools were "opportunistic critiques" without ideology.[110] One of the most well-known examples of medieval folly was the "festival of fools," organised by the lower clergy in different versions all over Europe. Central elements were cross dressing, eating forbidden food, riding on a donkey with head towards tail, electing a choir boy for bishop, playing dice in front of the altar and in various ways reversing and turning conventions upside down. The tradition was condemned by the higher clergy, who interpreted it as a cover for pagan fertility traditions, but nevertheless continued for several hundred years. In the end it disappeared because of modernisation, not condemnation. According to Zidjerveld, folly was never intended as an ideological critique of power, but in its practice ended up as an important critique of the status quo. He thinks that the idea of folly as a safety valve needed for release once a year in order to keep unrest at bay at other times had nothing to do with reality. It was an argument invented by the lower clergy in order to be able to continue the traditions that they enjoyed.[111]

Another medieval tradition which Zijderveld takes a closer look at is the court jester of the 16th and 17th centuries. At this time the court jester was firmly established as an institution and started to depart from its roots among the medieval fools. Zidjerveld calls the court jesters "parasites of power", and sees

---

[110] Zijderveld, *Reality in a Looking-Glass: Rationality through an Analysis of Traditional Folly*: pp. 52-56.
[111] Zijderveld, *Reality in a Looking-Glass: Rationality through an Analysis of Traditional Folly*: p. 91.

them as an integrated part of the absolutist monarch institution. The idea of the court jester "speaking truth to power" might be more of a myth than reality, since the court jester was considered a kind of pet along with the royal dogs. The court jester would do everything to please his master and knew his tastes, which meant that he attacked other people in powerful positions, such as intellectuals or religious people, with spiteful words, or played tricks on those out of favour with the king. However, his own master would never be the butt of the joke.

The writings of Bakhtin and Zidjerveld illustrate that, just as with the political jokes of today, the historical role of humour in protest and social conflict is by no means straightforward. The same can be said of the humour during occupations and dictatorships which is the subject in the next section, where there exists considerable disagreement about its achievements.

Humour in occupations and dictatorships

Academic literature on humour as a method for protest in modern times is relatively limited, and even the literature which has been published in academic journals sometimes is more anecdotal than contributing to development of theoretical understanding. Humour from different occupations and dictatorships has been studied in various academic fields.

Already in 1942, Antonin J. Obrdlik wrote "'Gallows humor' – A Sociological Phenomenon" which was published in the American Journal of Sociology.[112] The article is interesting because it is an early contribution to the topic that this thesis is concerned with. Obrdlik gives a first-hand account of the Czech humour during the Nazi invasion of Czechoslovakia. He uses the term *gallows humour* to describe all the humour used by people in a difficult situation, no matter what they joke about. The claims in

---

[112] Antonin J. Obrdlik, "'Gallows Humor'- a Sociological Phenomenon," *The American Journal of Sociology* 47, no. 5 (1942).

the article are not very well documented, and it does not include a single reference. However, there is no reason to doubt the accuracy of the anecdotes and jokes Obrdlik recounts. Obrdlik makes two major claims about the social functions of humour:

1. That it helps increase morale among a repressed people. He also thinks that the amount and strength of humour is a sign of how morale is doing. If there is no humour directed against the occupier, he thinks it means that people have given up.

2. The second claim is that humour disintegrates the forces that it is directed against. There is no documentation of this claim, although Obrdlik attempts to justify it. His most convincing argument is that the Nazi's anger towards the humour is a proof that it hurts. Obrdlik argues that an enemy that felt in control would not take humour seriously. That humour directed against the occupation forces was severely punished, and that graffiti removed immediately, meant that the Nazis felt insecure.

Much later, humour from two other countries occupied by Nazi Germany from 1940-45, Denmark and Norway, has been described in academic literature. Nathaniel Hong in his article "Mow'em all down grandma: The 'weapon' of humor in two Danish World War II scrapbooks"[113] uses humour from two Danish scrapbooks from the occupation to discuss to what degree humour is a political weapon. He claims that most people who write about political humour overestimate its potential as a form of resistance without actually having any data behind their claims. Hong thinks that by using the scrapbooks as sources the

---

[113] Nathaniel Hong, "Mow 'Em All Down Grandma: The 'Weapon' of Humor in Two Danish World War II Occupation Scrapbooks," *Humor: International Journal of Humor Research* 23, no. 1 (2010).

way he does, he comes much closer to the everyday life of ordinary people and their use of humour than many other researchers. First and foremost, the scrapbooks show the complexity of the issue.

One of the collectors of humour who Hong looks at is called Jensen. He primarily seemed to use his book to get through these difficult years more easily and Hong thinks that the humour in his books became a substitute for real resistance. The other collector is called Holmboe, and he collected many examples of jokes in circulation and wrote down humorous anecdotes. Holmboe himself said that what he tried to do was document the mood of the Danish population during these years. His primary concern was the free flow of information, free speech and the way censorship prevented that. His family participated in many different forms of resistance activities, and according to Hong, the humour which Holmboe collected shows how humour can be part of a critical reflection. However, humour was only a minor part of Holmboe's huge material, which mainly consisted of newspaper articles.

Hong thinks the power of humour is overestimated, but his main focus is jokes, which do not engage with the enemy/opponent as long as they are whispered in private. Only a few of Hong's examples are public and therefore part of an interaction with the German occupier. Because of this focus on jokes, the article's conclusions have little relevance for this thesis. But although Hong uses written primary sources, we still know little about to what degree the private jokes contributed to creating a culture of resistance and a hidden transcript, a subject I will return to shortly. Although the humour turned out to be a safety valve for scrapbook writer Jensen, Hong presents no data to show that everyone else reacted the same way.

In her writings about the use of humour as resistance to the Nazi occupation in Norway 1940-45, Kathleen Stokker[114] notes that quisling humour (directed towards Vidkun Quisling, the leader of the Norwegian Nazi party) protected people's self-respect and gave the population some sort of control in an uncontrollable situation.[115] The jokes also served to break down isolation and create a solidarity and group identity within the population. Because so many people shared the jokes, their very existence contradicted the Nazi propaganda that people who did not join them would stand alone.[116] Stokker writes: "The jokes also provided an image of nation-wide solidarity that vitally assisted the resistance effort."[117] Stokker compares the Norwegian occupation humour with jokes from Eastern Europe during dictatorship, and finds that in Norwegian humour "everyone" fights back, and support for the resistance movement is found in the most unusual places, whereas in Eastern Europe, the jokes show that you should trust no one.[118]

In the post-war period, the jokes have helped create the myth that "everybody" participated in the resistance, and that nobody supported the occupation, which is contradicted by the fact that 60.000 Norwegians joined the Nazi party. Similarly, Patrick Merziger, writing about humour in Nazi Germany itself, has identified a post-war perception of whispered jokes that has

---

[114] Kathleen Stokker, "Quisling Humor in Hitler's Norway: Its Wartime Function and Postwar Legacy," *Humor* 14, no. 4 (2001); Kathleen Stokker, *Folklore Fights the Nazis: Humor in Occupied Norway, 1940-1945* (Madison, WI: University of Wisconsin Press, 1997).
[115] Stokker, "Quisling Humor in Hitler's Norway," p. 339.
[116] Stokker, "Quisling Humor in Hitler's Norway," p. 349.
[117] Stokker, "Quisling Humor in Hitler's Norway," p. 339.
[118] Stokker, *Folklore Fights the Nazis*: pp. 102-03.

served to overstate the distance between the German people and the Nazi party.[119]

Humour from a different occupation has also been collected and presented in an academic article. In "Humor of the Palestinian Intifada", Sharif Kanaana presents resistance humour from the occupied Palestinian territories from the first Intifada.[120] She and her assistants have collected around 200 different jokes and anecdotes about the Intifada from all parts of Palestine. The majority are about Palestinians triumphing over Israelis. The Israelis in the jokes are almost exclusively the Israeli Army, not Jews, and not even settlers. In a minority of the jokes collected, the butt are Palestinians who are not doing enough for the Intifada, and in a few cases, collected late in the Intifada, the target is the leadership of the Intifada.

In the stories about Palestinians triumphing over the Israeli soldiers, it is very often women and children from non-urban settings who are smarter than the soldiers and intuitively understand what the Intifada is about. The jokes are not violent towards the Israeli soldiers, even when the soldiers are captured. The strength of the Palestinians lies in their humiliation of the soldiers. The author also contrasts the intifada jokes to her perception of pre-intifada humour, where Palestinians made fun of themselves and seemed to lack self-respect.

Apart from dividing the humour into categories depending on their theme, the article does not contribute to any theoretical developments. However, it is an interesting finding that the humour during the Intifada was mainly nonviolent, and seeking

---

[119] Patrick Merziger, "Humour in Nazi Germany: Resistance and Propaganda? The Popular Desire for an All-Embracing Laughter," *International Review of Social History* 52, no. S15 (2007).
[120] Sharif Kanaana, "Humor of the Palestinian 'Intifada'," *Journal of Folklore Research* 27 no. 3 (1990).

out alternative ways of humiliating the enemy, rather than promoting violence.

A recent article about humour utilised against a dictatorship is Helmy and Frerichs' "Stripping the Boss: The Powerful Role of Humor in the Egyptian Revolution 2011".[121] They argue from a social psychological perspective that humour can be a "resource in power battles"[122], and conclude that humour was a stress buffer during the Egyptian revolution in February 2011. They even go as far as saying that without the extensive use of open ridicule of President Mubarak and other forms of public humour, it would not have been possible for the activists to sustain their occupation of Tahrir Square for the 18 days that was necessary for the revolution to bring down Mubarak.[123] Although I find it a very far reaching conclusion to consider humour such a decisive factor, their study is certainly convincing that humour was important. An anecdotal account of the same case is Iman Mersal's article about the spirit of solidarity created by humour on Tahrir Square.[124]

In his article "Political Humor in a Dictatorial State: The Case of Spain"[125], Oriol Pi-Sunyer does not tell how the data for the article were collected, and there is no systematic analysis of different categories regarding content. The article reads as Pi-Sunyer's own personal observations about the functions of

---

[121] Mohamed M. Helmy and S. Frerichs, "Stripping the Boss: The Powerful Role of Humor in the Egyptian Revolution 2011," *Integrative Psychological & Behavioral Science* 47, no. 4 (2013).
[122] Helmy and Frerichs, "Stripping the Boss: The Powerful Role of Humor in the Egyptian Revolution 2011," p. 451.
[123] Helmy and Frerichs, "Stripping the Boss: The Powerful Role of Humor in the Egyptian Revolution 2011," p. 469.
[124] Iman Mersal, "Revolutionary Humor," *Globalizations* 8, no. 5 (2011).
[125] Oriol Pi-Sunyer, "Political Humor in a Dictatorial State: The Case of Spain," *Ethnohistory* 24, no. 2 (1977).

humour. He sees it as a form of oral guerrilla warfare that every-one could, and almost everybody did, participate in. He also mentions how jokes, like other forms of oral communication, travel far and fast in times of uncertainty. Pi-Sunyer thinks that humour functioned as a way of alleviating anxiety.

Humour, power and gender

There is not much academic work which focuses particularly on power and humour. However, some aspects have been raised from a gender perspective.

Joanne R. Gilbert's book *Performing Marginality: Humor, Gender and Cultural Critique*[126] is an interesting starting point. In this book Gilbert focuses on how American women stand-up comedians perform their marginality as women. She points to the fact that they actually manage to get paid for subverting power relations by performing the age old role of the fool. Their entertainment is a disguised resistance that holds up a mirror so that society can see itself reflected.[127] She sees marginality as the perfect position for expressing critique, because it is a place between the inside and outside. As an example of this marginal position being used as disguised resistance, Gilbert shows how women who use self-deprecatory humour (e.g their body size or sexuality) and put themselves down in their show appear so non-threatening that they disarm their audience. But because they perform this in a comic context, they also subvert the status quo by raising subtle questions and critique.[128] This is an interesting thought to ex-plore in relation to other marginalised groups, such as those who are "just" politically marginalised. Gilbert is also critical of critiques which claim that women who use self-deprecatory humour are not feminist, and that what they do is harmful to

---

[126] Joanne R. Gilbert, *Performing Marginality: Humor, Gender, and Cultural Critique* (Detroit: Wayne State University Press, 2004).
[127] Gilbert, *Performing Marginality*: pp. xii- xiii, xvii.
[128] Gilbert, *Performing Marginality*: p. 114.

feminism. Gilbert thinks that they have missed a crucial point – that this is humour, not to be taken too seriously.

Gilbert draws on superiority and relief theories of humour to make her points, and thinks that political humour can be both conservative and contribute to maintaining the status quo as well as be liberating and subversive. This way, humour is both violating and affirming cultural norms and values.[129] Her finding is that women stand-up comedians (and other minority stand-up comedians) must appear as non-threatening fools in order to get access to the stage, and suggests that there is a difference between making the master laugh and undermining his power position. She considers the fool to have a double role – as a satirist to encourage critical self-reflection, and at the same time entertain to relieve tension.

Gilbert distinguishes between the victim and the butt of a joke.[130] They can be the same, but not necessarily. Although a victim might be a woman, the butt might be a man, or society. Another thing she points out is how the "just joking" can be a defence that disguises attacks, something I will return to later.[131]

Although Gilbert acknowledges humour's ability to express subtle critique in a non-threatening way, and mentions that humour can be a "rehearsal for the revolution", she does not believe in any "comic activism." The very existence of female stand-up comedians is a subversive act, and is contributing to demolition of the hegemonic wall, but in itself it will not change real power relations. Even subversive humour will never be taken seriously. For this reason she thinks that "true believers" in any cause will never be good comedians.[132] I think the following

---

[129] Gilbert, *Performing Marginality*: p. 18.
[130] Gilbert, *Performing Marginality*: p. 160.
[131] Gilbert, *Performing Marginality*: p. 12.
[132] Gilbert, *Performing Marginality*: pp. 165-79.

pages will prove her wrong. Although these political activists are not professional comedians, their humour is still good enough to make many people laugh.

Someone who has more faith in the potential to affect power relations through humour is Anna Johansson. In a chapter in a Swedish book about resistance studies, she writes about humour among Nicaraguan women living in a workers' area of the city Leon.[133] She investigates how humour has a potential to both strengthen established power relations and resist them. The kind of humour the women in Nicaragua produce is very often about men, and it is done behind their backs. Johansson uses James Scott's concept of hidden transcripts to analyse the situations. She shows how it is possible to see the joking about men's sexual relations with other women as revenge. Johansson does not think that humorous resistance is a question of either-or. The humour she observed in Leon certainly reinforced existing stereotypes of how men are and what masculine behaviour is. But at the same time their humour is part of an everyday resistance against male domination. The women overcome their fear through humour, which makes men's power and domination seem less dangerous. However short and fragile the moment is, everyday resistance humour is a play with existing power structures, and a break in the routine of men's domination.

In an article called "Laughing when it hurts: Humor and violence in the lives of Costa Rican Prostitutes"[134], Pamela J. Downe looks at how sex workers in Costa Rica use humour. Just like Johansson, her main focus is the women's everyday lives, and the group solidarity they build among themselves. The prostitutes

[133] Anna Johansson, "Skratt, Humor Och Karnevalistisk Praktik Bland Nicaraguanska Kvinnor: Om Genus, Makt Och Motstånd," in *Motstånd*, ed. Mona Lilja and Stellan Vinthagen (Malmö: Liber, 2009).
[134] Pamela J. Downe, "Laughing When It Hurts: Humor and Violence in the Lives of Costa Rican Prostitutes," *Women's Studies International Forum* 22, no. 1 (1999).

use humour behind the scene to laugh at violent costumers and ridicule them when they are not present. In the very beginning of the text Downe also provides an example of how the prostitutes used humour during a demonstration to protest new laws that required them to carry a medical health card. The women thought that the government was neglecting the abuse and violence directed against the sex workers, and focusing too much on them as a problem, in spite of prostitution being legal in Costa Rica. During the demonstration, one politician came out to talk to the women, and in a prepared action, one woman used a balloon looking like a penis to mock the politician.

A different performance described in the text was conducted by another woman, who during the national AIDS day started a street performance telling jokes about prostitutes being a problem in Costa Rica. Dressed for work and in a self-deprecating tone, she focused on how prostitutes spread disease. When she had the attention of the mainly female audience she changed the style and instead attacked the prejudice of the women, accusing them of ignoring the fact that it was men like their own husbands who are her customers. The audience stopped laughing, but she still had their attention. Although she was not a professional stand-up comedian like the women in Gilbert's book, her self-deprecation became a way of raising serious critique.

A perspective which is not very different from Gilbert's is Case and Lippard's article, "Humorous Assaults on Patriarchal Ideology".[135] This is a description of a research project about women/feminist humour, and categorises American jokes of this kind. More than 60 percent of the collected jokes are about male stereotypes, where men are useless, stupid, hypersexual or disgusting. Very few of the jokes are about "feminist subtleties",

---

[135] Charles E. Case and Cameron D. Lippard, "Humorous Assaults on Patriarchal Ideology," *Sociological Inquiry* 79, no. 2 (2009).

that is questioning gender hierarchy or about equal rights. The authors conclude with noticing that almost all of the humour they have recorded upholds stereotypes about men and women being very different from each other, and this way contribute to sustaining divisions. However, they also see the very existence of this kind of humour as a proof that men's supremacy and patriarchy is being challenged.

The research on humour done within gender studies shows that there are different opinions regarding humour's ability to affect gender relations. Disagreement is also apparent within organisational theory concerned with humour and employer-employee relations which is the next theme.

Organisational theory and humour

Within organisational studies, there has also been some research on humour. Taylor and Bain in their article "Subterranean Worksick Blues: Humour as Subversion in Two Call Centres"[136] from 2003 includes a good overview of this literature. Their own research, using ethnographic data collection methods, shows how humour can be part of resistance in two call centres. In one call centre, humour was used to undermine management, for example by circulating emails which clearly suggested that management did not do its work properly. Another habit which challenged management ideals was to mock customers behind their backs but within earshot of the other workers.

Taylor and Bain's other case study is even more interesting from my perspective. In a call centre where management actively worked against unions, a group of workers consciously used humour as a tactic to undermine management and create support for a union. Taylor and Bain document how it was difficult for management to find appropriate responses, especially towards

---

[136] Phil Taylor and Peter Bain, "'Subterranean Worksick Blues': Humour as Subversion in Two Call Centres," *Organization Studies* 24, no. 9 (2003).

one openly homosexual man. He made use of prejudice and ambivalence towards gay men to get away with things for which others would have been punished. The humour was sometimes very hostile, but was used against people in superior positions. The authors demonstrate that humour can contribute to collective resistance even in a working environment as controlled as a call centre. An example of a collective humorous action was directed against new regulations demanding that the workers wear a shirt and tie. Since this is a call centre, the workers found it unnecessary. On the first day with the new regulations, a large number of workers did come to work in shirt and tie. But they had collectively organised to look as unprofessional as possible, by selecting patterns and colours not considered to go well together.

In their article "Having Fun? Humour as resistance in Brazil"[137], Rodrigues & Collinson argue that in the work place, workers' humour is not just a way to let off steam, something they find to be a persistent idea in organisational theory. Through a case study from Brazil, they show that humour is complex and can force management to change practices. In a big company, the union newspaper used humour (primarily cartoons), to expose bad management practices. This kind of humour was not encouraged by the leadership. By drawing on familiar images from mainstream Brazilian culture, such as comparisons with animals, the anonymous cartoons made such an impression that the company management was forced to improve working conditions and to change a practice regarding selection of employees.[138]

---

[137] Rodrigues and Collinson, "'Having Fun'? Humour as Resistance in Brazil."
[138] Rodrigues and Collinson, "'Having Fun'? Humour as Resistance in Brazil," p. 756.

Another article which primarily draws on organisational theory is "Jokes in a Garment Workshop in Hanoi: How does Humour Foster the Perception of Community in Social Movements?"[139] by Nghiem Lien Huong. In spite of its title, the article has no references to social movement literature. The author analyses two jokes from a garment factory in Hanoi and the most important point is that the jokes help to foster a sense of communi-community among workers on the shop floor and reflect a collective reality. Huong thinks that the jokes help to relieve tensions in a tough working environment. In the two jokes which are mentioned, the workers joke about themselves (in one of them about their perceived stupidity), while at the same time the jokes illustrate how terrible the working environment is, and how workers are pressured to lie to working condition inspectors. The author also claims that these kind of jokes lie somewhere between obedience and resistance, that they are neither one nor the other. However, that the jokes are told among the workers and not a way of confronting the employer makes it difficult to see how they can be more than part of Scott's hidden transcript of not-yet declared resistance.[140]

Humour as nonviolent resistance

The basic question that this thesis asks is what happens when political activists use humour in an encounter with persons and institutions they consider more powerful than themselves. Among scholars of humour, the opinions about this issue diverge considerably, and scepticism towards the rebellious potential of humour is not unusual. Billig, for example, wants to show how humour also serves to enforce social order through ridicule and mockery, a subject he thinks has been neglected in

---

[139] Nghiem Lien Huong, "Jokes in a Garment Workshop in Hanoi: How Does Humour Foster the Perception of Community in Social Movements?," *International Review of Social History* 52, no. S15 (2007).
[140] James C. Scott, *Domination and the Arts of Resistance: Hidden Transcripts* (New Haven, CT: Yale University Press, 1990).

humour research.[141] Some of the researchers who focus on political jokes or medieval folly also have a tendency to become sceptical.[142] However, as shown above, studies with organisational theory as their point of departure found that there can be much humour in the workplace at the expense of those on top of the hierarchies, including in places with very hard working conditions and systematic suppression of unions.[143]

In her book *Irony's edge*, Linda Hutcheon calls irony *transideological*, meaning that in itself irony is not radical or conservative. It is not a mode of oppression or a mode of resistance; it is just a particular way of communicating. Irony can be labelled in all sorts of ways depending on how it has been applied, and who you ask to have an opinion about it.[144] Although not all humour is ironic, I think that this particular observation is valid for all kinds of humour.

The dismissal of humour's rebellious potential is still going on. Tsakona and Popa in their introduction to *Studies in Political Humour* from 2012 continue the argumentation of people like

---

[141] Billig, *Laughter and Ridicule: Towards a Social Critique of Laughter.* p. 200.
[142] Hong, "Mow 'Em All Down Grandma: The 'Weapon' of Humor in Two Danish World War II Occupation Scrapbooks."; Benton, "The Origins of the Political Joke."; Zijderveld, *Reality in a Looking-Glass: Rationality through an Analysis of Traditional Folly.*
[143] Taylor and Bain, "'Subterranean Worksick Blues': Humour as Subversion in Two Call Centres."; Lien Huong, "Jokes in a Garment Workshop in Hanoi: How Does Humour Foster the Perception of Community in Social Movements?."; Rodrigues and Collinson, "'Having Fun'? Humour as Resistance in Brazil."
[144] Hutcheon, *Irony's Edge*: chapter 1. Along similar lines, Hariman says about parody that "Needless to say, parody is neither radical nor conservative, but both at once". Hariman, "Political Parody and Public Culture," p. 254.

Benton, Davies and Hong, although in a slightly moderated phrasing. They claim to identify this myth:

> Political humour is considered to be subversive and leading to political change: by offering a different perspective on political issues, it not only leads the audience to question the effectiveness of political decisions and practices, but also serves as a means of resistance to, or even rebellion against, political oppression and social injustice.[145]

In their introduction they say that all of this is just a popular myth and claim that even when humour conveys criticism, it "recycles and reinforces dominant values and views on politics"[146] This might be a fair conclusion based on the data they have looked at, but it should not be generalised to all political humour. It is especially problematic when they are basing it on a literature review that neglects findings that point in a different direction. So while Hong's findings (which are based on just two personal diaries) are referred to at length, they do not include Barker, Branagan, Downe, Huong, Rodrigues & Collinson, Taylor & Bain, Stokker and Sørensen in their review.[147]

What is particularly problematic about these humour scholars' way of discussing what happens in political humour is the dichotomous understandings of power, resistance and change underlying their line of argumentation. They do not appear to take into consideration that power, change and resistance is not a question of either-or.

---

[145] Villy Tsakona and Diana Elena Popa, "Humour in Politics and the Politics of Humour: An Introduction," in *Studies in Political Humour: In between Political Critique and Public Entertainment*, ed. Villy Tsakona and Diana Elena Popa (Amsterdam: John Benjamins, 2011), p. 1.
[146] Tsakona and Popa, "Humour in Politics and the Politics of Humour: An Introduction," p. 2.
[147] Tsakona and Popa, "Humour in Politics and the Politics of Humour: An Introduction."

James Scott's concept of hidden transcripts and everyday resistance is one of the most nuanced yet also very concrete ways
of explaining the complexity. Scott developed the idea of the
hidden transcripts as a way to describe the behaviours of people in
extreme subordinate positions, such as slaves and serfs, behind
the backs of their masters. In the *public transcript* which they
display to their masters, they might appear humble, subdued and
passive, but when they are out of sight, they might work slower,
steal and ridicule the master. In Scott's opinion they are wise to
do this behind the scenes. These sorts of resistance activities
might never become an open confrontation, but according to
Scott it is unlikely that a public declaration of resistance is going
to happen without being preceded by a well-developed hidden
transcript.[148]

Asef Bayat is another author who has nuanced perceptions of
what resistance can look like and how organised it has to be in
order to have an effect. Although Bayat criticises Scott for his
emphasis on intention, they do have much in common. Bayat
has coined the expression *quiet encroachment of the ordinary* to
describe the way for example street vendors and slum dwellers in
the cities of the global south carve out niches of public space for
themselves in order to improve their lives. They spread out their
businesses on the pavements, sell merchandise comprising major
brands, build their homes without permission and illegally tap
into the power grid. People do this as part of their everyday lives,
individually and fragmented and without guidance from ideology
or leaders. Because they are so many, the practices change societies. This quiet encroachment of the ordinary Bayat calls *social
nonmovements*. What they do is not an obvious political protest,
since they are not protesting on the streets *demanding* to get a
better life, but day by day *creating* it. Like Scott, Bayat gives much
agency to ordinary people who "understand the constraints yet

---

[148] Scott, *Domination and the Arts of Resistance: Hidden Transcripts.*

recognize and discover opportunities and take advantage of the spaces that are available to enhance their life-chances."[149] Only when their gains are under attack do these social nonmovements act collectively, for instance in defending their homes and business opportunities. The social nonmovements might one day become social movements, but that is not what is most interesting about them. Bayat's major contribution is to document how their impact can be measured by the way they transform societies through the quiet encroachment.[150] Bayat's findings are not of direct relevance to the study of humorous political stunts which are not part of ordinary, daily activities, but his studies broadens the horizon when it comes to understanding the complexities of resistance. Just as the slaves and serfs that Scott writes about, the resistance of the urban poor is more successful the more discreet and unnoticed it manages to be. A major implication of Scott's and Bayat's work is that hidden resistance might have an influence even if it does not lead to immediate results or is organised.

People like of Benton and Tsakona & Popa imply that only a more organised resistance is real resistance. However, much resistance is covert, opportunity based, and goes on behind the scenes. It is in its nature not to be discovered. It can happen totally without humour – but humour is also likely to be part of the folklore that keeps the cultures of resistance alive.

In my own previous work I combined Scott's concept of hidden transcripts with theory of nonviolence to develop a framework for understanding humour as nonviolent resistance to oppression.[151] I documented how those who think like Benton have too

---

[149] Asef Bayat, *Life as Politics: How Ordinary People Change the Middle East* (Stanford, CA: Stanford University Press, 2010). p. 26.
[150] Bayat, *Life as Politics: How Ordinary People Change the Middle East.*
[151] Majken Jul Sørensen, "Humor as a Serious Strategy of Nonviolent Resistance to Oppression," *Peace & Change* 33, no. 2 (2008); Majken Jul Sørensen, "Humour as Nonviolent Resistance to Oppression" (MA Thesis, Coventry University, 2006).

simple a view of power and resistance when they claim jokes are a vent which cannot contribute to resistance. I suggested that humour as a form of nonviolent resistance to oppression has three different functions:

1. As a way of reaching out to people who are not already part of a nonviolent resistance movement, it can facilitate outreach and mobilisation.

2. Within an already established resistance movement, humour can facilitate a culture of resistance by building solidarity and strengthening the individual's capacity for participating in resistance. Colin Barker in his book chapter "The Making of Solidarity at the Lenin Shipyard in Gdansk" about the emergence of the independent trade union Solidarity in Poland in 1980 explains how political jokes were an expression of distrust in the ruling system that contributed to people distancing themselves emotionally from the regime.[152] His findings support my own stance, and provide a challenge to authors such as Davies and Benton who dismiss the potential contribution of whispered jokes to resistance. Political jokes themselves do not automatically lead to resistance, but they can potentially be crucial in shaping independent thinking that assists moves towards open resistance.

3. Humour can affect the relationship between the nonviolent resistance movement and the oppressor. This last function has the most powerful potential, because it can affect the relationship between the oppressor and the oppressed.

---

[152] Colin Barker, "The Making of Solidarity at the Lenin Shipyard in Gdansk," in *Passionate Politics: Emotions and Social Movements*, ed. Jeff Goodwin, James M. Jasper, and Francesca Polletta (Chicago: University of Chicago Press, 2001).

This framework was originally developed to understand humour which was part of a resistance to oppression, and its main source of empirical data was humorous actions carried out by a Serbian group called *Otpor* between 1998-2000. These actions were successful as part of a strategy to resist the dictatorship in Serbia during the rule of Slobodan Milošević. However, I now find that the dichotomy of oppressor-oppressed is too narrow and simplistic to adequately address relations of power. I provide a less dichotomous definition below.

The only other major work which explicitly analyses the use of humour within nonviolence theory is Janjira Sombutpoonsiri's PhD thesis "The Use of Humour as a Vehicle for Nonviolent Struggle: Serbia's 1996-7 Protests and the OTPOR (Resistance) Movement".[153] It is a thorough documentation of the use of humour in Serbian nonviolent resistance to the rule of Milošević in the late 1990's and 2000 based on interviews with the organisers of the nonviolent actions and analysis of media reports. It investigates how humour was used or not used in different cities and towns depending on Otpor's cooperation or lack of cooperation with the opposition parties, NGO's and access to independent media. Sombutpoonsiri places the use of humour in its cultural context, characterised by Serbian black humour, absurd theatre and the political situation for the opposition in the 1990's. Sombutpoonsiri is well aware that her findings based on a single case study cannot be generalised to all use of humour in nonviolent struggles without testing them on other cases. With this in mind, she offers the following theoretical contribution:

> ... humour works as a vehicle of nonviolent struggle in three ways. First, it subverts the propaganda of ruling elites, enabling protesters to turn that propaganda against its creators. Second, humour channels the antagonistic at-

---

[153] Sombutpoonsiri, "The Use of Humour as a Vehicle for Nonviolent Struggle."

mosphere of street protests into cheerfulness, helping to avoid clashes between protesters and the security forces. Third, humour offers a metaphor of emancipation from an oppressive polity, encouraging the oppressed to make this metaphor become reality.[154]

Sombutpoonsiri uses the concepts of *excorporation* and the *carnivalesque* to analyse humour's unique contribution to nonviolent resistance. The concept of *excorporation* was introduced by John Fiske, and by applying that to the use of humour in nonviolence, Sombutpoonsiri takes critiques of Sharp's theory of consent into consideration. Excorporation means that resistance to a system does not require a total withdrawal from that system, something which critiques of Sharp said was not possible. Sombutpoonsiri writes:

> 'Excorporation' suggest a method of subverting hegemonic power without suspending the entire system of domination. The concept is based on the understanding that domination and resistance can take place in the same space.[155]

Sombutpoonsiri documents many examples of Serbian use of excorporation through satire and parody against Milošević's regime, both in the 1996-97 protests and in Otpor's street skits. It twisted the regime's propaganda thus invalidating its truth claims without making the critique explicit.[156]

During carnivals, Sombutpoonsiri thinks that multiple voices can exist at the same time thus fostering an atmosphere of dialogue despite the existence of prejudices and antagonism. She explains

---

[154] Sombutpoonsiri, "The Use of Humour as a Vehicle for Nonviolent Struggle," p. 1.

[155] Sombutpoonsiri, "The Use of Humour as a Vehicle for Nonviolent Struggle," p. 44.

[156] Sombutpoonsiri, "The Use of Humour as a Vehicle for Nonviolent Struggle," pp. 279-85.

"The carnivalesque world offers a scenario where alternative realities to the seemingly fixed present one may just be possible".[157] Again this is thoroughly documented with many examples of how the carnivalesque speaks to the imagination of other possible realities and channels anger into positive emotions.[158] A joyful atmosphere transforms hostility between protesters and authorities and helps maintain nonviolent discipline. It also becomes a way for protesters to overcome the dilemma between their anger and frustration over the situation, and the seemingly impossible demand from advocates of principled nonviolence to "love the enemy". Sombutpoonsiri expresses it this way:

> In a nonviolent conflict, carnivalesque humour constitutes an alternative means of expressing emotion that overcomes the dilemma of choosing between getting angry at those responsible for the oppression being resisted, or loving them in spite of it.[159]

In spite of the limited interest in humour from scholars of nonviolence, some other studies that are relevant exist. They use social movement theory as their point of departure rather than theory of nonviolence. In 2007, an interesting collection of articles were published in the book *Humour and Social Protest* edited by Marjolein 't Hart and Dennis Bos,[160] containing both historical and contemporary examples of humorous protest. Some of them I have already mentioned in the relevant sections about jokes, occupations and organisational theory. The intro-

---

[157] Sombutpoonsiri, "The Use of Humour as a Vehicle for Nonviolent Struggle," p. 58.
[158] Sombutpoonsiri, "The Use of Humour as a Vehicle for Nonviolent Struggle," pp. 285-95.
[159] Sombutpoonsiri, "The Use of Humour as a Vehicle for Nonviolent Struggle," p. 289.
[160] Marjolein C. 't Hart and Dennis Bos, eds., *Humour and Social Protest* (Cambridge: University of Cambridge Press, 2007).

duction to the book includes an overview of the study of humour and protest and suggests the social movement theory concerned with identity and emotions as an interesting tool for analysing humour and protest. Thomas Olesen in his article "The Funny Side of Globalization: Humour and Humanity in Zapatista Framing",[161] shows how the Zapatistas' humour was one strategy for framing their struggle in a way which could be understood globally. They used a universal humour referring to humanity and human beings' shortcomings in order to have resonance with their audience, thus using the symbolic and emotional aspects of humour to bridge differences between them and their audience.

Lisiunia A. Romanienko's contribution "Antagonism, Absurdity, and the Avant-Garde: Dismantling Soviet Oppression through the Use of Theatrical Devices by Poland's Solidarity Movement",[162] is also using a frame of social movement theory to highlight how the Polish group *Orange Alternative* through their absurd happenings in the late 1980's found a way of protesting which was difficult for the Polish authorities to respond to. In his book *A Carnival of Revolution - Central Europe 1989,* Padraic Kenney shows how groups like the Orange Alternative, the *Society for a Merrier Present* in Czechoslovakia and the *Czech Children* contributed to a carnivalesque atmosphere in Central Europe and a transformation of "how to do protest" in the late 1980's. The change was essential for preparing the ground for the

---

[161] Thomas Olesen, "The Funny Side of Globalization: Humour and Humanity in Zapatista Framing," *International Review of Social History* 52, no. S15 (2007).
[162] Lisiunia A. Romanienko, "Antagonism, Absurdity, and the Avant-Garde: Dismantling Soviet Oppression through the Use of Theatrical Devices by Poland's Solidarity Movement," *International Review of Social History* 52, no. S15 (2007).

revolutions of 1989 and is neglected in most accounts of the events.[163]

The Orange Alternative is a group whose stunts will be analysed in Chapter 3. Another scholar which has used the Orange Alternative as a case study is M. Lane Bruner in his article "Carnivalesque Protest and the Humorless State".[164] Bruner thinks that conditions need to be favourable in order for carnivalesque protest to succeed, but when they are, this form of protest can be the most effective way to challenge corruption. Also he notices that humour, in contrast to serious protest, can be difficult to respond to, since arresting elves and turtles means bad publicity for the state. In his discussion about carnival he points out (like Zijderveld) that although authorities might intend carnivals to be an outlet for frustration and a way of retaining social control, they have no guarantee that they do not end up as a challenge to power. The same conclusion is reached by Anna Lundberg in her contribution to *Humour and Social Protest*. In "Queering Laughter in the Stockholm Pride Parade"[165] she also finds that carnival has a political *potential* because of its rejection of what is considered normal.

Simon Teune is also interested in how the use of humour affects the relationship between a social movement and the authorities it reacts against. In "Humour as a Guerrilla Tactic: The West German Student Movement's Mockery of the Establishment "he investigates how the student movement in the conservative and authoritarian Republic of Germany was influenced by the concept of *Spassguerrilla* (fun-guerrilla) towards the end of the

---

[163] Padraic Kenney, *A Carnival of Revolution - Central Europe 1989* (Princeton, NJ: Princeton University Press, 2002).
[164] M. Lane Bruner, "Carnivalesque Protest and the Humorless State," *Text and Performance Quarterly* 25, no. 2 (2005).
[165] Anna Lundberg, "Queering Laughter in the Stockholm Pride Parade," *International Review of Social History* 52, no. S15 (2007).

1960's.[166] He uses examples of actions carried out by *Kommune 1*, the most widely known group that to a large degree set the tone in the early stages of the student movement. Their ironic actions provoked strong reactions from the state and from the populist media, and in this way radicalised members of the student movement and drew new members to it. Kommune 1 used their court cases to continue ridiculing authority, and in this way showed how difficult it is to respond to humorous attacks. However, their tactics were not embraced by everyone in the student movement. The biggest student organisation preferred a strategy of rational argumentation, and did not perceive the ambiguity and irony that Spassguerrilla represented as a fruitful path to pursue.

An early attempt to point out that humour is an under re-searched area of social movement studies was done by Harry Hiller in his article "Humor and Hostility: A Neglected Aspect of Social Movement Analysis".[167] He set up a model for how to explain humour and used the case study of the Western Canadi-an separatist movement to illustrate how most of the humour used by social movements ought to be considered resistance-oriented and can be a way of expressing hostility in a social conflict. At the time of his case study in the early 1980's, many people in Western Canada felt that they were being neglected by the Canadian central authorities in spite of their contributions to the national economy. Hiller looks at humorous novelty items such as bumper stickers, t-shirts and caps from a social move-ment working for independence for Western Canada. A message like "Republic of Western Canada" on a cap is ambiguous be-

---

[166] Simon Teune, "Humour as a Guerrilla Tactic: The West German Student Movement's Mockery of the Establishment," *International Review of Social History* 52, no. SupplementS15 (2007).
[167] Harry H. Hiller, "Humor and Hostility: A Neglected Aspect of Social Movement Analysis," *Qualitative Sociology* 6, no. 3 (1983).

cause people cannot be sure if the person who wears it is serious or making fun of this idea. This ambiguity means that the carrier of this message is not held responsible the same way she would normally be, and that people can adjust to the idea of an independent Western Canada slowly. Even if some will wear it because they are committed to the idea, others will buy it because they like to play with an idea they are not yet fully commit-committed to.

Marty Branagan in his article "The last laugh: humour in community activism"[168] writes from his own experience as a participant in social justice and eco-pax movements in Australia. He describes many positive functions of using humour as a supplement to serious communication, especially relating to internal dynamics in the movements. He observes that humour makes popular education more interesting and contributes to a more inclusive movement. It can also make activism more sustainable by preventing burnout, contribute to transforming anger into more positive emotions and help maintain nonviolent discipline in spite of provocations. In relation to people who are not involved in a movement themselves, he notes how the use of inclusive humour improved relations with police during events he observed.

Culture jamming, pranks and tactical carnival

Research traditions (and practices of activism) that frequently include humour but are not limited to humour are *culture jamming, pranks* and *tactical carnival*. These genres share a playful attitude towards expression of dissent and use various creative or artistic ways of communicating. A couple of activist accounts and documentations are Joel Schechter's *Satiric Impersonations*[169] and a

---

[168] Marty Branagan, "The Last Laugh: Humour in Community Activism," *Community Development Journal* 42, no. 4 (2007).
[169] Joel Schechter, *Satiric Impersonations: From Aristophanes to the Guerrilla Girls* (Carbondale, IL: Southern Illinois University Press, 1994).

collection of stories and interviews about "creative disruption of everyday life" called *The Interventionists*.[170] Many examples of these practices are also included in the handbook *Beautiful Trouble: A Toolbox for Revolution*.[171]

The boundaries between various forms of art, interventions, and pranks are porous. In her book *Satire and Dissent: Interventions in Contemporary Political Debate*, Amber Day writes about the differences and similarities between some of them.[172] She primarily uses US examples, and focuses on parody news shows (like the The Daily Show), satiric documentaries (like Michael Moore's movies) and ironic activism (similar to what I call humorous political stunts).

An important inspiration for many of these activist-artists was the *Situationist International*, which originated in France from 1957 and worked against the way that society had become a *spectacle*, a phrase introduced by Guy Debord.[173] As part of the spectacle, citizens were expected to consume ready-made cultural products instead of inventing their own. The situationists found that people were no longer important as workers and producers; their major role was as consumers.[174] Responding to this development, the situationists aimed to deconstruct the ready-made, and had several strategies for this. The most well-known is *détournement*.[175] Harold defines this as "a detouring of pre-existing

[170] Nato Thompson et al., *The Interventionists: Users' Manual for the Creative Disruption of Everyday Life* (North Adams, MA: MASS MoCA, 2004).
[171] Andrew Boyd and Dave Oswald Mitchell, *Beautiful Trouble: A Toolbox for Revolution* (New York: OR Books, 2012).
[172] Amber Day, *Satire and Dissent: Interventions in Contemporary Political Debate* (Bloomington, IN: Indiana University Press, 2011).
[173] Guy Debord, *Society of the Spectacle* (Detroit: Black & Red, 1970).
[174] Christine Harold, *Ourspace: Resisting the Corporate Control of Culture* (Minneapolis, MN: University of Minnesota Press, 2007). pp. 2-3.
[175] Harold, *Ourspace*: p. 8; Day, *Satire and Dissent*.

Spectacular [sic] messages and images in an effort to subvert and reclaim them."[176] That means an altering of original concepts into something different that can express a deeper message.

The French situationists and Debord's détournement were important inspirations for what later became known as *culture jamming* and the idea of the detour is present in many humorous political stunts. The American Yippies have been a similar inspiration coming from a different direction. The group was not formally founded until December 31st, 1967, but already earlier in 1967, two of the would be yippies, Jerry Rubin and Abbie Hoffman, had been the front figures of performances that would fit into my definition of humorous political stunts.

On August 24, 1967, Abbie Hoffman and a group of people entered the New York Stock Exchange, and from the gallery threw dollar bills down on the floor. What actually happened and how the stockbrokers reacted has been the subject of much mythmaking – and Hoffman has deliberately been vague about it. However, the lack of exact documentation has most likely caused many to imagine greedy stockbrokers crawling around on the floor to grab the money. No media were inside, and there are no photos of the event. One person claimed that they threw 1000 dollars, others that it was just 30-40 one dollar bills. Hoffman himself wrote that the stock dealers "let out a mighty cheer,"[177] while the New York Times reported mixed reactions of smiles and shouts.[178] After being escorted out, the activists

---

[176] Harold, *Ourspace*: p. 8.
[177] Quoted in Ashley Duree, "Greed at the New York Stock Exchange and the Levitation of the Pentagon: Early Protest Theatre by Abbie Hoffman and Jerry Rubin," *Voces Novae: Chapman University Historical Review* 1, no. 1 (2009): p. 56.
[178] Duree, "Greed at the New York Stock Exchange and the Levitation of the Pentagon: Early Protest Theatre by Abbie Hoffman and Jerry Rubin," p. 57.

also burned dollar bills outside of the stock exchange. Although this was certainly not the first time performers tried to blur the line between audiences and performers, according to Duree, the demonstration created "a form of protest that happened in the midst of the spectators, whether the spectators wanted to be involved or not".[179]

Later culture jammers have mainly focused on resisting corporate control of public space, for example through *billboard liberation*. The involved groups and networks have been numerous and frequently anonymous. An early Australian example was *Billboard Utilising Graffitists Against Unhealthy Promotions*, or for short B.U.G.A U.P, which in the 1980's especially targeted cigarette commercials and was influential in changing the laws regulating cigarette advertising in Australia.[180]

A few years later, Naomi Klein's book *No logo*[181] and Kalle Lasn's *Culture Jam*[182] quickly became classics for activists from the global justice movement. Today companies rely on branding to sell their products – Coca Cola is not just a soft drink, and Nike not just a shoe, but brands that aim to sell an image of a cool lifestyle filled with beauty, youth and happiness. Companies spend millions of dollars on developing their brands, but the brands also become vulnerable to attack by so-called *subvertising*.[183] Well

---

[179] Duree, "Greed at the New York Stock Exchange and the Levitation of the Pentagon: Early Protest Theatre by Abbie Hoffman and Jerry Rubin," p. 58.

[180] Iain McIntyre, *How to Make Trouble and Influence People: Pranks, Hoaxes, Graffiti & Political Mischief-Making from across Australia* (Melbourne: Breakdown Press, 2009).

[181] Naomi Klein, *No Logo: No Space, No Choice, No Jobs* (London: Flamingo, 2001).

[182] Kalle Lasn, *Culture Jam: The Uncooling of America*, 1st ed. (New York: Eagle Brook, 1999).

[183] Harold, *Ourspace*: p. 34.

done subvertising does not just express a general critique of consumerism, but use parody to attack the vulnerable aspects of a particular product. Subvertising uses the brand's own imagery to talk back to it, and reveal consequences of consuming the product or the production methods which the producers would prefer to keep away from the public mind. This can be to connect cigarettes with cancer or Nike with *sweatshop* production where workers in the global south work long hours in horrible working conditions and are paid wages they cannot live on. Harold quotes Robert Phiddian to suggest that the parodies do not destroy a brand, but instead deconstruct it by making potential consumers associate the brand with something other than what was intended.[184]

Harold herself suggests the term *rhetorical jiu-jitsu* to catch how the force of the brand is turned against itself like in the martial art.[185] Harold does not refer to Sharp, but this is an echo of his concept political jiu-jitsu from theory of nonviolent action. When the company Calvin Klein was advertising the perfume *Obsession* using a very thin young female model, the magazine *Adbusters'* parody ad used the brand's own style to attack it. In Adbusters' version, the skinny model is not just young and pretty, but vomiting over the toilet bowl, indicating that in order to look like the skinny models, women develop eating disorders.[186] To do this kind of subvertising in a way that makes sense to the audiences, requires familiarity with the brand and its ads, otherwise they just become meaningless.

Harold also points to the limitation of this type of activism – it does not provide alternatives, since there is no suggestions of how to replace the desires the brands tempt with. There is also a risk of co-optation, of the anti-logo becoming the new cool logo

---

[184] Harold, *Ourspace*: p. 35.
[185] Harold, *Ourspace*: p. 37.
[186] Harold, *Ourspace*: pp. 39- 40.

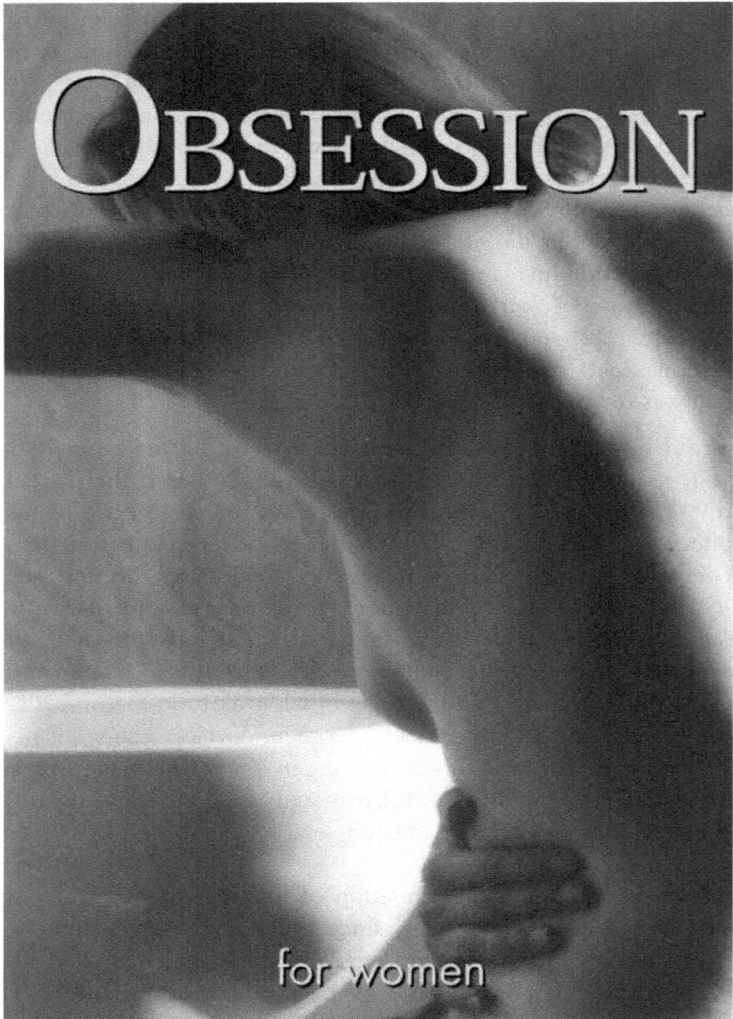

Illustration 3. Parody of Obsession ad that uses skinny model. © Adbusters, reprinted with permission.

for those who are the avant-garde trendsetters. Already the situationists were aware of this risk. They wrote that the spectacle was so sophisticated that it would be possible for the companies to take over the critique and make it their own, repackage it in a slightly different version and sell it back as the latest trend.[187] Today the rebels, culture jamming and anti-logo culture itself become cool and you can buy merchandise with jams. This all leads Harold to ask: "I can only wonder: Is the rhetoric and imagery of rebellion bankrupt?"[188]

Harold refers to Derrida when she says that the parodies are not really deconstructions, because a real deconstruction requires a double reading, not just the sabotaging of the establishment.[189] In search of deconstructions that do not provide the recipe of what is "correct thought" and where the performer/artist/activist does not talk down to the audience, Harold turns to pranks, hoaxes, and comedy. She writes: "Whereas the parodist attempts to change things in the name of a presupposed value, the comedian diagnoses her situation and tries something to see how people respond."[190]

An example of a prank in Harold's understanding is the Barbie Liberation Organization which since 1989 has liberated the Barbie doll and the G.I Joe action figure from gender stereotypes. A group of people bought a number of talking dolls, and switched the voice boxes from these two figures around. Afterwards they put the boxes back on the shelves without the staff noticing, an activity called *shopdropping*. When the children opened their Christmas presents, Barbie said "Dead men tell no

---

[187] Harold, *Ourspace*: pp. 12, 30-31.
[188] Harold, *Ourspace*: p. 72.
[189] Harold, *Ourspace*: p. 56.
[190] Harold, *Ourspace*: p. 74.

lies" instead of giggling "let's plan our dream wedding." G.I Joe said things like "I love shopping." The reaction from Mattel that produces Barbie was to downplay it all and say they had had no complaints from customers.[191]

In this example of shopdropping, like many types of pranking, the pranksters are not explicit with why they do this. The whole idea is to stimulate independent thinking without telling people what to think. The deception is all part of the drama, and serves an important purpose – when people realise they have been exposed to a prank, and maybe temporarily fooled by it, their daily routines are broken.[192]

In his book *Electoral Guerrilla Theatre: Radical Ridicule and Social Movements* L. M. Bogad identified what he calls *electoral guerrilla theatre*, as a recently added tactic in the repertoire of contention. Electoral guerrilla theatre is used by activists within liberal democracies to ridicule these highly ritualised arenas, either by attacking the whole electoral system or sabotaging a particular candidate's possibility for being taken seriously. Bogad uses three case studies from the Netherlands, Australia and USA to show how this has been an innovative way for social movements to confront a right wing candidate in Australia (Pauline Pantsdown ridiculed Pauline Hanson), criticism of heteronormativity in the US (drag queen Miss Joan Jettblakk) and confronting the establishment in the Netherlands (the Kabouters).[193]

Bogad has also analysed various performance elements in traditional demonstrations, calling them *tactical carnival*. It is both a

---

[191] Harold, *Ourspace*: pp. 80-81.
[192] Hilary Beth Tellesen, "Alternative Subterfuge: Pranking Rhetoric in Shopdropping and Identity Correction" (MA Thesis, California State University, 2009).
[193] L. M. Bogad, *Electoral Guerrilla Theatre: Radical Ridicule and Social Movements* (New York: Routledge, 2005).

way to confront some of the dogmas within the traditional left and can contribute to opening up public space as well as "create a joyous counterculture that can sustain long-term participation in a movement".[194] The goals of tactical carnival are to occupy space, present a friendly face to outsiders, provide an alternative to the existing world order, help overcome fear and create a culture of active defiance.[195] In *Queer Political Performance and Protest*, Benjamin Shepard is not concerned with a particular tactic, but shows how performance, show and the carnivalesque have a long tradition within queer protest in the US. The group ACT UP, focused on HIV and AIDS, was crucial in setting the example for how protest could be performed in a more carnivalesque atmosphere.[196] The carnivalesque is one way of doing *aesthetic politics* as Kenneth Tucker calls it. In his book *Workers of the World, Enjoy!* he ties the increase in aesthetics to the crisis in modernity where truth and knowledge are no longer given.[197]

Theoretically, Bogad makes a distinction between the Bakhtian carnival that turns the world upside down, and the tactical carnival that suggests that other worlds are possible. The tactical carnival of today is not the same as the carnival carried out in

---

[194] L. M. Bogad, "Tactical Carnival: Social Movements, Demonstrations, and Dialogical Performance," in *A Boal Companion: Dialogues on Theatre and Cultural Politics*, ed. Jan Cohen-Cruz and Mady Schutzman (New York: Routledge, 2006), p. 52.
[195] L. M. Bogad, "Carnivals against Capital: Radical Clowning and the Global Justice Movement," *Social Identities* 16, no. 4 (2010): pp. 542-43.
[196] Benjamin Heim Shepard, *Queer Political Performance and Protest: Play, Pleasure and Social Movement* (New York: Routledge, 2010); Day, *Satire and Dissent*: p. 154.
[197] Kenneth H. Tucker, *Workers of the World, Enjoy! Aesthetic Politics from Revolutionary Syndicalism to the Global Justice Movement* (Philadelphia, PA: Temple University Press, 2010). p. 5.

medieval times or as described by Bakhtin. Instead it is a reclaim-ing of the idea of carnival for the purpose of the activists.[198]

From a similar activist-academic performance studies tradition, Kristina Schriver and Donna Marie Nudd write about their experiences with the *Mickee Faust Club* in Florida in the US.[199] One of the two examples they give is a prank where some of the performers made an intervention in a controversial parade. They suggest a distinction between *celebratory* and *interventionist* types of protest performances but unfortunately they do not eleborate on this distinction.

In their article "Performing vs. the Insurmountable", Benjamin Shepard, L. M. Bogad and Stephen Duncombe enter the debate about power and effective activism from the perspective of playful activism. This type of activism has been accused of the same shortcomings as humour – not being effective and taking away energy from forms of activism which really matter. The three authors, who all have participated in playful organising for social change, use their own experiences to show how playful activism can increase outreach to media, recruit new members by inviting them in to play, contribute to creating communities of resistance and play with relations of power. They write that:

> At its most basic level, play as political performance is about freedom – of the mind and the body – from any number of repressive forces, from the state to the super ego, the cop in the head."[200]

Bogad, "Carnivals against Capital," pp. 547,56.
[199] Kristina Schriver and Donna Marie Nudd, "Mickee Faust Club's Performative Protest Events," *Text and Performance Quarterly* 22, no. 3 (2002).
[200] Benjamin Shepard, L.M. Bogad, and Stephen Duncombe, "Performing Vs. The Insurmountable: Theatrics, Activism, and Social Movements," *Liminalities: A Journal of Performance Studies* 4, no. 3 (2008): p. 2.

In an article Shepard wrote on his own, he emphasised joyfulness as an important aspect of community organising.[201]

Shepard, Bogad and Duncombe write that "play and political performance creates spaces where activists feel compelled to challenge seemingly insurmountable targets".[202] One of the criticisms they counter is that only the middle class can afford to play.[203] Instead of seeing the playful as something alien to the struggle itself, they show how it is an integrated part of people's lives and struggles and playful elements in protest can make people remain committed over a long period of time. And even if much creativity is directed towards the already converted, it helps make these networks denser.[204]

In their text Shepard, Bogad and Duncombe reflect together with Jennifer Miller, founder of New York based *Circus Amok*, about the importance of doing something, even if it is not the most "effective" way of behaving:

> "This insurmountable thing is where cynicism comes from," Circus Amok founder Jennifer Miller concedes. "It's insurmountable, we've got to become capitalists." Yet, the flip side of such thinking remains. The logic of play is that it defies conventional logic. It invites people to stay engaged within subjects that are far more serious than can be dealt with in an earnest fashion. Some issues are far too important to be dealt with a straight face. Rather, jokes, ridicule, and play may be the most post potent tools activists have, especially in the face of overwhelming obstacles.

---

[201] Ben Shepard, "The Use of Joyfulness as a Community Organizing Strategy," *Peace & Change* 30, no. 4 (2005).

[202] Shepard, Bogad, and Duncombe, "Performing Vs. The Insurmountable," p. 3.

[203] Shepard, Bogad, and Duncombe, "Performing Vs. The Insurmountable," p.12.

[204] Shepard, Bogad, and Duncombe, "Performing Vs. The Insurmountable," p.14.

Such a spirit of defiance is sometimes all one can do; sometimes it is just enough. "That opens up space for activism," Miller reflects. It makes the predictable not so predictable for just a minute. "It makes working in the face of the insurmountable a reasonable choice [. . .] It's not the most efficient thing to do, but it's the only thing we can do [. . .] there is so much joy in being able to shout in our anger together.[205]

Finally, with a reference to Schechner, Shepard, Bogad and Duncombe write that "Much of the politics of play involves shifting debate about who plays, on what terms, by whose rules, and on whose playing field".[206]

This section with the overall heading "humour, politics, protest and social conflict" has included seven subheadings aimed at summing up and discussing the possibilities and limitations of a number of different academic traditions relevant to the subject of humorous political stunts. It has included perspectives from studies of political jokes, traditional folly, humour in occupations, gender studies, organisational theory, nonviolent resistance and finally culture jamming, pranks and tactical carnival. After this long introduction, I will conclude the chapter by defining the central concepts of the thesis and discussing the ethical aspects of humour.

Power, resistance, activism and discourse

Power is one of the most contested terms in social science. My approach to the issue is inspired by a number of authors, including the scholars of nonviolence that I referred to above. Steven Lukes' classic essay *Power: A Radical View* and the three views on

---

[205] Shepard, Bogad, and Duncombe, "Performing Vs. The Insurmountable," p. 10.
[206] Shepard, Bogad, and Duncombe, "Performing Vs. The Insurmountable," pp. 20-21.

power he presents are a good starting point for a multifaceted understanding of power.[207] Chapter 4 in April Carter's book *People Power and Political Change*[208] gives a good overview of the limitations with the consent perspective dominant in theory of nonviolence. Foucault's thinking on power has inspired Vinthagen, but otherwise his perspectives are rather absent in theory of nonviolent action. Foucault worked from the assumption that power only exists in people's relations to other people, which means that power is multi-dimensional.[209] Although Foucault wrote very little about how power can be resisted, he did point out that resistance was a place to start investigating how power works.[210] An interesting application of Foucault's perspective in relation to nonviolence can also be found in Bleiker's concept of *transversal dissent*.[211]

Power is not something people have or do not have, and therefore resistance cannot be a question of either or. Nevertheless, some people appear more powerful than others. A person or a group of people might perceive themselves to be in power, and others might view them as extremely powerful. If this dominant group control resources, and can induce other people to do things that are in the interest of these apparently powerful, then this becomes a self-reinforcing cycle. Those already in power get the opportunity to set the agenda, and become the representatives of dominant discourses. This does not imply that the resisters are powerless, that alternative discourses are non-

---

[207] Steven Lukes, *Power: A Radical View* (London: Macmillan, 1974).
[208] Carter, *People Power and Political Change: Key Issues and Concepts*.
[209] Michel Foucault, "Disciplinary Power and Subjection," in *Power*, ed. Steven Lukes, *Readings in Social and Political Theory* (New York: New York University Press, 1976).
[210] Michel Foucault, "The Subject and Power," *Critical Inquiry* 8, no. 4 (1982): p. 780.
[211] Roland Bleiker, *Popular Dissent, Human Agency, and Global Politics* (Cambridge: Cambridge University Press, 2000).

existent or that the power relations cannot change. Nevertheless the activists themselves experience their position as marginal, subordinate and asymmetric. The apparently powerful can experience moments of slipping control, but under most circumstance this is only temporarily.

Dominant discourses are those well-established "truths" and taken for granted knowledges which rule a certain domain without being appreciably affected or displaced by challenges. I will not discuss in detail how the dominant discourses manifest themselves and to what degree they dominate. Sufficient for the purpose here is to recognise that some people consider them dominant enough, and are disturbed enough by this dominance, to set out to challenge them.

Although dominant and apparently powerful, even in the most brutal dictatorship or situations of oppression the dictator cannot have total control. Dissenters always manage to carve out small niches outside of the apparently almighty's control. These pockets of resistance are important for expanding resistance. As an overall name, I refer to these dissenters as "activists". Most of the activists that appear in the examples here are from groups concerned with social justice, peace, anti-consumerism and the environment since they appear to be the ones using humorous political stunts in their activism. However, activists can just as well be marginalised right wing extremists and conservatives and I do not exclude the possibility that they can use humorous political stunts as well.

In most arenas the activists are subordinate towards representatives of the state and big companies who control resources like money, land, legal violence, well-educated employees, and have the law on their side. In spite of these enormous obstacles, activists are not just fighting against people and groups who are more powerful than them, but also the discourses of what is true, right and just that the apparently powerful uphold. In order for the writing not to become monotone, I will refer to these inter-changeably as "dominant discourse", "truth" and "rationality" and to the people who represent these views as "representatives of the dominant discourses" and "the powerful". Sometimes I will modify with "apparently powerful" and similar expressions.

In order to take these nuanced understandings of relations of power into consideration when studying political humour, it is necessary not just to judge the immediate outcome of telling a joke, painting a humorous graffiti or doing a humorous action in public by its ability to change policies or actual circumstances. One also has to ask if humour contributes to reaching out to various audiences, mobilising new activists and creating a culture of resistance that makes activism sustainable. And in what ways can humour be part of challenging established relations of power and undermine dominant discourses?

Humour and ethics

In the context of political humour it is also relevant to raise the question of ethics. In 2005, two scholars independent of each other published books about ethical considerations regarding laughter and ridicule. Michael Billig's *Laughter and Ridicule: Towards a Social Critique of Laughter* is written from the perspective of critical sociology, and sets out to question common sense beliefs that humour is necessarily positive and good.[212] *The Pleasure of Fools: Essays in the Ethics of Laughter* by Jure Gantar[213] takes a very different approach. His point of departure is philosophy about ethics. For Gantar there is no question that some laughter is unethical, but he wants to investigate if this is a characteristic of *all* laughter, or if it is possible to have construc-

---

[212] Billig, *Laughter and Ridicule: Towards a Social Critique of Laughter*.
[213] Jure Gantar, *The Pleasure of Fools: Essays in the Ethics of Laughter* (London: McGill-Queen's University Press, 2005).

tive and inclusive laughter.[214] The sources for Gantar's investigations are various forms of classic literature – from Greek comedies to Oscar Wilde.

Gantar finds no shortage of people who throughout history have considered laughter unethical, and he writes that "Of all these different kinds of laughter the one that is most frequently associated with the unethical is satirical laughter".[215] Since much political humour involves satire, Gantar's findings are of interest. The reason satire is considered unethical is because its target is very often a real person, and satire is based on contempt for this person. No matter how much they deserve it, there is always someone who gets hurt by satire. As an example, Gantar notes how Adolf Hitler was upset by Charlie Chaplin's movie *The Dictator*. However, Gantar emphasises that it is also possible to argue that satirical laughter is most ethical. Satire is social correction, and it corrects what is morally wrong.[216]

Gantar also recognises humour's subversive potential, and thinks that it can be ethical to laugh at the oppressor.[217] He then proceeds to see if there will be any laughter at all in Utopia, when all social inequality has been abolished. He finds that the prospect for laughter is bleak in the perfect world that various authors have dreamed about.

Gantar's conclusion is both interesting and surprising. After he has carefully demonstrated how all types of laughter can potentially be unethical, he declares that he has found himself at "an epistemological dead end".[218] The problem is that ethical criticism of laughter either ends up censoring laughter, or keeps

---

[214] Gantar, *The Pleasure of Fools*: pp. 10, 14-16.
[215] Gantar, *The Pleasure of Fools*: p. 32.
[216] Gantar, *The Pleasure of Fools*: p. 48.
[217] Gantar, *The Pleasure of Fools*: pp. 92-93.
[218] Gantar, *The Pleasure of Fools*: p. 158.

looking for an innocent laughter that does not exist. He concludes that the subject of ethics "is incapable of dealing with laughter."[219] The reason is that ethical criticism does not have the capacity to distinguish between a joke and an insult; it will all look the same. So Gantar ends up concluding that "When we laugh, we should not care about offending. And when we investigate laughter critically, we should forget about ethics".[220]

Billig's approach to laughter and ridicule differs greatly from Gantar's, since his starting point is not ethics, but critical sociology. His aim is to question the taken for granted assumption that humour is something good and positive which is dominant in today's western societies. He reminds his readers that much humour also serves to enforce social order through ridicule and mockery, and that this aspect is a neglected area in studies of humour.[221] Billig is aware that humour can both disrupt and impose social order. However, in the tradition of critical sociology his focus is the social control he thinks others have neglected and what appear to be contrary to dominant common sense beliefs. Nevertheless, this one-sidedness becomes problematic because Billig almost ends up with the opposite one-sidedness. He makes generalisations from everyday ridicule which cannot be justified to apply to humorous political stunts as well.

Billig shows that the concept of *a good sense of humour* as a positive character trait historically is a rather new phenomenon, which was first used in the 1840s, but did not become common until the 1870's. In his critical investigation, Billig also points out that contrary to common sense impressions, the medical evidence on the benefits of humour is "weak and inconclusive".[222] He claims that the idea that humour helps us heal and prevents diseases, as

---

[219] Gantar, *The Pleasure of Fools*: p. 158.
[220] Gantar, *The Pleasure of Fools*: p. 158.
[221] Billig, *Laughter and Ridicule: Towards a Social Critique of Laughter*: pp. 2-3.
[222] Billig, *Laughter and Ridicule: Towards a Social Critique of Laughter*: p. 21.

stressed by many self-help books, is not based on solid evidence. Psychology's focus on the individual's capacity to handle stress and negative events by laughing and looking at what is positive is also problematic. Such a perspective of learning to live with whatever the problem is and get the best out of the circumstance is an implicit discouragement of struggles for social change.[223] The origin of many people's problems is not a lack of capacity to cope, but their social position in an unfair and unequal world where wealth is the privilege of the few.

Previously I mentioned Palmer's point that humorous intent does not automatically mean that the audience agrees that something is humorous. Differing perceptions of the same situation are also a theme for Billig who points out that "one person's harmless bit of teasing will be another's cruelty".[224] This is most obvious when it comes to ridicule and mockery. In everyday interactions, few people are willing to admit that they ridicule and mock others. What the target considers inappropriate, the person who is responsible for it instead refers to as "friendly teasing". When someone is accused of mocking or ridicule during the interactions of daily life, many respond that no harm was meant or that they were "just joking".[225] Billig has named this response the *tease spray*, which the person offending can spray around her to cover up the bad smell of ridicule. Billig's arguments about how children learn this behaviour by being mocked and ridiculed by their own parents through their up-bringing are convincing[226], and there is little doubt that the same "tease spray" is used by political activists. On the other hand, people exposed to ridicule do not have to laugh, but can turn to

---

[223] Billig, *Laughter and Ridicule: Towards a Social Critique of Laughter.* p. 32.
[224] Billig, *Laughter and Ridicule: Towards a Social Critique of Laughter.* p. 8.
[225] Billig, *Laughter and Ridicule: Towards a Social Critique of Laughter.* p. 25.
[226] Billig, *Laughter and Ridicule: Towards a Social Critique of Laughter.* pp. 196-98.

what Billig calls *unlaughter*. Unlaughter is not the same at not laughing because one does not understand; it is a way of showing disapproval when others laugh.[227] Unlaughter easily becomes the target of ridicule, as will be apparent in chapter 3 about humorous political stunts.

Billig belongs to the group of humour researchers that think that instead of producing "real" rebellion, humour becomes a safety valve.[228] The problems with this position were addressed in detail above and Billig does not add anything new to the debate. He suggests that there are some life circumstances people ought to rebel against. Nevertheless, his focus on how ridicule maintains social order in daily life has led him to sound as if ridicule is always something morally problematic. He acknowledges that ridiculing a child as a form of discipline might be considered a milder form of punishment than violence, but this is not discussed in relation to humour's rebellious potential.[229] If the example of the ridiculed child is transferred to societal level, the equivalent would be that a mocking would be better than a violent crackdown on protesters. Although he provides an example of a child ridiculing its parent this is not transferred to an ethical discussion about what it means when a subordinate political group ridicules those in power.

Conclusion

Both nonviolence and humour have been researched academically as multidisciplinary fields. Humour as a form of protest has caught the attention of many authors, studying themes as diverse as political jokes, traditional folly, culture jamming and humour during occupations. They come from various backgrounds,

---

[227] Billig, *Laughter and Ridicule: Towards a Social Critique of Laughter.* p. 192.
[228] Billig, *Laughter and Ridicule: Towards a Social Critique of Laughter.* pp. 211-13.
[229] Billig, *Laughter and Ridicule: Towards a Social Critique of Laughter.* p. 205.

including everything from sociology, folklore research and gender studies, to organisational theory and community studies. Many scholars have contributed with insights through case studies focusing on particular circumstances or specific forms of humour, but few have been interested in humour as an aspect of nonviolent resistance.

Theories of Sharp and Gandhi were used to introduce the variety in approaches to nonviolent action. These theories range from viewing nonviolence as a pragmatic choice, which increases the odds for success, to the only morally acceptable way to strive for social change, involving the activist's whole life. The four rationalities of dialogue facilitation, power breaking, utopian enactment and normative regulation suggested by Vinthagen provide a framework for understanding nonviolent action which takes its complexities into consideration. In chapter 7 I will investigate how the different rationalities might be affected by diverse forms of humour.

Within humour studies what is called the incongruity tradition is most dominant, and this aspect is also included in the definition of humour used here. However, the opposite of humour is routinely called "serious" both in academia and everyday language – a use of terminology which creates an artificial and misleading dichotomy between the "serious" and the humorous. I consider it more useful to refer to the opposite of humour as "rational" or "non-humorous", a distinction that takes into account that some humour is indeed deadly serious.

There are two important works on the ethics of humour. Billig thinks that ridicule plays an underestimated role in social control, but has not investigated political humour aimed at kicking upwards. Gantar concluded that it is impossible to judge humour through the lens of ethics.

Often the data for analysing humorous protest has been whispered jokes, which by their very nature do not engage with the

106

opponents. The emphasis of this source of data is probably one reason why there have been so few investigations into the interactions between humorous nonviolent resisters and their opponents.

For decades it has been debated whether humour contributes to resistance or if it is "just" a vent for frustration that either has no impact or is counterproductive because it takes time and energy away from activities that would make a real difference. For me it is impossible to frame this as a question of either-or. Some political humour probably has very little influence on relations of power, but to claim humour will never contribute to resisting dictatorship, abuse and injustice is a very strong statement. Those who are proponents of these ideas seem to have a rudimentary understanding of power and resistance. The insights that authors such as Foucault, Scott and Bayat have provided about the complexity of power and the subtle and discreet ways that resistance is practiced behind the scenes are absent from these scholars' writings. In addition it is not clear what they actually think constitutes "real" change and resistance.

Dominant discourses and powerful institutions are unlikely to be dismantled overnight, but through the centuries, social movements have succeeded in changing societies dramatically. The question is not if humour can create this change by itself, which is of course very unlikely, but rather the question guiding my research: *What role* can humour play in facilitating resistance to dominant discourses and powerful institutions and people?

Chapter 2: A methodology for emancipation and social change

Introduction

The literature review revealed that relatively little is known about my research questions regarding subordinate and marginalised political groups' use of humour in public to expose, ridicule and influence those they consider more powerful than themselves. This chapter outlines how I have gathered information and discusses the possibilities and limitations to the knowledge that can be generated based on this data. My case study data collection strategy is described, followed by the methods used for later chapters. Afterwards I discuss the assumptions behind the decisions I made along the way.

Data collection – a case study strategy

In the previous research on the role of humour in nonviolent resistance done by myself and others, the Serbian group Otpor had been used as a single case study to discuss the relations between humour and nonviolence.[230] This time I wanted to broaden the data in order to discuss the questions on a more general basis and not be limited by the circumstances around this or another particular case. I decided to look at many instances of the use of humour and in addition explore how humour was used in relation to other non-humorous methods of challenging relations of power. Conducting several case studies appeared to be a way to approach the subject.

---

[230] Sørensen, "Humour as Nonviolent Resistance to Oppression." This line of inquiry was continued by Sombutpoonsiri, "The Use of Humour as a Vehicle for Nonviolent Struggle." with her in-depth study of Otpor.

In "The Case Study and the Study of Social Movements" Snow and Trom describe what they call the "the core defining characteristics of the case study" as:

> (a) investigation and analysis of an instance or variant of some bounded social phenomenon that (b) seek to generate a richly detailed and "thick" elaboration of the phenomenon studied through (c) the use and triangulation of multiple methods or procedures that include but are not limited to qualitative techniques[231]

The "bounded social phenomenon" that I study is political activists' use of humorous political stunts. Chapters 5 and 6, the case studies of Ofog and KMV, illustrate how two different but comparable "instances and variants" of this phenomenon have utilised humour in their struggles against militarism.[232]

Snow and Trom write that using case studies is a research strategy rather than a particular method:

---

[231] David A. Snow and Danny Trom, "The Case Study and the Study of Social Movements," in *Methods of Social Movement Research*, ed. Bert Klandermans and Suzanne Staggenborg (Minneapolis, MN: University of Minnesota Press, 2002), p. 147.

[232] The two case studies are both about groups working on "anti-militarism". When participants in the peace movement use the terms "militarism" and "anti-militarism" they do not necessarily mean and imply the same things. When I use the terms I refer to the dominant and deeply enhanced discourse that military might give most power and that an army is the best way to protect a country. In Sweden and Norway, the armed forces and arms producers are institutions and companies that rely on the discourse of militarism in order to justify their existence. However, upholders of the discourse are also governments, a number of government institutions as well as a large proportion of the general public. "Anti-militarists", on the other hand, are people who contribute to the counter-discourse of anti-militarism that rejects or at least questions the assumptions inherent in militarism.

> a case study is not a method per se as are ethnography, survey research, laboratory experimentation, and historical/comparative research. Rather, we argue that the case study is more appropriately conceptualized as a research strategy that is associated with a number of data-gathering methods or procedures.[233]

This means that researchers who use case studies as a data collection strategy still have to specify what methods they have used in order to collect the data for the case study. For both my case studies I have used a triangulation of methods which is described in detail below.

In order to get even more information about the social phenomenon of humorous political stunts, I also collected the examples that are part of chapter 3. They are not detailed and "thick" enough to deserve the label case studies, but illustrate a part of the diversity of the phenomenon of humorous political stunts, thus broadening the study and making it possible to generalise more than what would have been possible with just the two case studies.

I have not used any quantitative methods, for the simple reason that they would not be appropriate in order to gather useful information about this subject. Although qualitative and quantitative methods do have a different epistemological history, I agree with Howard S. Becker that the difference is not as big as some people make it. "Practitioners of qualitative and quantitative methods may seem to have different philosophies of science, but they really just work in different situations and ask different questions."[234] At the moment, so little is known about humour

---

[233] Snow and Trom, "The Case Study and the Study of Social Movements," p. 151.

[234] Howard S. Becker, "The Epistemology of Qualitative Research," in *Contemporary Field Research: Perspectives and Formulations*, ed. Robert M. Emerson (Prospect Heights, IL: Waveland Press, 2001), p. 328.

and political activism that little valuable information can be gathered through a method like a large survey.

Selection of cases

Why these particular cases? With so little information about humorous political stunts available, I aimed to look for case studies that are rich in information and where it was possible to establish that humour had been or is playing a role for the political activists. This means that I have used what Patton calls "Extreme or deviant case sampling", a special type of purposeful sampling.[235] These cases are not to be considered typical of the way that grassroots political activists use humour. The two groups in the case studies use or have used humour to a much larger degree than the average political activist group. At the same time, I was interested in the interplay between humorous and non-humorous activities, which ruled out groups that have humour as their primary strategy, such as the Yes Men and Billionaires for Bush.

Many factors play a role in a sampling strategy. As a PhD student, I was constrained by a time limit and limited economic resources. I also felt it was important that I use my skills with Scandinavian languages to prioritise Scandinavian experiences in order for these to be included as research available in English.

It was not a sampling criterion that the political activists were concerned about the same or similar themes, but as it turned out, both Ofog and KMV are/were radical anti-militarists organised like networks that work as marginalised groups within a democratic setting. Even among radical activists they are quite marginal. These similarities have led me to offer some conclusions that would not have been possible with less comparable cases. Nevertheless, there are also major differences. An obvious

---

[235] Michael Quinn Patton, *Qualitative Research and Evaluation Methods*, 3 ed. (Thousand Oaks, CA: Sage Publications, 2002). p. 230.

one is the separation in time, so while Ofog is still an active network, KMV dissolved many years ago. The most decisive difference for my analysis is that KMV worked on a campaign with one particular aim in mind, while Ofog's focus is much broader.

The purpose of the 15 examples in Chapter 3 is to illustrate the diversity of the phenomenon of humorous political stunts with examples that cover different political issues, varying political circumstances and differing across time, geography, culture and language. Other differences have more to do with the way the stunt was carried out – the humorous techniques, mediums used and degree of professionalism. This number of examples is not required to establish that the phenomenon I have labelled humorous political stunts exist, but they are useful to illustrate how much such stunts can vary.

In the selection process for the examples in Chapter 3, I started out with cases that are described in the literature on nonviolent activism or well known via the mass media. After I started researching, many activists, researchers, friends and family pointed me towards examples I had not heard about before. When deciding on which cases to include and which to leave out, my criteria for inclusion were that they:

- Illustrate the diversity of the phenomena when it comes to the type of stunt or humorous technique
- Contribute diversity in terms of geography, time, language or culture
- Are not well described in academic literature already

However, although this was the ideal, in reality there is an apparent excess of European and Scandinavian examples. Those not European are all from the English speaking part of the world. Another limitation is that the majority of the examples come from groups concerned with social justice, peace, human rights and the environment. These selection biases might be because it is mainly this type of groups that uses humorous political stunts, but especially when it comes to language it is also a reflection of my language skills and the spheres of interest for people who have suggested cases to me.

Some well documented cases, such as Yes Men, are also included because they are useful illustrative cases for certain types of stunts, or when the reactions to them can contribute to a better analysis. Almost all new examples I have come across fit within the model since they use one of the five types of stunts. It is a limitation of the study that it does not include more examples from the "global south" something which would in all likelihood have shown an even greater diversity. However, other scholars and activists can in the future investigate to what degree this typology of humorous political stunts is valid outside of the "western world".

Data collection process for the case study with Ofog

Chapters 4 and 5 present the results from the case study I did together with the Swedish anti-militarist network Ofog.

Sandra L. Kirby, Lorraine Greaves, and Colleen Reid in their book *Experience Research Social Change: Methods Beyond the Mainstream* identify three different techniques for gathering information in qualitative research: 1. Listening (such as interviews) 2. Observing   and 3. Examination of records and historical traces.[236] In this case study, I used all these three techniques in order to gather data. However, the overall approach was *participatory action research* and the intention to produce knowledge that can contribute to social change. I consider

---

[236] Sandra L. Kirby, Lorraine Greaves, and Colleen Reid, *Experience Research Social Change: Methods Beyond the Mainstream*, 2nd ed. (Toronto: University of Toronto Press, 2010). p. 13.

participatory action research a strategy more than a method in itself, the same way that Snow and Trom speak about the case study as a strategy rather than a method per se. This way of understanding participatory action research is also in line with McTaggart who writes that

> Action research is not a 'method' or a 'procedure' for research but a series of commitments to observe and problematize through practice a series of principles for conducting social enquiry...[237]

In the sections below I describe this overall approach of participatory action research and the methods of participant observation, semi-structured interviews, workshop facilitation as well as data collection from written documents. I also describe what expectations the Ofog activists had of the research project and me and how the research developed.

Participatory action research

The term *participatory action research* can be used in different ways, but starts from the assumption that research should contribute to creating change for the better. Participatory action research is a collaborative process that people do together and on equal terms in spite of differences in formal qualifications and training. It is used in many different fields such as education, social work and development work. Usually one avoids loaded terms that indicate that a neutral researcher do research *on* someone else. In the end of this chapter I have included a discussion on the theoretical aspects of research and power and the epistemological assumptions behind the whole thesis. In this section I discuss the way participatory action research inspired the case study with Ofog in practice.

---

[237] Robin McTaggart, "Issues for Participatory Action Researchers," in *New Directions in Action Research*, ed. Ortrun Zuber-Skerritt (London: Falmer Press, 1996), p. 248.

Bridget Somekh's eight principles of action research sum up nicely what participatory action research is about:

1. Action research integrates research and action
2. Action research is conducted by a collaborative partnership of participants and researchers
3. Action research involves the development of knowledge and understanding of a unique kind
4. Action research starts from a vision of social transformation and aspirations for greater social justice for all
5. Action research involves a high level of reflexivity
6. Action research involves exploratory engagement with a wide range of existing knowledge
7. Action research engenders powerful learning for participants
8. Action research locates the inquiry in an understanding of broader historical, political and ideological contexts.[238]

These eight principles guided the research process with Ofog, but translating the ideals into a concrete project within a specific context that set certain limitations was a challenge.

In the "ideal" action research situation, the person who initiates the research is herself part of an already established group, for example a group of colleagues or volunteers. If this ideal is followed, there is no boss who can dominate or direct the process or an outside expert who knows how research is supposed to be done. In reality, this spontaneous formation rarely happens, and the action research process is initiated by outsiders.[239] Another ideal is that the research is carried out collaboratively by

---

[238] Bridget Somekh, *Action Research: A Methodology for Change and Development* (Maidenhead: Open University Press, 2006). p. 6.
[239] Graham Webb, "Becoming Critical of Action Research for Development," in *New Directions in Action Research*, ed. Ortrun Zuber-Skerritt (London: Falmer Press, 1996).

the whole group, on a subject that they together have decided is worth researching. However, much research is done under the label participatory action research where one of more of these premises is set aside. This was also the case with my work together with Ofog, where none of these three ideals were in place. Although I was a long term "insider" to the peace movement, I did not know anybody in Ofog well and thus approached the group as an "outsider". In addition, I already had a particular topic that I considered worth researching – the use of humour as a way to challenge people in power. Since the premises for the case study divert so much from the ideals, I consider the case study to be *inspired* by participatory action research rather than an example of participatory action research, although in the beginning I did talk with Ofog about it as if it was a participatory action research project. However, the principles of combining action and research, contributing to greater social justice for all through a highly reflexive learning process on equal terms were indeed guiding the process. Therefore the project were in many ways more "faithful" to other important principles of participatory action research than many projects that do not hesitate to use this label. I will return to some of these critiques of specific action research projects shortly.

Because the participatory element is so important to participatory action research I will describe the research process at some length. This is both a story about how I have become a part of Ofog, and how we together approached the subject of humour.

I had been aware of the existence of Ofog for a couple of years before I started this research project through my own involvement in War Resisters' International (WRI), a network of pacifist and anti-militarist organisations from around the world. I had been active in WRI for more than a decade, and Ofog was in the process of becoming an associate organisation.

When I started to look for case studies for this project which would be rich in information and the groups open to working together with me, Ofog came naturally to mind since my impression was that it was a network which was expanding and favouring creative radical anti-militarist work. I had met a couple of people who were active in Ofog, and contacted one of them about my research project and asked him if he thought Ofog would be interested in working with me and how I should proceed to find out. He suggested presenting the project on an open email list, which I did. Already in this first document I stressed that I was interested in doing participatory action research *with* Ofog, and not research *on* them. When I did not get any response I asked the same person again if he had suggestions for people I could contact directly. He gave me a name, and shortly afterwards I was invited to a meeting in Gothenburg. After the meeting, I summarized our agreement this way:

Ofog expectations:

1. In the day to day work of the organization, *Ofog* activists generally don't spend enough time on reflecting on their work. Actions are often prepared at short notice and under time pressure. They would like support from Majken in facilitating a process for reflections around how *Ofog* has used *humor* in the past and can use it in the future. *Ofog* also welcomes the idea of trying to evaluate the use of *humor* in order to try out improved methods in the next round.

2. *Ofog* likes the idea of Majken presenting an overview of how different humorous methods have been used by different groups across time and space.

3. *Ofog* expects that the documentation of their experiences that Majken will do through her thesis will be reflected back in a form that is

117

accessible for nonviolent activists both in Sweden and in other places.

The mutual agreement is now:

Majken certainly aims to fulfil the expectations mentioned above.

Ofog and Majken will investigate the potential of humour together. Majken will facilitate the process, and the experiences will be documented in Majken's PhD thesis at Wollongong University, Australia. In the thesis, *Ofog* will be identified as an organization, but all individuals will be anonymous unless they have agreed otherwise.

The first step will be a workshop to take place in mid May 2011. Majken will facilitate the content of the day, *Ofog* Gothenburg will arrange a place to meet and invite participants from other parts of Sweden. The day will focus on 1. Lessons learned from past experiences of *humour* from *Ofog*, 2. introduce examples of humour as they have been used in other places and contexts, and 3. try to develop ideas that can be used during the action camp in Luleå in July.

The research method that Majken uses is called participatory action research. This means that Majken is a participating observer in the process. In addition to this, she will also interview people. Before the workshop in May, Majken would like to make some interviews with people.[240]

I immediately felt very welcome in Ofog, already after this first meeting. When we talked about the possibility of going through Ofog's archive, one person said to me that "we never let journalists into this office. When we meet with them, we meet

---

[240] Email from Majken to Ofog Gothenburg after meeting February 10th, 2011 Spelling mistakes corrected.

somewhere else. But you are one of us."[241] I am not sure where this trust in me came from, but have assumed that it was based on my background in the peace movement. However, to my knowledge I was never checked to make sure that I was not an infiltrator.

Although this project differs from the ideal participatory action research project because I was not a part of Ofog beforehand and already had decided on the topic of our research, I think the process has worked well and benefited both me and Ofog. Although I was going to earn a degree with the material, the project has not been haunted by many of the power problems that other projects labelled action research struggle with. Graham Webb, for instance, is critical of how so-called action research is used in the area of staff development, where the staff developer functions as a catalyst or consultant. To Webb, this means that the staff developer automatically has the upper hand. To him, the idea of equality is a myth which might be declared in various "ground rules", but disguises that the established power relations remain intact.[242]

A related critique is articulated by Richard Weiskopf and Stephan Laske[243] who analysed the power dynamics of a project they were involved in. They think that action research that does not take unequal power relations into consideration easily contributes to a reproduction of power. In the project they worked on, a major employer had to close down, but reopened as a cooperative run by the former workers. Weiskopf and Laske's project was about how the new cooperative could survive in the tough business

---

[241] Personal observation February 10th, 2011,
[242] Webb, "Becoming Critical of Action Research for Development," p. 154.
[243] Richard Weiskopf and Stephan Laske, "Emanicipatory Action Research: A Critical Alternative to Personnel Development or a New Way of Patronising People," in *New Directions in Action Research*, ed. Ortrun Zuber-Skerritt (London: Falmer Press, 1996).

environment and they were given the role as consultants and outsiders rather than insiders. Their interest in the project differed heavily from that of the former workers and it turned out to be difficult to create an environment free from power and domination. According to them, the label action research became a camouflage for new power relationships.[244] Weiskopf and Laske found that thanks to their academic schooling they and the former management were the ones who got to name the problems instead of those who worked on the ground. Although there was a mutual dependence between the researchers and the workers who needed each other to "succeed" with the project, it was still an unequal relationship with no common interest regarding what constituted success. As an example they mention that written reports are not a neutral medium of communication, but favour those who are most familiar with producing and reading text.[245]

Although there is much to say about power within a network like Ofog, it was not the challenges mentioned by Webb, Weiskopf and Laske that were most problematic in this research project. Although some might say that affiliation with a university and status as a researcher will automatically give one more power, I definitely did not feel that I had a more powerful position. On the contrary, I was totally dependent on Ofog for getting data, the network was not depending on me in any way, and I had not yet proven that I had the "qualifications" that give status within Ofog.

My status as a PhD student was probably a plus and gave me undeserved respect among a few people in the beginning, but within Ofog academic schooling is not as prestigious as in many other settings. My impression was that most Ofog activists were

---

[244] Weiskopf and Laske, "Emanicipatory Action Research," p. 125.
[245] Weiskopf and Laske, "Emanicipatory Action Research," p. 129.

indifferent towards research and did not expect social science to contribute to developing more effective nonviolent activism. My history with WRI probably gave me more credibility than doing a research project. About six months into the research process, I made a list of five things that appeared give status within Ofog:

- Time spent on Ofog work per week and over the years
- Self confidence
- Having done civil disobedience
- Having been to prison for a civil disobedience action
- Having been convicted to pay huge amounts in criminal damage for a civil disobedience action[246]

Since I had not spent any time working for Ofog, never been to prison, no criminal damage and only did my first civil disobedience action after I became involved with Ofog, this only left me with a bit of self-confidence and general social skills to rely on. I reflected:

> My lack of history with Ofog and civil disobedience make sure that I'm not something special. To me it is quite obvious that I need Ofog in order to get data much more than the rest of the group needs me (...) I have no way of imposing anything on Ofog. People do as they please anyway.

The last sentence reflected my feeling that even if I had tried to pressure for more use of humour in order to get more data to work with, it would have been unlikely to work in this network of independent local groups and affinity groups.

There is one particular area where the research I did is unquestionably an unavoidable exercise of power, and that is the interpretation of the material. Although all readers of Ofog's mailing list were given the opportunity to comment on drafts of

---

[246] Research diary entry October 3, 2011, edited.

this thesis, only one person did. However, these comments were not about the conclusions regarding Ofog's use of humour. This lack of interest in commenting is a power issue that is seldom addressed. The emphasis on long written texts within academia is potentially a much bigger barrier than the status that comes with academic degrees.

Relationships in research projects like this develop over time. After the initial workshop focusing on humour, I participated in a couple of meetings and interviewed some of the most active participants in the Gothenburg group. The next big event I took part in was a summer peace camp in July 2011 in Luleå in the north of Sweden. During this camp I noticed that I switched from talking about Ofog as "them" to "us", clearly identifying as a participant myself.

My interaction with other people in Ofog has taken various forms during the research project. Below I distinguish between four different types of methods I used for data collection together with Ofog.

Participant observation

Participant observation has a long tradition and is a well-established method within anthropology and ethnography. In the introduction to *Contemporary Field Research: Perspectives and Formulations*,[247] Robert M. Emerson traces its history back to the 19th century and British and American interest in the "natives" and "savages". The principles of participant observation have developed much since then and previous ideas of naturalistic observing and recording abandoned. They have been replaced with reflexivity and acknowledgement that an "observer" will influence the situation in the field. Another obvious point which

---

[247] Robert M. Emerson, *Contemporary Field Research: Perspectives and Formulations*, 2nd ed. (Prospect Heights, IL: Waveland Press, 2001).

is now widely recognised is that two people are unlikely to make exactly the same observations.

Because researchers know little about humour and political activism, participant observation within an action research framework seemed like a good way of supplementing other methods of data gathering. Participant observation is usually used to observe various forms of everyday life, and is also suggested as a method to gain insights into a subject that little is known about.[248] Introductions to the method emphasise that the researcher should aim at being a natural part of the everyday that disturbs as little as possible, striving towards becoming an insider of whatever group is of interest.[249] However, in a setting like Ofog it is impossible to be an "insider" without "disturbing" both the group itself and the society that Ofog aims to change. To sit passively in a meeting, taking notes and not participate in the discussion would be more disturbing to the social interaction and everyday life of Ofog than to contribute with personal opinions.

Between May 2011 and October 2013 I participated in a number of the meetings in the local group in Gothenburg and in most of the bigger activities at the national level such as camps, the celebration of Ofog's 10 year anniversary and yearly national meetings that decided on organisational matters and made some plans for the future. I also participated in some humorous actions, but not all. In this way, I was very much a participant observer of the everyday life of Ofog. However, because I was not interested in studying Ofog as a group, but in working together to study the phenomena of humour, this is not a traditional ethnographic study. Much could be written about the interactions and dynamics within Ofog, but that would be a

---

[248] Danny L. Jorgensen, *Participant Observation: A Methodology for Human Studies* (London: Sage, 1989). p. 12.

[249] Jorgensen, *Participant Observation: A Methodology for Human Studies.*

different study. After each meeting or action I wrote field notes, but the only topics I systematically wrote about were ideas about humorous actions that had been suggested and attitudes towards the use of humour.

As a result of this participation through two and a half years, I have indeed become an "insider" in the sense that I consider myself a fully accepted participant in Ofog in my own right, and not just as a researcher. At the end of the research project, I am also very likely to continue my involvement in the group. However, I write the term "insider" in quotation marks because I agree with Kirby, Greaves and Reid that it is more helpful to speak about reflexivity than a rigid insider-outsider dichotomy.[250] By reading and discussing methodology with other people in university environments I have developed my ability to have a reflexive attitude towards both my own and others' taken-for-granted assumptions. By sometimes taking a step back from my "insider" role, I can "travel" back and forth between the different positions. This is not a skill that one acquires for good, but an attitude that requires continued attention. As someone who is now an active participant in Ofog, I aim to present the point of view of other "insiders" as accurately as I can. Although I do not claim to speak for everyone in Ofog on all subjects, it is possible to present the point of view of other people relatively accurately without having lived exactly the same experience.

The advantage of being part of Ofog myself is that I see from the "inside" how people talk about humour and how humour is treated as a subject when I or someone else have come up with humorous ideas. Nevertheless, being so close also has some disadvantages. Especially as time passed, my impression is that many people came to view me more and more like any other Ofog activist, and less and less as a facilitator of a research

---

[250] Kirby, Greaves, and Reid, *Experience Research Social Change*: pp. 38-39.

process we were doing together. This is of course a very good sign of trust and acceptance, but it also meant that I lost the possibility of being seen to be an "outsider".

Participant observation regarding peace, war and conflict is not unusual.[251] Patrick Coy's study of *Peace Brigades International*, an organisation that offers accompaniment to peace, union and human rights activist in high risk environments, discusses a number of ethical dilemmas.[252] Although his work is a traditional ethnographic study in a situation of armed conflict that does not involve participatory action research, some of the dilemmas he faced have similarities with mine. For instance, Coy had to juggle with the issue of having more than one "agenda". He appears to have been a committed participant in Peace Brigades International during his time in Sri Lanka and writes that he was more involved in the work of the organisation than what is usually the norm in ethnographic studies.[253] From his writing it seems obvious that he valued the interests of those he was there to protect as well as his fellow activists high. Nevertheless, like me, he also had his research agenda, and for Coy that influenced the risks he was willing to take.

Barrie Thorne in her research on the draft resistance movement in the US in the 1960's encountered some of the same challenges when she decided to avoid participating in activities that meant a

[251] See for instance Lorraine Dowler, "The Four Square Laundry: Participant Observation in a War Zone," *Geographical Review* 91, no. 1/2 (2001).
[252] Patrick G. Coy, "Shared Risks and Research Dilemmas on a Peace Brigades International Team in Sri Lanka," *Journal of Contemporary Ethnography* 30, no. 5 (2001).
[253] Coy, "Shared Risks and Research Dilemmas on a Peace Brigades International Team in Sri Lanka," p. 589.

risk of spending time in jail.[254] In my research project with Ofog, the dilemma has not been what kind of risks I was willing to take, but how much I should encourage the use of humour. I truly believed (and still do) that carefully planned humorous political stunts would be a very effective method for us to use. At the same time, I continually had to consider if I argued in favour of humour because I thought it to be a wise strategy, or because it would generate interesting data for me to analyse. In the chapters on Ofog I have aimed to describe my own involvement in the discussions, development and performance of the humorous political stunts as accurately as possible.

Coy also discusses the dilemma of informed consent in fluid arrangements where participants come and go and consent has to be renegotiated continually.[255] In my case, Ofog's network structure and lack of a formal hierarchy on some occasions made informed consent problematic. Because of its decentralised structure, very few decisions in Ofog are made at the national level. As described above, it was the Gothenburg group that agreed to do the participatory action research project together with me. When meeting new people at the national level or when new people joined the Gothenburg group, I have done my best to tell them that I was doing this project. Nevertheless, it is very likely that there are some people who have never heard about it (for example if they only participated in part of a meeting) or maybe forgotten that I told them. When it came to particular humorous actions and I was part of an affinity group, I was careful to obtain oral consent from everyone else in the group to use material from our joint action in my thesis. I described what

---

[254] Barrie Thorne, "Political Activist as Participant Observer: Conflicts of Commitment in a Study of the Draft Resistance Movement of the 1960's," *Symbolic Interaction* 2, no. 1 (1979).
[255] Coy, "Shared Risks and Research Dilemmas on a Peace Brigades International Team in Sri Lanka," p. 578.

I was writing about, the basic principles of participatory action research and promised that I would not disclose their names or any other information that could identify them in anything I wrote.

A final theme that Coy raises which is also relevant for me is the integration of the activist and academic self. For Coy, his research project together with Peace Brigades International made it possible for him to combine his long-time interest in peace and justice with his academic career.[256] In an article specifically about activist academics, Divinski et al. define these as "academics who attempt to integrate their academic and activist identities".[257] The authors outline some of the problems of conflicting roles and expectations. The main obstacle to integration of activist and academic selves is that academic's work for social change is seldom rewarded academically and that academic institutions generally uphold the status quo rather than work for change. Obstacles also occur when activist organisations do not see the relevance of academic research to their work. For example, expectations may differ considerably when it comes to timing and complexity. Academic research takes time and emphasises complexity, while activists frequently are concerned with the need for immediate action and conclusions that can be boiled down to a bumper sticker slogan.[258] Although it has sometimes been a challenge to integrate my activist and academic self, my experience of working together with Ofog on the use of humour is that it has made it possible to combine my passion for radical anti-militarist peace work with my academic interest.

[256] Coy, "Shared Risks and Research Dilemmas on a Peace Brigades International Team in Sri Lanka," p. 593.
[257] Randy Divinski et al., "Social Change as Applied Social Science," *Peace & Change* 19, no. 1 (1994): p. 6.
[258] Divinski et al., "Social Change as Applied Social Science."

Semi-structured interviews

The second method for data gathering I have used within the overall strategy of participatory action research in the case study on Ofog has been to make formal semi-structured interviews with ten people about the use of humour.

Semi-structured interviewing is another well-established method used to get a number of different types of information.[259] With interviews it becomes especially obvious that data are not something which is just "out there" waiting to be collected. It is created through the interviewer's and the interviewee's interaction.[260]

All interviews were done on a one-on-one basis, except one where two persons were good friends, had participated in many of the same events and preferred to do the interview together. Most of the interviews took place in quiet environments either at Ofog's office or in the activists' own home or a friend's home. Two of the interviews were focused on a certain action I wanted to know more about. The remaining eight were longer interviews about many aspects of humour. I had prepared a set of questions to be asked and tried to make the conversation as natural as possible. I aimed to focus on events that the interviewees had participated in, but some also spoke more generally. Very often people on their own initiative brought up themes that I had planned to ask later, and I did not have the opportunity to phrase the question exactly as I had planned. I just made sure that we had covered all the themes that interested me. The great benefit of the semi-structured interview is the possibility for

---

[259] See for instance Patton, *Qualitative Research and Evaluation Methods*; Kirby, Greaves, and Reid, *Experience Research Social Change*.
[260] Kathy Charmaz, "Grounded Theory," in *Contemporary Field Research: Perspectives and Formulations*, ed. Robert M. Emerson (Prospect Heights, IL: Waveland Press, 2001), p. 339.

people to describe things in their own words, and for the opportunity to ask them to elaborate on interesting or unexpected things.

The eight longer interviews were audio recorded and some parts transcribed. The purpose of the interviews was twofold. They provided facts about events that I had not observed myself and they gave an impression of what the humour means to those who tell about it. When it comes to research about perceptions of humour, I have aimed to be as accurate as possible. Becker writes that all researchers attribute points of view to those they do research together with. The question is not if they should or not, but how well they do it – how accurate they are. Nobody can be perfect, but a good researcher does better than zero when describing what other people think.[261]

Some informants are quoted at length in order to give the reader as vivid an impression of the situation described as possible, especially when it comes to particular humorous political stunts. This also gives the reader the opportunity to agree or disagree with my interpretation and analysis. In other places I chose to paraphrase what someone said in order to provide a better flow in the text.

Everyone I interviewed signed a written consent form before the interview. After deciding what to include I send a draft of the text about Ofog to everyone I had interviewed so they could see any direct quotes or a paraphrasing of something they had said within the context of what others said and my analysis. Everyone was invited to check the quotes and paraphrasing and given two months to reply. I explained that if I did not hear back from them, I assumed that it meant that they were satisfied with the way I had used the interviews. Almost everyone responded saying that it looked fine. To me this indicates that the interview data in this chapter are reliable and have a high credibility. After

---

[261] Becker, "The Epistemology of Qualitative Research."

this initial round I edited the text considerably, and I also decided that it would increase readability without disturbing the meaning to edit the transcribed quotes to some degree. Since the purpose of the quotes is not a word by word analysis, it was more important that they are easy to read also for readers who are not used to reading oral accounts. Thus natural parts of oral language, such as ehh, uhh, etc. have been removed. I also cut out repetition and instead of putting implied meanings in square brackets, as is common, they are included in the text in most places. Everyone I interviewed were given the opportunity to comment on the final version of the text as well.

In the case study on Ofog, all the informants have pseudonyms. In the other case study, some of the informants insisted that I use their real names and I have respected this wish. The reason I have not done the same regarding the interviews with Ofog activists is first and foremost that no one has asked me to. As well, many of the Ofog activists I spoke to have not been exposed much in media and even if they had insisted that I use their names, it would have taken much convincing for me to agree. Even if someone had insisted it would have been problematic to present some with pseudonyms and others with their real names, making it too easy for the rest of Ofog to identify everyone I had interviewed.

The development of the research process

The third type of method that I used for triangulating information was facilitating workshops about humour with Ofog. Workshops are not a standard data gathering method for researchers, but a common way of sharing knowledge among activists. Workshops can be done internally within a group where people already know each other, or can be a way to bring together activists who are not familiar with each other to share knowledge about a particular topic. The facilitator does not necessarily have special knowledge about the subject but is there to guide the process. However, often someone who has a special interest in a topic offers or is asked to facilitate a workshop about it.[262] To use workshops as a method seemed to be very much in line with the letter and spirit of participatory action research and a familiar way of working together and organising collective learning in Ofog.

The workshops that I facilitated were a type of participant observation where I took a leading role and the purpose specifically was for us together to learn more about humour. In practice a workshop shares many similarities with a focus group interview where a researcher usually interview 6-10 people about a particular topic in order to gather information efficiently both from the individuals and from the discussions that arise among the participants. Sometimes the people in the focus group know each other, but frequently they have not met before.[263] The major difference between a workshop and a focus group interview is that in a workshop the purpose is to share knowledge that everyone will benefit from. A focus group is conducted in order for outside researchers to gather data and if anyone happens to learn something from the experience that is just a side effect.

Early in the research process with Ofog I facilitated three workshops in Gothenburg, Luleå and Malmö between May and September 2011. At the time I described how I would implement the approach of participatory action research to my colleagues at the university like this:

> In the context of my thesis this means that I sit down with activists and ask: What questions are you working on?

---

[262] For more information and to get an impression of the ideas and spirit of workshops and facilitation see for instance Robert Chambers, *Participatory Workshops: A Sourcebook of 21 Sets of Ideas and Activities* (London: Earthscan, 2002).
[263] Patton, *Qualitative Research and Evaluation Methods*: pp. 385-90.

What is important to you? If you should try to do something humorous, what could it be? Do you want to try out
your ideas? Afterwards I will continue: How do you think
it went? Is there anything you would do differently if you
should try this again?[264]

The first four questions were addressed in the workshops in
Gothenburg and Malmö as well as in the interviews. These two
workshops lasted about six hours each and were structured as a
sharing about past experiences of humour and a one hour talk by
me presenting a number of humorous political stunts carried out
by others to inspire. The longest part of the workshop was spent
working on the question "If you should try to do something
humorous, what could it be?" Many ideas and suggestions came
up, but most of them were never carried out. The last two
questions had the character of an evaluation and I aimed to
address them in the affinity groups I participated in that actually
carried out humorous political stunts. The workshop held in
Luleå was considerably shorter than the others and the purpose
was to inspire the activists participating in the camp rather than a
genuine sharing.

In order to get an impression of what perceptions people in
Ofog had about humour and political activism, I started both
interviews and workshops by asking what people thought could
be achieved by using humour, before saying much about my own
ideas. However, the very action of asking the network to be part
of the research project and inviting participants to a workshop
on humour provides the idea that this is a topic worthy of their
time and thoughts. I have no illusion that I have not been an
"influence" from the very first email, and I assume that I have
caused more talk and thoughts about humour than would otherwise have happened. Lena, who I interviewed after the first

---

[264] Research Plan First Year Research Proposal Review, University of
Wollongong 22 November 2011.

workshop in Gothenburg, mentioned this spontaneously during our conversation. Spending a whole day on humour had made her realise how much humour Ofog used, and it had been very revealing for her to think about Ofog's activities along those lines.

Informed consent for the workshops was sought in a tacit way. In all written invitations to workshops there was a reference to the fact that the workshop was part of an ongoing participatory action research project and the insights from the workshop would be used in my thesis.

The four questions to the participants in the workshops were phrased like this:

1. What is the best example of a humorous nonviolent action that you know of?
2. What do you think can be achieved by using humour as a method in nonviolent actions?
3. How can humour influence relations with the military, media, arms producers and police in nonviolent actions?
4. Can there be any problems with using humour as a method in nonviolent actions?

The answers to question 1 became background information for me. During the analysis the answers to numbers 2 and 3 were divided into the four categories:

a) facilitating outreach and mobilisation
b) facilitating a culture of resistance
c) challenging power relations
d) others

These categories are almost equivalent to subheadings in Chapters 4 and 5 and together with information from the interviews some of the answers are included here as part of the analysis of the effect and meaning of humour.

Participant observation, interviews and the workshops were all part of the triangulation. I also used the interviews in the spirit of participatory action research to ask people what expectations they had of the project and of me as a researcher. Some focused on what had been mentioned already during the initial meeting – that they would like more focused discussions about strategy, and how humour could be part of that. Another recurring topic was to be inspired and learn about how humour had been used by other groups in other contexts. In addition, there were also suggestions for particular ideas to look more into. Two of them can also give an impression on how the research process worked. Clowning was a theme that came up in almost all interviews and many expressed interest in developing this further. When I specifically asked if they thought it would be interesting to look at clowning in connection with counter recruitment (discouraging people from enlisting in the military), I received several positive responses, and it is something we worked on during the workshop in Malmö. Therefore it is also an idea I spent time investigating and contributed to organising.

It is a natural part of the process of discussing ideas that some of them have not been carried out and maybe never will. Several people expressed interest in looking into another topic, how humour could be used in the legal system, for instance during court cases. So far Ofog had always been very serious during the court procedures and tried to appear as otherwise "ordinary" citizens who were only breaking a particular law. However, in a research process like this such a suggestion requires not just that it is an interesting idea, but that someone who has a court case coming up would like to carry it out, and that did not happen.

Asking people how they would like to work with humour is an unusual starting point in an activist context, and this is also the source of the biggest tension in the project. My primary interest was to explore humour, and it did not matter much to me if it was done in relation to military exercises, arms production or military recruitment. For everyone else in Ofog, this was a strange order of things, since they wanted to start either with a particular theme that they were most concerned about, like recruitment, or think strategically about areas where they thought Ofog could have most influence. When I asked Lisa if she was interested in participating in humorous actions directed outwards, she is the one who expressed this most directly when she said:

> I really don't know at all, I don't know what I want to do with Ofog in the future. That depends on what most people seem interested in doing and if I feel inspired by that in particular. I really can't say that I want to do something funny, because it is not that I want to be funny (…)I want to do what I think is best, (…) otherwise it is a bit like a weird end to start in.

When I started the project I had expected that it would result in more use of outward directed humour than what it did. Of course it is not possible to say what kinds of humorous political stunts, if any, would have been carried out without the research project. But in my naïve perception about what role I could play, I had hoped that my enthusiasm for humour would be more contagious. As it turned out, Ofog had a peak event in July 2011 quite early in the process. After that some of the most driving people reduced their commitment to Ofog.

My original idea was to do follow-up workshops, but it never became possible to do them the way I planned. In Malmö, the small group was hibernating when it was time to do a follow-up workshop a year later. In Gothenburg the group was still active, but with considerably less activity than the year before. For this reason I decided to suggest a one hour feedback of the preliminary results rather than push for a longer event where very few people were likely to show up. This short session took place in September 2012. None of the participants were interested in focusing particularly on humour in the near future, but together we identified a need for a workshop about strategy. Although

135

some humorous ideas came up here, most people considered it more important to work on long term organisational issues where humour would not be appropriate. I think this was a wise strategy although it meant that I obtained less data than I originally expected.

My attempt to honour the wish that material from the research project became available to activists in a non-academic form has also taken different formats. The first was a booklet called "Humour and political activism – inspiring examples from around the world". It includes examples which are described in chapter 3. The first version of this was printed in July 2011 and sold for a very reasonable price to cover printing costs during the camp "War starts here." The second type was the one hour feedback mentioned above where I presented my findings relating to Ofog and the typology presented in Chapter 3.

Other methods

The three methods of participant observation, interviews and workshops generated a rather large amount of data about the use and perception of humour in Ofog. In addition I collected written documents like press releases and photos produced by Ofog as well as media coverage of Ofog actions provided by newspapers, radio or websites. This material supplements the data from the three other methods.

Chapter 4 focuses on Ofog's experiences with the rebel clown army. In order to make comparisons with the original British Clandestine Insurgent Rebel Clown Army (CIRCA) and other ways of using clowning in political activism I also analysed 10 videos from YouTube featuring rebel clowns. The main purpose was to document how seldom rebel clowns use *incompetence* in their performances, something which is a staple ingredient in traditional clowning. The videos were all downloaded from youtube.com on October 22 2013. It is a random selection of the videos that appeared when searching for "clandestine insurgent rebel clown army" and where it was obvious from the picture and/or the description that they were about rebel clowning. I picked out videos from different clown actions in different cities, taking place between 2005 and 2013.

As part of the joint effort with Ofog to understand humour better, I also did another type of interview/observation that is neither participant observation nor semi-structured interview. In August 2012 while other Ofog activists did a gym session against the military training area in the north of Sweden called NEAT, I dressed as neutrally as possible and talked to people who stopped to watch the performance. I was able to talk to 15 people during the 45 minutes the action lasted and get their impression about what they were watching. The purpose was to find out to what degree the action was successful in getting the anti-militarist message across.

Data collection process for the case study on KMV

The case studies on Ofog and KMV have some similarities, but also obvious differences. With KMV the events now belong to history with all the advantages and disadvantages that poses for a researcher. Looking from a distance, some things become clearer. With KMV, it is easier to see the role of humour within an overall approach – when it comes to Ofog, the events are too close both emotionally and time-wise to get the same clarity. Most of the key people in KMV are still alive, but 30 years is a long time for busy people who since then have moved on with their lives. People who only encountered KMV in the outskirts of their life are likely to remember this time as even more distant.

KMV's history and role in the Scandinavian peace movements is hardly documented at all, except that one of the participants has written a little about it.[265] For the triangulation of this case I have used four types of sources: Newspaper reports from the period, KMV's own documents, interviews with four key informants – three activists and one representative from the government – as well as the official documents about the law change that eventually took place.

Newspaper reports of KMV's activities

Analysing written documents is a standard method for data gathering, especially used by historians who trawl the archives for information. However, searching the official archives is not likely to produce much evidence of KMV's existence. Official documents from the ministry of justice would be about individual men who refused conscription, not about the organisation. Although the media are not known to be the best source for facts, in this case they provide the most reliable data available about when things happened and approximately how many participated. The newspaper coverage also gives an impression of how some of the activities of KMV were perceived by the surrounding society. I have used the articles to better understand KMV's use of humour rather than a content analysis of the media coverage. My main interest has not been what the media write about KMV and why, but to get closer to KMV, the thinking within the group and what responses the authorities provided through the media.

The limitation of this data source is that the newspapers' objective is to sell as many papers as possible, inclining them to focus on the issues they think their readers will be interested in. The decisions about what to print reflect the fact that news produc-

---

[265] Åsne Berre Persen and Jørgen Johansen, *Den Nødvendige Ulydigheten* (Oslo: FMK, 1998); Jørgen Johansen, "Humor as a Political Force, or How to Open the Eyes of Ordinary People in Social Democratic Countries," *Philosophy and Social Action* 17, no. 3-4 (1991).

tion is geared towards writing about conflict rather than reconciliation and the spectacular and unexpected rather than the everyday and ordinary. Thus they covered spectacular actions carried out by KMV, but not the more hidden or less conflict oriented aspects. The newspapers, for instance, do not write about internal organising or lobbying activities. The materials I have obtained from newspapers also reflect that some individuals within KMV had a greater wish to and were more skilled at generating attention toward their individual conscientious objector cases than others.

The news reports are from both local, regional and national Norwegian newspapers. In addition I have included one TV report which two people I interviewed considered very important. Most of the articles I have obtained from KMV participants' personal archives; the TV broadcast I bought from the Norwegian national TV archive. Although I knew KMV activists themselves had collected most of the published material, I was interested in finding out if the coverage was as extensive as some of the people I interviewed thought. For this reason I also did a wide search for KMV in seven selected mainstream regional and national newspapers for the period 1980-1989 (*Aftenposten, Adresseavisen, Hamar Arbeiderblad, Klassekampen, Morgenbladet, Nationen, Nordlys and Stavanger Aftenblad*). These newspapers can be searched electronically at the National Library in Oslo. For these wide searches I used the search words "Kampanjen mot verneplikt" (campaign against conscription), "siviltjeneste i fengsel" (substitute service in prison) and "nektet siviltjeneste" (refused substitute service). In the same newspapers I also searched specifically for two particular actions, narrowing the search period to June 24-27 1983 and September 20-21 1983, but with the broad search words "fengsel" (prison) and "aktor" (prosecutor). I also searched manually through the microfilms of six other national and regional newspapers (*Arbeiderbladet, Dagbladet, VG, Finmarksposten, Fædrelandsvennen, and Bergens Tidende*) for the same narrow time periods. Neither the manual nor the electronic searches are perfect, which I discovered by doing both for the two newspapers *Nordlys* and *Stavanger Aftenblad*. In the first, I found an article in the manual search that did not appear in the electronic search. In the second, I found a piece in the electronic search that I had missed with the manual. Nevertheless, although there is a possibility that I have missed some small mentions here and there, I feel confident that I have had access to the large majority of the relevant news coverage.

KMV documents

The most central source for this case study is the documents produced by KMV itself. The newsletter *Rundbrev*[266] which was distributed to all subscribers with irregular intervals from 1 to 6 times per year, turned out to provide valuable information. I am especially grateful to Ulf Norenius and Jørgen Johansen for giving me a complete collection of the KMV newsletter from 1982-1990 as well as many other documents. The information in Rundbrev includes minutes from the *grand meetings* which were KMV's "decision making body", invitations to various meetings and reports and documentation of the network's activities. Some items were produced by KMV, but frequently the newsletter contained photocopies of the newspaper coverage. Where it has been possible to identify which newspaper it is, these articles are referenced as a regular newspaper article. On the few occasions where KMV photocopied them without writing which newspaper or which date I have not prioritised tracking down this information, but instead referred to the relevant newsletter. Where this is the case it is clearly indicated in the footnotes.

KMV also produced some posters, flyers and a booklet. This type of data are characterised by being made for an immediate purpose. It gives a very good impression of what was considered important information to the participants of KMV at the mo-

---

[266] *Rundbrev* just means newsletter.

ment, a snapshot of the group's daily life. Unfortunately these items were usually not dated. This means that they give an impression of KMV in the 1980's, but it would be very difficult to use them to trace developments in the arguments KMV used over time.

Both KMV's own documents and the newspaper coverage are mainly descriptions of events and include almost no analysis. The details of the debates about what KMV activists thought would be most effective are lost. The only thing left as "evidence" is what was actually done – presumably what KMV considered most effective given the human and economic resources available.

The most analytical document is the booklet *Verneplikt: Statlig Tvangsarbeid* (Conscription: State forced labour) published for the launch of KMV in 1981, which explains conscientious objection as a strategy against militarism.[267] KMV's own documents include almost no self-evaluation and analysis of what is effective. Only several years later did one of the participants, Jørgen Johansen, analyse his experiences in two different pieces of writing.[268]

Interviews

The third type of data gathering technique for the KMV case study is interviews with three of the most central activists from the early 1980's and one person who represented the Norwegian state and the department of justice in questions regarding conscientious objection.

---

[267] ICR Skandinavia, *Verneplikt: Statlig Tvangsarbeid: Et Hefte Fra ICR - Skandinavia* (Bergen: FMK, 1981).
[268] Johansen, "Humor as a Political Force, or How to Open the Eyes of Ordinary People in Social Democratic Countries."; Persen and Johansen, *Den Nødvendige Ulydigheten.*

Like in the case of Ofog, these four interviews were done in a semi-structured way. The interviews with the three KMV activists provided information about some of the aspects of KMV activities not captured by the news coverage and internal documents. For many of the individuals concerned these activities were central in forming them as politically conscious members of society. They can provide detailed memories of events and their thinking about them. Nevertheless, the time gap of almost 30 years means that much has been forgotten and many events "rewritten" in the participants' minds. They have been told as a good story many times, but 30 years later the order of things, the time that lapsed between certain events, the number of participants and so on are no longer reliable.

My awareness of the case of KMV and the humorous political stunts they performed stems from my close relationship with one of the most active participants in the group. Jørgen Johansen has been my partner since 1999, and I have heard him tell some of the stories in this chapter on numerous private and public occasions. There is therefore a risk that my account and analysis of the events are biased towards his version. However, both his and the other oral accounts have been cross checked against the written documentation. Generally I have considered *Rundbrev* and newspaper coverage of facts such as dates, times and numbers more reliable than the interviews.

My relationships with Johansen made it easy to contact other key people in KMV, and they readily agreed to be interviewed and help with access to their personal archives. Other researchers might have experienced intense questioning about their motives for doing this research and be met with a more reserved attitude. On the other hand, there is a possibility that our relationship can have caused some to withhold information about the personal dynamics within KMV. However, since it is the outward directed activities that are the focus here rather than the internal organising, this has had little if any impact on the analysis and conclusions.

Johansen was one of the driving forces within KMV, and some of the activities where he was a key figure take up much space in this chapter. I have carefully considered whether he is getting undue attention and come to the conclusion that I have not given him and his case more space than what is required to give a fair account and analysis of KMV. The only exception is the description of his first court hearing. The reason that it is his case and not someone else's is simply that Johansen's personal archive includes extensive media coverage from the local newspaper that would have been time consuming or maybe even impossible to obtain through a library search on another case.

By only interviewing three of the most central participants in KMV, there is a risk that the material is biased towards those who took on leadership roles in this otherwise non-hierarchical network. It does not include the perspectives of those who only participated for shorter periods of time or observed from the periphery. This is a conscious decision reflecting my wish to talk to people who might remember discussions about the choice of strategy and the role of humour rather than get an overall impression of how KMV worked – that is an issue for future research. For this chapter, I discussed with the informants how to treat their identity. I considered it unlikely that people who had been active in KMV and knew Johansen would not be able to guess who I had talked to. Promising total confidentiality was not realistic. All three informants also said that they would like me to use their real names. I ended up deciding this would be the most ethical thing to do. These people are grownups who spent many years of their adult life organising KMV activities. They have appeared with names and photos in countless media interviews, and are very proud of what they did.

The first interview with Ulf Norenius was done in 2012 before I had finished writing up the events described in the written documentation. I was surprised that he did not remember more details and discussions, and therefore decided to postpone the rest of the interviews while I did some more writing. Before I interviewed Johansen and Øyvind Solberg, I asked them to read a draft of chapter 6 so we could begin the interviews with their comments and reflections on that. Interviewing the two good old friends together also seemed to prod their memories.

Solberg suggested several people who represented the Norwegian state that I could talk to, and one of them was willing to be interviewed. This person is introduced with the pseudonym Jens Jensen. Because of the time that had passed there were many details that he did not remember. However, when he looked at the timing of various events he did not doubt that it was the total resisters themselves that played the decisive role in bringing about the law change that they were working for. This interview is an important confirmation of what appear as a logical conclusion from the official documents about the law change.

Official documents

KMV's major success was a change in the law that sent the total resisters to prison for 16 months but did not call it a punishment. In the archive of the Norwegian parliament, *Stortinget*, I tracked down all the relevant documents about the preparations for the law change, including white papers, official reports, suggestions for decisions from the justice committee and the transcription of the debate in parliament.

Epistemological assumptions

After this detailed tour through all the data collection methods and selection criteria for case studies and examples, I finish this chapter on methodology with some more general reflections on the epistemological assumptions underlying the thesis and a discussion about research and power.

Generally speaking, normative approaches to research are more the rule than the exception – most research in medicine and social work is either explicitly or implicitly conducted with the purpose of improving people's lives.[269] As a peace and nonviolence researcher, I use what Abigail Fuller calls an "emancipatory methodology".[270] In addition to contributing to an increased scholarly understanding of nonviolence and humour, I also hope my findings will be meaningful to nonviolent activists who are interested in developing their strategies and experiments with humour as a way to challenge power.

There are many labels in use for methods claiming to work in the tradition of emancipation: Action research, participatory action research, feminist action research, institutional ethnography, anti-oppressive research, participatory research, collaborative research to name some of the most popular. Action research is probably the most well-known of these, and has also inspired my approach. The term was first used by sociologist Kurt Lewin in 1946 in an article about the problems that minorities in the US faced.[271] Many authors have traced the historical developments of the different types of emancipatory research strategies and identified the finer points of their differences and similarities.[272]

---

[269] This is for instance the case with "intervention research" within social work. See for example Robert F. Schilling, "Developing Intervention Research Programs in Social Work," *Social Work Research* 21, no. 3 (1997); Mark W. Fraser and Maeda J. Galinsky, "Steps in Intervention Research: Designing and Developing Social Programs," *Research on Social Work Practice* 20, no. 5 (2010).

[270] Abigail A. Fuller, "Toward an Emancipatory Methodology for Peace Research," *Peace & Change* 17, no. 3 (1992).

[271] Kurt Lewin, "Action Research and Minority Problems," *Journal of Social Issues* 2, no. 4 (1946).

[272] There is no reason to repeat that here, see the following footnotes for sources.

Emancipatory research approaches has been used most frequently in the areas of education, social work and development where researchers have worked together with marginalised and subordinate groups in order to improve their situation. Examples of introductions to these approaches include *Participatory Action Research* by Alice McIntyre[273], *Action Research* by Ernest T. Stringer[274], *Action Research: A Methodology for Change and Development* by Bridget Somekh,[275] *Revolutions in Development Inquiry* by Robert Chambers,[276] and *New Directions in Action Research* edited by Ortrun Zuber-Skerritt.[277] The research on nonviolence, social movements and humour introduced in chapter 1 rarely makes use of these normative research methodologies. Even within a well-established field such as social movement research where one might expect to find emancipatory research, this is not the case. For instance, none of the approaches named above is mentioned in Bert Klandermans and Suzanne Staggenborg's book *Methods of Social Movement Research,* which solely focuses on methodology for social movement research. The book otherwise offers introductions to everything from surveys to semi-structured interviews and historical research.[278] Jason MacLeod's recent PhD thesis is an exception. MacLeod carried out an extensive participatory action research project together with the

---

[273] Alice McIntyre, *Participatory Action Research* (Los Angeles: Sage Publications, 2008).

[274] Ernest T. Stringer, *Action Research*, 3rd ed. (Los Angeles: Sage Publications, 2007).

[275] Somekh, *Action Research: A Methodology for Change and Development.*

[276] Robert Chambers, *Revolutions in Development Inquiry* (London: Earthscan, 2008).

[277] Ortrun Zuber-Skerritt, *New Directions in Action Research* (London: Falmer Press, 1996).

[278] Bert Klandermans and Suzanne Staggenborg, *Methods of Social Movement Research* (Minneapolis, MN: University of Minnesota Press, 2002).

resistance movement in West Papua to explore the potential of nonviolence.[279]

Dorothy Smith and the feminist standpoint theory she developed has been another inspiration for my investigations. In this tradition one acknowledges that there is no neutral point from which to start researching and that people's position in the social world determines how that world looks and what constitutes the right kind of knowledge. For Smith, this meant doing sociology from the perspective of women's everyday and experiences. The result was sociology very different from what was the norm of her time where the so-called neutral and objective sociology in reality almost exclusively reflected the standpoint of white affluent men with a Eurocentric perspective. In the volume *Sociology for Changing the World*[280] Caelie Frampton and her co-editors celebrate the legacy of Dorothy Smith's work related to institutional ethnography. This in turn led George Smith to his work on the *ruling regimes* and *ruling relations*.[281] Although the research I present here is not a piece of institutional ethnography, institutional ethnographers' attempt to bridge the gap between academia and activism and produce knowledge which is useful for activists has been a great inspiration and in that sense I attempt to follow their lead.

Another inspiration has been Leslie Brown and Susan Strega's book *Research as Resistance: Critical, Indigenous and Anti-Oppressive*

---

[279] Jason MacLeod, "Civil Resistance in West Papua (Perlawanan Tanpa Kekerasan Di Tanah Papua)" (PhD thesis, The University of Queensland, 2012). Forthcoming as Jason MacLeod, *Civil Resistance in West Papua* (Brisbane: University of Queensland Press, 2015, in press).
[280] Caelie Frampton et al., eds., *Sociology for Changing the World: Social Movements/Social Research* (Black Point: Fernwood, 2006).
[281] George W. Smith, "Political Activist as Ethnographer," in *Sociology for Changing the World: Social Movements/Social Research*, ed. Caelie Frampton, et al. (Black Point: Fernwood, [1990] 2006).

Approaches.[282] They use the term anti-oppressive research, but are engaged in a similar journey towards a methodology that emphasises social justice in a world of unequal power relations. They want to engage in the discussion about what constitutes knowledge and write:

> Framing the discussion about what constitutes knowledge within the discourse of positivism obscures important questions about how the development of knowledge is socially constructed and controlled, how knowledge is used, and whose interests knowledge serves.[283]

Brown and Strega are concerned with what they call "research from, by and with the Margins" and continue:

> Marginalization refers to the context in which those who routinely experience inequality, injustice, and exploitation live their lives. Being marginalized refers not just to experiences of injustice or discrimination or lack of access to resources. In the research context, it acknowledges that knowledge production has long been organized, as have assessments of the ways producing knowledge can be "legitimate", so that only certain information, generated by certain people in certain ways, is accepted or can qualify as "truth".[284]

What Brown and Strega say here is that traditional types of research contribute to upholding the status quo, even when researchers have no intention of this, as long as it keeps limiting what are "real" truth, knowledge and science. For them, it means that any researcher who wants to claim that he or she is doing anti-oppressive research also has to look towards unconventional

---

[282] Leslie Brown and Susan Strega, eds., *Research as Resistance: Critical, Indigenous and Anti-Oppressive Approaches* (Toronto: Canadian Scholars' Press, 2005).

[283] Brown and Strega, *Research as Resistance*, p. 6.

[284] Brown and Strega, *Research as Resistance*. pp. 6-7.

research methodologies: "We take the position that research cannot challenge relations of dominance and subordination unless it also challenges the hegemony of current research paradigms."[285]

Although I agree with Brown and Strega that traditional ways of researching have a strong tendency to limit what can be considered "real" knowledge and that the voices of the marginalised are seldom heard, I think their picture is very black and white with little space for nuances. Blaming certain methods for the ways they have been applied is like blaming the gun for a murder. For instance, statistical analysis – a conventional research method – can contribute to liberation. An example of this is the study by Erica Chenoweth and Maria Stephan about nonviolent resistance that was introduced in Chapter 1.[286] They used statistical analysis to document how nonviolence is more effective than violence, a finding which has a strong potential for contributing to emancipation when this knowledge spread among activists.

Kirby et al. define research as a "systematic inquiry into a phenomenon of interest".[287] They identify three research paradigms:

1. The instrumental paradigm, the traditional positivist paradigm which is often based on quantitative methods. Here the emphasis is on controlling the environment in a way which means that other researchers can reproduce the research and get the same results.
2. The interactive paradigm, which includes constructionist and ethnographic approaches. Here the focus is on lived experience and the construction of meaning. The theoretical base is in phenomenology, symbolic interactionism and grounded theory. For the researcher importance is on credibility.

---

[285] Brown and Strega, *Research as Resistance*, p. 10.
[286] Chenoweth and Stephan, *Why Civil Resistance Works*.
[287] Kirby, Greaves, and Reid, *Experience Research Social Change*: p. 11.

3. The critical paradigm focuses on reflexive knowledge and is founded on materialist, structural, feminist, and queer theory. Here the focus is on power relations as well as what is right and just.[288]

My approach to this study has been inspired by the critical paradigm. I wanted to explore how activists use humour to challenge established relations of power. But I was also interested in activists' own reflections about humour, and the meaning they attribute to it. This part of the research belongs in the interactive paradigm and is mainly included in the case study with Ofog.

In the concluding chapter of *Research as Resistance: Critical, Indigenous and Anti-Oppressive Approaches* Karen Potts and Leslie Brown provide three statements that convey what it means to be an anti-oppressive researcher:

- Anti-oppressive research is social justice and resistance in process and in outcome
- Anti-oppressive research recognizes that all knowledge is socially constructed and political
- The anti-oppressive research process is all about power and relationships[289]

These statements are very radical and have far reaching consequences for how research should be done. However, as the introductions to the methods above indicated, it is not so much the choice of a particular method that makes the difference, but the way it is applied in practice, the assumptions about

---

[288] Kirby, Greaves, and Reid, *Experience Research Social Change*: pp. 13-14.
[289] Karen Potts and Leslie Brown, "Becoming an Anti-Oppressive Researcher," in *Research as Resistance: Critical, Indigenous and Anti-Oppressive Approaches*, ed. Leslie Brown and Susan Strega (Toronto, ON: Canadian Scholars' Press, 2005), pp. 260-62.

knowledge that is behind it, who is going to benefit from the research and what the goal of the research is. Also crucial is the choice of what topic to study, something seldom discussed in the focus on methods.

In her call for peace researchers to conduct emancipatory research, Fuller refers to Dorothy Smith and feminist standpoint theory as the epistemological background for suggesting that in order to work for social change, one needs to work together with the oppressed in order to get results which are more scientifically valid.[290] Researchers do not start their projects from a neutral point. Their own position in the world determines what they consider worth researching, and how the research is carried out. Both the choice of subject and the interpretation of the results are influenced by who the researcher is and knows. Interpretation is not just something one does when the data have been collected, but part of the research process from start to finish. What researchers consider important to ask guides what kind of information they are able to gather. All researchers construct meaning, and what kind of meaning they are able to see and make sense of depends on the point from where they look. Methods are not just a toolbox to pick and choose from, they all come with assumptions about the world and what can be known about it.[291]

Researchers have a standpoint in relation to their research whether they declare it or not, and even if they are not aware of it.[292] When choosing the subject for my thesis, I made a conscious decision to investigate a subject that I thought would be of interest to nonviolent activists striving for social change, and enable activists to make informed decisions about the possibili-

---

[290] Fuller, "Toward an Emancipatory Methodology for Peace Research," pp. 295, 99.
[291] Kirby, Greaves, and Reid, *Experience Research Social Change*: pp. 4-5.
[292] Kirby, Greaves, and Reid, *Experience Research Social Change*: p. 37.

ties and limitations of using humour as a strategy in the struggle. I strongly believe more knowledge in this area can contribute positively to activists' goals and make activism more fun, effective, sustainable and welcoming to newcomers. My background for this choice was that I had been an activist and organiser, contributing to peace and anti-militarist work for almost two decades before I embarked on this research journey. There are some disadvantages with choosing a subject I feel so passionately about. It has been a constant challenge to distinguish between what I and other activists would like to be the result of humorous political stunts and perceive have happened, and what conclusions it is reasonable to draw based on the information available. However, this is a problem many researchers face when studying groups they personally support. The proximity to my area of study has made me acutely aware of the limitations with the data, an awareness that might not have been so obvious for researchers who believe they have a greater distance to the subject of their inquiry.

Much of the literature on emancipatory methodologies mentioned above speaks about conducting research which is meaningful to subordinate groups or the *margins* as Brown and Strega call it. Talking about "margins" can give a wrong impression, since in some cases the "margins" are actually the numerical majority, for instance in some of the nonviolent revolutions mentioned previously.

In these texts, subordination is either explicitly or implicitly understood to be poor or disadvantaged communities, or victims of discrimination and harassment. Although some of these subordinate groups take up nonviolent struggle and might be inspired to use humour effectively, many nonviolent activists whose stunts are included here are not subordinate in this sense. On the contrary, they are frequently well educated, white, have middle class incomes and no problem speaking up for themselves. Nevertheless, activist groups working on peace, justice and environmental issues are indeed subordinate and highly marginalised in relation to the governments, multinational corporations, and authorities with state backing that they are challenging.

Research and power

That power is a complex phenomenon became clear already in Chapter 1 when I discussed power, resistance and the possibilities for change through humour. The Foucaudian perspective on power as relational and multidimensional that I advocated clashes somewhat with part of the action research tradition. Action research has its roots in the Enlightenment and ideas of progress, reason and improvement that Foucault was critical of and only saw as contributing to ever more sophisticated ways of exercising control. However, some researchers have drawn from both approaches. Somekh's inspiration by Foucault is reflected in the eight principles of action research quoted above. She emphasises that power is not something negative, but constructed in social interaction. It is not something one person does to another, but part of social formations.[293] In "Exposing Discourses through Action Research", Leonie E. Jennings and Anne P. Graham try to reconcile the modern tradition of action research with based in rationality and progress with the postmodern "moment" and Foucault's poststructuralism. They remind action researchers that postmodern ideas are not a rejection of struggles against oppression and suggest discourse analysis to be a useful way for action researchers to deconstruct established dominant discourses. There might be more than one "truth" and interpretation, depending on which perspective one look from. They also draw attention to some of the commonali-

---

[293] Somekh, *Action Research: A Methodology for Change and Development*. chapter 1.

153

ties between action research and postmodern approaches, such as concerns with power and knowledge.[294]

Many action research projects work from the assumption that the conditions for the marginalised can be improved. This is also the normative approach taken in this research project. However, in some of the literature on participatory action research and related approaches, there seems to be an assumption that policy makers will change policies towards social justice once they know better and if they are included in the process.[295] This implicit or explicit assumption appears rather naïve, but can probably be explained by action research's roots in the Enlightenment. Policymakers might sometimes change laws and regulations when better informed, but there is nothing automatic in this process. In a chapter about young people's transition from care, Deb Rutman et al. write:

> ... the common objectives in doing participatory action research are for shared ownership, learning and action. This often pits researchers and clients/subjects against authority and resources; indeed, the solutions to issues that emerge do not have to be acceptable to those who hold power and control over resources.[296]

Some issues are more contested than others, and it would probably be difficult for Rutman et al. to find policymakers who do not use rhetoric about providing the best transition from care as

---

[294] Leonie E. Jennings and Anne P. Graham, "Exposing Discourses through Action Research," in *New Directions in Action Research*, ed. Ortrun Zuber-Skerritt (London: Falmer Press, 1996).

[295] See for example Stringer, *Action Research*. pp. 20-21.

[296] Deb Rutman et al., "Supporting Young People's Transition from Care: Reflections on Doing Participatory Action Research with Youth from Care," in *Research as Resistance: Critical, Indigenous and Anti-Oppressive Approaches*, ed. Leslie Brown and Susan Strega (Toronto, ON: Canadian Scholars' Press, 2005), p. 155.

possible. The disagreements would arise about the best way to do it and how this service should be prioritised when compared with other tasks competing for the same resources. In the Scandinavian countries where my case studies were carried out, it would be difficult to find a politician who would say that acting against poverty and discrimination is undesirable. Research on poverty and discrimination might be areas where these politicians would change policies if they are better informed and included in the process of finding solutions together with disadvantaged groups. However, when it comes to areas such as arms export, military exercises and conscription, the political rhetoric is very different. Here one should be careful not to underestimate the vested interests in upholding the status quo and the active and deliberate marginalisation of those who want to change it. As Fuller writes, "historically those with power have not been known to relinquish it."[297]

Robin McTaggart writes that people underestimate how much oppressive structures are upheld deliberately by those who actively strive to avoid change and how much time must be spent on just avoiding regression. In his response to some of the criticisms of action research he also points out that there are frequently unrealistic expectations about what can be achieved in a short time.[298] The radical peace and anti-militarist groups whose humour is the core of this thesis are very aware that they are considered peripheral by those in power. The voices of these volunteer networks are easily drowned when they stand up to companies, states and institutions that have enormous economic and human resources at their disposal. Any conclusions about the effects of humour also have to reflect this inequality. It is quite unrealistic to expect a handful of anti-militarist activists armed with a humorous political stunt to overturn such a domi-

---

[297] Fuller, "Toward an Emancipatory Methodology for Peace Research," p. 290.
[298] McTaggart, "Issues for Participatory Action Researchers," pp. 243-45.

nant discourse as militarism overnight. Finally McTaggart stresses that emancipation is not some ideal stage. For him the central question is not "are we emancipated yet?" but "are things better than they were?"[299] For some contexts, one could also ask, "did we prevent it from getting worse?"

Another way the term "power" is relevant when discussing methodology has to do with the way research is carried out. The research approaches emphasising emancipation and change that I have referred to above are becoming increasingly popular, but sometimes they are now used in ways which dilute concepts of change and participation of meaning and very far from their roots of liberation.[300] For instance, Ortrun Zuber-Skerritt writes about how action research can make organisations more effective.[301] It is a major problem with her approach that she talks about more effective organisations without discussing what these organisations are doing. Where is the emancipation in becoming more effective if this effectiveness is used to become even better at being violent and destructive? Developing more effective gas chambers together with Adolf Hitler during World War II using an action research model would probably have been quite possible. But it would never become emancipatory as long as it is based on the Nazi ideology and the result is more effective killing of Jews, homosexuals, gypsies and others considered unworthy of life. This is an extreme example, but many institutions, also in democracies, have at least some goals that

---

[299] McTaggart, "Issues for Participatory Action Researchers," p. 245.
[300] For this critique, see for example Kirby, Greaves, and Reid, *Experience Research Social Change.* p. 43 and Potts and Brown, "Becoming an Anti-Oppressive Researcher," p. 256.
[301] Ortrun Zuber-Skerritt, "Emanicipatory Action Research for Organisational Change and Management Development," in *New Directions in Action Research*, ed. Ortrun Zuber-Skerritt (London: Falmer Press, 1996).

might have violent and destructive consequences. Weapons manufactured in Sweden are used in wars around the world, although the companies' stated intention is to make a profit and not that people die. When the Norwegian court system functioned smoothly regarding the total resisters, it contributed to upholding a law that sent young men to prison for 16 months because of their beliefs.

A final power issue to make note of is that unequal relations of power do not just go away because one is aware of their existence. It is not enough to have good intentions about including the marginalised and subordinate in a research process in order to make it happen in reality.

Conclusion

Using a case study strategy as my main approach, I have used many conventional methods for data gathering, such as participant observation, semi-structured interviews and document analysis of newsletters and media reports. In addition I have relied on some more unconventional methods as part of the participatory action research project I did with Ofog, for example facilitating workshops about humour and nonviolence.

Another researcher would have approached this subject in a different way, but by being open about my own standpoint and role in the research process others have the possibility to follow the development of the project and judge the way data have been gathered and analysed. My long-term commitment to the peace movement has provided openings for me that would not have been there for others, but it also has some limitations.

Humorous political stunts take place within a context, and my perspective has primarily been from those who initiate these stunts. The research hardly includes any firsthand accounts about how they were perceived from the "other side". When analysing the responses and reactions, I have relied on what can be observed and what is stated in public, and this is probably the biggest limitation with this project. Hopefully future research can get closer to those who are the targets of the humorous political stunts.

This research process has been guided by an epistemological assumption about social science's obligation to contribute to creating a society based on respect for diversity and social justice for all. A positivist research paradigm seldom contribute to this emancipation, but instead is a part of upholding the status quo by accrediting more value to a certain kind of knowledge gathered by certain kinds of people. Although not all research that claims to be participatory and liberating is this in reality, awareness of the power relations in a research project should increase the chance that these relations do not determine what will count as valuable knowledge. By focusing on humour's role in nonviolent action my hope is to develop knowledge which is meaningful and useful for nonviolent activists in their struggles for more peaceful and just societies.

Chapter 3: Humorous political stunts

Introduction

Humorous political stunts are confrontational performances/actions carried out openly which attempt to undermine dominant discourses. An original model consisting of five different types of stunts provides the structure for this chapter. Before the model is presented I described how I developed the concept of the humorous political stunt and discuss how to define it.

The five types in distinct ways challenge the prevailing order and transcend established power relations. I have named them *supportive, corrective, naive, absurd* and *provocative*. Each category is presented with two to four examples from different political contexts that can illustrate some of the diversity within each type of stunt. *Supportive* stunts are framed as ostensible attempts to help and protect from harm. *Corrective* stunts present an alternative version of the power holders' truth, and the *naive* stunt challenges from behind a pretended innocence. The *absurd* stunt defies all rationality and in the *provocative* stunt the pranksters transcend power by appearing not to care about the consequences of infuriating the powerful. In all instances, humour is the tool of serious dissent and protest attempting to humiliate and undermine the powerful. The model is based on the way the stunt relates to the perception of what is true, rational and logical that the representatives of the dominant discourses aim to uphold.

In the analysis of 15 examples I start with identifying the humorous techniques they use to generate an amusing incongruity. Then a metaphor of theatre is applied to these "plays of politics". The theatre metaphor has four different dimensions that analyse the cases from the perspectives of who the *actors* are, what *stage* they play on, how the *audience* is included and interpret the performance and the *timing* of the whole affair.

159

After the analysis of all the individual examples, the similarities and differences between the different types of stunts are discussed in relation to a table that summarises the core characteristics of the different types of stunts. Humorous political stunts are very diverse when it comes to the mediums they use, the settings they take place in, and the degree of professionalism in the performance. Identifying this complexity helps illustrate how power and resistance cannot be considered a simple question of either-or, but is a multi-dimensional struggle.

In the end of the chapter the humorous political stunts are discussed in relation to public jokes, theatre and graffiti.

Defining humorous political stunts

This is what I mean by humorous political stunts:

A humorous political stunt is a performance/action carried out in public which attempts to undermine a dominant discourse. It is either so confrontational that it cannot be ignored or involves a deception that blurs the line between performers and audiences. It includes or comments on a political incongruity in a way that is perceived as amusing by at least some people who did not initiate it.

The discourses which are challenged can be major and all-pervading discourses like militarism, consumerism or neo-liberalism, or it can be more limited discourses controlled by a powerful political party. This challenge can be directly aimed at a person or institution considered an opponent, or it can be communicated to other audiences using a variety of media. That the humorous political stunt takes place in public means that this is more than a humorous critical comment or joke whispered in secret. One can observe someone doing something without hiding it, although they might try to hide their identity. The stunts are political in the broad sense that they comment on a political theme of how society should be organised. Humorous political stunts also have to be humorous. Since what people consider funny varies greatly, not everyone will necessarily find the stunts below amusing.

Among nonviolent activists and scholars the type of activity which I refer to as *stunts* are known as *actions*, but within cultural and performance studies terms such as *performance, happening, hoax* or *prank* are more common. I decided on the term stunt because it is not so clearly associated with one particular activist or academic tradition. I have not used Day's notion *ironic activism* because not all of the humorous political stunts rely on the technique of irony. Later I compare humorous political stunts with *conventional/ordinary* protest. With these terms I refer to the stereotypical ideal type of non-humorous, rational routine demonstrations, speeches, posters, blockades and leafleting. Of course non-humorous protest can be creative, disruptive and everything but ordinary and conventional, but nevertheless a rather big proportion of political activism usually consists of these stereotypical activities.

The focus here is on stunts performed by grassroots political activists, but in order to illustrate the potential two stunts performed by professional comedians are included as well. These stunts could have been performed by grassroots activists since they do not in themselves require access to a professional stage, although in these cases it certainly helped spreading the ideas. Humorous political stunts seem primarily to be a tactic chosen by those who communicate critiques or alternatives to the prevailing order from a subordinate or marginal position, aiming to disrupt or transform the status quo. I have not identified any stunts in favour of the status quo, but this possibility is not excluded by the definition.

The logic of humorous political stunts differs from what goes on in theatre performances, graffiti, stand-up comedies and cartoons that can also be examples of political humour. The stunts include a confrontation or blurring between audiences and performers which is usually absent in political humour that uses these traditional mediums. Stand-up comedies are based on jokes which can be repeated from one stage to the next. The stand-up comedy can be provocative, but the audiences remain audiences and the comedian the comedian. As long as the comedy happens on stage there is usually not enough confrontation to create a humorous political stunt. The act of making graffiti or a political cartoon can be confrontational, but the images that result are clearly distinct from their viewers. In most theatre performances there is a distinction between the actors and the audiences. An exception from this is the "invisible theatre", which does blur the lines when people are not aware that they have been exposed to a piece of theatre.[302] Invisible theatre is usually not amusing, although it does provide interesting avenues for humorous political stunts.

A stunt is not a joke, a text or an image which can be transferred from one stage or show to the next and have the same effect. The performance of a humorous political stunt is in itself the critique, and although it can be turned into a narrative that can be retold, the critique and confrontation occur in the original encounter, not in the retelling. Thus, if something is a stunt or not depends very much on the situation it takes place within. Some comedians (like Michael Moore, Mark Thomas and The

---

[302] Augusto Boal designed invisible theatre as a response to severe political repression, but it can be used everywhere. The "actors" perform an apparently everyday scene in a public place. It could be an example of sexual harassment, where one passenger on a bus apparently is harassing another passenger. Instead of ignoring this, which is what would often happen, another passenger intervenes and ask the harasser to stop. This way, a drama of social responsibiliy and possible solutions can be enacted without the other passengers knowing that they have been exposed to a piece of theatre. Hopefully the other passengers will talk about and reflect on what happened. Jan Cohen-Cruz and Mady Schutzman, *A Boal Companion: Dialogues on Theatre and Cultural Politics* (New York: Routledge, 2006). p. 3.

Chasers) perform stunts which are filmed and included in their TV shows in order to reach a larger audience.[303] Repetitions can also have effect on power relations, but it is not the encounter which is repeated, only the story about it.

Humorous political stunts have much in common with phenomena such as culture jamming, satiric theatre and news show parodies, and some examples of oppositional counter culture like graffiti painting or protest music. When I started researching humorous political stunts I did not have a name for this phenomenon. The definition and explanation developed over time. I knew that there was a type of actions and performances taking place which to me was different from other forms of political humour. I had an idea about what my ideal types were – the actions carried out by Otpor which I had studied before, the Yes Men identity corrections and CIRCA's clowning that will appear below, and the KMV actions I will return to in Chapter 6. When I came across examples of political humour they sometimes fitted my ideal type, but frequently they did not. Cartoons, theatre, TV and movies were seldom relevant, although there were a few exceptions.

---

[303] Two humorous political stunts carried out by Mark Thomas and the Chasers are included in the examples. A typical Michael Moore stunt is included in *The awful truth*. Moore and a group of people who have lost their voice because of smoking and have voice-boxes go to visit the big tobacco companies to sing Christmas hymns. In their ironic support, the choir says that they want to cheer up the tobacco industry because it has had such a bad year due to many lawsuits. The sounds they are able to make with the voice-boxes are indescribable, and are an extreme contrast to common perceptions of what constitutes beautiful singing. The tobacco companies insisted on driving their visitors out as quickly as possible, but the scenes were broadcast to TV viewers as part of Moore's program. Tom Gianas and Michael Moore, "The Awful Truth," (UK Channel 41999).

The definition was developed by going back and forth between the theoretical definition and the examples, trying to narrow down what they had in common and what separated them from related phenomena that others had described in the literature under labels such as *culture jamming* and *tactical carnival*. In a conceptual exploration like this, I have intentionally been clear about what is the core of the phenomenon, but vague about the borders. The purpose of this is to remain open about what can possibly be counted as a humorous political stunt in order not to exclude what might shed light on the subject. I have also taken the point of departure in the practice of what activists actually do, rather than a theoretical desk definition. Further research might make it clearer where the humorous political stunt ends.

Analysing humorous political stunts as "play of politics"

This chapter presents and analyses 15 examples of humorous political stunts according to my model of five different types of stunts. The distinction between the different types developed during the process of defining what a humorous political stunt is. Through this process I approached the examples from different perspectives. An important one was to look at the 45 different techniques of humour which Arthur Asa Berger had identified in his book *An Anatomy of Humor*.[304] Berger divides the 45 techniques in four categories, depending on whether they have to do with language, logic, identity or action.

In an attempt to understand the examples better, I started out identifying what techniques they use in order to generate their humour. Berger's framework is widely known within humour studies and professes to be a tool to understand all types of humour. Although Berger's techniques were useful to describe

---

[304] Arthur Asa Berger, *An Anatomy of Humor* (New Brunswick, NJ: Transaction, 1993).

what is funny in most of the examples, I also have some cases which did not fit very well. However, Berger did not have political humour in mind when he described the 45 techniques, so that should be no surprise that this technical framework is not enough when one wants to investigate what happens in power relationships where humour is involved. I do not intend to engage in a discussion about whether Berger's techniques are appropriate for describing all kinds of humour or if this is a good description of them, but those that I have drawn on are useful for analysing these examples. In addition to the techniques described by Berger, I suggest a few additional techniques necessary to explain what makes some of the examples funny.

When the technical approach to humour did not bring new insights about the power relationship, I started to look at the ways the activists use humour to undermine and transcend dominant discourses. Above I described how I went back and forth between the theoretical definition and the examples I had as my ideal types until I could narrow down what I was interested in. In parallel I also noticed that even within the phenomenon of the humorous political stunt that I wanted to study, there was a huge variation in how they were performed and carried out. I found that the pretence that the stunt is not a form of protest was a central element in almost all of them, and arrived at five different ways that this pretence is presented, each challenging the relations of power in different ways.

The five types in my model are not based on the humorous techniques they use, but on the different ways they attempt to undermine the discourse of their opponent, and transcend the established relations of power. They are not meant to replace the techniques identified by Berger, since they meet a different need. As with all categorisations, some cases are more clear-cut than others. Nevertheless these five types transcend power relations in distinct ways, independent of the techniques used to generate the humour. For example, exaggeration and irony are central in much political humour and can be found in several of the categories.

The 15 examples included here are not intended to be representative of all humorous stunts, but to illustrate their diversity.[305] Many groups are well known for performances that fit into my definition of humorous political stunts, but not included here. Among those are US Reverend Billy and his "church of life after shopping",[306] and the Guerrilla Girls that drew attention to the lack of women in the US art world from 1985 and onwards.[307] Billionaires for Bush, who change their name depending on the situation and for instance became Billionaires for Bailouts during the 2008 Wall Street meltdown, are a well-documented case.[308] A historic example is the dropping of dollar bills at the New York Stock Exchange mentioned in chapter 1. Other individuals, networks and organisations are radical cheerleaders[309], Raging Grannies[310], Laboratory of Insur-

---

[305] The selection process is described in Chapter 2.

[306] Day, *Satire and Dissent*: pp. 176-81.

[307] Day, *Satire and Dissent*: pp. 162-63; Schechter, *Satiric Impersonations: From Aristophanes to the Guerrilla Girls*: chapter 2.

[308] Day, *Satire and Dissent*; Angelique Haugerud, "Satire and Dissent in the Age of Billionaires," *Social Research* 79, no. 1 (2012); Kavita Kulkarni, "Billionaires for Bush: Parody as Political Intervention," http://hemi.nyu.edu/journal/1_1/kulkarni.html; L. M. Bogad, "A Place for Protest: The Billionaires for Bush Interrupt the Hegemonologue," in *Performance and Place*, ed. Leslie and Helen Paris Hill (London: Palgrave Macmillan, 2006); Angelique Haugerud, *No Billionaire Left Behind: Satirical Activism in America* (Stanford, CA: Stanford University Press, 2013).

[309] Jeanne Vacarro, "Give Me an F: Radical Cheerleading and Feminist Performance," http://hemi.nyu.edu/journal/1_1/cheerleaders.html.

[310] Carole Roy, "The Irreverent Raging Grannies: Humour as Protest," *Canadian Woman Studies* 25, no. 3/4 (2006); Carole Roy, "When Wisdom

rectionary Imagination[311] and The Space Hijackers.[312] The recent Spanish *M15* movement has used much humour in its protests about the financial crisis[313], and in Russia and Belarus, when people were banned from demonstrating in 2012, the idea spread about toys holding a protest.[314]

Several authors have suggested that pranking, culture jamming and creative activism are becoming more frequent, constitute a new type of activism and are spreading all around the world.[315] I am not convinced these types of activities are all that new – some of my examples go back 40 years – and it is difficult to judge to what extend it is global since primarily European and US examples have been studied. However, academic interest in the phenomena certainly seems to have increased, at least as measured in the number of publications.

Speaks Sparks Fly: Raging Grannies Perform Humor as Protest," *Women's Studies Quarterly* 35, no. 3/4 (2007).

[311] The Laboratory of Insurrectionary Imagination, "The Laboratory of Insurrectionary Imagination," http://labofii.net/.

[312] The Space Hijackers, "The Space Hijackers " http://www.spacehijackers.org/html/history.html.

[313] Romanos, Eduardo. "The Strategic Use of Humor in the Spanish 15m Movement." In *Crisis and Social Mobilization in Contemporary Spain: The 15m Movement*, edited by B. Tejerina and I. Perugorría. (Farnham: Ashgate, 2015, in press).

[314] Oleg Kupchinsky, "Toys for Democracy: In a Siberian City, Activists Find a Creative Way to Protest " *rferl.org*, January 16 2012; RFE/RL, "'Police Detain Stuffed Animals' in Minsk Toy Protest " *rferl.org*, February 10 2012.

[315] Silas Harrebye, "Cracks: Creative Activism – Priming Pump for the Political Imagination or a New Compromising Form of Democratic Participation Balancing between Critique, Cooperation, and Cooptation on the Margins of the Repertoire of Contention?" (PhD Thesis, Roskilde University, 2012), p. 4; Day, *Satire and Dissent*: pp. 150-51. Romanos, Eduardo. "The Strategic Use of Humor in the Spanish 15m Movement".

Supportive stunts are framed as ostensible attempts to help and protect from harm by exaggerating and over-emphasising the discourse and claims to truth upheld by those in power. *Corrective* stunts also use exaggeration to present an alternative version of the power holders' truth, but they hijack the identity or message of those in power and declare their protest from this disguise. In the *naïve* stunts, the challengers put forward their critique from behind a pretended innocence that seems unaware that a dominant discourse exists. It provides the possibility to act as if the pranksters do not understand that what they do can be interpreted as protest. *Absurd* stunts attempt to defy all rationality and ignore all dominant discourses. Finally, in the *provocative* stunts the pranksters transcend power by appearing not to care about the consequences of infuriating the powerful.

Table 1 presents a summary of my model. After looking at the 15 examples I will return to an expanded version of this summary table.

For each example I have aimed to do a number of different things. First of all the humour is explained within its context in order to enable readers to grasp what is going on. Without knowing what the situation is about, most of the examples here become meaningless. Where it has been possible to identify the goals of the activists and reactions from the audiences these are included in order to analyse the dynamic of the interaction. In addition to identifying the techniques used to generate amusement [316], I also explain what makes a certain stunt supportive, corrective, naïve, absurd or provocative. Finally the examples are analysed using a *metaphor of theatre* in order to better understand what happens when a humorous political stunt is staged.

---

[316] The descriptions of the different techniques are based on Berger, *An Anatomy of Humor.* pp. 15-55.

Table 1. A schematic overview of five different types of stunts. Short version that shows how those who carry out the stunts position themselves in relation to the dominant discourses.

Type	Description	Position in relation to dominant discourse	Dominant humorous techniques
Supportive	Activists appear supportive and pretend to support, celebrate, help, protect from harm etc, but stunt is a way of invalidating the target	Exaggerate the dominant discourse, play along with it, overemphasise it	Irony, parody, unmasking
Corrective	Activists appear rational but hijack the identity or message of their target in order to reveal a correction	Exaggerate the dominant discourse, play along with it, over-emphasise it	Unmasking
Naïve	Activists appear naïve and innocent and pretend not to understand that their action can be interpreted as a protest	Appear not to understand dominant discourse	Pretended coincidence
Absurd	Activists appear as innocent clowns but point towards absurdities	Ignore dominant discourse altogether	Absurdity, slapstick
Provocative	Activists openly act as provocateurs in order to expose vulnerabilities	Don't care about dominant discourse	Ridicule, insult

169

In his ground-breaking study about how individuals keep up a certain front, Erving Goffman showed how metaphors of play, drama and theatre can be used to show how individuals stage their own appearance in front of others.[317] Studies of social movements have also used theatre metaphors to describe and analyse the interactions between movements and their audiences[318], and it is not unusual to refer to politics as a game where politicians play politics on the public stage.[319] Since humorous political stunts are performed in public they literally make political issues into a piece of theatre, when their attacks on dominant discourses disrupt, subvert, oppose and transform what I call the *play of politics*.[320]

Dominant discourses operate almost unchallenged on the political *scene*. The representatives of these power formations decide who play the lead roles and the minor roles, and what props should be on the stage. Under all political circumstances there are also some people who will insist on playing roles such as opposition, protesters and critical journalists. In democracies, these roles have been written into the play, although representatives of dominant discourses do their best to control or sideline them. Journalists are handled through carefully scripted press conferences and well prepared answers in interviews, and protesters are tolerated or even welcomed as a sign of true democracy. Mass demonstrations and marches get police escorts and the organisers cooperate with the representatives of the

---

[317] Erving Goffman, *The Presentation of Self in Everyday Life* (Garden City, NY: Doubleday, 1959).
[318] Kathleen Blee and Amy McDowell, "Social Movement Audiences," *Sociological Forum* 27, no. 1 (2012).
[319] See for instance Tucker, *Workers of the World, Enjoy! Aesthetic Politics from Revolutionary Syndicalism to the Global Justice Movement*: p. 11.
[320] I am grateful to Stellan Vinthagen for his suggestion to explore this metaphor of theatre and the play of politics.

dominant discourses for the protest to be carried out in an orderly manner without risks for the participants. These types of protests are all part of the ordinary play of politics, and although the participants might be satisfied by this staged opportunity to express their opinion, it can also be understood as what Marcuse called *repressive tolerance.*[321]

Although the activists are those who disrupt the usual play, they are not the only ones "playing". The metaphor also takes into account that those who are already on the stage representing a dominant discourse perform and enact a drama when they are conducting "business as usual".

Sometimes, someone shows up and interrupts the ordinary drama, insisting on playing a part not included in the script at all. What is at stake during the interruption is the ability to determine what is right and wrong, true and false regarding the issue. The surprise does not have to be humorous, but one type of unexpected disruption is the humorous political stunt. When the usual rules of the game are broken the ordinary play being performed changes, since the challengers on stage have to be dealt with somehow. How the play unfolds in these cases depend on many factors, some controlled by the newcomers, some outside of their control. Four major aspects for the theatre can be identified – 1. the *stage*, 2. the *actors*, 3. the *audiences* and 4. the *timing*. These four aspects are ideal type analytical categories developed to assist the analysis, but since they are all part of the play of politics they are closely linked to each other and the choices activists make in relation to one will influence what is possible in the others.

1.   What type of *stage* is it that the pranksters attempt to enter or create? Is it a physical location, or is it a virtual stage like a

---

[321] Herbert Marcuse, "Repressive Tolerance," in *A Critique of Pure Tolerance*, ed. Robert Paul Wolff, Barrington Moore, and Herbert Marcuse (Boston: Beacon Press, 1969).

TV show or a webpage? What significance does this stage have? Is it a major, established stage with high symbolic value such as a national parliament or a world famous building already closely observed by media, politicians and political commentators? Is it a little scene outside of the spotlight? Or do the challengers try to establish their own stage and capture attention from there, regardless of which venues others consider important?

Space and location have a high significance for many forms of resistance. Certain places are associated with those in power, while other locations are traditional sites of protest. As will be apparent in some of the examples, there is a high symbolic value when certain places are "invaded" by pranksters. In Scott's concept of the hidden transcript it is significant that resistance is invisible and happens under the radar of those in power. In the humorous political stunt, it is a characteristic that it takes place openly and can be observed by various audiences, frequently attempting to temporarily control a space usually controlled by others.[322]

2. Who are the *actors* performing in the play of politics about to be disrupted? Lead actors considered very important, such as presidents, royalties and other celebrities, or minor characters who might be important on their own little stage? Sometimes it can be difficult to separate the factors of stage and actors, since lead actors have a tendency to create a major stage wherever they go because of their fame. The new actors in the show who initiate the stunt I have termed the *challengers*, and their identity matters as well. Are they already famous or well-known from other plays, such as professional comedians? How many are they, how unexpected is their appearance, how convincing are they in their new roles, and what is it that they do, once they

---

[322] Anna Johansson and Stellan Vinthagen, "Dimensions of Everyday Resistance: An Analytical Framework," *Critical Sociology* (2014, in press).

have gained access to the stage? How much have they prepared their script, and how good are they at improvising?

An important element is how well the challengers play their roles in the new drama. Do they manage to take it all the way when they have chosen a certain path? It is not uncommon that activists who are used to playing the ordinary role of protester find it hard to leave this role behind. If they bring symbols of protest along in the stunt, there is a risk of the stunt losing focus: it is neither a pure traditional protest, nor a pure humorous stunt.

In Chapter 1 the complexities of understanding relations of power were discussed. Applying this metaphor of theatre by looking at both the apparently powerful and the challengers as people performing roles highlights how much impressions of who is powerful are in the eye of the beholder. It becomes more obvious that in order for a discourse to remain dominant, the actors who uphold it also have to convincingly perform as if they believe the discourse to be right and true.

3. The *audiences* include many different people who can be friendly, hostile or indifferent from the outset. In his article about parody's role in sustaining a democratic public culture, Hariman speaks about the audience as "unruly, mixed, possibly drunk or stoned, maybe crazy, and at times also stupid, deluded, out of work, or otherwise deviant from the norms of serious, respectable, daytime routine."[323] Seldom do activists take such diversity into consideration. Audiences include both people who already know about the issue and those who are new to it. Kathleen Blee and Amy McDowell have written about how social movement groups construct their audiences and how that construction can develop over time. Blee and McDowell emphasise the performance studies perspective that focuses on the interaction taking place in the encounter: "… audiences typically do not exist *a priori*, as natural or given categories of social life; rather,

---

[323] Hariman, "Political Parody and Public Culture," p. 255.

audiences are discursive constructions, created by social actors through social interaction."[324] Even more importantly, social movements have perceptions about who their audiences are and how they want them to think and react. One of the findings of Blee and McDowell is that social movements seldom have a neutral perception of their audiences. If they are not constructed as people who can fulfil a need for the group, such as providing more activists or serving as allies, then they are seen as "needy" of knowledge and information.[325]

In some instances where a stunt is about to take place, the audience is not aware that a piece of theatre is going on at all. In other cases, the audience has already directed its attention towards a stage or an actor, expecting something to happen. Stages with a significant symbolic value are frequently under constant surveillance, and major actors have a tendency to draw a big audience wherever they go. An interesting question is also how the challengers treat the audience – as an audience, or as part of the play? Challengers frequently design their stunts to appeal to the type of audience with access to media, in order to be able to reach larger audiences, but some challengers are more concerned with reaching out to the general public and communicating directly with them.

Perhaps the most important aspect regarding the audience is how they interpret the performance according to their own previous knowledge, cultural references, experiences and expectations. What do audience members think is happening and what does it mean to them? In order for a humorous political stunt to succeed, the challengers almost always depend on challenging

---

[324] Blee and McDowell, "Social Movement Audiences," p. 4. Emphasis in original.
[325] Blee and McDowell, "Social Movement Audiences," p. 16.

audience expectations. The interruption of the ordinary drama includes a surprise which turns the world upside down.

4. Finally, the *timing* of the whole affair matters: Is the stage already occupied when the new actors enter, or do they sneak in while the spotlight is off? How long do they stay, and how frequently do they appear? The answers to these questions determine how the dynamic of the power relations between the challengers and the old actors will develop. The timing can also be analysed in a broader perspective – are the humorous political stunts part of a social movement expressing similar kinds of critique, or is it a one-time event?

The theatre metaphor does not in any way indicate that the play of politics is not serious. All the actors, both those who represent a dominant discourse and the challengers, consider this game highly serious. As discussed previously, that some activists decide to use humour in no way implies that they are not serious about the issue. However, using the theatre metaphor allows us to take a step back in order to better see what happens in the unscripted meeting when the "non-protesting protesters" enter the stage.

Supportive Humorous Stunts

Supportive humorous stunts are framed as attempts to help, support, protect from harm, and celebrate. Those who carry out supportive stunts appear supportive and rational, but what happens is that the target is invalidated. On the political scene, those assumed to be in power and control are joined up front by the pranksters. Apparently the pranksters do not dismiss the truth and rationality the representatives of the dominant discourses present, instead it is exaggerated and overemphasised. Usually irony plays an important role in supportive humorous stunts, since they are not supportive at all, but instead attempt to disconfirm their targets. The targets will know that they are being watched, and the audiences are presented with an image of the

175

power holders' vulnerable sides. Here the protesters do not appear irrational in their relation to what they actually oppose, they are constructive, helpful and supportive. By acting in this way they attempt to undermine their opponents' claims to truth and transcend the unequal relations of power. Compared to conventional political protest, at first glance supportive stunts look like real support, but a closer look reveals an underlying message that exposes and disconfirms. Below are three examples of supportive stunts from Australia, Britain and Belgium challenging the dominant discourses of a conservative prime minster, the Indonesian government's denial of human rights abuses and a bank's investment in land mines and cluster munitions.

John Howard Ladies' Auxiliary Fan Club

Australia's conservative prime minister from 1996 to 2007 had an extraordinary fan club consisting of four young women plus their driver and camera women. In character as Bea Wight, Bea Wright, Bea Rich and Bea Strait they mocked him and his politics during the last part of his time as prime minister. In an interview, the women explained how the names "reflect the key pillars of Howardism – being white, right, rich and straight."[326] The women were provoked by Howard's conservative politics and what they saw as his attempt to bring Australia back to the 1950s. They set out to confront his politics in an unusual manner, starting with the 2004 election. Dressed up in silly hats, pearls, long white gloves, lots of makeup and frocks, representing the stereotypical Australian housewife of the 1950s, they tried to confront him with these ironic personas. In 2004 they did not get closer than 50 metres, but in the following years the characters were developed. Prior to the 2007 election campaign, they did their first public performance on a tram. Here they launched the "White blindfold campaign" and explained to the

---

[326] McIntyre, *How to Make Trouble and Influence People*: p. 118.

passengers "Now, this is the official John Howard view of history. What happens with the white blindfold is that you put it on and you can't see a thing. It completely whites out everything. All you can see is white."[327] Then they had a "patriotic" Australian history quiz, satirising Howard's perception of what Australia's history was like. Responses from the passengers were positive, and even Howard supporters thought it was funny.[328]

Getting a chance to get close to Howard during the election campaign was difficult, since his schedule was kept secret, but in 2007 they finally found themselves at the right hotel. While the journalists were waiting for Howard, the women got a chance to introduce themselves as the *John Howard Ladies' Auxiliary Fan Club*. They had a number of gags, e.g. playing on the *electoral Viagra* they had prepared for Mr. Howard and the *race card* that he could play during the election (which Howard had done in previous elections) and uranium export to Iran and North Korea. Later that day, they finally met him in the botanical gardens in Melbourne. Bea Wight asked Howard if he would like some yellowcake, referring to a form of uranium concentrate powder, and Howard's recent signing of an agreement with Russia about export of Australian uranium. Bea Wight explains what happened: "He looked at us and smiled as though all his dreams had come at once. He smiled. He was happy, just for one split second, and then he realised – 'Electoral Viagra' – that we were evil."[329]

The fan club continued to follow Howard, including by going to a horse race he attended. Here they found their way into the exclusion zone with their pink fluffy hats and white gloves in order to encourage Howard to play the race card. When security

---

[327] McIntyre, *How to Make Trouble and Influence People*: p. 118.
[328] McIntyre, *How to Make Trouble and Influence People*.
[329] McIntyre, *How to Make Trouble and Influence People*: p. 119.

guards wanted to escort them out, they explained that "Johnny" had asked them to be there, and that they were his fan club.

Next time they tried to get to Howard, their costumes helped them though several security points, since they looked cute and harmless. That gave the four ladies time with Howard's people and an opportunity to offer them xenophobia pills, with words like "Are you afraid of muslims dear, please take this pill it will help you." They had white pills for fear of muslims, pink for gay people, purple for feminists and red ones for communists and unionists – all minority groups the fan club thought were attacked by Howard's politics.[330]

The fan club managed to get away with many stunts without being arrested or fined, and made it to the national TV news.[331] They think themselves that because they presented themselves as absolute Howard lovers and behaved so non-threateningly, they were perceived more as performers than as activists. It also helped that they were four small white women.[332] And they were convincing. A news reporter starts her account of the offering of yellowcake "Even if their message is not quite your cup of tea, it's hard not to admire the commitment of the four mothers of the John Howard Ladies Auxiliary Fan Club."[333]

Mark Thomas' PR training for dictatorships

Mark Thomas is a British professional comedian who has done numerous humorous political stunts. His work combines serious investigative journalism with deeply felt opinions about what is

---

[330] McIntyre, *How to Make Trouble and Influence People*.
[331] Michael Brissenden, "7:30 Report - Australian Broadcasting Corportion - Campaign Focuses on Rates Fallout," (Sydney: Australian Broadcasting Corporation, 2007).
[332] McIntyre, *How to Make Trouble and Influence People*: pp. 117-21.
[333] Julie Szego, "Four Play First Thing in the Morning: That's Some Fan Club," *The Age*, November 2 2007.

right and wrong. He has disclosed his investigative findings in his immensely popular performances as a stand-up comedian and in TV shows. In his book *As used on the famous Nelson Mandela*[334] Thomas describes his "underground adventures in the arms and torture trade." One of the adventures led Thomas and his colleague Chris Martin to the Defendory Arms Fair in Athens in 1998. Here their self-invented PR company *McKintosh Morley* offered advice to the arms dealers and potential buyers on how to deal with accusations of human rights violations. The organiser of the arms fair thought it was very interesting to have a PR company for the first time and told them that "PR is absolutely vital."[335]

With two large posters proclaiming "Are you ready when Amnesty International comes knocking on your door?" And "Who's Winning the War on Words?" outside their stall, Thomas and his helpers tried to attract attention from customers from countries with a record of human rights violations. They presented their services with words like:

> We offer media training and advice on how to minimise the negative impact of the human rights industry. We teach crisis management, damage limitation, pre-crisis preparation, and we focus on training the trainers so that when we leave our work continues. We can't solve your problems with Amnesty but we can teach you how you can solve them.[336]

Arms fair participants who showed interest got a realistic free media training, where Martin interviewed them in front of a camera, while Thomas gave them advice on how to improve their public appearance. Their basic advice was that when ac-

---

[334] Mark Thomas, *As Used on the Famous Nelson Mandela* (London: Ebury, 2007).
[335] Thomas, *As Used on the Famous Nelson Mandela*: p. 31.
[336] Thomas, *As Used on the Famous Nelson Mandela*: p. 31.

cused of human rights violations, it is better to admit a little of the truth – the part that is least damaging – than to deny everything. One of the visitors to the free media training in the stall was a high ranking officer from Kenya who in front of the camera told Martin and Thomas that beating your wife is a way of showing love and affection, and that the women really want it. This episode made its way into Thomas' show. However, their biggest exposure came when Major General Widjojo from Indonesia visited the stall.

Indonesia has a long record of severe human rights violations. From 1965 to 1998 the country was ruled by a military dictatorship, headed by President General Suharto. Amnesty International had many reports on human rights violations in Indonesia, but no official had ever admitted to them in public. During the media training, Thomas and Martin gained Major General Widjojo's trust and on video he appears to be an open-minded officer who is willing to learn something new. Apparently he really believed that they had skills to offer that would help him cover up human rights abuses.

During the interview Thomas had different relaxation exercises for the officer. This included making big waves with his arms, which meant that he made a fool of himself in front of the camera. He was also given different toys as a positive reinforcement when Thomas judged that he did something well. All the time, Thomas was playing his part as the self-help coach and his colleague that of a reporter asking critical questions. In the end of the training, Major General Widjojo admitted in front of the camera that occasionally the Indonesian army practiced torture, and that it was "in order to protect the security of the society". When asked why they did this, he said that the Indonesian government occasionally needed to torture some people in order give other people freedom of expression, freedom to move and the right to education.[337]

After the interview, Major General Widjojo was pleased with the experience, and inquired if it would be possible for McKintosh Morley to come to Jakarta to teach a six week military media course. This did not go ahead, but Major General Widjojo's positive experience became the entry ticket for McKintosh Morley to meet Defence Attaché Colonel Halim Nawhe at the Indonesian Embassy in London. Major General Widjojo was a friend of his, and Colonel Halim Nawhe was easily talked into trying the free media training himself, this time in a studio in London.

The advice to Colonel Halim Nawhe was the same as to Major General Widjojo – admit to some of the minor things you are accused of, and continue to lie about what is most grave to you. With Colonel Halim Nawhe in the studio, Thomas and Martin gave him a list of some of the recent troubling accusations. He was then asked to decide what was most sensitive and should be lied about, and pick a few that he considered the least damaging. One of the issues that Thomas and Martin presented him with was the use of British produced military equipment in East Timor during Indonesian occupation. For years, this had been a controversial case in Britain, and the British government had been assured that British produced arms had not been part of the occupation. However, this was one of the things on the list that the Colonel said he could admit to, and he confessed that tanks made in Britain had been used in East Timor. As Thomas wrote "The colonel's selection of 'sensitive' issues is based on what would be most embarrassing to the Indonesian government. They are not, however, the issues most sensitive to the British government."[338]

---

[337] Thomas, *As Used on the Famous Nelson Mandela*: pp. 37-38.
[338] Thomas, *As Used on the Famous Nelson Mandela*: p. 45.

In spite of these confessions, nothing changed regarding the export of British produced arms to Indonesia. Both Colonel Halim Nawhe and Major General Widjojo denied the confessions.[339] A British newspaper reported that:

> Diplomatic sources in Jakarta said that the programme was a "set-up". "The officers were entrapped and were co-operating with the PR company in the spirit of a game, almost," said an Indonesian spokesman. "This does not prove anything."[340]

Mark Thomas is an unusual comedian, who is not even sure if he would rather be called an activist or an investigative journalist. One reviewer of his work calls him an *investigative comic*.[341] Where many comedians pride themselves of being ready to ridicule everything and everyone, Thomas has strong opinions about how to choose the subject of his humour. To him, everything is political. As he says, "it's a political decision to believe that people just want a good night out without having to think." [342] He does not believe in objectivity, on the contrary. Looking at the state of the world, his duty as a comedian is to present a critical corrective of the ruling elite. In addition, people should have a good laugh and be encouraged to work for change themselves.[343]

Searching for landmines at the Belgian bank AXA

In Belgium a network working against landmines and cluster munitions sent a landmine clearance team to the headquarter of

---

[339] Amy Otchet, "Mark Thomas: Method and Madness of a TV Comic," *The UNESCO Courier* 1999.

[340] Andrew Gilligan, "Indonesians Admit Torture in TV 'Sting' " *Sunday Telegraph* January 17 1999.

[341] Simon Hattenstone, "Joking Aside," *The Guardian*, July 1 2006.

[342] Otchet, "Mark Thomas: Method and Madness of a TV Comic."

[343] Otchet, "Mark Thomas: Method and Madness of a TV Comic."

AXA, a bank which had increased its investment in mines while other banks where reducing their investment in this industry. In the press release they wrote:

> Today, 18th October, activists from the campaign "My Money. Clear Conscience?" symbolically demined the headquarters of AXA in Brussels. A landmine clearance team went in search of landmines, cluster munitions and other controversial weapons. This action is needed more than ever, as research from Netwerk Vlaanderen reveals that AXA invests heavily in two new US landmine producers.[344]

The demining team of approximately 10 people used orange and white tape to close of the area and displayed signs saying "danger, mines" and "demining in progress". In a three minute video about the action which enabled the continuation of the performance across time and space, the employees in AXA show emotions like bewilderment, surprise, amusement and worry.[345] It seems apparent that they do not know what to do with the deminers. Landmines and cluster monitions is a serious issue, and there should be no doubt that the organisation is serious in its critique of AXA's continued investment in this type of weapons. At the time of the action the Ottawa Treaty, an international ban on anti-personnel landmines, had been in place for 8 years. *Netwerk Vlaanderen* had been campaigning for more ethical investments for three years, and while most banks had decreased their investment in weapons, AXA had not been willing to cooperate with the group.[346] To make this more public, the group decided to do the demining action.

---

[344] Netwerk Vlaanderen, "Demining Team Begins Its Work at AXA," Netwerk Vlaanderen
http://www.netwerkvlaanderen.be/en/index.php?option=com_content&task=view&id=47&Itemid=268.
[345] Netwerk Vlaanderen, "Demining Action 18/10/2005," (2005).
[346] Netwerk Vlaanderen, "Demining Team Begins Its Work at AXA".

Although this was only pretence and the employees seemed more bewildered than scared and we as viewers knew that the landmine clearance team would not find any landmines or cluster munitions at the AXA headquarters in Brussels, it is obvious that they approached the conflict with a logic which differed from conventional protest.

Confronting power through support

In order to better understand the incongruity that generates amusement in the examples above, Berger's list of 45 humorous techniques is useful. Both Netwerk Vlaanderen and the fan club used the technique of *irony*.[347] They say that they are there to search for landmines and profess to love Howard and his politics although the real purpose is to highlight AXA's investments and critique Howard's social politics. A standard definition of *irony* is to say one thing but mean something else or in another way make a gap between what is said and what is meant. Encyclopædia Britannica distinguishes between *verbal irony* and *dramatic irony*. In verbal irony, "the real meaning is concealed or contradicted by the literal meanings of the words." Verbal irony arises from a sophisticated or resigned awareness of contrast between what is and what ought to be. In dramatic irony, "there is an incongruity between what is expected and what occurs."[348] However, Linda Hutcheon suggests understanding irony in relational terms. She is critical both of those who focus on the ironic intent and the skills of the one who aims to be ironic as well at those who understand irony to require a certain competence from the interpreter. Instead she says that irony "happens" when the ironist and the interpreter share enough knowledge about the subject being ironised about, that they belong to the same "discursive communities". For irony to happen, compe-

---

[347] Humorous techniques in italics always refer to Berger's 45 techniques.
[348] Encyclopædia Britannica Online, "Irony," (2012).

tence is not the key word, but everyone involved shares at least some assumptions about the world and about communication.[349]

All humour risks being misinterpreted and there is always a chance that the audiences will not "get it". This risk appears to be especially present when it comes to the technique of irony where the fact that the literal meaning can be the complete opposite of the intended meaning poses an extra risk.[350] Most other techniques will just generate confusion or bewilderment if the signals to indicate humorous intent are not communicated obviously enough to the audience.

Impersonation is another technique used in several of the supportive stunts. Impersonation can be "theft" of a person's identity or of a profession (occupational identity). The three examples illustrate how diverse the "theft" can be. Mark Thomas impersonated a PR consultant, the deminers impersonated the role of a mine clearance team, and the fan club appear as caricatures of a white middle-class Australian woman from the 1950s.

In addition *allusion* is used to hint at AXA's investment in landmines. *Allusions* are hinting at something, referring to something which is not present. Much everyday humour consists of allusions, where just the mentioning of the name of a person who has done something stupid is enough to cause laughter. The fan club used the technique of *exaggeration*, which is to make things smaller, bigger, higher, worse, better etc. than what the

---

[349] Hutcheon, *Irony's Edge*: pp. 94-98.
[350] For an interesting analysis about the problems related to interpreting irony, see Lauren L. Martin, "Bombs, Bodies, and Biopolitics: Securitizing the Subject at the Airport Security Checkpoint," *Social & Cultural Geography* 11, no. 1 (2010). This is an examination of the fact that people make jokes about carrying bombs or poison when going through airport security, and the authorities' difficulties with dealing with this.

audience expects them to be or what is generally considered "normal".

Unmasking and Revelation of Character is also a technique used by both Thomas and Netwerk Vlaanderen to reveal the true colours of the AXA and the Indonesian military. Berger describes it this way: "The emphasis in unmasking is on the process and effects of discovery (...) what is revealed or discovered often leads to embarrassment and humiliation."[351]

Thomas is a popular comedian, and his shows draw large audiences. This episode was not just causing little smiles; his professional skills when it comes to timing and building up expectations meant that the episode was hilarious. The techniques are the *mistakes* that the officer makes. The audience is aware that this is a trap, and enjoy that a highly disliked figure makes the mistake of thinking this was real. Mistakes can be humorous when someone shows poor judgement, does something considered stupid or makes an error. Berger thinks that we laugh at others' mistakes because we feel superior to them.

Identifying these techniques might help understand what is funny to the audiences in these cases, but it does not tell anything about the relationship between the different actors and or their power relationship.

Conventional protest can easily be identified as such by the use of leaflets, posters, critical speeches, blockades etc. Ordinary protesters use rational argumentation in their efforts to convince others to join them. In contrast the activists performing these supportive stunts offered help, support and concern for other's safety. The landmine clearance team, dressed in orange wests, protective helmets and equipped with instruments for mine detection looked out for the safety of the employees of AXA,

---

[351]Berger, *An Anatomy of Humor.* p. 54.

while John Howard Ladies' Auxiliary Fan Club was there to support their hero through difficult times. Mark Thomas did not appear to criticise human rights abuses, but to support those who carry them out. This way, they all engaged with their opponent by applying a different type of logic to what the conflict was about, although in very different ways.

Applying the theatre metaphor it is obvious that the fan club tried to enter the stage where "Australian politics" was being played, casting one of the main actors – the prime minister. He did what he could to ignore his fan club, but could not avoid them getting attention nevertheless. Because they used irony and said they were his biggest supporters, it was difficult to force them into the ordinary protester role and the political play was disrupted in a way that transformed the meaning of support and opposition. What happened with the landmine action had both similarities and differences. The activists did not play the usual protester role here either, but entered a scene where they were not expected at all. Their apparent help made it easier for them to remain on the scene in order to stage their own play about landmines than would have been possible had they acted as conventional protesters. Mark Thomas' strategy was different yet. He entered an established scene (the arms fair) under disguise, and managed to set up a "sub-stage" where he was in control of the rules. He lured important participants from the main stage onto his sub-stage. One must assume that McKintosh Morley's presence on the main stage made the Indonesian Major General less cautious than he would otherwise have been. The real intentions of Thomas was not revealed until he was on stage as himself months later, so there was no direct confrontation where anyone had to decide how to respond to the stunt – no one was aware that they have been subjected to a stunt until it was too late.

The audiences for these stunts varied a lot. In all three cases there were immediate audiences, for example passing by and bank employees. However, all these humorous political stunts were filmed, making it possible for many more to watch the confrontations. When it comes to the factor of timing, it was important for the fan club to time its activities around the schedule of the prime minister. The PR training depended on being present at the arms fair, while Netwerk Vlaanderen had the possibility to show up at AXA bank any day they liked, since the investment in landmines was ongoing.

Corrective Humorous Stunts

Corrective humorous stunts aim to transcend the inequality in power by presenting an alternative version of "the truth". They hijack the identity or the message of their target in order to reveal a correction. This type of stunt unmasks the dominant discourse by disclosing a more nuanced version of persons, institutions or messages. Just like in the supportive stunt, this happens when the discourse and rationality of the target are exaggerated and overemphasised. Returning to the metaphor of theatre, the pranksters do not enter the scene right in the face of the powerful as in the supportive stunt, but sneak in behind their back while the main actors look the other way or are busy somewhere else. Then they reveal what they consider a more correct version of who the target really is. They choose a scene usually controlled by the powerful. This way, the pranksters communicate to the power holders that they are being watched, but the correction is usually more directed towards the audience to whom the true colours of the target is revealed. Corrective humorous stunts frequently share their goal with conventional protests – they want to inform the public about an alternative version of the truth.

Corrective stunts subvert a dominant message by using a distorted version of the message that those in power use. The dynamics are illustrated below with examples from two groups: The *Yes Men* hijacked the identity of the World Trade Organisation and a multinational corporation and *Netwerk Vlaanderen* created a bank that invested in arms, oil and child labour.

The Yes Men: Hijacking WTO and Dow

The Yes Men is a small US based activist group which has challenged the World Trade Organisation (WTO) and multinational corporations with different stunts in order to expose the shortcomings of their neoliberal ideology. The predecessor to what is now the WTO was called GATT, and in first years after the change, it was not uncommon for people to talk about GATT meaning the WTO. The Yes Men established a web site on www.GATT.org, which was a parody of the WTO. Through this site, they have been contacted by conference organisers who thought they had come to the official WTO site and wanted to invite a speaker. The Yes Men have posed as WTO representatives on several occasions, and have been able to say the most outrageous things apparently without anybody taking notice. At a conference in Salzburg in Austria they suggested the idea of making democracy more profitable – that a voter should be able to sell his/her vote on an auction to the highest bidder. At another occasion they announced "might equaled right... that there ought to be a market in human rights abuses."[352]

The Yes Men were surprised by the lack of response, so when they got a new invitation to the WTO they decided to do something more spectacular. The Tempere University of Technology in Finland was hosting a textile industry conference in August 2000, and Andy Bichlbaum went together with his colleague Mike Bonnano. Bichlbaum was posing as *Hank Hardy Unruh*, and this time they wanted to visualize the ridiculousness in what he said from the podium. In his speech, Bichlbaum told the participants that slavery was inefficient in producing the economic results that their owners wanted, and that exploitation of third world labour was much more efficient. New technology   would

---

[352] Harold, *Ourspace*: p. 88.

189

Illustration 4. Andy Bichlbaum from the Yes Men posing as Hank Hardy Unruh, representing the WTO at Tempere University of Technology in Finland, August 2000. The photo is in the creative commons.

make it possible for management to control their workers by keeping them under constant surveillance, transferring the idea of the prison panopticon to the new technology. He then presented the *Management Leisure Suit* as the WTO solution to management difficulties. He tore off his ordinary clothes, and underneath the audience could see his golden *leisure suit*. He continued to introduce the audience to the core features of the suit, and when he unzipped the front of it, a three foot long golden phallus was inflated in front of him. The audience clapped. Hank Hardy Unruh then told his audience about the *Employee Visualisation Appendage* which with an electronic device could communicate with chips implanted in the worker's bodies.[353]

---

[353] Andy Bichlbaum and Mike Bonanno, "The Yes Men Fix the World," (Docudramafilms, 2009); Andy Bichlbaum, Mike Bonanno,

In this stunt, the Yes Men used a traditional conference lecture as their medium, and the potential audience was expanded when film was used to spread the story of the stunt. Their agenda was to attack the WTO and its promotion of neo-liberal economics. At this occasion it was the abuse of cheap labour in the sweat shops of the textile industry which was under attack. The Yes Men did not seem to design their action to make the conference audience laugh, but just to make them react and be outraged at what they head. But that failed, as it had done before when the Yes Men criticised free trade and the idea that it should be possible to make a profit from anything. Only the people who were present know what they actually thought about the situation. From the data available there is no way of telling if they were upset by the speech but too shy to stand up and say that this was ridiculous. They might have understood this was a stunt, been amused but chose not to say anything. All we know is that the audiences who watch the movie are amused, but they have also been given many clues that this was a stunt about to happen.

The WTO could either choose to ignore a stunt like this, or make a public announcement that this is not their opinion. From the WTO point of view, it was probably wise to ignore it.

In 2002, the Yes Men thought it was time to end their careers as WTO representatives, and decided to do it properly by shutting down the organisation. After the event in Finland, the WTO had put a warning on their website about www.gatt.org, and the Yes Men did not expect to get any more invitations. Nevertheless, an accountants' association in Australia invited the WTO to Sydney to talk about "Agribusiness Globalisation".[354] When the Yes Men arrived as WTO representatives they explained that there

and Bob Spunkmeyer, *The Yes Men: The True Story of the End of the World Trade Organization* (New York: Disinformation, 2004); Harold, *Ourspace*: pp. 87-92.
[354] Bichlbaum, Bonanno, and Spunkmeyer, *The Yes Men*: p. 115.

had been a change in plans that prevented them from talking about the topic of agribusiness. Instead Bichlbaum, this time going by the name Kinnithrung Sprat, explained that the WTO had initiated an internal evaluation of its work, and that the conclusion was that the organisation would close down shortly. The speech went through much documentation of the short-comings of the WTO and the neo-liberal doctrine of "free market" and how it had been unjust and prevented poor countries from prospering. Sprat announced that the WTO would be re-launched under the name Trade Regulation Organisation, but that much was still uncertain about this new organisation. However, it would certainly have its basis in the UN Charter of Human Rights, in order to secure that the needs of *all* human beings counted more than profit and free trade.[355]

Also after this stunt, the Yes Men were surprised by the reactions. The audience was actually happy to hear this announcement, thought it was a good idea and came up with many suggestions for how to make the new Trade Regulation Organisation good. The stunt was convincing enough to make a Canadian MP ask in parliament what the consequences of the closure of the WTO would be for the Canadian people. The official WTO had to reply to at least one journalist that this was a hoax.[356]

Another Yes Men stunt had its background in serious accident which took place in the city Bhopal in India on December 3rd, 1984. Poisonous gas leaked out from a pesticide plant that was owned by the company Union Carbide. 5000 people died immediately after the accident, while 15,000 more died over the next 20 years as a result of the gas. Another 120,000 are estimated to need lifelong medical care. The victims of the disaster have

---

[355] Bichlbaum, Bonanno, and Spunkmeyer, *The Yes Men*: pp. 158-75.
[356] Bichlbaum, Bonanno, and Spunkmeyer, *The Yes Men*: pp. 176-77.

fought for compensation and a clean-up of the site ever since. Union Carbide left India shortly after, and in 2001 the company was sold to another company, Dow Chemical.

20 years later, on December 3rd 2004, the BBC asked the company for a comment about the case. On live TV from Paris, the Dow Chemical representative Jude Finisterra appeared. To everyone's surprise he said that Dow Chemical was finally ready to take full responsibility for cleaning up and paying compensation to all the victims. At the same time he apologised that it had taken so long for the company to take this step. On film it looks as if the BBC reporter was quite surprised by the announcement, and in the next hours the value of Dow on the stock exchange

Illustration 5. Andy Bichlbaum from the Yes Men posing as Jude Finisterra on the BBC in 2004. As a spokesperson for Dow Chemicals, Finisterra announced that the company would finally take full responsibility for the Bhopal catastrophe. The photo is in the creative commons.

193

fell with two billion American dollars.[357] Jude Finisterra turned out to be Bichlbaum from Yes Men, and again appeared live on BBC, this time posing as himself. He explained the rationale behind the action – that the Yes Men were helping Dow improve. The Yes Men received some criticism for bringing the victims false hope, but argued that it was Dow that denied the victims what they deserved. Just as in the case with the WTO, it was the Yes Men's alternative webpage for Dow and a mistake by the BBC that made the stunt possible at all.[358]

The message of the Yes Men is difficult to argue about: That Dow should take full responsibility for compensating victims and cleaning up. Their medium of choice for communicating this message is not unusual – activists around the world dream about access to the BBC to communicate their message.

ACE bank for ethical investments

In the category of supportive stunts, Netwerk Vlaanderen's demining of AXA was one example. The same organisation was behind a more elaborate deception. Focusing on the same issues as when searching for landmines – banks' responsibilities for what they invest in – they decided to set up a new bank, ACE bank. The bank opened an office in central Brussels and advertised that it was investigating if there was a market for its special way of doing banking. The bank wanted to specialise in investments in dubious areas such as arms and oil production as well as child labour. It claimed to be ethical and transparent because in contrast to other banks it did not try to hide what it invested in. On the contrary, they exclusively invested in these areas in order to provide the best possible interest rate to their customers. In a video about ACE bank the viewer sees potential bank

---

[357] Ryan Gilbey, "Jokers to the Left, Jokers to the Right," *http://www.theguardian.com*, July 17 2009.
[358] Bichlbaum and Bonanno, "The Yes Men Fix the World."

customers being introduced to the idea. Some are very sceptical; others appear seriously interested, some thought it was a parody. The new bank made headlines in the TV news and in newspapers – but after a week of speculation it was closed down by the Belgian bank authorities. Apparently furious about the decision, ACE bank called for a press conference. Here they named all the major banks and their investment in similar products and demanded that if ACE bank had to close because of its investment practices, then all the other banks had to be closed as well. Finally they revealed that it was Vlaanderen Netwerk which was responsible.[359]

Confronting power by correcting it

Returning to Berger's techniques, *impersonation* was used in most of the examples of the corrective stunt, just as it was a popular technique in the supportive stunt. Yes Men impersonated WTO and Dow representatives, and Netwerk Vlaanderen's activists took on the role of bankers when they created ACE bank.

Exaggeration is another technique that appeared again, this time in the Yes Men's performance at the textile conference in Finland where they exaggerated the neo-liberal policies of the WTO in order to provoke a reaction from the conference participants. When Berger describes this technique, he mentions that exaggeration has to be combined with one or more other techniques in order to be funny. Here they combine it with *absurdity*. The giant golden penis was so absurd that it seems unbelievable that the conference audience did not understand that this was a joke. This way, the technique to make the spectators of the movie laugh is the *ignorance* of the conference audience. According to Berger, ignorance works as a technique because we like to feel superior to those we consider stupid.[360] The absurdity in the speech is created by the extreme exaggeration of the possibility

---

[359] Pieter De Vos, *The Ace-Bank Hoax*, (2006).
[360] Berger, *An Anatomy of Humor.* pp. 36-37.

and wish for control. No matter what one thinks about the WTO, their statements have not yet been as outrageous as what the Yes Men made them say.

ACE bank is a *parody* of the real banks. In Berger's understanding of the term, parody is a "verbal mimicry" of a particular person, where his or her style is imitated. ACE bank is not an example of this kind of parody, but a parody of an institution.

Unmasking is another technique used in examples of both supportive and corrective stunts. The Yes Men showed that it would in fact have been possible for Dow to offer compensation to the victims in Bhopal, and in a similar type of unmasking, Netwerk Vlaanderen exposed the double standards of the ordinary banks. Some audiences might also have enjoyed the *mistakes* of the potential customers which were fooled by the false bank.

The Yes Men themselves write about what they do as "identity correction" (although someone suggested the term to them *after* they had already done some of their stunts). Amber Day talks about "identity nabbing".[361] Dow and the WTO uphold an image of themselves that the Yes Men do not think covers the whole truth. The WTO neglects to talk about some of the devastating consequences of its neo-liberal policies, and Dow pretended that it could not do anything about Bhopal. The Yes Men set out to correct this self-presentation by revealing the true colours or providing alternative causes of actions.

At one point, it was suggested to me to call this category honest – however, that implies that those who are being corrected are lying. Although they might frequently do this, corrective stunts can also be used in cases where someone make statements they

---

[361] Bichlbaum, Bonanno, and Spunkmeyer, *The Yes Men*: p. 11. Day, *Satire and Dissent*: p. 146.

themselves believe in. Therefore it is more appropriate to talk about different understandings of the truth rather than *the* truth.

On the surface, the corrective stunt seems to be acting within the frame of logic and rationality, and again the metaphor of theatre can be useful for illustrating what is going on. The stages that the pranksters entered vary a lot: The play that the Yes Men attempted to disrupt was an ordinary conference about textiles. ACE bank set up an alternative stage and lured their audience in there, just like Mark Thomas did in his supportive stunt. Who the correcting activists considered the audiences and what they wanted to communicate differed, but they all had in common that they wanted to provide an alternative. The Yes Men wanted to present a more correct picture of what the WTO is, and what ideology the organisation represents. The activists behind ACE bank wanted to bring the issue of banking investment practices in dubious areas to the attention of the general public. On these various stages, no one appeared to be playing a protester role, neither did they want to "help" in the way the participants in the supportive stunt did.

What they did was different again, and the timing of the stunts was important. They had to appear at exactly the right moment and control the stage for a while in order to communicate an alternative point of view to the audience. Netwerk Vlaanderen brought in a new actor – a new bank – in order to expose the old banks already on the scene. The Yes Men did not change the play by bringing in new actors; they just let one of the ordinary actors exaggerate his part. In the direct interaction with the conference audience, this failed when nobody seemed to notice anything wrong. They were not even treated like ordinary protesters and ordered out of the conference room. The WTO was not put in a position where they were forced to react. From this perspective, the prank was a complete failure. Nevertheless, the Yes Men reached a much larger audience through their film: viewers were given the clues that this was a joke.

When it comes to the audience element of the play metaphor, it is difficult to know if members of the general public changed their perception of the neo-liberal discourse targeted by the Yes Men because of these stunts. Neither will we ever know if ACE bank influenced investment habits in Belgium. Even if it is possible to trace a change in behaviour people can always claim that this is a coincidence or that other factors caused the change. However, although it might be due to a selection bias it is striking that the examples of corrective stunts I have come across have been very effective in getting media attention.[362] It would be worth investigating further if there is something about this type of stunt that is especially appealing to media.

Naïve Humorous Stunts

Naive humorous stunts deal with the power holders' truth and rationality in a way which differs from the supportive and corrective stunt. By appearing naïve and innocent, protesters pretend not to understand that what they do can be interpreted as a protest and this way point to the unequal relations of power by only hinting at them. Where the supportive and corrective stunts exaggerate and overemphasise the rationality of the power holders in order to get their message across, those who carry out naïve stunts pretend that they are not aware that they have challenged any power. In terms of the theatre metaphor, they enter a scene but pretend that they are not aware that there was a play going on. If anything looks like a protest, that must be a coincidence. The story of the good solider Svejk who challenged

---

[362] Another example of a corrective stunt that was effective in getting media attention was the Swedish peace organisation SPAS's parody webpage of a government agency established to support arms export. Majken Jul Sørensen, "Humorous Political Stunts: Speaking "Truth" to Power?," *European Journal of Humour Research* 1, no. 2 (2013).

the authority of the army without ever framing his actions as protest is a classic literary example of a naïve prankster.[363]

The purpose of the naïve stunt is not to present a more correct version or unmasking, but under the disguise of naiveté to simply utter a dissenting message. Below four short examples illustrate the diversity of the naïve stunt. The first is an advertisement for sausages during the Nazi occupation of Denmark, followed by a Serbian blood donation action. The third example involved a number of Poles who took their TVs for a walk. I conclude with another Danish example where Santa came to town just before Christmas in 1974.

Innocent advertising during the Nazi occupation of Denmark

During WWII, both Denmark and Norway were occupied by the Nazis from 1940-1945. In these countries, jokes ridiculing the occupation forces were widespread and to some degree contributed to creating a culture of resistance. Examples of humour which was public and therefore part of an interaction with the German occupier are less common. In his article about Danish occupation humour, which mainly focuses on whispered jokes, Hong provides an unusual example from a butchers van in the town Esbjerg. On the back of double doors the butcher had written:

"Salted down sausages. N.S Jensen, Butcher. Delivery Anywhere. England Road 22, Esbjerg." But when the right door was opened, the words on the left door then read "Down with N.S [National Socialism], Long Live England.[364]

---

[363] Jaroslav Hašek, *The Good Soldier Švejk and His Fortunes in the World War* (New York: Crowell, 1974).
[364] Hong, "Mow 'Em All Down Grandma: The 'Weapon' of Humor in Two Danish World War II Occupation Scrapbooks," pp. 43-44. For a

This anti-Nazi message, which is also a support of England, took place under very serious conditions. Repression from the Nazis was harsh and the butcher was taking a great risk. The medium used in this case was a traditional advertising on the door, which should not pose any threat to the Nazis. Only upon closer inspection does the message turn out to be far from innocent.[365]

Donating blood to avoid bloodshed in Serbia

In November 1996 there were elections in Serbia, and at the local level the coalition *Zadjeno* opposing Slobodan Milošević won in more than a hundred municipalities, including Belgrade and other important cities. When the regime refused to accept the result, this sparked more than three months of mass demonstrations. The students played a major role in bringing a carnivalesque atmosphere to the protest. One event, called *blood transfusion*, was an example of a naïve stunt. It was based on a statement by Mirjana Markovic, the leader of the Yoguslav Left Party and the wife of Slobodan Milošević. She had threatened to use violence against the protesters when she said that "a lot of blood had been shed for the introduction of communism into

---

general discussion about humour's contribution to creating a culture of resistance, see Sørensen, "Humor as a Serious Strategy of Nonviolent Resistance to Oppression." About Norway, see Stokker, "Quisling Humor in Hitler's Norway." Already in 1942, Obrdlik wrote that humour was important for Czech resistance to Nazi occupation in: Obrdlik, "'Gallows Humor'- a Sociological Phenomenon." Nathaniel Hong, who has documented this Danish example and has studied Danish anti-Nazi humour during the occupation, thinks that the power of humour is overestimated. However, his main focus is jokes, which by their nature of being whispered in secret do not engage with the enemy/opponent. This example of open use of humour is an exception from most of the examples in his article.
[365] An example of a similar tactic used by a sports magazine in Burma is included in Sørensen, "Humorous Political Stunts: Speaking "Truth" to Power?."

Yoguslavia and that it [the Communist Party] would never go without blood".[366] Some students initiated a campaign to collect blood and then said "here is our blood, now you can go".[367]

Poland – taking the TV for a walk

The independent trade union Solidarity in Poland called for a boycott of the official TV news in 1982. Since the creation of Solidarity in August 1980, the union had been a huge challenge to the communist government. On December 13, 1981, the enforcement of martial law put a temporary stop to the democratization movement when tanks rolled through the streets of Poland. However, this was not the end of resistance. From underground, Solidarity called for a boycott of the news on TV, which was filled with lies from the regime. But how would anybody get an idea about how many people participated in the boycott?

In the town of Swidnik in the east of Poland, the inhabitants started the habit of going for a walk, just as the half-hour news report began at 7.30 pm. The streets would be full of people chatting with each other. Before they went out, some people would place their TV in the window, pointing to the street with a blank screen. Others took their unconnected TV with them in a stroller for children or something else with wheels. The habit soon spread to other places, and apparently the authorities were furious, but felt there was little they could do. After all, the chance of being ridiculed increase even more if you decide to arrest people for taking their TV for a walk.

The authorities' "solution" was to move the start of the curfew forward from 10 pm to 7pm. The answer from the people of Swidnik was to take their walk during the 5pm news instead.[368]

---

[366] Sombutpoonsiri, "The Use of Humour as a Vehicle for Nonviolent Struggle," p. 129.
[367] Sombutpoonsiri, "The Use of Humour as a Vehicle for Nonviolent Struggle," p. 129.

This humorous twist to a boycott depends on many people participating in order to have an effect, which it apparently did have in Poland in 1982 – if not, why should the regime had bothered to change the timing of the curfew?

The message from the people is straightforward – we don't believe in your news, therefore we don't want to watch it and by taking our walk where everybody can see us, we show you (and each other) how many we are.

Santas hand out gifts from the shop shelves

In the week leading up to Christmas 1974 100 Santas visited Denmark's capital Copenhagen. This week long action/performance was created by the theatre group *Solvognen* that wanted to bring public attention to the rising unemployment and commercialisation of Christmas.[369] The action had many different parts, ranging from friendly Santas singing to the elderly and giving away hot chocolate to a symbolic attack on the court of industrial relations which were renamed a class court.

The culmination came late afternoon on December 22, when the army of Santas visited the shopping centre Magasin. The place was filled with people buying last minute presents, and here Santa set out to do what Santas are supposed to do, hand out presents. The Santas had brought some books with them, but also picked books from the shop shelves and handed them to the customers with a "merry Christmas" and words like "no,

---

[368] Steve Crawshaw and John Jackson, *Small Acts of Resistance: How Courage, Tenacity, and Ingenuity Can Change the World* (New York: Union Square Press, 2010). pp. 5-6.
[369] The Santas from the theatre group Solvognen, "Solvognen: Derfor Malede Vi Byen I Folkets Farve," [Solvognen: The reason we painted the city in the colour of the people] *B.T.*, December 23 1974. Solvognen, "Solvognens Julemandshær (Synopsis Og Invitation)," (1974).

Illustration 6. The Santas marching through central Copenhagen with their Christmas goose, December 1974. ©: Nils Vest 1974, reprinted with permission.

today it does not cost anything, today it is free."[370] A film about
the event shows how some customers smile and laugh, some
ignore the Santas, and over the loudspeaker system the management of Magasin declares:

> Announcement to all our customers. Please be aware that
> the persons in Father Christmas costumes that hand out
> goods from the shelves, do *not* belong to the staff of Ma-
> gasin. We kindly request our customers to return items
> they have already received at the checkout counters. The
> police have been called."[371]

The police arrived and children cried when the Santas were
arrested and rather roughly led out with their arms behind their
backs. Outside the shopping centre, the passers-by which had
stopped to watch were on the side of Santa. They sang Christmas carols and tried to prevent the police from taking the Santas
to the waiting police vans.[372] A group of Santas who had not
been arrested proceeded to another shopping centre called Illum,
where they repeated the performance before they were arrested
as well.

The shopping centre did not want to press charges against the
Santas for theft, but the prosecutor raised a case for disturbing
public order against 45 Santas. In the first trial they were acquit-

---

[370] The most detailed description about the week long action is Nina
Rasmussen, *Solvognen: Fortællinger Fra Vores Ungdom* (Copenhagen:
Rosinante, 2002). pp. 192-217. The only source in English is Aage
Jorgensen, "Touring the 1970's with the Solvognen in Denmark," *The
Drama Review: TDR* 26, no. 3 (1982).
[371] Jon Bang Carlsen, "Dejlig Er Den Himmel Blå [Beautiful Is the
Blue Sky]," (C&C productions Aps, 1975).
[372] Else Sander, "Julemænd Anholdt under Gaveuddeling," *Ekstra
Bladet*, December 23 1974.

ted, but when the prosecutor appealed the case they were later convicted and received small fines.[373]

During the week of the action, Solvognen succeed in gaining extensive media coverage that to a large degree was fair and unbiased.[374] Later there was much debate and even more coverage after Solvognen received a grant from a stately art fund. More than 30 years later the stunt became part of the Danish cultural canon. The performance is considered one of 108 cultural expressions that is part of the Danish cultural heritage.[375]

Confronting power with naiveté

It is more difficult to explain what causes amusement in the naïve stunts using Berger's techniques than with the supportive

---

[373] Rasmussen, *Solvognen: Fortællinger Fra Vores Ungdom*: pp. 192-217.

[374] I did an extensive search and analysis of the media coverage from the seven national Danish newspapers *Aktuelt, B.T, Berlingske Tidende, Ekstra Bladet, Information, Jyllands-Posten* and *Politiken.* These are all the major national Danish newspapers from this time period. All the findings are too long to include here, but from the 17th to the 24th of December, Solvognen was the main item in 31 articles. The majority, 24, were news reports. Four articles are categorised as "other", such as a portrait of the day and short notes on the front page referring to a different page in the newspapers. In addition there were three editorials published on December 24th, and between December 23 and 29, there were six letters to the editors about Solvognen. That the action became the subject of three editorials indicate that Solvognen had touched a subject the editors found interesting. Two of these are very supportive and one is very critical. Berlingske Tidende, "Bedrevidende Julenisser," [Know-all Santas] *Berlingske Tidende,* December 24 1974. lip, "Sol(Hverv)Vognen," [Untranslatable wordplay] *Information,* December 24 1974. Ekstra Bladet, "De Røde Julemænd " [The red Santas] *Ekstra Bladet,* December 24 1974.

[375] Kanonudvalget, "Julemandshæren [the Santa Claus Army]," Det danske kulturministerium, http://kulturkanon.kum.dk/scenekunst/julemandshaeren/Begrundelse _Julemandshaeren/.

and corrective stunts. Although pretence plays a role in most humorous stunts, it is crucial for understanding the apparently naive, and none of the 45 techniques captures pretence. In order to stay within Berger's technical perspective, one would have to add categories that included the *pretended coincidence* and *pretended innocence* present in these cases. Berger does describe techniques for coincidences, innocence, misunderstandings and ignorance, but the way he uses the terms varies considerably from what is happening in the examples above. For instance, Berger explains a kind of coincidence which is based on embarrassment, and in his description of ignorance people laugh at those who are ignorant.[376] That situation changes when someone is pretending to be innocent or ignorant – instead of laughing *at* them, we laugh *with* them. In the donation of blood episode in Serbia, Markovic intended to mean "blood by using violence", an implicit understanding which the students pretended not to understand. Berger has a technique for ignorance where people laugh because they feel superior to others who are stupid.[377] But here we laugh at Mira Markovic, not the activists who pretend to misunderstand her statement. Therefore it is inappropriate to talk about mistakes and misunderstandings as the techniques used, since the Nazis, Polish, Danish and Serbian authorities were not fooled and fully understood that this was only pretended innocence.

Berger mentions pretence when he writes about taking on a different identity, like impersonation, but that differs from the mechanism of defining the whole situation as something else. In the Polish example, the timing of the TV walk with the beginning of the TV news was crucial, although it of course was a "coincidence" and not intended as a protest – should anybody from the authorities ask. The Danish butcher wrote an innocent message which by "mistake" happened to be anti-Nazi.

---

[376] Berger, *An Anatomy of Humor.* 29.
[377] Berger, *An Anatomy of Humor.* pp. 36-37.

Although Berger's techniques are inadequate for fully explaining these examples, some of his techniques are present. The result of the Danish butcher's "mistake" is an *insult* to the Nazis, something which can be funny to an audience when they dislike a person or a group, but generally it has to be combined with some other technique in order to be amusing. The TV walk is both an example of the *absurd* and *eccentric*. I will return to the technique of absurdity when describing the absurd stunt, but *eccentricity* is a technique that builds on people's eccentric behaviour or appearance. It would have been eccentric to walk around with your TV in a stroller had the circumstances been different. Had it happened out of a context like this, we would not have made much sense of it. It is a technique which in many ways is similar to the absurd, but Berger operates with a distinction between strangeness connected to identity (eccentric) and our sense of logic (absurdity).

There is also a *literalness* of the boycott of the TV news. To Berger, literalness is when the same word or statement gets a different meaning when you look at the actual words. However, it is possible to understand the technique of literalness much more broadly than Berger, and not just connected to language.

These types of stunts are naive – not because the activists would be called naïve by their opponents, on the contrary, but because they frame what they do so on the surface they are not doing anything wrong at all. They pretend to avoid the logic of power and protest altogether. This can be by doing something which is actually quite normal, like advertising sausages, donating blood and Santa handing out presents. In other cases the behaviour cannot be called normal, such as taking the TV for a walk, but it can still be framed as completely harmless.

Solvognen's army of Santas played on Danish mythology where Santa is naive, friendly, helpful and more than anything else associated with giving away gifts to children. The humour in the stunt arises when Santa performs his role in a way which clashes with other societal norms, such as not stealing. When the police was called out to perform their law enforcement role and did that dutifully, it became funny because Santas in handcuffs being taken away by police is completely incongruous with the image of the naïve gift-giving Santa.

Most of the examples of naïve stunts that I have come across took place in situations of relatively severe oppression. For those living with oppression, framing oneself as naïve might be the only possibility for protest they consider available at all. The Santas in Denmark are an exception and together the four examples show how diverse the naïve stunts can be.

Returning to the theatre metaphor, it is not the major stages that these activists aim for, but whatever scene that seems to be within reach. The Danish butcher used his own van, the Polish TV walkers their own streets and their own TVs. The Serbian students provided their own blood, but were depending on media coverage in order to spread the message of what they had done. The same was the case with the Santas. The cases from dictatorships attempted to disrupt the pieces of theatre called "everything is normal" which these dictatorial regimes aimed to uphold, and any disruption, however minor, fulfilled this purpose. They did not attempt to hijack the character of someone else as in the corrective stunts, and there were no major actors like prime ministers and presidents nearby. There is little data to tell how the audiences reacted and interpreted the stunts taking place in severely oppressive circumstances. In the Santa example Solvognen received extensive media coverage, and the media reported that many of the customers who witnessed the event were supportive, although many was confused about what was going on and some accused the Santas of stealing.

In some of the examples, timing was important – had the Poles walked out with their TV half an hour later it would not have made any sense, and the Santas depended on it being Christmas time. The Serbian students could have donated their blood at any time after Markovic's statement, but the closer in time the more sense it would make. For the butcher timing was less crucial – the ad would work during the whole occupation.

The naive stunt has a different way of refusing the rationality of those in power than the corrective and supportive stunts; those who carry it out simply appear not to be aware of how the play of politics works. However, since there is logic to what they do, which presents an alternative message; they do leave themselves vulnerable to persecution, and the authorities can respond accordingly. There is no documentation of what happened to the Danish butcher. For the Polish regime, there was no obvious way of reacting when the TV walkers entered and started their absurd play. The communist regime had seen plenty of protest in 1980-81 and knew how to react to strikes and other outspoken protests, but since this was different, it did not seem wise to remove them with force. But the theatre of normalcy was disrupted enough to cause a change in the curfew time.

Absurd Humorous Stunts

In absurd humorous stunts, the activists frame themselves as innocent clowns who point towards society's absurdities. Their relation to the rationality of the dominant discourse is to defy it altogether. The absurd stunt shares some similarities with the naïve stunt regarding the apparent naiveté of the activists, but whereas the participants in the naïve stunt appear not to understand, the absurd pranksters refuse to acknowledge any kind of rationality. Returning to the theatre metaphor, those who carry out absurd stunts can capture any stage, anywhere. They might invade a major scene right in the power holder's face, or they might sneak in behind someone's back on a smaller and less guarded scene. Their message is that the whole world is absurd, including the apparently powerful. All claims to power and truth are challenged with silliness, slapstick or total craziness. Everyone is assumed to be participants in the play and no one is being chased away, but the previously prevailing rules and roles are altered. The absurd pranksters are unlikely to suggest that this has anything to do with protest; it is only the context and the audiences' interpretations which can reveal any critical intent. The *Orange Alternative's* happenings in Poland during the late 1980's and the British *Clandestine Insurgent Rebel Clown Army* serve as examples of this type of stunt.

Poland's Orange Alternative

During martial law in the early 1980's in Poland, at around the same time as the inhabitants in Swidnik took their TVs for a walk, graffiti in favour of the now illegal trade union Solidarity was quickly painted over by the authorities. This left "blobs" on the walls, so that everyone knew that they covered graffiti. Activists who identified with a new group called *Orange Alternative* started to work on the blobs by giving them arms and legs so that they became little elves. According to Kenney, who has written about the Orange Alternative and its place in the fall of the communist regimes in central Europe, elves made passers-by "consider the point of the struggle over wall space, and wonder why little elves were threatening to the communists".[378]

Several years later, the elves came to life at an Orange Alternative happening on Children's day, June 1st 1987, one of the happenings which became what Kenney calls a "catalyst" for the Orange Alternative. An invitation to the happening was distributed at schools and universities around the city Wroclaw, and almost 1000 young people showed up. Here they got a red cap, and then they became elves. Since it was Children's day, they handed out candy to people, danced and sang children's songs. The leader of the Orange Alternative called himself Major Fyderych, but he could not be present himself this day, since he was arrested just before the happening began. Nevertheless the

---

[378] Kenney, *A Carnival of Revolution*: p. 158.

happening went ahead and the guitar player Jakubczak, another central person in the Orange Alternative, played and sang with the crowd. When the police started to take the elves to the police cars they followed without protesting, kissing the police and throwing candy out through the windows. Then the crowd started to shout "elves are real", and accounts of this surreal celebration of Children's day went around Poland in the underground press, providing new images of what protest could look like.[379]

Orange Alternative was a small group that mainly worked in the city Wroclaw, but later spread to other cities in Poland. They initiated happenings which brought colour and carnival to the greyness which characterised both the communist regime and the opposition in Solidarity. Instead of staging a protest march or a fast as other protesters did, they arranged events which involved the audience. In addition to candy, on other occasions they also handed out toilet paper or sanitary pads (scarce under communism). The concept of *socialist surrealism* mocking the socialist realities guided the happenings, but the Orange Alternative was a co-organiser of events, not *the* organiser, since the police and passers-by also had a say in what was to happen.[380] The happenings were never an open expression of dissent, but *any* independent organising, no matter the reason, was a threat to the communist desire for total control.

In 1987 and 1988, there was a happening on average once or twice a month,[381] and another major event took place on February 16, 1988. This was carnival time, and Orange Alternative

---

[379] Kenney, *A Carnival of Revolution*.
[380] Mirosław Peczak and Anna Krajewska-Wieczorek, "The Orange Ones, the Street, and the Background," *Performing Arts Journal* 13, no. 2 (1991): p. 51.
[381] Bronislaw Misztal, "Between the State and Solidarity: One Movement, Two Interpretations - the Orange Alternative Movement in Poland," *British Journal of Sociology* 43, no. 1 (1992).

211

invited everyone to the surreal version of carnival in socialist Poland – the "ProletaRIO Carnival". This time the only dress code was carnival costume, and the crowd of 3-5000 people included a skeleton, Ku Klux Klan men, smurfs, and Red Riding Hood together with a wolf. Official radio first reported the invitation, thinking it was an idea invented by the authorities. Finally bluehelmet police joined the crowd, but they were not there to party, but to take the carnival to the police station. In the official press the events was framed as student foolishness that had to be stopped in order not to create traffic chaos in the afternoon peak period.[382]

In contrast to Solidarity, Orange Alternative was unpredictable and the regime never knew what would come next. The little elves did not resist arrest, but they kissed the police and gave them flowers. This way, they became difficult for the regime to suppress, since arresting someone for playing an elf seems ridiculous, even for the communists. In the beginning, Orange Alternative was not just critical of the communist regime, but also of Solidarity and the church because of its belief that the Bible provided the answers. It was the regime itself which pushed the Alternative more and more in the direction of pro-test.[383] The happenings became a training ground for protest and socialised people to the idea of speaking out. They encouraged people to come out on the streets where they noticed that a few hours of detention was not that dangerous after all.[384] This way, by lowering levels of fear, Orange Alternative prepared people for toppling the regime a few years later.

---

[382] Kenney, *A Carnival of Revolution*: p. 1.
[383] Misztal, "Between the State and Solidarity," p. 61.
[384] Misztal, "Between the State and Solidarity," p. 62; Kenney, *A Carnival of Revolution*: p. 190.

CIRCA – Clandestine Insurgent Rebel Clown Army

Clandestine Insurgent Rebel Clown Army (CIRCA) is a UK based network of clowns that uses nonviolent action against symbols of capitalism and militarism, e.g at military recruitment offices and G8 meetings.[385] They explain why they are clowns:

> We are *clowns* because what else can one be in such a stupid world. Because inside everyone is a lawless clown trying to escape. Because nothing undermines authority like holding it up to ridicule (…) We are *circa* because we are approximate and ambivalent, neither here nor there, but in the most powerful of all places, the place in-between order and chaos.[386]

Clowning is visual, so to experience CIRCA, one needs to see it rather than read a description. At the very least, it is worth quoting one clown's own description of what happened at a military recruitment office in Leeds in the UK. Kolonel Klepto from the Clandestine Insurgent Rebel Clown Army explains:

> …15 clownbatants from the Clandestine Insurgent Rebel Clown Army (CIRCA), dressed head to toe in combat gear delicately trimmed with pink and green fuzzy-fur and sporting sparkling steel colanders helmets, had marched into the [recruitment] centre and asked the recruiting officers if they could join up. In high pitched clown voices we told them about our previous experience in the clown army, displaying skills such as silly salutes, showing subversive slapstick drills, exhibiting the art of telling jokes that disarm and explaining that where their bombs fail we might

---

[385] CIRCA is part of the anti-globalisation/globalisation-critical/globalisation-from-below movement which also has a strong "carnival" component. Notes from Nowhere, *We Are Everywhere: The Irresistible Rise of Global Anticapitalism* (London: Verso, 2003). pp. 173-183.

[386] CIRCA, "Clandestine Insurgent Rebel Clown Army " http://www.clownarmy.org/.

be able to succeed with laughter (...)But they hadn't taken our desire to join their army seriously, and a very large and extremely un-amused commando from the Royal Marines tried to throw us out of the centre with the help of a growing number of police officers. But it's hard to move a rebel clown, they don't resist in a conventional sense, but tend to slip out of the clutches of authority like wobbly jelly and distract them from their duties with loud gaffaws and stinging mockery. The more our pleas to join the army fell on deaf ears - "Please teach us how to liberate people!" "Where are the application forms? " "Why can't we have really really big guns like yours?" - the more chaotic the scene in the recruitment office became. Very long sausage ballons started screaming across the space sounding like ammunition about to explode, sherbert filled toy aeroplanes did manic loop the loops over the RAF desks, one clown crawled around the floor polishing soldiers boots with his feather duster while another read out loud the latest communique from CIRCA...[387]

Confronting power with absurdity

In CIRCA's action in the recruitment office, the 15 clowns participating used a number of different techniques. The whole situation with its chaos and unexpected behaviour can be called an example of *slapstick*, which might best be described as the refusal to let someone be comfortable in their role as adults. Berger explains:

Slapstick is physical humour, often involving degradation by action (...) It is an "attack" on our claims to adulthood, importance, and status of any kind. As such, it feeds on an inner sense of egalitarianism we have (...) a kind of "dem-

---

[387] CIRCA, "Clandestine Insurgent Rebel Clown Army ".

ocratic" degradation that is tied to a sense we have that we
are all humans…[388]

When CIRCA turned the situation in the recruitment office into
chaos, they refused to let the military and police carry out their
adult roles with dignity. CIRCA also uses irony, a technique
already encountered in other examples. The clowns asked to
learn how to become soldiers, but they did not really want to be
recruited. Another technique they used is *ridicule* of military
behaviour and statements, for example when they said "please
teach us how to liberate people." *Ridicule* happens when we
expose people in a way that put them in a bad light. No one likes
to be ridiculed, so humour which humiliates people risks causing
strong reactions. Berger calls ridicule a "direct verbal attack
against a person, thing or idea"[389] and mentions different forms
of ridicule, such as mocking, taunting and deriding. Ridicule and
its consequences will be discussed in more detail in Chapter 5.

Berger also includes the technique of absurdity in his list, something also found in these two examples of absurd stunts.
Absurdity is a common technique for creating humour, and
occurs when something or someone seems completely out of
place. We find things absurd when we think it is obvious that
they do not belong together in any way. Berger explains how the
absurd causes us to be puzzled and sometimes amused when our
sense of order and logic is challenged. He also thinks that the
absurd is used to communicate human beings' "possibilities in an
irrational universe."[390] Watching CIRCA, there is *absurdity* in the
contrast between the clown figures and the military recruitment
office, especially between the military uniforms and the little silly
clowning attributes that go with them, pink and green fuzzy fur.
Also the idea that their experiences from the clown army should

---

[388] Berger, *An Anatomy of Humor.* p. 51.
[389] Berger, *An Anatomy of Humor.* p. 48.
[390] Berger, *An Anatomy of Humor.* p. 19.

make them fit for military service is absurd. The whole episode is one big incongruity between military behaviour and expectations, and clowning behaviour and expectations.

The incongruity which Orange Alternative exposed was between the everyday life under communist rule and the propaganda of the regime. The technique they primarily relied on was absurdity, evoking images from people's childhood which were transformed into the socialist surrealism of the Alternative. Sometimes they also made *parodies* of communist slogans and ideology.

The role of the clown is familiar to a western audience: just the sight of red noses and other clowning paraphernalia increase expectations of being amused. Many people automatically shift to the play frame and expect certain behaviour.

The absurd stunt is not a direct confrontation, but an attempt to be an eye-opener. It is the type of stunt which is furthest away from protest, since it might just as well expose hierarchies, rigidity and domination within a protest movement. To the degree it is possible to talk about design at all with this type of stunt, it is designed to make people question everything they hear and see. The absurd stunt does not provide any answers, but questions dogmas.

The absurd stunts refuses rationality altogether, and in this tradition the activists respond to all reactions from those in power with further absurdity, as both CIRCA and the Orange Alternative did. When trying to give rational responses, the opponent finds herself confronted with even more silliness and absurdity, with the world turned upside down. The only thing predictable is that the performers will continue to be unpredictable. All attempts to deal with this as conventional political opposition will only contribute new components to their absurd plays. However, since the absurd is bound to remain within the absurd, it cannot suggest alternatives and improvements without

leaving its position. If the participants in an absurd stunt suddenly should decide to suggest solutions to a problem in a rational
way, they leave themselves vulnerable to critique that they are
(mis)using the absurdity for their own purposes, and not ready to
criticise all and everyone.

CIRCA in the recruitment office appeared where there were
already other actors performing their own play. Unlike prime
ministers and gatherings with many politicians, recruiting officers
are not even used to the usual role of protesters appearing in
their daily show. The recruiters felt forced to shut down the
recruitment office and get someone to carry the clowns away.
The daily show had been successfully interrupted from CIRCA's
point of view, but police and military insisted on treating them as
ordinary protesters and removing them from the scene. This
episode did not generate big headlines, presumably because the
police and military description of them as ordinary protesters
was accepted. The description and video of the episode is available to everyone who is interested, but CIRCA did not force
themselves upon a scene with world leaders, and as soon as the
clowns were removed they could be ignored. However, clowns
appearing at every recruitment office every day for an extended
period of time would probably be a different story.

Through their happenings, Orange Alternative took their play
right into the everyday life of the Polish people. Just like CIRCA,
Orange Alternative depended very little on what others did. Any
reaction, also being ignored, contributed one way or the other.
In these two examples, everyone who came along – police,
passers-by, recruiting officers - was treated as partners in the
show. Accounts of these two examples include some descriptions on reactions from part of the audience, the authorities.
Both the Orange Alternative and CIRCA expected to be removed from the scene by the police. However, these arrests just
added to the absurdity that the activists apparently attempted to
point towards. After all, clowns and elves should hardly pose any
threat to a communist regime and the military. These absurd

stunts did not depend on any particular timing – the recruitment office could have been visited any day to the same effect, and the Orange Alternative could always find an excuse for a happening, although its particular design could be fitted to the circumstances.

Provocative Humorous Stunts

Provocative humorous stunts are the type of stunt closest to conventional protest since they generate their humour simply by daring to directly confront those in power, usually without the pretence that is so central to the other stunts. The pranksters do not deny the unequal relations of power as in absurd stunts or present any alternatives like the supportive or corrective stunts; they simply appear not to care. In this way they amuse and impress parts of their audiences with their boldness and devil-may-care attitudes. The "almighties" become ridiculous when they turn out not to have total control anyway. The activists openly act as provocateurs in order to expose vulnerabilities and hurt big egos. They capture any scene, openly or secretly, and aim to control it long enough to humiliate the target. They speak a message of lack of fear both to the target and to other audiences. Three examples from Serbia, Russia and Belarus illustrate what humorous provocations can look like when the secret police forces are insulted and teddy bears fall from the sky.

Otpor: Dinar za Smenu

Earlier Serbian students' action to donate blood was mentioned as an example of a naive stunt. A few years later, the youth and student-led movement *Otpor*, which played a decisive role in bringing Slobodan Milošević from power, carried on the tradition of humorous political stunts. One of Otpor's popular actions was mocking an initiative taken by Milošević's government. To support agriculture, Milošević placed boxes in shops and public places asking people to donate one *dinar* (the Serbian currency) for sowing and planting crops. As a response, Otpor arranged its own collection called *Dinar za Smenu. Smenu* is a Serbian word with many meanings: *Change, resignation, dismissal, pension* and *purge*. This action was repeated several times in different places in Serbia, and consisted of a big barrel with a photo of Milošević, a stick and instructions for passers-by to use the stick to hit the barrel after donating one dinar. On at least one occasion, the sign suggested that if people did not have any money because of Milošević's politics, they should bang the barrel twice. Another day it suggested to hit harder. Usually there were no activists present, something which decreased the risks. When the police removed the barrel, Otpor said in a press release that the police had arrested the barrel. They also claimed that the action was a huge success, because they had collected enough money for Milošević's retirement, and that the police were going to hand over the money to Milošević.[391]

President Milošević himself, as the prime symbol of bad government in Serbia, was the target in this example. Although the action did not make much sense on its own other than expressing hostile feelings towards Milošević, it was part of a larger campaign to de-legitimize the regime in Serbia, expose its double standards and show how its politics was damaging to ordinary Serbian citizens. The regime had the choice between removing the barrel, and thereby exposing their intolerance to critique, or let it stay and continue a public display of disapproval.

Voina: Insulting bridge painting

In Russia, an art collective called *Voina* has made itself loved and infamous because of its creative stunts that expose Russian authorities. In June 2010, they painted a giant penis on Liteiny Bridge in St. Petersburg in just 23 seconds. Liteiny Bridge is a bascule bridge, and the action was done just before it was

---

[391] Sørensen, "Humour as Nonviolent Resistance to Oppression." Sombutpoonsiri, "The Use of Humour as a Vehicle for Nonviolent Struggle."

opened to let a ship pass. When that happened, the penis was standing erect for several hours just in front of the unpopular secret police (FSB) headquarters in St. Petersburg. Members of Voina are facing prison sentences for this and similar actions.[392]

Illustration 7. Voina's penis painting on Liteiny Bridge in St. Petersburg, June 2010. Courtesy of http://plucer.livejournal.com.

[392] Marina Galperina, "Why Russian Art Group Voina 'Dicked' a St. Petersburg Bridge," http://animalnewyork.com/2010/06/why-russian-art-group-voina-dicked-a-st-petersburg-bridge/; Nick Sturdee, "Don't Raise the Bridge: Voina, Russia's Art Terrorists," *The Guardian*, 12 April 2011.

The circumstances in authoritarian Russia make this different from performing the same stunt in a more democratic country.

Teddy bears over Belarus

In July 2012, a small airplane took off from Lithuania and flew over Belarus. On board were two Swedish PR management consultants turned human rights activists. The plane was loaded with 879 teddy bears each in a parachute and carrying the message "We support the Belarusian struggle for free speech" in English and Belarusian. The stunt was a response to naive stunts performed inside Belarus earlier in the year. Local activists from the campaign "Tell the Truth" had arranged stuffed animals at Minsk's Independence Square with little signs telling President Lukashenka to "free the people!", asking "Where is freedom of the press?" and saying "Toys against lawlessness" and "Cops tore my eye out."[393] One person, who says he was just watching the toys, was later sentenced to 10 days in prison for holding an unsanctioned toy protest.[394]

One of the Swedes who dropped teddy bears over Belarus in support of the stuffed animals said to a Norwegian TV station, "Our campaign was to support the teddy bears [in Belarus], from teddy bears all over the world".[395] To Euronews, he said "A dictator can be feared and he can be hated, but when people

---

[393] RFE/RL, "'Police Detain Stuffed Animals' in Minsk Toy Protest ". The toy protest was inspired by toy protests first carried out in the town Barnaul in Siberia in Russia in January 2012, where teddy bears, plastic figures and others toys carried anti Putin slogans and demanded freedom and respect for human rights. See Kupchinsky, "Toys for Democracy: In a Siberian City, Activists Find a Creative Way to Protest ".
[394] RFE/RL, "Belarusian 'Toy Protest' Inmate Goes on Hunger Strike " *rferl.org*, February 22 2012.
[395] Birger Henriksen, "Svensker Teddy-Bombet Hviterussland " [Swede teddy-bombed Belarus] *www.TV2.no*, August 2 2012.

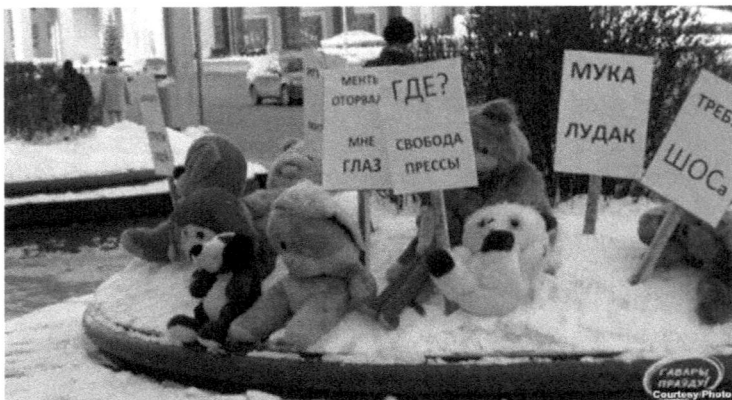

Illustration 8. Toy protest in Belarus. Courtesy photo.

Illustration 9. Teddy bears in parachutes landing in Belarus in support for human rights July 2012. Photo reprinted with permission from Studio Total.

start to laugh at him, his days are numbered. So, that was the objective."[396] He and his colleagues run *Studio Total*, a Swedish PR and marketing company. On its webpage, the company says that they did this pro bono in support of the Belarusian opposition, and tells how the PR consultants became interested in the fate of the Belarusian opposition by a coincidence. When it turned out that no pilot was willing to risk dropping the teddy bears, they decided to learn how to fly and bought a little airplane.[397]

Belarusian authorities first denied that the stunt had taken place, but soon said that it was a provocation. The stunt had direct consequences for high ranking officials and journalists in Belarus. The heads of border control and the air force were sacked,[398] and two people detained accused of assisting the Swedes and publishing photos of the teddy bears on the internet.[399] The affair also turned into a diplomatic crisis between Belarus, Sweden and other members of the European Union. Although the stunt was not mentioned specifically, shortly afterwards the Swedish ambassador to Belarus was expelled from Belarus and accused of having too close relations with the opposition. As a response, the new Belarusian ambassador to Sweden was no longer welcome.[400]

For this stunt, there is a little information available about Belarusian citizens' support for the event. The group *Independent Institute of Socio-Economic and Political Studies* made a survey shortly

[396] Euronews, "Swedish Activists Behind Belarus Teddy Bear Stunt," *euronews.com*, August 2 2012.
[397] Studio Total, "Why We Did It," http://www.studiototal.se/teddybears/why-we-did-it.html.
[398] Henriksen, "Svensker Teddy-Bombet Hviterussland ".
[399] Belarusian Human Rights House, "Two Belarusians Detained on Charges of "Teddy Bear Drop"," *humanrightshouse.org*, July 23 2012.
[400] Mats Carlbom, "Vitryssland Utvisar Sveriges Ambassadör," [Belarus expels Sweden's ambassador] *dn.se*, August 3 2012.

afterwards about Belarusian attitudes to Russia and the European Union which included the question: "In July a group of Swedish citizens made an unauthorized flight to Belarus and dropped teddy bears over Ivenets and Minsk with slogans that called for freedom of speech in Belarus. How do you evaluate this action?"[401] 1502 people were asked, and about one third replied that they did not know about the action, and 13.8% that it was a provocation by Western intelligence. 23%, almost one in four, considered it "a courageous protest against the violation of human rights". However, the largest group, 31.7% responded that "it was a silly action". This category is rather ambiguous and reflects the general problem with both academic and everyday understandings of humour mentioned previously. The categories in the survey are not mutually exclusive since it is quite possible to think it was a silly action and in addition consider it either a courageous protest or a provocation by Western intelligence. In spite of this methodological problem with the possible answers, the 23% that express a supportive attitude by accepting the word

---

[401] Independent Institute of Socio-Economic and Political Studies, "Teddy-Bear Landing – How the Belarusians Evaluated It," (Independent Institute of Socio-Economic and Political Studies, 2012). The Independent Institute of Socio-Economic and Political Studies describes itself this way: "Independent Institute of Socio-Economic and Political Studies (IISEPS) was established in February 1992 by group of academics, journalists, politicians and businessmen. Now IISEPS is registered as public institution in the Lithuanian Republic. IISEPS' mission is to promote formation of civil society and free market economy in Belarus through study socio-economic and political process of transition from totalitarianism to democracy and active promotion of values and principles of liberalism." Quote downloaded from http://www.iiseps.org/o_nisepi/lang/en September 3 2013. There is no apparent reason to doubt that the survey was not done using accepted survey methodology, but the reader should keep in mind that Belarus is a dictatorship and respondents might have been doubtful about revealing their attitudes to a stranger.

"courageous" can be understood as a relatively high level of support for the action.[402]

Variants of answer[403]	%
It was a silly action.	31.7
It was a courageous protest against the violation of human rights.	23.0
It was a provocation by Western intelligence.	13.8
I don't know what you are talking about.	31.2
Difficult to answer.	0.3

Confronting power with provocation

Applying Berger's techniques to these three provocative stunts, new techniques appear. In Otpor's Dinar za Smenu action five different techniques are present simultaneously. The action was both a *parody* and a *ridicule* of the government's campaign, as well as an insult. In addition, it used a *wordplay* on the word *smenu* with its multiple meanings. *Puns/wordplay* happens when one word can have more than one meaning. Such words differ from language to language, but in Serbian *smenu* is such a word. When the barrel was removed, the word play continued when Otpor activists said that Milošević had accepted the money and was now going to retire, playing on the *pension* meaning of smenu. The word play also contains an *allusion* to Milošević's retirement.

A technique used by Voina was the *grotesque*, in the form of an over dimensioned phallus. Placed on the rising bridge, it became

---

[402] Independent Institute of Socio-Economic and Political Studies, "Teddy-Bear Landing – How the Belarusians Evaluated It," p. 2.
[403] Adapted from Independent Institute of Socio-Economic and Political Studies, "Teddy-Bear Landing – How the Belarusians Evaluated It," p. 2, table 4.

a severe *insult* to the FSB. Berger explains that the grotesque can be both comic and scary, and that the framing of the grotesque determine our response. As with the other giant penis that the Yes Men used at the conference about the textile industry, this is a loaded sexual symbol. Under these circumstances it can hardly be interpreted as anything else than a provocation. Of course the Russian authorities had the option to ignore it, but taking their usual reactions to protest into consideration, it is doubtful that the option was considered.

Like the absurd stunt, the provocative stunt also refuses rationality. As described in the examples above, the provocative stunts display a devil-may-care attitude which causes amusement when the almighty, such as the Russian secret police, Belarusian or Serbian regimes, are shown to be unable to prevent such attacks right under their noses. Even those supposed to exert total control can be brought down from their pedestals.

Although the corrective, innocent, constructive and absurd stunts are confrontational as well, the provocative stunts appear to depend especially on whether the audiences recognise the irreverent attitude of the activists. Therefore it is no surprise that the technique of insulting is present in two of the provocative examples.

From sympathetic bystanders, provocative activists get a "wow, how courageous". However, many other nonviolent actions can generate that feeling without being humorous at all. For instance, the *Freedom Flotillas* that in 2010 and 2011 attempted to break the Israeli blockade of Gaza were also considered bold actions. In 2010, nine activists were killed during this attempt to bring humanitarian aid to Gaza. The convoy was attacked by Israeli soldiers while it was still in International waters.[404] *The Plough-*

---

[404] Majken Jul Sørensen and Brian Martin, "The Dilemma Action: Analysis of an Activist Technique," *Peace & Change* 39 no. 1 (2014).

shares is another example of a nonviolent movement that has not involved any humour and might be considered courageous by some. Using hammers as a symbolic reference to the Bible verse of turning swords into ploughshares, they enter arms factories and military areas in Europe and the US in order to start the disarmament process themselves. Afterwards they await the police. Especially in the US, these actions have resulted in long prison terms, causing numerous people within the peace movement to understand these acts as bold and courageous.[405] They are also provocative, but not humorous at all, so there is more to the provocative humorous stunt than boldness and courage.

What makes the provocative stunts different are the initiators' attitude towards those they attack, and their expectations of reactions. The Freedom Flotilla movement and the ploughshare activists care a great deal about the reactions of states and companies and thereby indirectly recognise their power and the rationality they represent. Although their actions use much symbolism, they are not just a performance and their approach to their opponents is rational. In contrast, the participants in a provocative stunt do not appear to be concerned about the power of the institutions they attack at all and deny them their claims to rationality. The provocative stunts do not seem to have any other purpose than to provoke and communicate to a large audience: "We do not care very much about potential consequences." The actions by Voina, Studio Total and Otpor tease and humiliate the target with the message "You are not that powerful after all, because we can do this right under your nose, and we refuse to be scared of you." And to the wider audience it adds "Why are you so scared?" "See, they just pretend to be powerful! Why do you believe that?" With this refusal to be intimidated they contribute to transcending the rationality of the so-called powerful. When someone finally says that the emperor

---

[405] Sharon Erickson Nepstad, *Religion and War Resistance in the Plowshares Movement* (New York: Cambridge University Press, 2008).

227

has no clothes, people's fear may start to decrease. In addition some of these stunts include other humorous techniques, such as the parodies and wordplays in Otpor's Dinar za Smenu action, and the absurdity and naïveté in the Belarusian case.

The case with dropping teddy bears over Belarus is a little different from the other two examples. It is certainly provocative, but because the Swedes behind it are not a local activist group that has to continue working inside Belarus, the edge of "we don't care" is not so sharp as in the other provocative stunts. Although there was a risk involved, as soon as their plane left Belarus they were safe, meaning that the typical statement of "what are you afraid of?" to the audience was lost. People who live in Belarus would have reason to be afraid if they had done this. Just publishing the photos on the internet got one blogger in trouble.[406] The way the humour is generated in this example is also different from the other provocative stunts where what causes amusement is ridicule and insults. Although the authorities are insulted, the stunt would not have been humorous if the Swedes had just violated the airspace to show that they could. It is the teddy bears – a symbol of naïveté – that causes amusement when they parachute to Belarus in an absurd show of solidarity from the teddy bears around the world.

The provocative stunt does not attempt to appear as a serious threat to those in power – from a rational point of view what authoritarian state leader would be scared because someone drops teddy bears, paints a giant penis or shows contempt by hitting a photo of them? After all, they have armed police and military troops ready to back them up. Nevertheless, that authorities bother to react can be interpreted as a sign that these types of humorous stunts are indeed considered threatening. One can

---

[406] Belarusian Human Rights House, "Two Belarusians Detained on Charges of "Teddy Bear Drop"."

understand them as kind of *guerrilla attack*, but not a violent physical attack. Instead they are attacking the dominant discourse as part of the *discursive guerrilla war*.[407] With this concept I mean to say that if one believes Foucault to be right when he claimed that the most important way of dominating a society is through discourse, then it also follows that an important way to resist is by combatting dominant discourses. All humorous political stunts can be understood from this perspective, but the attack is perhaps the most obvious in the provocative stunts.

The provocative stunt is the least friendly and dialogue oriented type of stunt. The laughter it generates is not based on wittiness and inclusiveness, but on establishing a clear we and they divide, where "the other" can be mocked and ridiculed. Although it happens without violence and against violence, there is no aspect of the type of nonviolence that aims to include the opponents and win them over.

Stunts overlapping different categories

This typology of five different kinds of humorous political stunts divides the examples according to the way the pranksters relate to the power holders' rationality and claims to truth. In some cases, it is possible to identify traces from more than one type of stunt in work at the same time. Where this is the case, I have included them in the type of stunt which is most prominent. For instance, I have placed the Polish TV walkers in the naive category, because naiveté is the most crucial aspect in their way of relating to the authorities. However, it does have some absurd

---

[407] The inspiration for the term is Pi-Sunyer, "Political Humor in a Dictatorial State: The Case of Spain." Pi-Sunyer refers to "oral guerrilla warfare" that everyone could participate in during the Franco dictatorship in Spain. However, with the term "discursive guerrilla warfare" I want to emphasise not just that everyone can contribute to resistance, but that the whole issue of what is true, right and just is at stake.

elements as well with the TV's in the strollers in the street. In the Yes Men's hijacking of the WTO the corrective aspects of the stunt were most dominant. However, the *Management Leisure Suit* that they introduced was also a way to "help" managers keep better track of their workers, and the outfit was rather absurd, showing traces of the supportive and absurd stunt as well. The dropping of teddy bears over Belarus in support for the opposition was mainly a provocative stunt, but did also include absurd and naïve elements – the teddy bears are naïve, and the idea of them protesting and showing solidarity is rather absurd.

One stunt in particular that I have come across is difficult to place in only one category. A performance by the comedians from *The Chaser* team during an APEC meeting in Australia in 2007 draws on aspects from both the corrective and supportive stunt.

In 2007, the Asia-Pacific Economic Co-operation (APEC) held a summit in Australia. Representatives from the 21 member states gathered for a week in Sydney for *Leaders week*. Many heads of state participated, and security in downtown city was supposed to be tight. Official figures show a cost of 170 million Australian dollars for security arrangements.[408] The popular comedy team The Chaser and their TV show *The Chaser's War on Everything* decided to do a stunt to ridicule the security arrangements, although they had been warned not to do it.[409] Posing as Canadian participants in the summit, they made it through several security checkpoints with their motorcade of three black limousines and a motorcycle. Their ID cards were stamped with the word *joke* clearly visible. When they arrived ten metres outside

---

[408] Jim Dickins, "APEC Security to Cost $24m a Day "
http://www.news.com.au, June 3 2007.
[409] David Braithwaite, "Chaser Bust 'Proves Security Success'," *The Age (Melbourne)*, September 6 2007

Intercontinental Hotel where the US participants were staying, a Chaser team member dressed as Osama Bin Laden stepped out of one of the cars and said to the police "I'm a world leader. Why haven't I been invited to APEC too?"

Julian Morrow who directed the stunt later said: "It was an attempt to satirise in a silly way the very heavy security and the spin surrounding that security. It was a test of the old adage that if you want to get in somewhere the best way is right through the front door."[410]

Australian authorities refused to be amused and charged the team with offences under the new security laws. In Australia the action caused much debate, and later all charges were dropped. The rationale was that when the police did not stop the comedy team at the checkpoint, it had given "tacit" permission for them to be in the restricted zone. The Chasers have themselves said that they were surprised by their own success. When they planned the stunt, they had prepared for every possible scenario along the way, except this. They have also claimed to have regretted the prank, saying that it was stupid and went too far.[411]

The Chaser's stunt was a *ridicule* of the whole APEC summit, especially the security arrangements. Talking about security is absurd if it is possible for someone who looks like the world's most wanted man to pass security check points with an ID card stamped *joke*. In this case, the target of the ridicule was not a particular person, but absurd security arrangements around a summit of world leaders. Since the Australian authorities were responsible for security, they were the ones who ended up humiliated.

---

[410] Paul Bibby, "Chaser Comics Say APEC Stunt Went Too Far," *The Age (Melbourne)*, September 12 2007.
[411] Bibby, "Chaser Comics Say APEC Stunt Went Too Far."

Members of the The Chaser team do not consider themselves political activists, but are professional comedians ready to ridicule everyone and everything.[412] However, no matter what their intentions were, the message of the action is a critique of the security hysteria, and forces its audience to ask questions like: When people speak about security, what is it they expect will create a safe environment – and for whom? Just for world leaders, or for everyone? Why are some people's lives considered worth more than others? How to create a world where everyone is safe? How can fences and weapons which separate people instead of uniting them bring more safety?

The comedy team used their professional characters to make a stunt. The incident became widely known because they brought their TV crew with them and it later became part of their TV show. Almost three million viewers watched this episode of the show.[413]

The stunt is difficult to place in the typology of humorous political stunts. The way they hijacked the identity of bin Laden resembles the hijacking of identities for corrective purposes, but although they suggest that bin Laden ought to have been invited as well since he was a world leader, this was not their message. The other corrective stunts have a serious intent in their correction, but no one really thought that the Chaser's cared if bin Laden was present or not. Neither did they sneak in on the scene as is one of the characteristics of the corrective stunt; they invaded the major scene in Sydney, right in the face of the authorities. This is more closely related to the provocative stunt. The way they made their way through the security arrangements

---

[412] McIntyre, *How to Make Trouble and Influence People*: p. 10.
Braithwaite, "Chaser Bust 'Proves Security Success'."
[413] Matthew Ricketson, "Chaser Ratings Rocket on APEC Antics," *The Age (Melbourne)*, September 13 2007.

with an identity card stamped *joke* brings the absurd to mind, and the provocative aspect of the stunt might warrant a place in the provocative category. However, it did not have the element of "what are you afraid of?" that the other provocative stunts have. That the Chaser's stunt is ambiguous and does not fit in the typology might be a reflection that the Chaser's do not really have a political message apart from ridiculing the security arrangements.

There is nothing in this typology preventing activists from combining aspects from the different types of stunts and having overlaps. However, in most cases there is an internal logic within each type, and the stunts dilute their meanings if this coherence is abandoned. The rebel clowns don't suddenly explain rationally what the clowning is about, and John Howard's Fan club do not step out of character to announce "we don't really mean this".

The APEC stunt showed that it was quite easy to challenge security arrangements, and afterwards this became the main issue. A real Osama Bin Laden with bad intention could have caused a lot of damage, so the stunt easily plays into the hands of the advocates of even more security.

The diversity of humorous political stunts

As one would expect, context matters a lot for understanding humour. Language and political situation are probably two of the most important circumstances. Hearing about people who take their TV for a walk during the news broadcasting make little sense if one is not aware of the political situation in Poland at the time and know about the appeal for a boycott of the TV news. Serbian word plays need explanation in order to become comprehensible for non-Serbian speakers. That context matters might sound obvious, but comedians, activists or anyone else aiming to produce humour need to take into consideration what the intended audience knows in advance – especially if an international audience is involved. Likewise, awareness about cultural

233

differences regarding what are acceptable objects of humour matter for everyone aiming to produce humorous political stunts.

There seems to be no limit to the mediums available for political humour. Everything from a lecture, a bridge, a double door, or a shopping centre opens up possibilities for the creative prankster. It is also likely that the more creative the use of the medium is, the more attention one will get. Most of the examples presented here were communicated via mass media – if not to the whole world, then at least to a national audience. But even in times with less media attention, local messages can have an effect if many people participate. The numerous Polish TV-walkers got their message across. The Danish anti-Nazi writing on double doors were apparently a one-time only experiment from a creative butcher. But had it been used systematically in half the shops in occupied Denmark, who knows what would have happened?

When a medium is unusual or is used creatively there is a risk that the medium receives more attention than the issue the actionists want to raise awareness about. The Chaser's APEC stunt put more focus on them being in the restricted area than on the reason for establishing such a zone. A similar observation can be made regarding the Yes Men on the BBC as a Dow representative – the discussion ended up being about how Yes Men created false hope for the victims of the disaster, not about the company's responsibilities for cleaning up and compensating victims.

Some individuals have easier access to mass media than others. Professional comedians already have an established platform that they can use for political humour. Some of them use this platform to make fun of all dogmatism no matter who is behind it, whereas others have an agenda. Joanne Gilbert in her writing on women stand-up comedians suggests that "true believers" in any cause will never be able to joke about what they believe to be right because they take it too seriously.[414] Although the Chaser's might agree with Gilbert, and some people might choose not to joke about what is most sacred to them, there is little doubt that the majority of the activists presented here are dedicated to seriously challenging their targets and that their style appeals to many people's sense of humour.[415]

The examples I have given above all carry a message that I personally support. As Peter Berger writes, "Those who laugh together, belong together"[416], and that people laugh more at humour expressing political messages they support than ones they disagree with should be no surprise. Nevertheless, what people appreciate also depends on what techniques are used, and what kind of techniques they prefer. Most people can find things funny if they recognise the stereotype they are based on or because they like certain techniques without agreeing with the message of a piece of political humour.[417]

---

[414] Gilbert, *Performing Marginality*: p. 179.
[415] Over the years I have shared many of the examples in this chapter with numerous students at workshops and in university courses. In spite of my limited skills as a performer the stories have never failed to cause laughter and amusement. However, not everyone has found everything amusing.
[416] Berger, *Redeeming Laughter*: p. 57.
[417] A personal example: Shortly after I had decided on the theme for my thesis, but before I had read the classics about humour theory, I stumbled upon an article in a Norwegian newspaper about the Tea Party in the US. Together with the article came a photo of a Tea Party activist carrying a homemade poster which said "I'll keep my Guns, Freedom & money – You can Keep the 'Change'". See Martin Burcharth, "Krampetrekning Før Valget," [Dying twitch before election] *Klassekampen*, October 30 2010. I disagree with the politics of the Tea Party movement in the US, but I did laugh loudly at the wordplay on the word "change", a word used numerous times by President Obama in his election campaign.

Humorous political stunts and the play of politics

Humorous stunts are games of pretence, interpretation and appearance. They operate within a play frame, and depend on establishing a resonance with one or more audiences that this is humorous, and that ambiguity and multiple meanings and interpretations are acceptable. Nevertheless, the play frame and humour do not mean that stunts are not serious, in some cases even deadly serious for the people involved. Some of the games are played with regimes such as the Nazi occupiers which did not hesitate to kill those who dared challenge their version of truth. The examples provided here point to the need to question the idea within humour studies that the contrast to the humorous is the serious. Humorous stunts are just one method in a larger struggle which is not playful at all. What is at stake is a question of life/death; of democracy/dictatorship; of censorship/freedom of speech.

The humorous political stunts illustrate a shortcoming with a purely technical approach to understanding why something is funny. Although one or more of the techniques described by Berger could be found in most of the aforementioned cases, the techniques were not sufficient to explain the political context the stunts are an integrated part of. In particular the provocative and naïve types do not make sense from a purely technical point of view. Humorous stunts are so much part of a power struggle that one cannot fully understand them without analysing them within their context.

My model with a classification of five different types of stunts provides a starting point for analysing how pranksters relate to those they confront. The essential aspect of this typology is the way the activists present themselves and position the different stunts in relation to the rationality, logic and claims to truth that the different representatives of power aim to uphold in this play of politics. The purpose of including so many examples has been to illustrate that there can be much diversity also within each type of stunt, although each one still depends on the same logic.

In reviewing the different theories of humour, I mentioned how the incongruity tradition is today considered the most important theoretical perspective when explaining what causes amusement. The humorous political stunts fit well within this theory. In these examples, the incongruities that cause the audiences to smile and laugh are closely connected to the relations of power. Those who consider these episodes funny are likely to enjoy watching the pranksters from the minority position outsmarting the apparently powerful and almighty companies, governments, institutions and agencies. A reason for the enjoyment is for a short while seeing the roles turned upside down and the established relations of power challenged. At least temporarily, these representatives of vested interests with so much money and/or force at their disposal are brought down to earth by a few clever activists.

More specific incongruities can also be identified. In the example of the John Howard Ladies' Auxiliary Fan Club there is an incongruity connected to the use of irony. The fan club members present two incompatible statements of critique and celebration at the same time. Returning to Mark Thomas and his exposure of the Indonesian military officer, there is an enormous incongruity between the seriousness of the human rights abuses he uncovered and the relaxation exercises he convinced Major General Widjojo to perform. The Yes Men at the textile conference made an incongruous presentation where the apparently serious message of the presentation did not correspond with the absurd outfit.

As mentioned earlier, the cases included here are not representative. However, a hypothesis that can be tested by future research is whether the same five strategies for dealing with power holders through humorous stunts are relevant in a variety of cultural contexts.

237

Type	Description	Position in relation to dominant discourse	Theatre metaphor
Supportive	Activists appear supportive and pretend to support, celebrate, help, protect from harm etc, but stunt is a way of invalidating the target	Exaggerate the dominant discourse, play along with it, overemphasise it	Pranksters invade any scene right in the face of the power holders
Corrective	Activists appear rational but hijack the identity or message of their target in order to reveal a correction	Exaggerate the dominant discourse, play along with it, overemphasise it	Pranksters invade a scene usually controlled by the power holders, hold it temporarily behind power holders' backs in order to reveal a correction
Naive	Activists appear naive and innocent and pretend not to understand that their action can be interpreted as a protest	Appear not to understand dominant discourse	Pranksters sneak in on any stage
Absurd	Activists appear as innocent clowns but point towards absurdities	Ignore dominant discourse altogether	Pranksters get on stage by capturing it, invading it or sneaking in, in power holders' face or behind their backs
Provocative	Activists openly act as provocateurs in order to expose vulnerabilities	Don't care about dominant discourse	Pranksters capture or invade any scene

Statement to power holders	Statement to audience	Dominant humorous techniques	Relation to non-humorous protest	Examples
We join you on the scene to invalidate and disconfirm you, beware that we watch you and are ready to expose you	See who they really are	Irony, parody, unmasking	Opposite of conventional protest, celebration rather than protest	John Howard Ladies' Auxiliary Fan Club, Search for landmines at AXA
We hijack your scene to show you that we watch you, and reveal your true colours to others	See who they really are	Unmasking	Conventional protest also attempt to control the stage	Yes Men as DOW representative on BBC
Sorry, was that wrong? We did not know there was a play going on	Look at them	Pretended coincidence	No apparent protest	Otpor's donation of blood, Danish butcher's van door
Let's all play together in this absurd world	The world is absurd, including the apparently powerful	Absurdity, slapstick	No apparent protest	Orange Alternative CIRCA
Fuck you. This is our scene too, and now we control it	What are you afraid of?	Ridicule, insult	Obvious protest	Voina's penis on bridge, Otpor's Dinar za Smenu

Table 2. (previous pages) A schematic overview of five different types of stunts.

In all examples, pretence is a central element, since no one wants to play the ordinary protester on the stage of the political theatre. These five types of stunts represent different ways of undermining dominant discourses and thereby transforming the play of politics, at least temporarily. They attempt to disrupt, subvert or transform relations of power because they highlight the contradictions and weaknesses of the dominant discourse, using a format that is recognisable and accepted as humorous.

Table 2 is an expanded version of table 1. In addition to the columns of description, position in relation to dominant discourse and dominant humorous techniques which were included in table 2, the table now includes a summary of the theatre metaphor, the "statement" that the stunt can be understood to make to power holders as well as other audiences. Finally, in the last column I have suggested some examples of each stunt that can be said to be typical and show all the characteristics of this particular type of stunt.

Both the supportive and corrective stunts position themselves as rational and logical, but exaggerate, play along with and overemphasise the discourse of those in power. In the corrective stunt, this is done by hijacking the message or the identity of the target, whereas in the supportive stunt identification with the target to help and support is the key. The supportive stunt happens right in the face of the powerful, while a characteristic of the corrective stunt it that it usually happens behind the power holders' back. In these two types of stunts the messages to the audiences are also similar – to expose the powerful and show who they really are. On the surface both the supportive and corrective stunts appear as if their statements should be taken at face value. But that is only at first glance. After that initial apparent acceptance of the discourse of the powerful, they base their challenge to power on the moment where the audiences must ask themselves if this is meant to be taken literally, or if someone is joking. Although this is an area that has not been studied yet, the people who carry out these stunts assume that something important happens in that moment of uncertainty. When a reader or viewer asks herself "is this serious? Do they really mean this?", the perception is that she is more open to new information and new perspectives. When political arguments are presented rationally using traditional ways of disseminating information such as leaflets, posters and speeches, most people meet the arguments with an already formed opinion. However, humour can provide a cognitive "detour" or a "psychological circuit breaker" creating this moment of openness. If that moment will really change a person's view and deepen the insight depends on a number of factors, but at least there appear to be a possibility for getting the audience to re-examine its assumptions.

The naïve, absurd and provocative stunts each has a different way of relating to the discourse of those they aim to challenge. Those performing naïve stunts appear not to understand that what they do can be interpreted as a challenge of anyone's rationality, whereas the absurd pranksters defy rationality altogether. Initiators of provocative stunts seem not care about the rationality and logic of the powerful at all.

In both the absurd and naïve stunts the pranksters appear as innocent clowns. In the absurd stunts, those who carry them out can partly protect themselves from prosecution because there is usually little logic to what they do. This possibility is not available to those performing a naïve stunt, since there is usually a logic behind their naiveté which can be disclosed. It is not the mistakes of the authorities which cause laughter, because they are not fooled, but the daring to challenge and hide behind the innocence which appeals to friendly audiences. This boldness is something the naïve stunt has in common with the provocative, but they differ in how they display their courage. Whereas the

241

provocateurs of the provocative stunt seem not to care, the innocent appear not to understand.

Through the theatre metaphor, other differences between the stunts become visible. In the supportive stunt, the pranksters invade any scene right in the face of the power holders in order to show their apparent support. For this type of stunt, there would be no point in hiding away, and they are depending on the sharing of the scene with the representatives of the dominant discourse. If the power holders are not there, they cannot offer their help, support and protection. If the political situation makes it too dangerous or too difficult to invade a scene right in the face of the power holders, potential pranksters can consider trying other types of stunts. In the corrective stunt, the pranksters also aim for a scene usually controlled by the power holders. However, in order to display the correction that they want to communicate, they depend on capturing and holding this scene for a while. In order to do this, they calculate on not being discovered or removed from the scene for as long as it takes to generate the confusion about whether this is a joke or not.

A characteristic of several naïve stunts are that the pranksters sneak in on the stage and display their message more or less in secret; if they did it openly it would rather be a provocative stunt. However, the Santas are an exception since the logic of their stunt depended on the gifts being given away openly. In their case, the naïveté was generated by the use of the mythological Father Christmas figure. For the absurd stunts, there is no specific scene to aim for, and the absurd performers can stage their play anywhere. Everyone who happens to be present or show up will become part of the absurdities. Depending on the situation and what point they want to make, they can be bold and invade a scene, or they can sneak in on the stage and remain discreet until it suits them to reveal themselves. A characteristic of the provocative stunt is that the provocateurs attempt to capture or invade a scene as loudly as possible; it would be a contradiction if they tried to be discreet.

The audiences to the humorous political stunts are numerous. They can include the target/butt of the prank, media, people on the scene, random passers-by and other activists. Sometimes those who initiate a stunt have a specific audience in mind, but most of the stunts presented here appear to have the general public as their main target and the aim is to encourage a critical perspective on the dominant discourse. In many of the stunts the initiators deliberately aim to blur the line between audiences and performers. Everyone who happened to be present on the street when Orange Alternative staged their happenings became part of the event. The employees at the AXA bank and the visitors to the arms fair in Greece became unwilling main characters in the shows when Netwerk Vlaanderen and Mark Thomas showed up with their land mine clearance team and PR training.

Within social movement research there has been much focus on how activists frame their activities and messages, but relatively little is known about how audiences actually perceive it. From media studies it is well known that audiences are not "empty vessels" waiting to be filled with propaganda, but actively interpret what they see and hear depending on their own previous knowledge, experience and expectations.

Whether audiences accept something as humorous is not straightforward and self-evident. There is a struggle over what meaning to attribute to what is said or done, and the outcome depends on the context, as Palmer has pointed out.[418] The example from the Yes Men at the textile conference in Finland showed that humour is a fragile thing. With the original conference audience, the stunt was a complete failure. Not until the film reached a different audience was it recognised as humour. Palmer does not say that the butt of the joke or prank has to

---

[418] Palmer, *Taking Humour Seriously*.

agree that something is funny, but either the situation demands or the audience agrees that this was humorous. When audiences are moved from the rational mode to the humorous mode, they laugh. Laughter has the potential to undermine the dominant discourse, when it changes the scene of the political play so much that the ordinary play is temporarily disrupted. So far, no one has interrupted the play permanently, but that does not mean it cannot be done.

That protesters manage to interrupt the ordinary play of politics so much that they take over the scene is not unusual. This happened in Seattle in 1999, when the neo-liberal discourse was under attack and the WTO meeting was disrupted by 60,000 protesters. Many aspects of these protests had a carnivalesque atmosphere, for instance the 250 *turtle people* who contributed to reducing potential violence.[419] However, from the point of view of the WTO, these 60,000 still performed the usual protester roles; they just got out of control. And as long as most of the activists frame their actions as protest, this image will not be changed by a minority of clowns, Santas and turtles.

In most of the examples provided here, the situation is different from conventional protest because of the pretence that this is not a protest. The disruption through pretence opens up possibilities for transformation rather than opposition. Maybe except for the provocative stunt, the use of humour means that it is much more difficult for representatives of the dominant discourse to frame these actions as ordinary protest, although they certainly try and frequently succeed. Since non-protesting protesters cannot easily be categorised with the other protesters, the show on the scene is interrupted in a different way. The fan club was not protesting Howard's politics, they were celebrating him. The Yes Men did not disrupt WTO meetings, they just clarified

---

[419] Bruner, "Carnivalesque Protest and the Humorless State."

WTO's neoliberal position. The Polish TV walkers did not strike or march in a demonstration, they just took their TVs for a walk at a certain time. CIRCA did not say that war was wrong, they just wanted to contribute with their skills in the army as well. Therefore they did not fit into the ordinary play called "dominant discourse tolerates protest."

But what is different? The humorous techniques bring in new ideas on the stage, and if they cannot be considered part of the usual show, something else has to happen. Actors cannot continue playing Shakespeare when someone appears on the stage performing a children's play. Then they either have to stop playing and wait for security to remove the new actors, or improvise a completely new play.

The borders of the humorous political stunt

There is a close relationship between the concepts of culture jamming, pranking, creative activism and tactical carnival presented in chapter 1 and the humorous political stunt. Some of the examples provided by authors who write about these concepts obviously fit within the definition of humorous political stunts. There is especially a big overlap between culture jamming and the type of humorous political stunts I have called corrective. Åsa Wettergren considers fun and humour key ingredients in the culture jammer's resistance towards late capitalism's commodification of feelings. In culture jamming there is an emphasis on *creating* pleasure which is opposed to the pleasures that consumerism can buy.[420] The Adbusters version of the obsession ad mentioned in chapter 1 becomes a humorous political stunt when it is placed in public places. However, in Wettergren's definition it is not a requirement that culture jamming is humorous, and she restricts it to anti-corporate forms of

---

[420] Åsa Wettergren, "Fun and Laughter: Culture Jamming and the Emotional Regime of Late Capitalism," *Social Movement Studies* 8, no. 1 (2009).

protest.[421] That excludes the anti-militarist and regime-critical stunts included above.

Much of what takes place as part of the tactical carnival is humorous, but funny slogans, songs and posters generally lack the confrontational aspect that cannot be ignored which is required for something to be a humorous political stunt. Neither do they include a deception that blurs the line between the artists and the audiences.

The notions of culture jamming and tactical carnival were invented to investigate something other than relations of power and are not first and foremost concerned with how activists challenge power by positioning themselves humorously in relation to the rationality of dominant discourses. Figure 1 schematically sums up the relationship between the humorous political stunt and other concepts. It shows the overlap between culture jamming and the corrective stunts. All the types of humorous political stunts are placed within the circle *creative activism* which is a much broader concept. The two boxes to the left illustrate that the mediums for communicating political humour and the techniques used to generate amusement are independent of the humorous political stunts.

Political humour comes in many different forms, and much of it is not humorous political stunts in spite of it being both amusing and political. As mentioned in the beginning of the chapter, I have intentionally been clear about what I consider the core of the definition and the *ideal type* of a humorous political stunt and included examples that are indisputably included in the definition. On the other hand I have deliberately chosen to be vaguer about the borders in order for future research of the margins to

---

[421] Wettergren, "Fun and Laughter: Culture Jamming and the Emotional Regime of Late Capitalism," p. 2.

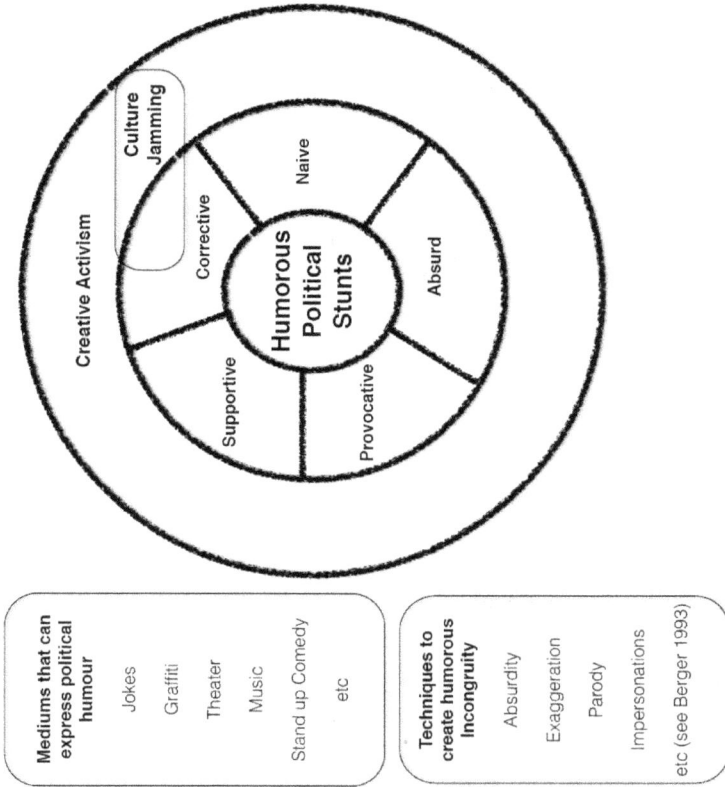

Figure 1. The relationship between the humorous political stunt and other concepts.

be able to bring new insights to the phenomenon. This section discusses some of the borders and grey zones using a few examples: political jokes told in public; theatre; and graffiti.

In some places and contexts, comedians perform at great risk to their own freedom, and just the telling of a joke in public becomes a political act. On several occasions, Burmese comedians who have criticised the military regime have been imprisoned. One of the most well-known is Zarganar (which is a stage name that translates as "tweezers"). Even from prison, Zarganar's jokes spread to the community. The prison guards enjoyed them, and passed them on to other people.[422] An example of a joke Zarganar's friend Htein Lin told to a visitor concerns electricity. Burma regularly has power cuts, but according to the official newspapers there is no shortage of power, and the opening of new power plants is regularly celebrated. So the story goes:

> Htein Lin once shared a house with Zarganar. One day they visited a teashop, run by another former political prisoner. As they drank tea, Zarganar told Htein Lin about a friend who had died. "That's terrible," said Htein Lin. The teashop owner overheard. "Poor guy," he said, "what happened?" Zarganar replied: "He touched a newspaper and was electrocuted".[423]

The punch line here makes a Burmese audience laugh, but can be puzzling to outsiders. The point is that the only way Burmese people get in touch with electricity is through the newspapers.

Other comedians have also had trouble with the military junta in Burma. *The Moustache Brothers* is a trio where two members have served several years in prison for their political humour. Now they only perform in their own home, where foreign tourists can watch the show and bring their criticism to the outside world. An example of their humour is this:

> Lu Maw is in pain. A toothache has robbed him of food, sleep and sanity; only a health professional can bring relief. Summoning the last of his strength he escapes across the Burmese border to Thailand, hoping that there he'll

---

[422]Anonymous, "Burmese Humour,"
http://www.freezarganar.org/Burmese-humour.asp.
[423] Anonymous, "Burmese Humour".

find the treatment he desperately needs. Finally Lu Maw finds a clinic. The dentist is perplexed. "Why have you come this far?" he asks. "Surely they have dentists in Burma." "Sure they do," replies Lu Maw, his face stretching to a grin. "But in Burma we're not allowed to open our mouths".[424]

Although clearly political and humorous, these jokes from Burma are not humorous political stunts even when they are performed in public. The element of deception which blurs the line between performers and audience or is too confrontational to be ignored is missing. That comedians perform is courageous and obviously confrontational, but the humour is not generated by the confrontation of doing a show, but the content in the show. It is what they say from the stage which is funny, not being on the stage.

Another arena for professional satire has been the theatre. Italian playwright and performer Dario Fo does not perform stunts the way I have defined them here, but his theatre production during half a century is obviously political. It is firmly grounded in a tradition of *carnivalesque subversion*,[425] but concerned with serious subjects such as rape, war and police repression. His use of the comic to explore these issues caused many to be surprised when he in 1997 was awarded the Nobel Prize for literature.[426] During years of writing and performing he has been condemned by both the communist party in Italy and the Catholic Church. Fo's work has been dominated by a concern for the poor and downtrodden and aimed at exposing the establishment.[427] He is especially

[424] Stephen Gray, "The Mustache Brothers," *thanassiscambanis.com* not dated.
[425] Antonio Scuderi, "Unmasking the Holy Jester Dario Fo," *Theatre Journal* 55, no. 2 (2003): p. 284.
[426] Scuderi, "Unmasking the Holy Jester Dario Fo," p. 286.
[427] Domenico Maceri, "Dario Fo: Jester of the Working Class," *World Literature Today* 72, no. 1 (1998).

concerned with restoring people's pride in their folk culture and is inspired by Bakhtin's work on carnival and Gramsci's work on hegemony. The process of hegemony devalues folk culture and make what is considered "culture" reflect the oppressor's view of the world.[428] Fo's performances and plays include both one man farces where Fo plays all the roles himself, and more traditional plays staging several actors.

An example of the later is "The Accidental Death of an Anarchist" which is a farce based on real events in Milan in 1969. The police claimed that the railway worker Giuseppe Pinelli, suspected of bombing a bank, felt so guilty that he committed suicide by throwing himself out of the window. Fo's play exposes all the contradictions in the official explanations and inquiries into the death.[429] Much of Fo's work are border cases of humorous political stunts. Just like with the jokes told by comedians in Burma, Fo's plays are humorous, political, told in public and confront authorities. However, because they are performed on stage they can be ignored, and again there is no deception blurring the line between performers and audiences. The incongruity is not created by being on the stage, but by what is being said from the stage.

A final example to explore the borders of the humorous political stunt is taken from the world of graffiti. Like adbusting, graffiti is based on the idea that the streets belong to everyone. People who create graffiti speak back to all the advertising in public spaces dominated by commercial interests.[430] Some graffiti carries an obvious political message that goes beyond saying "no", and some graffiti artists reach world fame. The prime

---

[428] Scuderi, "Unmasking the Holy Jester Dario Fo," p. 276.
[429] Dario Fo, *Plays*, 2 vols. (London: Methuen Drama, 1997); Maceri, "Dario Fo: Jester of the Working Class."
430 Steve Wright, *Home Sweet Home: Banksy's Bristol: The Unofficial Guide* (Bristol: Tangent, 2009). p. 54.

example is Banksy who started his career in Bristol in the mid 1980's, and is now well known around the world. Today he is considered an artist rather than a rebel, and his pieces are no longer removed from public spaces.

In his work, Banksy criticises everything from established art museums to war, consumerism and surveillance. Most of his pieces do not have an obvious political message, and they are not funny either. But some of his work is both political and amusing. Take for example the piece on the cover of the book *Wall and Piece*[431], a guy in a black jacket, with his face covered and his arm raised to throw something. What most people expect him to throw is a stone, but what appears in his hand on the back cover is a bunch of flowers with yellow, red, blue and green. The contradiction between expectation and what is actually in his hand is amusing.

In 2005 Banky painted on the separation wall which Israel has built on occupied Palestinian territory,[432] and in 2007, he was back to make more images in Bethlehem. One of them is an image of a little girl in a pink dress who is body searching an Israeli soldier in uniform. The incongruity in this situation, the unexpected reversal of roles makes this an amusing image to some people. It is also an image that can be used to discuss the borders between humorous political stunts and other political humour because it changes depending on the situation the image is placed in. When the painting appears in a place where it is seen by IDF soldiers passing it, it is a challenge to the power they practice every day towards civilians and can be understood as a humorous political stunt. However, now that it is a famous

---

431 Banksy, *Wall and Piece* (London: Century, 2006).
[432] The International Court of Justice has called the wall illegal and demanded its removal. Israel claims that the wall was build in order to increase security and prevent terrorist attacks. In several places, the wall has become the target of civilian Palestinian nonviolent resistance, like in the village Bil'in.

painting, it is used in many different places. I have it as a poster on my wall, and I find it both amusing and political. However, having it on my wall at home is not a stunt. Just like the jokes and the theatre play the image is not an amusing confrontation, but a *picture* of an amusing confrontation that does not blur the line between artist and audiences.

Illustration 10. Banky graffiti from Bethlehem. Photo by Pawel Ryszawa. Reprinted under GNU Free Documentation License.

Do humorous political stunts really make a difference?

In her book about irony, Hutcheon raises a puzzle about this particular mode of communication. Why bother with irony when it is so complex and the intentions can so easily be misunderstood?

> Why should anyone want to use this strange mode of discourse where you say something you don't actually mean and expect people to understand not only what you do mean but also your attitude toward it?[433]

Not all irony is humorous, and not all humorous political stunts are ironic. Nevertheless, Hutcheon's question is also relevant when it comes to humorous political stunts and in particular when the aim of a nonviolent action is to engage people in dialogue. Why use this method instead of saying what you mean without making communication more complicated? There are probably just as many answers to this as there are humorous activists, but a general answer is that the potential benefits are greater than the risks.

In chapter 1 I introduced the discussion within humour theory concerning whether humour really poses a challenge to those in positions of power, or if it is merely a vent for frustration. I indicated that it is necessary to leave the either-or dichotomy behind and instead discuss what role humour can play under what circumstances. Looking at one particular form of political humour, the humorous political stunt, and dividing it into different types is one way of probing the complexities of humour. Also the play metaphor and all the cases in this chapter can contribute to illustrating how complex it can be to analyse the effect of humorous political stunts on relations of power.

---

[433] Hutcheon, *Irony's Edge*: p. 2.

Some of the factors that are likely to have an influence can be approached through the theatre metaphor: Was the scene empty or were there already lead actors on the stage when the humourists attacked? How long did the disruption last? How frequent were the disruption(s)? How many people wanted to play a role not included in the script? How did those in power respond to the challenge? Were the lead actors put in a situation where they felt they themselves had to stop the play, or did the humourists stop it?

It seems that the more the challengers managed to enter the stage when there were already lead actors present, the easier it was to get attention from mass media and a large audience, something which the John Howard's Ladies Auxiliary Fan Club and Yes Men on BBC experienced. But if it is too difficult or too dangerous to interrupt lead actors, this can potentially be compensated by frequency or number of people, as shown in the example with the TV walkers. Maybe CIRCA could have increased its influence by performing more plays at the same time. Another factor affecting success is the new actors' ability to keep the focus on the dominant discourse, and not divert all attention to themselves or their way of performing.

The use of pretence combined with the ambiguity, incongruity and contradictions necessary for generating humour means that the attack on the dominant discourse can be both direct and indirect at the same time. The pretence that this is not a protest means that it is indirect. But sometimes there is a direct link between the technique used to generate the humour and the discourse to be undermined. The humorous techniques directly contribute to the deconstruction, at least for a little while, and serve to illustrate that the dominant discourse is not as almighty and unchallengeable as it appeared. The Fan Club used impersonations of a stereotypical idea of what women were and should be to satirise and exaggerate what they considered Howard's old fashioned vision for Australia. When the Polish people took their TVs for a walk, the absurd image of the TV in the stroller also directly dealt with the issue of false news on TV. The Yes Men's golden leisure suit with its *Employee Visualisation Appendage* was also in its own absurd way directly linked to the issue of workers' rights that the group wanted to highlight. CIRCA's slapstick was a direct attack on the military recruiters' claim to adulthood, and their clowning embodied values that directly contradicted the discourse of militarism. However, the link is not that strong in all cases. Voina's ridicule of the FSB via a bridge painting did not communicate what in particular they thought was wrong with the FSB, and Otpor's Dinar za Smenu did not show what the activists thought was problematic with Slobodan Milošević's regime.

Not surprisingly, the representatives of these dominant discourses did not agree to improvise a new play, but sometimes they were forced to do it. They did not accept the children's play but insisted on continuing with Shakespeare. In some cases it was possible to ignore the new actors, because they were too few, or because they presented themselves when no important actors were already on the stage. With ACE bank, Netwerk Vlaanderen could gain the attention of the general public, but they did not disrupt the functions of the major banks whose practice they wanted to criticise, and the banks could ignore them. In the Yes Men's stunt at the textile conference, WTO could also safely ignore these new actors. However, that those in power are not directly affected does not necessarily mean that a stunt has no effect. Other audiences might be directly or indirectly affected when they encounter the stunt on the street or through a YouTube video.

In some of the other cases, the activists interrupted the ongoing play so much that the representatives of the dominant discourses felt some kind of reaction was needed. The Fan Club, CIRCA and the Santas were physically prevented from being present on the stage where they wanted to be. In Poland, people from the Orange Alternative were arrested and put in detention, and in the case with the TV walkers, the government changed the rules for when the stage was open by changing the curfew time.

The question of effectiveness is important, but extremely difficult to estimate. In some cases, the pranks can be disruptive enough to catch world attention and force a reaction from those being undermined, something which happened to the Yes Men when they went on the BBC as representatives of Dow, and when The Chaser team were charged with offences under new security laws after the stunt ridiculing security during the APEC summit in Sydney. However, even when humorous political stunts are "just" short and symbolic interruptions, they are still contributions to the *discursive guerrilla war* that the activists are engaged in.

Summing up, it should by now be clear that a large number of factors are involved in determining the impact of a humorous political stunt. It is not just a question of directly challenging established relations of power, but also concerns the activists themselves and their commitment to a cause, as well as media, other activists and the general public.

Conclusion

Humorous political stunts are attempts to disrupt the smooth dominance of prevailing power formations. They are a unique type of resistance due to the way they utilise humorous incongruity. Except in the cases of provocative stunts, the pretence that this is not protest means that it is a challenge for those in power to frame these actions as ordinary protest. Because it is difficult to treat non-protesting protesters in the same way as other protesters, the *play of politics* either has to continue in a different way or be temporarily broken down and exposed as a play that is not totally dominant after all.

Humorous political stunts can be powerful stories because they frequently speak to the imagination. In Sweden, homosexuality was officially classified as a disease until 1979. The story goes that the movement for homosexual rights therefore organised a campaign where they asked people to call their employers and say that unfortunately they would not be able to work today, since they were feeling a little gay.[434] As a naïve stunt, this exposed the hypocrisy of considering homosexuality a disease by pretending that it was not meant to be considered a disease which should prevent people from working. In connection with an occupation of The National Board of Health and Welfare in 1979, a few people did indeed use this argument, but there is no basis for the stories of thousands of people calling in sick. However, the story strikes so many keys that several people independently of each other have told it to me as a true story. Likewise, the story of the Yippies throwing dollar bills in the New York Stock exchange has created images of greedy stock brokers crawling on the floor in many people's imagination.

Humorous political stunts are related to phenomena such as culture jamming and tactical carnival that other scholars have studied, but these concepts were developed with a different aim in mind. Although there are many overlaps these notions speak about something else. Likewise, Berger's 45 techniques of humour can provide insights about how the amusing incongruity is generated in a humorous political stunt, but his framework does not have much to say about humour and relations of power.

This chapter has identified the ideal type of a humorous political stunt where a dominant discourse is openly challenged by a confrontational performance/action. It is either so confrontational that it cannot be ignored or involves a deception that blurs the line between performers and audiences. I have intentionally been clear about the core of the phenomenon, but vague about

---

[434] RFSL, "Ockupationen Av Socialstyrelsen 1979 [the Occupation of the the National Board of Health and Welfare 1979]," http://www.rfsl.se/?p=987.

the borders in the hope that future research on borderline cases can bring more insight about the core as well. The many different examples showed that even within this ideal type, there is room for much diversity.

I formulated, examined and illustrated five main categories of humorous political stunts. Supportive, corrective, naïve, absurd and provocative types of stunts position themselves in relation to those in power in distinct ways. Almost all examples of humorous political stunts can be placed in one of these types because there is an internal logic to them, but the example of the Chaser's APEC stunt in Sydney demonstrates that this is not always the case.

The type of stunt says something about the broader picture, but by introducing so many different examples it also became apparent how much variety there can be within one type of stunt. Take for instance the three supportive stunts by the John Howard Ladies' Auxiliary Fan Club, Mark Thomas and the landmine clearing team in the AXA bank. They have the supportiveness in common, but even within this category there is much variety. Similarly for all the other four types.

The theatre model is a way of analysing the dynamics of each individual stunt. Investigating the four factors of stage, actors, audiences and timing separately brings insights about each stunt, but understanding the way each of the factors influences the others and how they play together shows how the humorous political stunt can be varied and how many possibilities there exist for creative activists. It also shows the complexities of power and resistance and how it is unfruitful to consider resistance a question of either futility or impact. Even when those in positions of power do not change their behaviours because of a single humorous political stunt, the pranks can be part of broader social movements. They can be inspiring, uplifting events in the discursive guerrilla war that bring attention, new energy and perhaps most importantly demonstrate the existence of alternative discourses.

The following chapter analyses rebel clowning, a particular type of an absurd humorous political stunt, in more detail. The two subsequent chapters are the case studies of Ofog and KMV. In all these chapters the five types of humorous political stunts and the theatre metaphor are tools that serve to analyse the humorous political stunts performed by these organisations.

Chapter 4: Radical clowning as humorous political activism

Introduction

In Chapter 3 I presented the British Clandestine Insurgent Rebel Clown Army (CIRCA) as an example of an absurd stunt. This chapter explores the phenomenon of radical clowning in more detail, drawing primarily on Ofog's experiences with clowning[435] and relating this to findings from the academic literature on CIRCA.

The analysis takes its point of departure in Peacock's clown theory with its focus on three central clown elements – *play, otherness* and *incompetence* and adds a fourth element which is prominent in Ofog's and CIRCA's clowning - *ridicule*. It shows under what circumstances rebel clowning can contribute to facilitating outreach and mobilisation, a culture of resistance and challenging relations of power. The chapter concludes with a discussion of clowning in relation to Vinthagen's theory of nonviolence and the contradictions and limitations of radical clowning.

Radical clowning with Ofog

The "clown army" is a concept that the Swedish anti-militarist network Ofog has used frequently during its nonviolent actions, both before and during our joint research project. It was often one of the first things people from Ofog mentioned when I talked with them about humour. Ofog's radical clowning is directly inspired by the British CIRCA.

The literature on clowning as a form of protest is growing. Poul Routledge and L. M. Bogad have both analysed their own and

---

[435] The data collection process is described in Chapter 2.

other "clownbattant" experiences in CIRCA in academic writing in their respective fields of critical geography and performance studies. The rebel clowns have also been used as a case in order to discuss citizenship[436] as well as humour and nonviolent resistance to oppression.[437] Routledge has described how the clowning is developed within a tradition of direct nonviolent action emphasising independent organising through affinity groups, a tradition that Ofog is also part of. These affinity groups take care of training, preparations and the participants' emotional well-being through what he calls *sensuous solidarities*.[438] CIRCA's activism has been placed within a larger trend of joyful, carnival-like protest that has been termed *carnivalesque*[439], the *ethical spectacle*[440], and *tactical carnival*[441] as described previously.

Bogad traces the history of CIRCA back to London 2003 and the recruitment tour through Britain that resulted in about 150 clowns participating in the protests against the G8 summit in Edinburgh in 2005.[442] In addition to contributing to the goals of tactical carnival, clowning is considered a way of countering our society's focus on individualism and celebrities. Since it is difficult to recognise people behind the makeup, clowning is seen as an equaliser.[443] The clowns in these very special armies dress in a mixture of military and clown clothing and use attributes from

---

[436] John Fletcher, "Of Minutemen and Rebel Clown Armies: Reconsidering Transformative Citizenship," *Text and Performance Quarterly* 29, no. 3 (2009).
[437] Sørensen, "Humor as a Serious Strategy of Nonviolent Resistance to Oppression."
[438] Paul Routledge, "Sensuous Solidarities: Emotion, Politics and Performance in the Clandestine Insurgent Rebel Clown Army," *Antipode* 44, no. 2 (2012).
[439] Bruner, "Carnivalesque Protest and the Humorless State."
[440] Duncombe, *Dream: Re-Imagining Progressive Politics in an Age of Fantasy.*
[441] Bogad, "Tactical Carnival."
[442] Bogad, "Carnivals against Capital."
[443] Bogad, "Carnivals against Capital."

the clowning sphere. While they are clowns in their hearts, their curiosity draws them to the exciting world of everything associated with police and military authority. Their absurd performances become a different way of challenging the discourse of militarism as well as police and military personnel that uphold this discourse. Clowning frequently opens up possibilities for interaction which are not available in the same form to "ordinary" protesters.

The people who initiated CIRCA had a well thought through idea about what they wanted to do and the purpose of the clowning. CIRCA's own statement *About the army* is a long explanation of the name Clandestine Insurgent Rebel Clown Army. *Clandestine* signifies a refusal of celebrity and resistance of surveillance, and *Insurgent* that "we have risen up from nowhere and are everywhere".[444] *Rebel* sends signals of changing the world in a rebellion that will continue forever and promise always to disobey those in power. *Clown* "because what else can one be in such a stupid world. Because inside everyone is a lawless clown trying to escape. Because nothing undermines authority like holding it up to ridicule."[445] Finally, in the section about why they are an *Army*, CIRCA says that a single clown is pathetic, but together an army of clowns is dangerous and can declare war on the absurdity of the world where money counts more than people and there is an absurd war going on in Iraq.[446]

Since CIRCA first introduced the idea of rebel clowning to the global social justice activist community in Europe, the idea has spread to many different struggles and under different circumstances in the so-called western world. Ofog's use of clowning is

---

[444] CIRCA, "Clandestine Insurgent Rebel Clown Army ".
[445] CIRCA, "Clandestine Insurgent Rebel Clown Army ".
[446] The war in Iraq is not mentioned explicitly in this document, but elsewhere. See for instance Routledge, "Sensuous Solidarities."

part of this spread and adapts the idea of rebel clowning to local circumstances.

In the written comments I collected during the first workshop with Ofog about humour, someone wrote:

> As clowns we are more unpredictable, one moment we imitate police, the next moment we play with each other and the third moment we play with the police(...) it is also possible to push the limits more as for example clowns, like passing barriers.

Unpredictability is a central aspect of the clown army, just as it is in conventional circus clowning. When clowning within Ofog was new to me, I wrote in my research notes:

> Ofog has used the concept of the clown army several times, and found it a useful way to question power and authority. (...)It is a good way to get a lighter tone, ease tension and get out the human side of the policeman or woman, who will maybe start to juggle with the clowns. Most people become happy when they see a clown, but sometimes the police get annoyed as well.[447]

Subsequently, I have explored the concept and the various ideas in the quotes above by interviewing people about their clowning experiences and through participatory observation as a clown.

None of the people with clowning experience that I have interviewed have had much training or referred to any theory about clowning. Within Ofog, there is knowledge about CIRCA, but little connection to the whole tradition of clowning. The three clown army actions in Luleå, Gothenburg and Belgium where I was a participant observer were organised in a typical Ofog manner. Preparations were done with short notice, ad hoc and with a mix of more and less experienced clowns. This way of preparing has its advantages and disadvantages. More people can

---

[447] Field notes May 22 2011.

participate if they are not required to spend long hours rehearsing and preparing. On the other hand, the performances might not be as good as they could otherwise have been. For example, Emma and Maria who participated in Luleå found it difficult to go in and out of their clown roles in different situations.[448] More training could probably have prepared them how to handle this.

For some Ofog activists it has been important to let the clowning be a way of taking action that everyone can participate in. Peter, who was an experienced clown when he joined Ofog, thinks that it is important that the clowning is unpretentious. If some people in an affinity group have clowned before and others not, people learn from each other:

> You can walk in there and just stand there, and then you still fulfil a function. Everyone does not have to do the same, go in to influence or establish a relation or do something more advanced.[449]

People engage in the clown army with multiple aims in mind, and there may be as many opinions about the purpose of clowning as there are clowns.

Peacock's clown theory

Several books provide instructions and practical exercises for people who want to practice clowning or other physical comedy[450], but academics have made surprisingly few attempts at theorising clowning. An exception is Louise Peacock's book *Serious Play: Modern Clown Performance*, which has a few pages on

---

[448] Interview September 2011.
[449] Interview September 2011.
[450] See for instance John Wright, *Why Is That So Funny? A Practical Exploration of Physical Comedy* (London: Nick Hern Books, 2006); Eli Simon, *The Art of Clowning: More Paths to Your Inner Clown*, 2nd ed. (New York: Palgrave Macmillan, 2012).

CIRCA. However, more interesting is her attempt to define the unique features of all clowning, including ceremonial clowning, the traditional circus clown, clowns in theatre and the recent use of clowns in hospitals. According to Peacock, clowning "allow[s] us to connect with deeper truths about human existence"[451], and she explains that:

> The clown clowns not simply to amuse his audience but because he [sic] has observations about the world, about life, to communicate to them, and play becomes a conduit to aid that communication.[452]

This wish to communicate observations about the world can also be found in CIRCA's aims. Kolonel Klepto, echoing CIRCA's webpage, explains:

> CIRCA aims to make clowning dangerous again, to bring it back to the street, reclaim its disobedience and give it back the social function it once had: its ability to disrupt, critique and heal society (…) creating coherence through confusion - adding disorder to the world in order to expose its lies and speak the truth.[453]

Peacock has identified three central aspects of clowning which will be the point of departure for my presentation of Ofog's clowning:

> The clown is distinguished from the actor by his or her ability to **play** with the audience and to create a sense of *complicité* with them by using play to connect with them. There is always something of the 'other' about clowns. This may be expressed in the way that they look different

---

[451] Louise Peacock, *Serious Play: Modern Clown Performance* (Bristol: Intellect Books, 2009). p.12.
[452] Peacock, *Serious Play: Modern Clown Performance*: p. 14.
[453] Kolonel Klepto, "Making War with Love: The Clandestine Insurgent Rebel Clown Army," *City* 8, no. 3 (2004): p. 407. See also CIRCA, "Clandestine Insurgent Rebel Clown Army ".

> from ordinary everyday people (through make-up, cos-
> tume, the use of a red nose), but the most striking feature
> of the clowns' **'otherness'** is their attitude to life as ex-
> pressed through their performance. Whilst the clown often
> fails to achieve what they set out to achieve, their **failure** is
> framed by their optimism and by the simplicity of their ap-
> proach to life.[454]

I have emphasised the three concepts I consider central in
Peacock's definition with bold - *play, otherness* and *failure*. Below I
treat them as techniques that can be more or less operationalised
in a performance and apply them to the data from Ofog. Later in
her book Peacock uses the expression *incompetence* interchangeably with *failure*, incompetence is a word I find more appropriate
and will use subsequently. In addition, I present the fourth
concept of *ridicule* which Peacock mentions, but did not find so
prominent in traditional clowning that it is included in her
definition.

It is the combination of play and otherness that sets this type of
activism apart from what I have called conventional/ordinary
protest and also from most other humorous political stunts.
Playful elements are part of many stunts, but they are seldom as
central as in radical clowning. Likewise it is not unusual to
emphasise otherness in some types of activism, for instance
queer performance, but then it frequently has an angry tone that
is not part of the clown performances the original CIRCA and
Ofog have tried to foster.

Working on humour together with Ofog I have come across
three different contexts where radical clowning has been used. In
legal demonstrations clowning has been a way to deescalate
tensions and reach out to police officers. In civil disobedience

---

[454] Peacock, *Serious Play: Modern Clown Performance*: p.14. The bold
emphasis added by me, the italics in the original.

actions clowning has served the additional purpose of physically challenging access to restricted space. In so-called counter-recruitment when Ofog has attempted to disrupt military recruitment of young people clowning has been a way to demon-demonstrate the absurdity of militarism. In all these situations two of the basic clowning concepts – play and otherness – are important features.

Play

Play is probably the most crucial element in clowning generally, and for rebel clowning too. By playing with each other and inviting others to play clowns can be understood to reach out. I observed how play can work for the first time during an international summer camp called "War Starts Here" organised by Ofog near Vidsel Test Range in July 2011. Vidsel Test Range, at the time known as NEAT (North European Aerospace Test range), is Europe's largest overland military test site, with an air space almost the size of Belgium.[455] This huge area in the north of Sweden is administered by the Swedish Defence Materiel Administration (FMV) and is routinely rented out to other countries' military forces to train and test new weapon systems.

During the day of direct action, 200 people held a pink carnival just outside the restricted test area.[456] I was part of an affinity group with 8 clowns which had two goals: 1. Challenge police perceptions of their own role, by trying to reach to the human beings behind the police uniform, and 2. distract the police to make other affinity groups achieve what they wanted, e.g. climb the fence in order to get to the military runway. I will return to the problematic aspects of trying to do these two things simultaneously.

---

[455] FMV, "Europe's Largest Overland Test Area," http://www.vidseltestrange.com/europe%E2%80%99s-largest.
[456] The following is based on participatory observation during Ofog's action July 26, 2011. Field notes July 2011.

The clowns were dressed in a mixture of clowning and military clothes, and brought jump ropes, soap bubbles, feather dusters, balloons etc. with them to play with. When all the 200 activists arrived outside of the restricted area, the clowns immediately spotted the police blocking the road, and decided to "help". As members of the clown army the idea was to show how they felt a community with others in uniform, although much of what the police do perplexes the clowns. Forming their own line across the road just in front of the police, the clowns assisted in stopping the rest of the activists from proceeding and helped direct the traffic that was allowed to pass where the protesters could not go. At this point all activists had agreed to respect the police line so the clowns' "help" did not really make a practical difference.

Most of the police seemed quite relaxed around the clowns, although they declined to try the soap bubbles and most of them politely said "no thanks" when offered sultanas and chocolate. Emma, who was part of our group, tells that when she started to clean the shoe of one policeman with her feather duster, to her surprise he just put forward his other foot as well.[457] However, one particular policewoman had been very hesitant in her interaction with the clowns. When they moved towards her, she moved away, and she definitely did not want chocolate or sultanas. However, a breakthrough came when the clown Sara claimed that her shoes were bigger than the policewoman's shoes and without words indicated that she wanted to measure. When Sara sat down on the ground, the policewoman followed her lead and put her boot against the clown's boot, revealing that Sara did in fact have the biggest shoes. A little while later, this same clown pretended to get stuck half way through the fence into the runway, were a number of activists where sitting under arrest and waiting to be escorted out. This performance was so good that I

---

[457] Interview September 2011.

thought Sara actually was stuck. It is the only example of a radical clown deliberately using the idea of incompetence that I have come across.

Later in the day, a group of around 50 people, including some of the clowns, decided to participate in a civil disobedience action when they entered the restricted military area by walking on the main road which leads through the zone. Cars can go through but are not allowed to stop. The place had been declared off-limits to Ofog, but the handful of police had no chance of stopping the group. On the walk to the fence which separate the road from the military run way, these 50 people were escorted by only two police officers – a man walking and a woman driving the police car. During this five kilometre walk, some of the clowns walked in the heels of this lonely policeman, sometimes one, sometimes three in a line, imitating his every move. If he walked fast, the clowns walked fast, if he talked in his radio, the clowns talked in their make believe radios. If he turned around to see what was going on, the clowns turned around as well.

Illustration 11. Ofog. Luleå July 26, 2011 clowns and police.

269

From the clown perspective, this was a game of "follow John", but in all likelihood it looked rather different from the policeman's point of view. His strategy for dealing with the clowns seemed to be to ignore them to the extent possible, and engage in conversations with the "civilian" protesters.

Another example of clown play during a civil disobedience action was described to me in several interviews. Bofors is one of Sweden's biggest arms manufacturers, and Ofog had held a demonstration against the company in June 2008. The police had

Illustration 12. Ofog. The clown army succeed through camouflage and silliness to get inside the enclosure. Outside arms producer Bofors' headquarters in Karlskoga June 17 2008.[458]

---

[458] Original photo text on Ofog's webpage.

closed off a zone in front of the building with red and white tape. A small delegation from the activists had just tried to deliver a letter to the CEO, but was driven out of the enclosed area. Everybody was a bit tired, it rained a little, and the activists were discussing if they should go home. Suddenly, three rebel clowns from the clown army arrived. All three did their best to hide together behind a small tree branch on this huge open parking lot. Pretending that they were invisible to the police, the three clowns snuck into the enclosed area, hid behind a flower pot and started playing clown games. Then the clowns became bolder, and tried to engage the police in their games and imitate the way the police officers stood and moved. Some of the police officers started to move differently in order to get the clowns to imitate them, and one policeman even blew soap bubbles that a clown offered.

Vera reflected about the episode:

> And then we appear, a group of clowns and kind of hide behind little twigs and roll around and fool around and we can stay there, and we reflected on that. But they just removed someone, and I don't think it was because the police got tired, they understood that it would probably be easier to let us stay in there. [459]

As Vera interpreted the situation, the police thought it would be easier to let the clowns stay inside the enclosed area and let them play since they did not do any harm. That the police apparently accepted the clowns as harmless meant that they had been successful in communicating their nonviolent intentions. Lena, another Ofog activist who participated in the same clown group, adds how the situation was perceived by the "ordinary" Ofog activists who were holding the demonstration outside of the enclosed area:

---

[459] Interview September 2011

271

> We kind of snuck in, you know we were very visible be-
> cause it was a totally open parking lot, but we pretended to
> sneak in and came all the way to the house and really
> played theatre. It was like a show for the others in the man-
> ifestation because it rained a little and was kind of "should
> we go home or what" atmosphere. [460]

Peter described a similar challenging of space in Luleå in 2009, where he and other clowns hid behind twigs and pretended to be completely hidden, in order to cross the police line.[461]

Illustration 13. Ofog. The clown army succeed through camouflage and silliness to get inside the enclosure. Outside arms producer Bofors' head-quarters in Karlskoga June 17 2008.[462]

---

[460] Interview June 2011.
[461] Interview September 2011.
[462] Original photo text on Ofog's webpage.

Peacock's emphasis on play and the rebel clowns' attempts to get the police to engage in play with them is also supported by John Wright's understanding of clowning. His book *Why Is That So Funny? A Practical Exploration of Physical Comedy*[463] provides many practical exercises for performers to help them find their *inner clown*. To Wright it is important that clowns are not acting, they just "are". Clowns exist in the here and now without pretence.[464] All clowning takes as its point of departure the *simple clown* whom he characterises as "fun-loving, childlike, amoral, irresponsible, mercurial, bizarre, destructive, chaotic and anarchic".[465] Central to the simple clown is stupidity, naivety and constant bafflement about what life has to offer.

Otherness

The second keyword from Peacock's definition of clowning, *otherness* also resonates well with radical clowning. By wearing parts of military uniforms, the clown army is partly like soldiers, but the clowning attributes and especially the red noses obviously make them part of the community of clowns. Ofog and CIRCA clowns belong everywhere – and nowhere. The otherness is also expressed in part of CIRCA's description of itself quoted in Chapter 3: "We are *circa* because we are approximate and ambivalent, neither here nor there, but in the most powerful of all places, the place in-between order and chaos."[466]

A telling example of otherness comes from Vera when her clown character pretended to fall in love with one of the police officers. She looked at him and flirted by hugging herself, and felt it was a

---

[463] Wright, *Why Is That So Funny? A Practical Exploration of Physical Comedy*.
[464] Wright, *Why Is That So Funny? A Practical Exploration of Physical Comedy*: p. 193.
[465] Wright, *Why Is That So Funny? A Practical Exploration of Physical Comedy*: pp. 203-04.
[466] CIRCA, "Clandestine Insurgent Rebel Clown Army ".

breakthrough that made him relax: "For me the symbolism became: You are here, but you are not my enemy. I rather think you should be with us instead."[467]

A comparable expression of radical clowning can be found in one of Bogad's articles. The clown Trixi confronted a line of very serious police in riot gear during the G8 summit in Edinburgh in 2005. During a rather tense situation, Trixie went along the line of police and kissed the plastic shields of all the policemen in the line, just after the shields had been used to shove people away in order to recreate police control of a street. A photo of this episode went around the world the next day as part of many reports of the protests. Bogad comments that the police who were exposed to Trixie and her fellow clowns expressed reactions ranging from amusement and surprise to asking her to "step away, from the shield please".[468] The clown performance continued with a number of different games, and after a while the police withdraw from this part of Edinburgh's streets. Bogad adds that there might have been other factors than *clown magic* involved, but for the people present it was a powerful moment.

Both Vera and Trixie used typical expressions of flirting to disarm and communicate friendliness. It is part of both traditional and rebel clowning to divert from established social norms in various ways. Peacock writes that "clown actions can also involve sexual antics which involve a level of obscenity that would not be acceptable in everyday society."[469] However, even if kissing and flirting are associated with sexuality, when done by a rebel clown confronting police it becomes disconnected from its ordinary use. Instead of the kisses' conventional associations with sexuality, they become a sign of otherness when social

[467] Interview September 2011.
[468] Bogad, "Carnivals against Capital," p. 539.
[469] Peacock, *Serious Play: Modern Clown Performance*: p. 26.

conventions about relations between protesters and police are broken.

Clowns behave in different ways, depending on the person underneath. They communicate multiple and sometimes contradictory messages which get interpreted in various ways by differ-different audiences. As a minimum almost all rebel clowns aim to communicate a non-threatening attitude, something that can be achieved through the play and otherness apparent in their actions and attitudes. It is impossible during the heat of the moment to communicate sophisticated understandings of non-violent action such as the whole of Vinthagen's theory, but most people that Ofog's rebel clowns have encountered seem to understand that no harm is intended.

Some clowns go further and want to express friendliness and demonstrate that police and protesters should not consider each other enemies. Vera was one of the people from Ofog I interviewed who expressed this aspect of clowning most clearly. When talking about clowning during larger demonstrations, she said she prefers to take the role of the curious clown who wants to include everyone in what is going on. She likes the clown figure because it does not make her "a hard and angry activist"[470], a notion she used to describe the stereotype of political activists. She wishes to communicate that the police are not the object of the activists' anger; they are just something that people in Ofog have to deal with as part of their anti-militarist activism. Vera is also the kind of clown who leaves police officers alone if they don't want to play, as she expresses it: "you know, it is not as fun to play with someone who thinks you are very annoying."[471] When Vera clowns, she gives everyone a chance to see what her intentions are:

---

[470] Interview September 2011.
[471] Interview September 2011.

Majken Jul Sorensen

> For me the point is that it should not just be fun for me, it has to be something that the police can appreciate as well. It should not exceed the limits, so if they don't seem to understand that after they have had the opportunity, then I leave them alone.[472]

Vera also explained how she used her high-pitched clown voice to communicate the potential bond between activists and police with words: "But if you take a helicopter, and you fly in over here, then you can let us down in the area of the arms factory where we would like to be, that is a good idea, isn't it?"[473] She thinks it is easier to get acceptance for the idea that activists and police have something in common when she is clowning compared to when she is in "civilian". Even if Vera never displays anger herself, her experience is that she is perceived as angry by the police when she is not clowning. However, she only pretended to fall in love with one particular policeman. With others she thought looked stricter, she practiced standing in line just as them. If she did not get any response she moved on to the next one. But everyone got a chance to see what her intentions were, including the head of the police.

Incompetence

According to Peacock, "failure or 'incompetence' is a staple ingredient of clown performance", and the third central aspect of clowning she identifies.[474] Weitz also describes how the western clown is inspired by the *country bumpkin* and draws on "physical, intellectual and social incompetence".[475] However, failure and incompetence are almost absent from the data about rebel clowns. Although CIRCA's recruitment video includes a

---

[472] Interview September 2011.
[473] Interview September 2011.
[474] Peacock, *Serious Play: Modern Clown Performance*: p. 24.
[475] Eric Weitz, "Failure as Success: On Clowns and Laughing Bodies," *Performance Research* 17, no. 1 (2012): p. 79.

276

sentence about "learning how to be stupid"[476] and CIRCA's statement has a reference to failure when discussing why they are clowns[477], the incompetence is not mentioned in the academic literature on CIRCA. As mentioned earlier, Sara getting stuck in the fence surrounding Vidsel Test Range/NEAT is the only example of incompetence I have observed or heard about. Since this is rather striking, I systematically looked for episodes of incompetence in ten randomly selected YouTube videos documenting rebel clown actions.[478] In none of them did I find anything resembling incompetence.

---

[476] Anonymous, *Circa Recruitment Video* (youtube.com, not dated).
[477] CIRCA, "Clandestine Insurgent Rebel Clown Army ".
[478] I randomly picked videos from different clown actions in different cities, taking place between 2005 and 2013. See Anonymous, *C.I.R.C.A G8 Road Blockade* (youtube.com: 2005); Anonymous, *Clandestine Insurgent Rebel Clown Army in Rostock 2007*, (youtube.com, 2007); Anonymous, *You Can Not Give an Anarchist Clown Directions (Especially While Wearing Riot Gear)* (youtube.com: 2013); Anonymous, *Glasgow Section of Clandestine Insurgent Rebel Clown Army* (youtube.com: not dated); Anonymous, *Rebel Clown Army Cologne* (youtube.com: not dated); Anonymous, *The Clown Army, Christiania 2005* (youtube.com: 2005); Anonymous, *G20 Toronto Protests Send in the Clowns* (youtube.com: not dated); Anonymous, *Circa Recruitment Video* ; Anonymous, *Rebel Clown Army at Faslane 08/07/2012* (youtube.com, 2012); Anonymous, *Clownplay with Policeman @ G8* (youtube.com, 2005).The length of the videos is between 1½ minute and 9½ minutes. I selected some with many views, and others with few. "Clandestine Insurgent Rebel Clown Army in Rostock 2007" had more than 22.700 views, while "G20 Toronto Protests Send in the Clowns" only had 30. Six of the videos appear to be the raw filming which is posted on YouTube without any additional sound, text or explanation, while four have some text to help the viewer understand what this is about. Two of these, some of the oldest videos from the original British CIRCA, also have music and are described as recruitment videos. The videos are not representative of all rebel clowning, but are a small selection of what has been filmed and found interesting enough to be posted on YouTube. This "selection

Peacock herself does not engage in a systematic discussion about the similarities and differences between what she describes as central clowning concepts and her analysis of CIRCA. Thus, she mentions how CIRCA clowns are playing and how they parody the military, but does not comment of the lack of incompetence in CIRCA clown behaviour.

There are most likely several reasons why there is so little incompetence in rebel clowning. Activists who have little knowledge of the clown tradition are unlikely to have thought much about what ought to be "staple ingredients" in their clowning. It also takes more practice and skills to be funny by appearing incompetent than most amateur rebel clowns have. In addition it requires a type of action/situation where there is enough time to establish a contact with the audiences. It is also possible that amateur clowns who are used to being "ordinary" protesters might find it relatively easy to play and ridicule others, but a challenge to humiliate themselves by appearing incompetent. However, it would require more research to know why incompetence is almost absent from rebel clowning.

An interesting question is if more use of incompetence would improve the rebel clowns' likelihood of achieving their goals. It would probably contribute to communicate the clowns' otherness at the same time as it reaches out and emphasises that we are all humans who can fail, activists and representatives of authorities alike. Where the non-humorous activists usually find it hard to deal with failure, this would be easier for clowns. Since

---

bias" is done by the film maker and cannot be controlled by a researcher. Nevertheless I see no better way to get an impression on the diversity of rebel clowning and confirm my impression about the lack of incompetence, since participant observation is extremely time consuming and cannot be used on historic cases. Moreover, the videos show the variety of ways that the idea of rebel clowning has been picked up and adopted to local circumstances.

clowns are constantly bewildered by the state of the world and their lack of success, they could serve as an embodiment of all activists' common failure to change the world. Likewise, daring to show incompetence, even though it in fact requires great skill to do it well, would make it more difficult to interpret the clown activists as self-righteous.

Ridicule

If incompetence is missing, rebel clowning instead includes a fourth feature which does not take such a prominent place in Peacock's theory, namely *ridicule*. Clowns standing next to police and military personnel and imitating their every move are a "staple ingredient" in actions I have observed and heard about. Peacock's clown theory does mention ridicule, but in radical clowning the use of ridicule is more striking than in conventional clowning. Rebel clowns address the issue of high and low status with their parodies of police and military signs of importance and prominence, for instance when body posture and ways of walking are imitated. The parodies ridicule law enforcement officers' attempts at displaying authority and for most people they come across as funny without much explanation. As Emma expressed it: "If you see a person with a red nose standing in exactly the same position, then it looks comical."[479]

Lena was one of the people I interviewed who emphasised how ridicule can be used to expose the ridiculousness in the police and military roles. She talked about a clowning experience from Luleå in 2009 this way:

> A lot of military personnel stood there guarding the military airport and we were mainly there to make fun of them. We had our own little exercise a kind of "practice peace" where we encouraged the soldiers to come with us and practice peace instead of practicing war. But we were also just hanging around them. You know, when you are

---

[479] Interview September 2011.

279

> dressed like a clown it is quite rewarding just to stand next
> to a police or a military, and then you kind of make them
> look stupid just by standing next to them.[480]

This use of ridicule is also outspoken when clowning has been
used as so-called "counter-recruitment". This is a term used
within the peace movement for activities aimed at providing
alternatives to or facts about military recruitment of young
people. The purpose of clowning in this context is to engage
directly with the army as an institution and not "just" interact
with the police present at larger demonstrations and civil disobedience actions confronting military exercises or arms production.

During the interviews I asked some people what they expected
would come out of clowning counter-recruitment, something
which Ofog had not practiced before and we were planning to
do. Gustav who had not been clowning himself, but was interested in doing it as part of the counter-recruitment, explained his
expectations of the clown figure like this:

> It is a way of ridiculing, or show (...) that militarism and
> military recruitment is quite silly. Especially if it is a clown
> which is recruiting I think it can be interesting. And first
> and foremost I also think that you can make people reflect
> a little more, hopefully ask "what is this really, why do
> they do this?" It is actually quite sick that you have people
> who recruit people to war.[481]

Here Gustav described how ridicule is part of rebel clowning,
and the purpose of it. Contrary to Lena he did not find it so
interesting in itself to ridicule people in uniform, but saw it as an
opportunity to make the audiences wonder what the clowns are
doing, what they mean. Instead of providing a definite statement

---

[480] Interview July 2011.
[481] Interview September 2011.

that military recruitment is bad, the absurdity of the clowns might make the audiences think for themselves.

The use of ridicule is not unproblematic. It is one of humour's darker sides, and its existence is often downplayed in writings focusing on the positive aspects of humour.[482] Below it will become apparent how ridicule is ambivalent in relation to the playful and friendly aspects of clowning, and in Chapter 5 I return to the risks of ridicule being experienced as abuse.

Analysis: Clowning the way to hearts and minds?

The first part of this chapter took its point of departure in Peacock's clown theory. It showed how radical clowning uses two of the three core features of clowning she identified: play and otherness. These two aspects of clowning are central in communicating friendliness and nonviolent intentions. However, Peacock's third feature, incompetence, is almost absent in radical clowning. Instead I identified ridicule as a fourth central feature, which sends very different signals than playfulness. In the analysis I will investigate how play, otherness and ridicule contribute to or hinder the clowns' ambitions when it comes to:

a)   facilitating outreach and mobilisation
b)   facilitating a culture of resistance
c)   challenging power relations[483]

Towards the end of the chapter I discuss play, otherness and ridicule in relation to theory of nonviolent action.

---

[482] Billig, *Laughter and Ridicule: Towards a Social Critique of Laughter.*
[483] The last three sub-headings are similar to the structure I presented in Chapter 1 which was based on my previous research. The difference is the name of category 3 which has been changed from "turning oppression up-side down" to "challenging power relations" in order to reflect the less dichotomous assumption about power relations discussed earlier.

Facilitating outreach and mobilisation

Frequently activists are very interested in getting media attention, since this is considered the gateway to getting information about an action to the general public. Although some activists are cautious about focusing too much on mainstream media because the journalists have the possibility to distort the image that the activists would like to present, few activists claim that unbiased or supportive coverage does not matter.

Bogad's experience from CIRCA in Edinburgh was that the clowning received a less hostile media coverage than most of the other protesters, and CIRCA's promise to "amuse, bemuse, but never bruise"[484] was quoted in several media reports.

On April 1st 2012 Ofog participated in an action called *NATO Game Over* in Brussels in Belgium. It was organised by a Belgian group and had participants from many European countries. We were a group of six clowns from Ofog, but there were several other clowning groups. The action was announced beforehand as a *humanitarian intervention*, and was a civil disobedience action where 500 people attempted to enter the headquarters of the military alliance NATO by climbing the fence. There were numerous journalists, film crews and photographers present while the action was taking place. They were filming and photographing the attempts to climb the fence and the arrests of the 500 activists. The number of photos showing clowns is out of proportion with the actual number of clowns, leaving the impression that clowns in handcuffs make good photos.[485] However, even if the media like the clown photos, clowns'

---

[484] Bogad, "Carnivals against Capital," p. 553.

[485] For instance a Finnish newspaper included two photos of me in its report about the arrest of a number of Finnish activists. "Suomalaiset Brysselissä: 19 Pidätetty, Odottelemme Epätietoisuudessa," *iltalehti.fi*, April 1 2012.

Illustration 14. Action pour la Paix. The author in clown handcuffed together with her buddy and taken away by a policeman.

relationship with media is ambivalent. It can be difficult to understand what the clown army is there for, something Johanna has noted:

> It is probably very difficult for media to comprehend why
> we are clowns, that is kind of a standard question from
> journalists, "why are you clowns?" I think the question is
> understandable because we work on something as serious
> as war preparation.[486]

Johanna continued reflecting that the clowning tries to communicate many different things about the military structures and
encourages people to reflect on this by twisting things around
and taking a step back, and concluded that "It is difficult to
explain all aspects quickly in a few sentences to a journalist in an
interview."[487]

However, explaining clowning is not just a challenge when it
comes to journalists, but to all outsiders. It is like explaining a
joke. As soon as you try to explain the punch line rationally, the
joke falls to pieces. However, some clown performances are
clearer than others.

In November 2011 I contributed to organising a group of rebel
clowns that wanted to stand next to the military and recruit to
the clown army at a big career and education fair in Gothenburg.
We produced a recruitment flyer which was a parody of some of
the elements in the military's recruitment. The Swedish armed
forces, Försvarsmakten, advertises itself with a focus on the high
tech equipment it uses, team work, and peace. It presents itself as
a good employer with many career opportunities, with almost no
mention of war or armed combat. The clown army took up the
competition with motivations such as

> a job in the clown army is not like any other job. With us
> you don't get pay and pension. Instead you get material
> benefits such as your own water pistol, a becoming red
> nose, a whole bottle of bubble soap and a totally round hu-

[486] Interview June 2011.
[487] Interview June 2011.

284

la hoop. In addition, you become part of the amazing clown community.[488]

At the education fair, a group of six clowns and two civilian Ofog activists were ready to enter the fair in order to recruit for the clown army next to the regular army. However, someone had been keeping an eye on Ofog and knew we were coming, so the clowns were turned away in the door. Nevertheless, one of the advantages of humorous political stunts is that an apparent defeat can easily be turned into a success. Ofog could claim that Försvarsmakten was scared of clowns.[489]

When the clowns were not allowed inside, they and the two civilian Ofog activists spent an hour outside handing out leaflets. However, the parody in the clown flyer got lost when the military's flyer was not being handed out right next to it. In spite of this, the civilian Ofog activists commented in the evaluation that the clowns had drawn a lot of attention from passers-by, making it easier for them to engage people in a conversation.[490] So even if the action did not achieve its goal of challenging a dominant discourse, the clowns still contributed to outreach.

Peter is one of the most experienced rebel clowns in Ofog. Talking about outreach he said that clowning has a huge potential, and it is a shame that it is not used more:

> The potential is to be able to reach to those you encounter in a different way. To loosen up the boundaries for what is allowed, and also to be able to create an atmosphere in an action that is positively appealing. Not only with police or military or other protesters, but also if there is someone watching. In the kind of environments where there are oth-

---

[488] Ofog, "Försvarsmakten Rädda För Clownarmén I Göteborg," http://ofog.org/nyheter/forsvarsmakten-radda-for-clownarmen-i-goteborg.
[489] Ofog, "Försvarsmakten Rädda För Clownarmén I Göteborg".
[490] Field notes November 11 2011.

clowning. After all, clowns are something people recognise, and it is more difficult to make a hostile caricature of
clowns. Dangerous clowns do not really exist, so it becomes more difficult to talk about dangerous protesters.
Clowns are something different.[491]

Here Peter mentioned several different aspects of clowning that
he thought increased the potential. Clowns can reach to others in
a way that is different from other forms of protest because the
clown figure creates certain associations for the passers-by. It is
difficult to frame clowns as dangerous and demonise them
because they are something people recognise and generally have
a positive attitude towards. However, among activist clowns it is
seldom mentioned that some people are scared of clowns or that
the clown figure has been heavily commercialised (think of the
McDonald's clown Ronald McDonald). Neither is it addressed
that the ambivalence of the clown figure has been used as an
extremely scary figure, for instance in Stephen King's novel *It* or
as the bad guy "the joker" in one of the Batman movies.

One of the potential problems with the spread of rebel clowning
that has been raised is that little or no preparation means that
people dress up as clowns rather than find their *inner clown* and
stay in clown.[492] A bad performance influences many aspects of
clowning, among them how it is perceived by others. Ofog has
been less systematic than the British CIRCA when it comes to
clown preparations and I suspect that some observers might be
critical of the way the preparations are done in Ofog. Routledge
for instance is critical of how the idea of CIRCA has been copied
in other parts of the world and the lack of training. Not only
does it take practice to stay in clown, but to Routledge CIRCA

---

[491] Interview September 2011.
[492] Boyd and Mitchell, *Beautiful Trouble: A Toolbox for Revolution*: p. 306;
Routledge, "Sensuous Solidarities."

was a method that was developed for the specific context of the "war on terror" and the G8 protests in 2005.[493] He thinks the concept becomes less coherent when people attempt to transfer the idea to a different time and place. The example of clowning that he appears to be most critical of was during the demonstrations against the UN climate talks in Copenhagen in 2009. I agree with Routledge that it is difficult to explain the clown army in the context of climate change, but the concept goes well with everything to do with war and war preparations, not just the war on terror. For Ofog radical clowning has also worked well in spite of short training sessions. Of course training makes it easier to *stay in clown*, but one should not underestimate the trouble at least some outsiders will have with understanding the clown army concept no matter how good and well thought through the performance is.

Facilitating a culture of resistance

Facilitating a culture of resistance is about the way groups build internal community and strengthen the individual's capacity for participating in resistance. In the example from Bofors mentioned above, Lena felt the performance of the three clowns gave new energy to the rest of the Ofog activists. In literature on CIRCA it is frequently noted how clowning affects the clowns themselves. Routledge reflects:

> CIRCA was not an excuse for activists to dress up as clowns and bring color and laughter to protests. Rather, the purpose was to develop a form of political activism that brought together the practices of clowning and non-violent direct action. The purpose was to develop a methodology that helped to transform and sustain the inner emotional

---

[493] Routledge, "Sensuous Solidarities."

life of the activists involved as well as being an effective technique for taking direct action.[494]

Whereas Routledge emphasises activists' emotional life, Bogad speaks about how CIRCA training sessions are a way for the participants to find their clown personas, something which goes beyond taking on a role in the moment of the action. In addition to figuring out how one should look and act as a clown, Bogad mentions the mutual relation between the individual and the group:

> It is also a much longer and deeper process that involves a great deal of thoughtful/playful exploration. Putting on the makeup before an action is a crucial part of the transformation, the re-entry into one's alternate clown persona. This celebration of individual creativity and identity through the development of one's own clown can hopefully enable CIRCA members to express themselves in the moment and mode of carnival while still feeling part of a larger group identity.[495]

These types of comments about the purpose of the training sessions have not been made by the Ofog activists I interviewed. The explanation for this is probably the much more ad-hoc approach to clowning that Ofog has had than CIRCA. However, all the clowns I interviewed said that clowning is fun and that they have enjoyed it themselves. Clowning and other types of humour have been important for many activists in finding the energy to keep working on such a depressing issue as war.

---

[494] Poul Routledge, "Toward a Relational Ethics of Struggle: Embodiment, Affinity, and Affect," in *Contemporary Anarchist Studies: An Introductory Anthology of Anarchy in the Academy*, ed. Randall Amster, et al. (New York: Routledge, 2009), p. 87.
[495] Bogad, "Carnivals against Capital," p. 550.

To see how clowning can be a personal liberation, some of my field notes say a lot. In my "normal" life, I am usually quite intimidated by representatives of authorities. During demonstrations I prefer to keep in the background and let others handle the interaction with the police. However, as a clown my fear was reduced considerably. At my first clowning experience in Luleå described above, I ended up interacting with the police in ways I had not even thought I would dare the day before. Straight after the action, I wrote in my hasty field notes:

> I found myself in new situations that I had not imagined [the day before]. I was imitating a policeman for several kilometres by following in his heels, and interacting with many of them.

Also during the NATO Game Over action in Belgium mentioned previously, clowning made me less scared of the encounter with the police. I thought that the chance of the police beating up clowns was smaller than violence against "ordinary" activists, something which Bogad also has noted. What is even more interesting is that I have been able to take this experience of fearlessness from my clowning persona and subsequently use it also in my "normal" life.

However, clowning is not necessarily personally liberating for everyone if people find it hard to find a way to use the clown role under the circumstances they encounter. Emma and Maria felt a little superfluous as clowns in Luleå in 2011 when there were so many protesters and so few police. When Emma had been at the action in Luleå two years previously, the atmosphere had been very different and there had been police and conscript soldiers everywhere. Maria had decided to be part of the clown army in Luleå in 2011 as a personal challenge, since she has never liked the clown figure much, not even as a child. Although it felt a bit strange for her to be a clown with this attitude behind her, she is glad that she tried. Sometimes during the action she had a good flow and it was cool, but at other times she did not really know what to do and would have liked to have more training and scenario planning beforehand.[496]

To sum up rebel clowning's impact on facilitating a culture of resistance, it can be a way to contribute to more energy and sustainability to the group, and a personal liberation for some clowns. However, it depends very much on the circumstances what the clowns can do.

Challenging power relations on the ground

Through play and otherness clowns present their friendliness and nonviolent intentions, but as soon as ridicule is added the whole affair becomes more ambivalent. When it comes to relations of power, the accounts of rebel clowning first and foremost attest to the way activists perceive and interact with police and military on the ground, since they are the representatives of dominant discourses that rebel clowns actually get to meet.

Although the police and soldiers on the ground are rarely what concerns activists the most – in the case of Ofog the main target is the dominant discourse of militarism – relations with the police frequently become the major topic for rebel clowns. Law enforcement officers respond to clowns in many different ways, but according to the clowns there is something disarming about the clown figure. Vera experienced this already when she was performing as a clown for the first time. She described how by being in her role as a clown, the police that she interacted with became more relaxed. Her experience was that at first they were quite stiff, but once they understood that the clowns did not intend to do anyone any harm, they responded by moving in ways which they expected the clowns to imitate.[497]

---

[496] Interview September 2011.
[497] Interview September 2011.

Earlier I described the action at Bofors' headquarters in 2008 where three clowns "snuck" inside the enclosure. Vera experienced a change in the dynamic of the interaction with the police:

> And we had very much fun, and in the end the police started to interact with us and blow soap bubbles. When we imitated them they started to do funny things because they knew we would imitate them, and it became an interaction instead of an angry demonstration.[498]

To Vera, situations like this show something about what it is that clowns can do that other protesters cannot do, and how disarming the clown figure can be:

> I experienced how big the difference can be between being a clown and an ordinary activist, and I thought it was really intense and cool. Not because it is very cool in itself to cross the enclosed area, but there is something very disarming with this figure, the symbol that the clown is.[499]

Lisa, an activist who observed this episode, viewed it as a little victory regarding space because the clowns managed to get a little further than what was allowed. That victory felt important, since the year before someone had been arrested and convicted just for being a few meters inside the enclosed area.[500] However, there is a limit to the clowns' ability to influence relations of power. Vera used the term *disarm* metaphorically to describe how the clowns charmed the police into a mutual recognition of each other as human beings. However, in spite of this "disarmament", the police literally remained armed and it is hard to imagine anything the clowns could have done that would change that.

---

[498] Interview September 2011.
[499] Interview September 2011.
[500] Interview September 2011.

Illustration 15. Ofog : A police blows soap bubbles outside Bofors headquarters.[501]

The challenge of space was mainly symbolic, since the clowns themselves did not have any clear plans about what they wanted to do once they were inside. It was the crossing itself that was seen as a victory, because it challenged the authority that the police was trying to uphold. Some people might consider this childish mischief, but in this context where the police were there to protect a big arms producer against nonviolent protest, and there was no obvious reason for having the restricted area exactly where it was placed, the challenging of space became an undermining of the rationality that the police were trying to uphold. By physically crossing the line of authority, the clowns showed that the location of the line was artificial and negotiable, since some people could be there and others not. By using an

---

[501] Original photo text from Ofog's webpage.

absurd humorous political stunt, they pointed towards the absurdity of the situation.

However, clowning will not have this effect of negotiating space in all types of situations. At the NATO Game Over action in 2012 the clowns found little space to manoeuvre because everything happened so fast and there was little we could do as clowns. I doubted how useful the clowning was because the timing of the action meant there were only a few minutes when we could interact with the police. My field notes describe how my clown character offered sultanas to a policewoman on a horse in this very short moment of opportunity:

> Then I tried to approach the police to offer my sultanas, but did not get very far before three police horses were cutting me off and I became a very small and scared clown. However, as a determined friendly and peaceful clown I still offered sultanas, and even in a situation like this the policewoman actually felt obliged to say "no thank you". That is an interesting observation, and although the police of course react individually, friendly clowning definitely helps break through. But no chance of imitation or playing games.[502]

My interpretation of the policewoman's polite reaction was that I had succeeded in communicating the nonviolent values that I intended to, and to me it felt like "breaking through" to the person behind the police role. It is possible that this is an over interpretation and she might have been friendly anyway, but during the heat of the moment I was satisfied with being able to bring about this reaction.

After the NATO Game Over action outside of NATO's headquarters we had to walk half a kilometre to an enclosure. On the way I tried to talk to several of the police. Some responded and some did not speak English or pretended not to. I asked them if

---

[502] Field notes April 2nd 2012.

they were scared of clowns, and when they said no as expected that became an opportunity to ask why they then arrested the clowns. No one answered that, but some of them smiled. I interpreted the smiles as if they did see the absurdity in the situation. However, another episode was a bit more peculiar and difficult to interpret. Before being put on the bus to the police detention, everyone was searched and everything that said "NATO Game Over" or otherwise expressed a critical opinion of the military was taken away and thrown in a pile. By then I had decided to stop clowning, and had put the red nose in a bum-bag. When I was searched, the policewoman threw away

Illustration 16. The author in clown offering sultanas. Photo by Olivier Vin, heymana.com.

my soap bubbles and my red nose, and no insisting that they were mine would bring them back. In my notes I wrote:

> This was just really ridiculous but that must be scary material, how else to interpret such an overreaction? It shows that clowning has some impact on them although I'm not sure what impact.[503]

I enquired of other clowns if this had been a systematic approach towards all clowns, but it appeared to be a random decision by one particular police person.

In several of the interviews, people from Ofog also commented on police reactions to clowns. Again it becomes obvious that clowns generate many different reactions. Emma and Maria observed the policeman in Luleå who walked several kilometres with one or more clowns in his heels. Emma's impression was "I think he thought it was quite comical,"[504] and she thought that he had a good attitude because he talked to some of the "civilian" demonstrators. To her it looked like he tried to interact a bit with the clowns, and smiled a little. Maria added that he was quite tolerant and did not overreact, but treated us like a good father when his kids were a bit naughty or out of line.[505]

Johanna had not been close to the police herself as a clown, but has observed the various responses to clowns: "The police laugh, and I think it is very difficult not to do that. However, I have also seen police who did not dare to laugh."[506]

As Johanna interpreted the police, most of them could not help but laugh, and in her opinion those who did not laugh did not dare. An alternative interpretation is of course that they were just not amused.

---

[503] Field notes April 2nd 2012.
[504] Interview September 2011.
[505] Interview September 2011.
[506] Interview June 2011.

Peter's experience has been that police and military do not really know how to react to clowns. According to him clowning creates uncertainty because they cannot react as they do with conventional protesters.

> I think there is such a liberty in the role of a clown. First of all, the limitlessness, what you can do as a person, it becomes more like play. I have noticed that police and soldiers do not really know how to meet clowns, they can't really behave as they usually do when they meet demonstrators. Instead they become a bit more cautious. They don't know exactly how to react, and therefore you can get away with more things than you usually would. It becomes a little less hostile.[507]

Peter has also had the experience that the police attempted to make the clowns become serious, asking them to stop clowning and being foolish. When I asked what he and the other activists did as a response, Peter painted a picture of the dilemma that absurd clowns pose to police who know how to deal with rational protest, but have little experience with absurdity:

> Peter (laughs): Then you just continue, that is the point. To be a clown is about giving those you meet a perspective on their own role, on how they react. So when I walk and pretend to be a soldier, and place myself next to a soldier then maybe they get a perspective. That is a part of the action as well, that you can reach to the human being in a different way. You go in as a clown and play either police or military or demonstrator, so everyone can see themselves in what they do.

> Majken: Have you seen any episodes where you have felt that break through the police role and reach the person who is behind it?

---

[507] Interview September 2011.

> Peter: That is difficult, because you never really know, actually. You feel that the police are uncomfortable, you can feel that. And then you have reached through in some way, because then they are not so certain in their role. Then you have kind of broken through, but it is difficult to see if there is any personal connection. But you feel that they must in some way reflect on how to react to this. And then you have reached across in some way.[508]

Peter thought it was difficult to know to what degree he and other clowns had connected with the persons behind the police role, but had the feeling they became uncomfortable and Peter interpreted the uncertainty as a kind of breakthrough. This is Peter's understanding of the situation, but to make someone who is usually sure of themselves and how to handle various situations uncertain is a big achievement from the clowning perspective. It is worth noting that Peter's experience is that when it comes to meeting clowns, confusion lead to less hostility. It is easy to imagine other situations where uncertainty would lead to more aggression.

Emma also spoke about the confusion clowning can create. She mentioned the example from the 2011 action in Luleå, where the clowns "stole" the police task of directing the traffic, and played police who told the other activists where they could be and not be (while the clowns were on the side where the activists could not be).[509] It became difficult for the police to uphold authority when clowns are standing next to them and performing the task that the police consider their job.

Maria brought up another theme connected to the relationship with the police which she had encountered when she tried to explain the clowning to some of her family members who are

---

Illustration 17. Ofog. Luleå July 26, 2011. The clown army "helps" the police stop the protesters approaching Vidsel Test Range.

not familiar with Ofog. They asked if clowning were not counterproductive if it risked making the police annoyed and angry? Even if clowning feels good for the clowns and the other activists, Maria suggested that clowning risks turning the focus too much on the police. She added something that many people in Ofog agree to: "I'm not involved in Ofog to be against the police."[510] Maria both saw the risk of clowning turning our attention away from the goal, and that the police get provoked and become rougher with protesters.[511]

---

[510] Interview September 2011.
[511] Interview September 2011.

Peter acknowledged the risks that Maria identified, but was not so worried about provoking the police and military.

> That can maybe happen, but it is not a general response I have felt. As a clown one's task is to touch somebody on a tender spot, ridiculing people, so of course that can happen. You are more challenging as a clown than as an ordinary political activist or protester, clowning is the weapon. It becomes more personal for the person you meet, that is obvious. If you meet a person who is a little more defensive, and feel that this is touchy, then of course that person can become more outward-reacting in an aggressive way. But it varies very much from person to person among the police, and generally I have not been met with more hostility from their side when I have been clowning.[512]

Among the clowns there is a worry of not being understood and concern that the clowning might backfire into hostile reactions to the clowns. However, those who have had most encounters with the law enforcement as clowns have felt that although they might cause confusion , they have not been met with hostility.

When it comes to the relations with the police, both Bogad and Routledge mention many of the same things that Ofog activists have told me and that I observed. Clowning changes the dynamic of the interaction when the police are not sure how to react, and it is an attempt to reach to the human being behind the uniform. Bogad explains how the clowns refuse to behave as "ordinary" protesters when they do not show fear or turn to anger:

> As the clowns greet the police as 'friends' and fail to either melt away in fear or raise the tension in anger, a shift in the paradigm and pattern of confrontation ensues. The true

---

[512] Interview September 2011.

challenge is to stay 'in clown' even when conventional power relationships assert themselves.[513]

Other protesters told Routledge how clowning can diffuse tensions and reach out to the human being behind the uniform:

> Various protestors at the G8 protests told us that such tactics had helped diffuse tense situations between them and the security forces during the protests. Moreover, CIRCA clowning attempted to access the person behind the police uniform. During CIRCA operations, I witnessed police officers smiling and laughing in interaction with rebel clowns, and even mimicking the clown salute.[514]

It is a challenge to sum up the reactions to clowns from authorities because so many factors are involved. There is the "big picture" about what type of action the clowns are involved in, since it makes a major difference if the clowns participate in a big legal demonstration, an attempted counter-recruitment or a civil disobedience action. It also matters a great deal how much time is available during the encounter, what the activists are planning to do, and what instructions the police have received from their superiors. Adding to the complexity is also the interactions at the individual level. Behind every clown and police officer is an individual who responds to micro signals from another individual – signals that might be intended or unintended and whose interpretation depends on how they are perceived. A clown like Vera thought it was ok to pretend to flirt and fall in love with one police officer, but she did not do it with others. A policewoman in Luleå had been hesitant towards all clowns, but finally gave in to a clown who was particularly skilful and convinced her to sit down and measure shoes.

---

[513] Bogad, "Carnivals against Capital," p. 550.
[514] Routledge, "Toward a Relational Ethics of Struggle," p. 88.

Above Emma and Maria expressed concern that clowns might provoke anger. However, a problem that was not really addressed by anyone in the interviews is the risk that clowning focuses on the interaction with the police and diverts attention away from the issue the activists are concerned about. After all, the discourse of militarism is the main interest of Ofog, not the individual low-ranking soldier or police officer.

Lena emphasised that it is not the people on the ground she wants to confront, but systems and people on top of the hierarchies. As an example she mentioned that she has never understood why people who are against the politics of former US president George W. Bush get hung up on his alcoholism or dyslexia, when what should be the focus is his politics. About the clowning and the soldiers she said:

> These food soldiers are furthest down the hierarchy, and it is not them as persons we want to get at. We want to reach those who decide about the structure.[515]

Nevertheless it is mainly those at the bottom of the hierarchy who are exposed to the clowns' mocking and ridicule of authoritative body language and commands, since the clowns usually do not have access to those on top of the hierarchies. This creates a contradiction between what the clowns intend to achieve and what they are actually able to do. Although the clowning is directed at the role that police and military perform, it is the individual police officer or soldier who knows how the experience feels for them.[516] Some police officers might laugh or smile at the ridicule if they have enough critical self-distance, but they can also be genuinely offended.

---

[515] Interview June 2011.
[516] As part of the research project I contacted the police in the north of Sweden and asked for an interview with the police officers who had been present during the *War Starts Here"* action in 2011. However, they never responded to the request.

Clowning – an absurd humorous political stunt

The accounts above illustrate that the clown army has multiple meanings for the people who engage in it. Some emphasise the playful and friendly aspects of clowning, others the ridicule. People get involved in rebel clowning with a huge variety of aims in mind to do with both the atmosphere within Ofog and with relations to other people, especially the police and military who are the state representatives that Ofog activists meet when they take action. The reactions to clowns also vary a lot – from indifference to laughs, smiles and play, as well as being told to stop being silly.

Maybe clowns are trying to do so many different things at the same time that it becomes almost incomprehensible to others. Certainly journalists have expressed confusion. However, to confuse someone who is usually sure of themselves and what they do is in the clowning perspective an achievement in itself. This is something that Peter touched on when he experienced the police's uncertainty about how to handle the situation as something positive.

Radical clowning is a version of the absurd stunt as described in Chapter 3, and challenges all claims to rationality and logic put forward by the police and military with a refusal to accept this perception of the world. Clowning aims to transcend established power relations using slapstick and absurdity. Through ridicule, parody and imitation, the police and military are denied the dignity of being adults in uniform performing their job. Clowns are "others", who do not dress and behave like the people uniformed officers usually have to deal with, but have adopted a role quite contrary to associations with both crime and conventional protest. This means that the police do not just go ahead and react as they usually do. Although representatives of law enforcement are unlikely to be fundamentally scattered in their view of the world, they have been placed in a position where there is no response that seems quite right.

When Vera pretended to fall in love, or suggested that the police help the activists get into the arms factory by providing a helicopter, she transcended the usual relations between these groups of people. Of course everyone involved is aware that the clown army is a performance and that the red nose is not real, but since all protest is a performance, at least for some clowns it becomes a way of including a sincere wish to communicate in the performance. Whether this intention comes across is of course another matter.

However, the absurd stunt and the clown role have some limitations. Clowns cannot attempt to present alternatives to militarism in rational terms at the same time as they are clowning. Here one is forced to choose. Rationally explaining the purpose of clowning requires that one bring along civilian friends or stop clowning.

In traditional clown performances, aggression and violence can be part of the show,[517] but the initiators of the original British CIRCA did not include this in their concept of rebel clowning. That nonviolence was central is indicated by the slogan "amuse, bemuse, but never bruise"[518], and any sign of violence would have been an obvious contradiction to the nonviolent values that the activists wanted to communicate. Had the clowns been aggressive in their play, this would have been a potential source of huge misunderstandings.

In his writing about the background to CIRCA, Bogad places it within the *carnival against capital*.[519] In this carnivalesque protest there is a focus on do-it-yourself direct action, taking personal

---

[517] Peacock, *Serious Play: Modern Clown Performance*: p. 26.
[518] Bogad, "Carnivals against Capital," p. 553.
[519] Bogad, "Carnivals against Capital," pp. 543-44.

control and protesting in ways that is not permitted by the state. Although most of what happens is nonviolent, this type of activism sometimes ends in vandalism and rioting.[520] In an account of a network of cycling clowns in New York, Shepard, Bogad and Duncombe mention an episode of a biking clown who intentionally hit a man who had parked on the bike lane.[521] They do not reflect on this, but such episodes are potentially much more damaging for the clown army concept than the lack of training which has been brought up as the biggest problem. It is one thing if the performance is confusing or meaningless, but if clowning becomes associated with what most audiences consider vandalism or assault, then there is a considerable risk of losing sympathy from otherwise friendly audiences who respond positively to the clown figure. Good-will might be lost if they perceive clowning as a disguise for vandalism, rather than a sincere wish to communicate the absurdity of the world order. Clowns who engage in or gets associated with violence have left the innocence of the clown figure behind.

To my knowledge, this type of incident is not something Ofog activists have experienced, and there is nothing that indicates that this happens frequently in rebel clowning. However, when searching for traces of incompetence I came across the video *You Can Not Give an Anarchist Clown Directions (Especially While Wearing Riot Gear)*.[522] It shows a man with clowning face paint arguing with a policeman. According to most observers the policeman is not wearing riot gear as the title suggests, but a bicycle helmet and an ordinary police uniform. The person who is identified as an "anarchist clown" called Gen'ral Malaise of the

---

[520] Bogad, "Carnivals against Capital," p. 543.
[521] Shepard, Bogad, and Duncombe, "Performing Vs. The Insurmountable."
[522] Anonymous, *You Can Not Give an Anarchist Clown Directions (Especially While Wearing Riot Gear)*

Salish CIRCA in the explanation that goes with the video seems to have left all playfulness behind. Instead of playing tricks with the policeman or teasing him, he is engaging in a relatively aggressive conversation that has nothing to do with the humorous mode. There is no absurdity, play, otherness or even ridicule. The film clip shows the limits of clowning. The person is obviously upset about an episode where a protester was hit by a policeman[523], but his clown persona found no way of dealing with this frustration within the limits of the role. Other clowns might have been able to use their clown roles to express their grief and horror about what had happened.

Just like with other aspects of humour and the carnivalesque, clowning's subversiveness has been debated and there is no consensus.[524] Not surprisingly there is a tendency to frame this as either-or, rather than ask under what circumstances clowning can be subversive. Weitz discusses different interpretations of traditional clowning, and finds that the clown can be seen as a way of enforcing social control that teaches children the "correct" response to failure – to be ashamed and disappointed. However, he adds that "it is also possible to read the clown's buoyant attitude toward setback as somehow liberating, shrugging off social expectation to shoulder the world playfully."[525] Weitz claims that even if the clown can get away with much "the status quo reasserts its primacy in the end, with the reins still

---

[523] The text that was published together with the video says: "Gen'ral Malaise of the Salish CIRCA (Clandestine Insurgent Rebel Clown Army) dismisses Sgt. Ryan Long of the Seattle Police Department during a march against Monsanto rally at Westlake Park, May 25th, 2013. At the El Comite Immigration Reform Rally on May 1st 2013, Ofcr. Jack Persons hit and ran a protester on a bicycle, which is what clownie is referencing in this video."

[524] Weitz, "Failure as Success: On Clowns and Laughing Bodies.";
Wright, *Why Is That So Funny? A Practical Exploration of Physical Comedy.*

[525] Weitz, "Failure as Success: On Clowns and Laughing Bodies," p. 80.

firmly in the hands of the dominant discourse – yes, we have had a good laugh, but what has changed?"[526]

What has changed is that some of the children grow up and take the liberating potential they saw with them into adult life. The very existence of the idea of rebel clowning shows how the clown figure has been an inspiration for resistance. It is a traditional figure that has been modified and interpreted in the context of protest, and if this is the result it is irrelevant that academics have found it to mean something different. Although clowning might be a way to enforce social control and teach children "correct" behaviour, at least some of the children later remember the subversive potential it showed them when they took clowning into their political activism.

Play, otherness, ridicule and theory of nonviolent action

Above I discussed the possibilities and limitations of clowning when it came to facilitating outreach and mobilisation, a culture of resistance and challenging power relationships based on their expressions of play, otherness and ridicule. In chapter 1 I presented Vinthagen's theory of nonviolent action with its four different dimensions. A nonviolent action (1) is dialogue oriented at the same time as (2) it aims to break power. An ideal nonviolent action is (3) an utopian enactment that demonstrates that (4) violence is not necessary and not normal.[527]

Above it became clear how many clowns use their clown personas to be dialogue oriented when they use play and otherness to express their nonviolent intentions. Even when clowns stay within the absurd in their relation with the police, some aspects of the ridicule might be considered a strong contradiction to nonviolent values and the dialogue oriented element of the

---

[526] Weitz, "Failure as Success: On Clowns and Laughing Bodies," p. 87.
[527] Vinthagen, *Ickevåldsaktion.*

action. Radical clowns might reach out to individual police officers, and be received in an atmosphere of mutual recognition of friendliness. Nevertheless, when the clowns at the same time aim to distract police officers in a dishonest attempt to divert attention away from what the police are there to do and thus prevent them from doing their job, they jeopardise the trust they have just built. The police are most likely perfectly aware of this double role of the clowns and never fully let their guard down as long as they are on the job. The clowns will never know if they have just failed a potential ally. The individual police officer might consider policing protest an undesirable aspect of her job that just has to be dealt with and support the activists' demands for global justice or nuclear disarmament – viewpoints that might be weakened if police feel badly treated. That clowning also can break power, at least temporarily, became apparent when it turned out to be difficult for the police to find an adequate reaction to the three clowns who "snuck" inside the enclosure outside Bofors. These clowns could be in places where other protesters were not allowed.

It is in the third dimension of Vinthagen's theory, the utopian enactment, that clowning is outstanding and quite distinct from other types of both humorous and non-humorous protest. According to Vinthagen, the power of utopian enactment is frequently underestimated and neglected when activists prepare for actions. An utopian enactment as part of a nonviolent action directly displays what an alternative reality would look like if the activists' vision of the world came into being. The activist should both believe and behave as if even the most brutal opponent at some point will be willing to change. This corresponds well with the naiveté and stupidity inherent in the clown role. Both traditional and rebel clowns should always behave as if the world is actually going to treat them well, an optimism which is emphasised by both Peacock and Wright. The nonviolent action should make visible that the utopian situation is possible in principle, at least for a short moment while the action is being carried out.

Instead of making abstract demands, one *shows* that world, even if just as a vague hint or fleeting glimpse. Good nonviolent actions help all parts in a conflict deal with hatred and enemy perceptions and undermine the idea that violence is normal. At the same time as the activists fight injustice, they should – to the degree it is possible – build the society they long for. The rebel clowns embody a vision of the world with space and tolerance for innocence, otherness and play.

Another aspect of the utopian enactment that Vinthagen emphasises is his modified version of the self-suffering that was important to Gandhi. In Vinthagen's theory the self-suffering is associated with the *willingness* to risk suffering and even death for one's cause. Looking at the clowns from this perspective, one can also speak about activists-as-clowns running a risk. Although the clowns ridicule others, the clowns also expose themselves considerably. Through their otherness, clowns accept the role as the outcast of society in order to comment from a marginal perspective. This aspect of the clown has not been explored in the literature on CIRCA or discussed in Ofog, but it is a way for the clowns to make a unique contribution to the nonviolent action. This self-accepted outcast role is of course limited because it is only temporary – radical clowns can slip back into their usual life as soon as the face paint and costume are removed – and is not comparable with risking death. Although the rebel clowns take their outcast position seriously, it is a privilege to be able to decide yourself when you are willing to be seen as an outcast.

Keeping the utopian enactment dimension of nonviolent action in mind, one should not underestimate the power of a hint of a better world. It is part of the "nature" of clowning that it cannot do more than hint. As an absurd humorous political stunt it is bound to remain absurd. As was pointed out above, convincing clowns have to stay in clown and perform from this position. It is impossible at the same time to give rational talks about how society ought to be organised.

Although hints of a possible better world are important, clowning certainly has its limitations. Peacock claims that the effect of CIRCA was limited[528], and Bogad reflects that in themselves, performances like these can only hint at a better world:

> These carnival-inspired power-plays can be problematic. While the experience of training and playing with CIRCA, or with carnivalesque protest in general, can be liberating for individual participants, these actions in and of themselves only hint at a better, possible world. Tactical carnival in and of itself does not change the fundamental relations of production or distribution in the greater society. The liberatory spaces it creates are quickly dispersed, either by the force of the state or by the inevitable need of its participants to eventually *get back to work*.[529]

It is important to be cautious when judging the effects the clowns have had. Creating friendly relations with the police might be considered an important aspect of a good nonviolent action, but it can hardly be the goal in itself. Of course a few clowns here and there cannot be expected to dismantle the discourse of militarism, but Ofog's clowns did not even get to meet representatives of NATO or Bofors and communicate the absurdity of the situation directly to them. Such a "meeting" only took place indirectly through the media. Thus, the most generous interpretation possible is to say that the clowns in these cases might have contributed to reaching out and created a little more attention to the issues of NATO and Swedish arms production and export. Clowning was also a positive experience for most of the activist clowns and can potentially contribute to creating a culture of resistance. Finally, radical clowning can under some

---

528 Peacock, *Serious Play: Modern Clown Performance*: p. 122.
529 Bogad, "Carnivals against Capital," p. 555 emphasis in original.

circumstances break established relations of power when it
becomes a way of negotiating physical space.

Conclusion

Ofog's clowns are an application of the rebel clown army concept developed by CIRCA. Rebel clowning is part of a tradition
of tactical carnival and playful protest which appears to be
increasingly popular in the global justice movement in the so-
called western world. Rebel clowns can play a natural part in
bigger actions like the pink carnival in Luleå or the humanitarian
intervention in Belgium where they provide some of the colour
and playfulness which are elements in the world that the activists
strive towards. In the counter-recruitment actions the ridicule of
military personnel provides a more obvious and direct challenge
where clown values clash with the ideals that militaries uphold.
Unpredictability is part of the clown figure and clowning can be
varied considerably, but like with all other types of actions it is a
challenge for clowns to remain unpredictable and not become
yet another routine within the *repertoire of contention*.[530]

Peacock's definition of clowning with its key concepts of play,
otherness and incompetence was a useful starting point for
investigating Ofog's rebel clowning. Both play and otherness
were found in abundance, but incompetence was almost absent.
A possible explanation for the absence of incompetence is that
convincingly pretending to be incompetent requires performance
skills that most activists have not acquired. However, rebel
clowning has another core feature, ridicule, which Peacock did
not find prominent enough in traditional clowning to include in
her definition.

---

[530] This term which is frequently used in social movement theory was
first coined by Charles Tilly, *Popular Contention in Great Britain, 1758-
1834* (Cambridge, MA: Harvard University Press, 1995).

The way individual rebel clowns and clown groups perform their versions of play, otherness and ridicule influence how the interactions with various audiences unfold. Although clowns cannot control the reactions of others, the ways they draw on these core features determine to what degree radical clowning can contribute to outreach, a culture of resistance and challenging relations of power.

When it comes to outreach, clowns appear to be confusing to media, at the same time as they are recognised as good images for photos. Since most audiences associate clowns with something positive, they are a way to communicate nonviolent values and present a non-threatening face to outsiders. Regarding the culture of resistance, clowning can be a personal liberation for individual activists and bring new energy that can be spent on other types of activism.

For those who engage in rebel clowning, the most interesting aspect is its ability to challenge power. Since the police are the state representatives Ofog activists meet most often when they take action, interactions with them become the centre of the clowns' attention. Rebel clowns have been met with many different types of reactions from authorities. At the education fair in Gothenburg, the clowns were turned away at the door. Offerings of food have been politely declined. The policeman in Luleå who walked for almost five kilometres with clowns imitating his every move ignored them most of the time. Some police officers respond to the clowns by moving in ways they expect to be imitated.

Many factors influence to what degree the clowns can reach out to the police and other audiences and if they succeed in challenging established relations of power. The time available to build a relationship with the audience, the skills of the clowns and the interactions that arise between individual clowns and audiences all matter. The varied reactions to clowns reflect the ambiguity of the clown performances and how they constantly shift position.

It is part of the role to be unpredictable and be difficult to place in a box. However, this also makes it difficult to predict exactly what the reactions might be, and the clowns' own focus on interaction with police officers can potentially risk diverting attention away from the issue the activists were originally concerned about.

I also investigated how the use of play, otherness and ridicule can be understood in light of Vinthagen's theory of nonviolent action. Some parts of clowning, especially play, make it dialogue oriented, while ridicule sends a contradictory message. However, it is especially when it comes to the aspect of the utopian enactment that clowning is highly unusual. The clowns show what another world can look like at the same time as they often aim to speak to a shared humanity that transcends roles of activists and police officers. Although clowning may only hint at another world, one should not underestimate the power of showing potential. It is part of the logic of absurd stunts that you cannot simultaneously be rational.

Even when they are considered annoying, nonviolent rebel clowns at some level appeal to the shared experience of what it means to be human. The clown figure can potentially speak to both the comic and tragic aspects of human life in addition to standing out from other types of humorous as well as non-humorous protest. However, it is not enough to put on a red nose and start imitating the police – the relations are still fragile, and if the performance is not experienced as sincere the possibility will collapse. That is why just a single violent clown should be a concern for the whole community of rebel clowns.

Militarism is a dominant discourse that manifests itself through a number of military institutions, most notably the armed forces. No single action or method is likely to significantly change that in the short term. It would be naïve to expect a group of clowns to do more than contribute to change, no matter how skilful and dedicated they are. However, it is worth taking into consideration that the experiments CIRCA, Ofog and similar groups have done so far have been small scale. Of course it is impossible to dismantle the military institutions and the discourses of militarism and neo-liberalism with 8 clowns here and 150 clowns there. However, it would be an interesting experiment to evaluate what effect a "standing army" of 1000 trained, creative, unpredictable yet persistent clowns could have in 10 years.

Chapter 5: Ofog - playful anti-militarist mischief

Introduction

The case study of the anti-militarist network Ofog begins with an introduction to what type of activities members of the network carry out, Ofog's nonviolent platform and views on civil disobedience, organisation and who Ofog activists are. The purpose of this is to place the use of humour within a broader context. In Chapter 4 I presented Ofog's clowning, a particular type of absurd stunt. In this chapter many of Ofog's other humorous political stunts are introduced together with a discussion of their place within Ofog's overall way of working and what meaning they have to Ofog activists.

Seven different public humorous actions or campaigns are presented. The type and amount of information are uneven: some are introduced briefly while others are discussed in great detail. The data about the actions originate from the interviews, workshops and participant observation I carried out as part of the participatory action research project supplemented with information from press releases, newspaper coverage and Ofog's webpage.[531] Although this is not an attempt to write the history of Ofog, I have chosen to include many details and anecdotes that are not documented elsewhere to give a fuller context for understanding Ofog's use of humour.

After summing up the findings from these humorous political stunts through the theatre metaphor I proceed to analyse Ofog's use of humour according to its ability to facilitate outreach, mobilisation, a culture of resistance and challenging power relations. Finally I discuss some interesting findings, namely how

---

[531] The data gathering process is described in Chapter 2.

314

the distinction between humour and other types of creative activities is experienced as artificial, and the risks with using humour in political activism. The conclusion sums up the chapter and points towards some possible future research areas.

The anti-militarist network Ofog

Ofog is a Swedish network of anti-militarist individuals and affinity groups doing direct action for peace in Sweden and abroad. The targets of its anti-militarism include NATO, Swedish arms production and export, military exercises and militarisation of Swedish society. The network uses methods such as participation in public debates, education and training in nonviolence as well as civil disobedience in its attempts to simultaneously challenge and raise awareness about the discourse of militarism and the institutions that uphold this worldview.

The network was formed in 2002 when a group of people began to participate in international peace actions in various places in Europe, such as "Trident Ploughshares" blockades of UK nuclear weapon facilities in Scotland and England and the Belgian "Bombspotting" campaign. Ofog started doing actions in Sweden in 2007 with a disarmament camp in Karlskoga, near the headquarters of one of Sweden's biggest arms producers, Bofors.[532] At this point, Ofog already had a tradition of combining the serious issues of anti-militarism and opposition to nuclear weapons with prankish ways of carrying out protest.

The name "Ofog" in itself is playful and has a humorous touch to it. On its webpage, Ofog explains its name this way in English:

> "Ofog" literally translates into "mischief". But Ofog is also a play with words. "Foga" is a Swedish verb meaning to conform, to obey. But in Swedish, if you put an O before a word, you turn it into its opposite. "Foga" also means,

---

[532] Ofog, "English," http://ofog.org/english.

roughly, fixating things together in a decided and un-
changeable form, so in this meaning of the word, when we
put the O before, this is an allusion to our function as a
flexible, dynamic network.[533]

Ofog is a network and not a formal organisation. Anyone who
agrees with the platform can take action in the name of Ofog.
The first part of Ofog's platform states:

> Ofog struggles for disarmament, international solidarity
> and a just, peaceful world. We work against the world's
> largest military war organisation NATO and the growing
> militarisation of the EU, against nuclear arms and the arms
> industry, the Swedish as well as the global.

> We are a network independent of religious societies and
> political parties, where everyone who endorses our plat-
> form is welcome to participate. Within the guidelines of
> the platform everyone is welcome to build their own group
> and carry out actions in the name of Ofog.

> Ofog's activities happen locally through independent local
> groups, nationally through coordinated actions and camps
> and internationally by travelling to actions in other coun-
> tries and cooperation with antimilitaristic networks and
> organisations in other countries.

> We work for peace through peaceful means, through opin-
> ion building, public awareness raising, active nonviolence,
> civil disobedience and other forms of peaceful direct ac-
> tion. Our working methods are characterised by openness,
> responsibility and respect towards everyone involved and
> care for our own and other's safety.

> We think it is important to challenge the obedience that
> makes repression, abuse and injustice possible. Because

---

[533] Ofog, "English".

> some laws allow abuse to be perpetrated some of us some-
> times choose to take action which breaks the law. Breaking
> laws is one of the many tools of resistance and that Ofog as
> a network sometimes break laws does not mean that every-
> one who participates in our activities choose to do so.[534]

My impression from the participant observation is that there is
congruity between the way Ofog present itself in the platform,
and the way the network operates in reality. The platform emphasises Ofog's network structure where affinity groups take
action independently. The embracement of civil disobedience in
the platform shows how some members are ready to take radical
steps in order to achieve change.

Civil disobedience

From the platform it is apparent that civil disobedience is central
to Ofog. Although many of the network's activities are also
focused on awareness raising, participation in public debates,
education about nonviolence and organising cafes and seminars,
the active support of civil disobedience is one of the keys to the
"feeling" of Ofog. Another central aspect is the light-heartedness
where the use of humour plays an important part.

A few Ofog activists have done disarmament civil disobedience
actions – which the arms producers call sabotage. The most
extensive actions of this type so far in Ofog's history occurred in
the *Disarm* campaign from 2008-2010, where five people in three
different actions disarmed parts of grenade launchers and can-
ons, and attempted to disarm a fighter plane, all produced in
Sweden. For this the activists were convicted to a combined total
of 2 years and 3 months in prison and 944,774 Swedish crowns
in criminal damage (approximately 140,000 Australian dollars).[535]

---

[534] Ofog, "Ofogs Plattform," http://ofog.org/ofogs-plattform.
[535] Ofog, "Aktioner," http://ofog.org/avrusta/aktioner.

317

However, the majority of those who decide to break the law limit their disobedience to activities that result in relatively small fines, such as entering a restricted military area to do a citizen inspection or mark out that war starts here. In spite of relatively minor direct consequences of this type of civil disobedience, for most of us these decisions to break laws do not come easily, and only after careful deliberations.[536]

On its webpage, under the heading "Civil disobedience", Ofog says:

> Ofog works against nuclear weapons and arms export in various ways, but our main form of action is civil disobedience. By civil disobedience we mean in openness and without violence breaking a law, an order or a tradition, with a political purpose. Why have we chosen this approach?
>
> There are many arguments in favour of civil disobedience against nuclear arms and arms export. Ofog has not made a joint statement; everyone has their own reason for working with the network.[537]

This is followed by a list of different arguments in favour of civil disobedience.

In this description of what is meant by civil disobedience, Ofog refers to four key concepts which are standard in most literature

---

[536] After my own first civil disobedience action with Ofog I wrote about how this decision had not come easily and how empowering the feeling was. A similar experience is expressed on the webpage under the heading "civil disobedience" this way: "It is a very strong feeling to take the step from trying to influence people in power to actually start changing it yourself." Ofog, "Civil Olydnad," http://ofog.org/civil-olydnad.

[537] Ofog, "Civil Olydnad".

on civil disobedience: 1. openness, 2. without violence 3. break a law 4. with a political purpose.

These four components do not differ considerably from John Rawls' classic definition:

> I shall begin by defining civil disobedience as a public, nonviolent, conscientious yet political act contrary to law usually done with the aim of bringing about a change in the law or policies of the government.[538]

Ofog's understanding of civil disobedience is also quite consistent with a standard Scandinavian definition suggested by Persen and Johansen:

> Civil disobedience (...) [involves] conscious, nonviolent, illegal actions done openly with the purpose of influencing social or ethical conditions considered serious by the participants. It is actions that fulfil at least five criteria: 1. Openness, 2. Nonviolence 3. Breaking the law 4. Serious conviction 5. Social and/or ethical purpose.[539]

The literature then continues with long discussions about these criteria, and when civil disobedience is justified and not. Although there might be disagreements about the finer points of the terminology, these definitions mean that civil disobedience differs considerably from other types of law breaking since it is not done for the benefit of the individual, but for what the participants consider important social or ethical reasons.

In Ofog's civil disobedience actions, activists act out of strong convictions and feelings of personal responsibility to prevent arms produced in Sweden reaching war zones and wars from being prepared in Sweden. The subsequent court cases are also

---

[538] John Rawls, "Definition and Justification of Civil Disobedience," in *Civil Disobedience in Focus*, ed. Hugo Adam Bedau (London: Routledge, 1991), p. 104.

[539] Persen and Johansen, *Den Nødvendige Ulydigheten* p. 24.

grave affairs where people frequently argue that they take action in self-defence[540] in order to prevent war crimes. I have not observed humour playing any role in this important aspect of Ofog's actions.

Ofog activists and activities

People in Ofog are diverse when it comes to age, gender, backgrounds and the lives that have led them to Ofog. The people I interviewed have been or are involved in a number of other issues including union work, prisoners' rights, animal rights, refugees, anti-racism, the environment, feminism and LBGTQ (Lesbian, Bisexual, Gay, Transgender, Queer) rights and activism. No one I interviewed had been involved in any other organisations that had the same style as Ofog or used humour to the same degree.

I have not tried to do a survey of people's backgrounds, but within the organisation there is a self-consciousness that Ofog is white, young and with a middleclass background. The network has an outspoken aim to be inclusive, and looking at the network as a whole reveals an age range from 16-75, and a more or less equal representation of men and women. However, even within networks like this, informal hierarchies emerge based on personality and experience. Ofog has tried to counter this by rotating roles and responsibilities and actively encouraging newcomers to contribute with ideas and share their points of view. This said, during the time of my fieldwork there did seem to be a core of people who others turned to when they had questions and there

---

[540] In the Swedish language activists and lawyers use the terms "nödvärn" and "nödrätt". Unlike the English term self-defence, the Swedish words do not have any component of "self" but refer to "emergency". Although the argumentation has rarely been accepted by the courts, the Swedish terminology makes it much easier than English to express that activists take action to prevent bigger crimes.

were uncertainties. These people might well disagree much among themselves, but my impression is that some people's words carried more weight than others on some occasions. This is probably unavoidable and it does make sense that others listens more to the experienced activist who has spent much time with Ofog than to the newcomer. What gives "status" in Ofog is how much time you spend working on Ofog's issues and if you have done civil disobedience and been to prison for it. Nevertheless, I have never spent time with any other group that makes such a conscious effort to be inclusive and take consensus decision making so seriously.

This atmosphere of tolerance and sharing creates an environment that stimulates creativity, including the use of humour. Although it is difficult to prove this causal relationship, it is probably not a coincidence that Ofog is a network that uses more humour than other organisations, according to the people I interviewed. Ofog's way of organising means that there is much less chance of someone saying no and disapproving of different ideas. Although other participants might not find an idea to be optimal, they are unlikely to express this loudly as long as there is an affinity group that wants to go ahead with the suggestion. In a hierarchical organisation where someone at the top makes the decision, there is a much higher risk that someone will say no. It only takes one leader that disapproves of humour whatever the reason for the whole organisation to turn away from humour.

Although civil disobedience actions are important and contribute to making Ofog different from other peace organisations in Sweden, locally much work is focused on opinion building and awareness raising, both with and without humour. To give some examples: In Stockholm the local group in December 2011 arranged a Nobel walk to all the places in Stockholm that contribute to war.[541] In Malmö, they arranged a five week summer course in nonviolence together with a local folk high school. One Christmas, they hung toy automatic weapons wrapped as gifts on the public Christmas tree. Under the banner "Sweden sends hard gifts to the world's children again this year," they collected signatures against arms export from the general public. They have also been present at the local arms producer which manufactures red dot sights exported to armies around the world. Here they have lit candles, read out the names of victims of the war in Iraq and tried to talk with the workers and leadership of the factory. During a trial against Ofog activists that had climbed the fence to the same factory they rented a jumping castle and arranged "jump for peace".[542] In Umeå they sang Christmas carols with a different text before Christmas 2011, and in Gothenburg the group has regularly arranged "anti-mili" cafes with various themes and speakers.

Ofog's public humour

In this section some of Ofog's campaigns and actions are presented with an emphasis on the use of humour. In some cases it becomes clear that humour is not easily defined, and that a campaign or action can have humorous elements although these are only a minor part. For each example I identify which type of stunt it is according to the model presented in Chapter 3 and apply the theatre metaphor to analyse them.

Reality AB

In the North of Sweden near the town Luleå, the Swedish Defence Materiel Administration (FMV), operates Europe's largest

---

[541] Ofog, "Stadsvandring I Krigsföretagens Och Fredsinitiativens Stockholm," http://ofog.org/nyheter/stadsvandring-i-krigsforetagens-och-fredsinitiativens-stockholm.
[542] Interviews in Malmö September 2011.

overland military test site now.[543] In 2009, NATO had permission to use this huge area, something which Ofog considered a sneaking erosion of Sweden's tradition of neutrality.

Ofog pretended to start a new company called "Reality AB", which saw this NATO exercise as an opportunity to do business. Although NATO had of course done everything possible to make its exercise realistic for its soldiers, Reality AB would help them make it even more realistic. With the company slogan "We die for you", what they could offer were the missing civilian victims – dead, wounded and traumatised. On the main street in Luleå, Ofog activists showed up dressed as serious business people to provide information about this new opportunity for a summer job in Luleå as a civilian victim of "collateral damage". Reality AB was especially eager to get women and children, and had a questionnaire for people to fill in where they could write about the kind of job they would prefer – did they want to die, be injured or get post traumatic stress disorder? On a couple of occasions they created a scenario in the main street in Luleå of civilians getting killed. Once they enacted the bombing of a wedding in Afghanistan, another time the NATO bombing in 1999 of a train with civilians in Grdulice in the South of Serbia. At the bottom of the invitation to participate in this scenario, it also said "With us, everyone is welcome. Even *you* can become a civilian casualty." The idea was also to take the civilians to the military base, but this part of the plan was never carried out.

This is an example of a supportive stunt according to the model introduced in chapter 3. Ofog framed its protest as an attempt to help NATO make its exercise more realistic and improve it. There are similarities with the way the John Howard Ladies' Auxhiliary Fan Club supported John Howard and how Netwerk

---

[543] Please see Chapter 4 for more details about this area now called Vidsel Test Range but formerly known as NEAT (North European Aerospace Test range).

Vlaanderen pretended to search for landmines in AXA in concern of everyone's safety. Irony was used to draw attention to the fact that most people killed in war are civilians. A large majority of the people Ofog met on the street also understood this irony, but two people took everything literally, and thought they had applied for a real summer job.

The incongruity Ofog aimed to expose was the military's attempt to present war as "clean" and a fight for human rights and development, while the reality on the ground is that civilians are wounded and killed. Since Ofog's show was on the street, and not directly confronting NATO, it could be ignored by the representatives of the dominant discourse. Had Ofog instead chosen to take the play to a place where NATO or Swedish authorities could not ignore it, the spectacle would have been different. Since they were not playing the ordinary protester role, it would with all likelihood have been difficult to respond adequately. However, the audience Ofog was targeting was the general public in the hope of increasing awareness about NATO's role in causing civilian suffering.

It is difficult to know if Ofog got their message across better through the use of irony, and one can only speculate if Reality AB managed to reach a different segment of the general public or if they reached them at a deeper level. Johanna, who was one of the recruiters on the street, reflects about how the general public usually know in advance what types of arguments they will meet from both the military and from protesters:

> I think it is difficult for most of us to reflect critically on the militarism we live in and get fed with every day. Therefore it is important to think about strategies that make people reflect. It can be easy for people to "switch off" and I think [the style of Reality AB] is a strategy one can use not to end up in this for and against. When we hand out leaflets about the tragic consequences of war and so forth, I think it is easy for people to switch off and kind of let go.

However, you reflect on something that seems to be somehow twisted. (…) Although I am angry at an unjust world order, I think it can be very difficult to get sympathies when you are angry. I think it can be easier to get people to join you if you make them laugh, and [make them see] that you have some kind of self-distance.

Here Johanna describes how she experienced Reality AB to be a strategy to reach out to people in a way that differed from conventional leafleting. Although she is angry about the state of the world, her experience is that it is more constructive to channel this anger into a type of action that is "twisted" and therefore makes people reflect about what Ofog "really" means.

During interviews, Reality AB is the action several people within Ofog have mentioned as Ofog's best humorous action. Both Johanna, Vera and Lena mentioned it as their favourite example of Ofog's use of humour. Vera exclaimed spontaneously when she remembered the action: "God, that was really smart. That was a typical genius thing". She was not in Luleå the year it took place, but thought it was a very successful action, a smart choice:

That was probably the best ever. Unfortunately I didn't have anything to do with it. But that was a really smart thing, and I was very impressed by those who got the idea.

The stories about Reality AB have become part of Ofog's "heritage" and are shared when humour is discussed within the network. However, it is not so pervasive that everyone I have interviewed had heard about it.

Refining recruitment ads from the armed forces

Ofog has also been working with "ad-refinement" or "ad-sabotage" of the Swedish military's public recruitment campaigns. Sweden ended conscription in 2010, and ads for the Swedish military, Försvarsmakten, were new in public space. To recruit enough soldiers, Försvarsmakten spends roughly 1 billion Swedish crowns (approximately 166 million Australian dollars)

325

every year on recruitment campaigns. The institution is acutely aware of the need to build a brand that appeals to young people, and that there is a huge difference between this brand and selling commercial products.[544] The first recruitment campaign had the slogan "Do you have what it takes?", and in addition to having the right physical and mental capacities, it also included references to having the right opinions. These ads stated things like "Your grandmother does not think it's a big deal if Sweden's airspace is violated. What do you think?" and "Your friend does not want any help during natural catastrophes. What do you think?" Ofog activists did a refinement of the ads by manually adding more text. The text "Your grandmother does not think it's a big deal if Sweden's airspace is violated" was supplemented with "But she is fucking outraged that USA is practicing bombing in Norrland" [area in the north of Sweden]. "Your friend does not want any help during natural catastrophes" was corrected with "By the military. Other help is welcome". "Do you have what it takes to have an opinion" and its reference to Försvarsmakten's webpage was modified with "We have what it takes" and a reference to Ofog's webpage. The ironic press release about the action began this way:

> Ofog shows that we have what it takes to have an opinion and refine Försvarsmakten's many million crown ad campaign. The military's colourful posters with biased messages were tonight expanded with a little more facts the military itself forgot to mention.[545]

This type of ad-refinement is an example of corrective humour as described in Chapter 3 and has many similarities with culture

---

[544] Christopher Holmbäck and Urban Hamid, "Framtidens Svenska Militärer Rekryteras Tidigt," Re:public 2012.
[545] Ofog, "Vi Har Vad Som Krävs För Att Ha En Åsikt!," http://ofog.org/nyheter/vi-har-vad-som-kr%C3%A4vs-f%C3%B6r-att-ha-en-%C3%A5sikt

Illustration 17 Ofog. The original text from Försvarsmakten, white on green background says "Your friend does not want any help during natural catastrophes." It has been refined with the text: "By the military. Other help is welcome". In the corner, the supplement text says: "We have what it takes" and a reference to Ofog's webpage.

jamming. Instead of just openly criticising the Swedish military forces, Ofog corrects the image that Försvarsmakten tries to portray of itself with a different version of what military reality is about. When the military attempted to sell itself as a helper during natural disasters, Ofog suggested that this should be a civilian task. When Försvarsmakten referred to violation of Swedish airspace, Ofog tried to draw attention to the fact that NATO is allowed to practice war in Swedish airspace. The provocative assumption in the posters, that if you do not agree

327

with Försvarsmakten's interpretation of reality, it means that you don't dare to have an opinion, is openly rejected. By the very act of ad-refinement, Ofog activists showed that they disagreed, and that they certainly had what it takes to have a different opinion.

Returning to the theatre metaphor, Ofog snuck in on the scene behind the back of Försvarsmakten, something which is a typical characteristic of the corrective stunt. There are no major actors present to be challenged, and there is no special requirements regarding timing, apart from doing the modification while Försvarsmakten's campaigns were running. Just like with Reality AB, Ofog's intended audience is the general public, maybe even specifically the young people that Försvarsmakten are targeting in their recruitment campaigns. To my knowledge, no one in Ofog has been caught doing ad-refinement and there has never been any other reaction from authorities and companies that provide spaces for ads than to remove the changes as quickly as possible. Lena, an experienced ad-refiner, has noticed that when she does the corrections openly on smaller posters on public transport, it becomes a way to discuss militarism with the other passengers.[546] Sneaking in on the stage without a direct confrontation and having the general public as the main audience means that it was unproblematic for authorities to ignore Ofog.

In these ad-refinements there are some similarities to the billboard liberators and adbusters mentioned in Chapter 3, but also some important differences. Ofog's modifications were a critique of this use of public space, and an attempt to interfere with a newly established brand – the Swedish armed forces, which now had to sell itself in a way that was not required before. But although Försvarsmakten has worked hard to create its own brand, Ofog's refinements were not a critique of consumerism

---

[546] Comment made by Lena during the War Starts Here seminar about counter recruitment July 24th 2011, Luleå.

like most adbusting. It also differed from the type of adbusting that Harold criticised for not presenting alternatives. It suggested joining Ofog instead of the armed forces, and this way showing that you have what it takes to have an opinion, just not the one Försvarsmakten would like to see. Compared to the Obsession example from chapter 3 Ofog's modifications were not very graphically and technically sophisticated in this case, but it provided a much more controversial message than reminding the audience that cigarettes cause cancer or that skinny models might contribute to young people's eating disorders. It also expressed Ofog's attitude of "do it yourself" with the means available.

Ironic posters and flyers

When the technical university in Lund arranged an open day and invited companies to have a stall and meet the students who were training as engineers, physicists etc., two people from Ofog also showed up. One of the companies that were invited was SAAB, one of Sweden's big arms producers. SAAB and the other companies used this as an opportunity to show themselves as good employers, in order to recruit the best students. Ofog took advantage of this, and decided to produce a satiric version of a SAAB recruitment flyer. The first three lines read:

> Do you have what it takes to create a world filled with suffering, death and misery? Then SAAB AB is the company for you. SAAB is world leading in the attack and war industry and our weapons are frequently used around the world.

The two activists discretely placed the flyers among SAAB's own recruitment material, and as far as they know, SAAB did not notice them. They have not heard about any reactions to the satiric flyers either.[547]

---

[547] Interview with Gustav September 2011.

329

This was an example of a corrective stunt that has the core characteristics of the challengers sneaking in on the scene behind the back of the actor they wanted to expose, in this case SAAB. They hijacked the recruitment flyer and in ironic terms phrased it as if this was produced by SAAB. As in the other corrective stunts, the activists aimed to bring attention to facts that the company would prefer to keep silent about. They targeted the same people as SAAB, those who were showing an interest in working for the company, presumably in the hope that this unmasking of the company might make people think twice about this employment choice.

A second satiric flyer was produced and handed out by the Malmö-Lund group during the election campaign for the parliamentary election in 2010. It was a parody of a sales ad and advertised Swedish arms. On the top it said "Sweden's war industry is booming, we celebrate that with an arms sale". On the bottom it said "you find us all over Sweden". In the middle were photos of three weapons produced in Sweden, the red dot sight from Aimpoint in Malmö, an Excalibur grenade and a Carl Gustaf grenade launcher. It did not have a direct connection with the election, and the person who made the flyer thought that the timing with the election was not ideal since it drowned among all the election flyers from the political parties.

The arms sales flyer was a supportive stunt, again using irony to bring attention to Swedish arms production and export. What at first glance can be interpreted as celebration for the arms industry used the easily recognisable language of a shoe or cloth sale to ironise about these products made in Sweden. The activists did not get any immediate reactions from their audiences, maybe because the timing of their show was not ideal, but as with many other stunts it is difficult to measure the effect.

In 2013 Ofog in Stockholm produced a series of satiric posters, and 7 of them were posted on Facebook in January and February. The posters were a parody of the newest recruitment campaign from Försvarsmakten called "what are you doing?" In this campaign Försvarsmakten produced a number of films and posters with people doing various arty/cultural/meaningless things, depending on who you asked. One showed a young

Illustration 18. Two flyers from Ofog Malmö-Lund used on two different occasions:

Left: Satiric ad for Swedish arms. On the top it says "Sweden's war industry is booming, we celebrate that with an arms sale". On the bottom it says "you find us all over Sweden". In the middle are photos of three weapons produced in Sweden, the red dot sight, Excalibur grenade and Carl Gustaf grenade launcher.

Right: Satiric recruitment flyer from the company SAAB, hidden among SAAB's own recruitment material during a job fair. The text begins: "Do you have what it takes to create a world filled with suffering, death and misery? Then SAAB AB is the company for you. SAAB is world leading in the attack and war industry and our weapons are frequently used around the world."

331

woman apparently sorting her books according to the colours on the back, another a young man making a piece of art/meaningless pattern with post-it notes in different colours. Below Försvarsmakten wrote something about what they do, for instance "What we are doing is making tracks during snow-storms, and rescuing people in the mountains. Service within Försvarsmakten is an opportunity to make a real difference". To some observers, the campaign was specifically ridiculing people doing something related to art, and the campaign generated

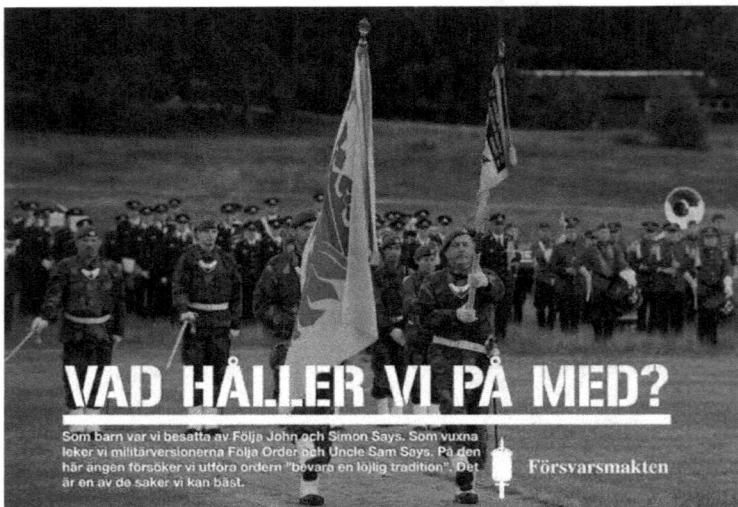

Illustration 19. Parody poster from Ofog. The text says "As children we were obsessed with Följa John [game where you imitate someone else] and Simon Says. As adults we play the military versions Follow Orders and Uncle Sam Says. On this meadow we are trying to follow the order 'preserve a ridiculous tradition'. That is one of the things we know best."

much controversy.[548] Ofog's posters, on the other hand, were ridiculing Försvarsmakten. A number of Försvarsmakten's own photos were adapted to imitate the "what are you doing?" campaign, with the main text changed into "what are we doing?" The texts in this corrective stunt was again referring to things that people in Ofog thought were missing from Försvarsmakten's own self-portrait. The first poster published showed what appears to be a military ceremony. The text from Ofog said:

> As children we were obsessed with Följa John [game where you imitate someone else] and Simon Says. As adults we play the military versions Follow Orders and Uncle Sam Says. On this meadow we are trying to follow the order 'preserve a ridiculous tradition'. That is one of the things we know best.

On Facebook, 242 people pressed "like" for this poster, and it generated 50 comments. However, most of the comments were critical comments from people who disapproved of Ofog. The other posters received between 31 and 120 "likes" and between 6 and 28 comments.

War Starts Here

Although the War Starts Here campaign was not developed with humour in mind, it had some humorous aspects. During this campaign Ofog marked all the places where war starts pink. The choice of the colour pink, the most un-militaristic colour available, does create some humorous associations for many people. One of the more spectacular actions happened in the town Umeå, where a new Ofog group had recently been started. On April 20th 2011 a tank placed in the public space outside the regiment was painted completely pink. In the press release, Ofog explained the action this way:

---

[548] See for instance Alex Schulman, "Och Vad Håller Sveriges Försvarsmakt På Med," [And what is Försvarsmakten doing?] *Aftonbladet*, January 27 2013.

The marking with pink of the tank is a part of a bigger campaign to mark out all military activity like weapon factories, military areas and other places representing milita-militarism. "We don't think that military symbols should be found undisturbed in public space", says Angelika, one of the people who participated in the action.[549]

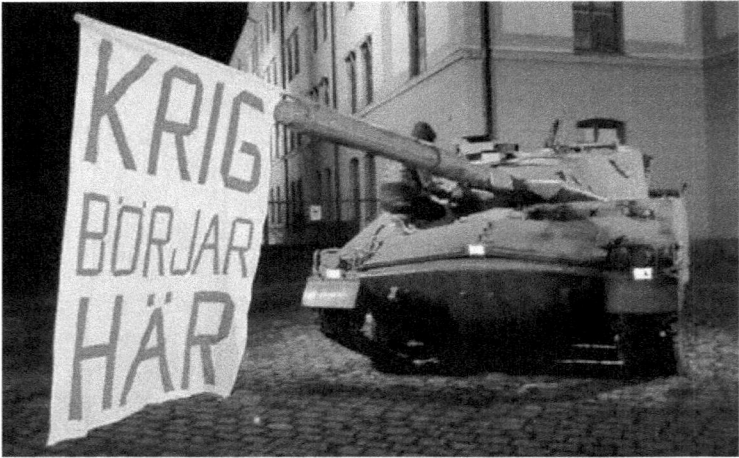

Illustration 20. Ofog. Umeå April 20th 2011, a tank outside the local regiment was painted completely pink. The text says: War Starts Here.

On May 18th, Ofog in Umeå wrote on Ofog's web page that now the tank had been removed from public space.[550]

---

[549] Ofog, "Rosa Stridsvagn - Pepp Inför Sommarens Massaktion!," http://ofog.org/pressmeddelanden/rosa-stridsvagn-pepp-infor-sommarens-massaktion.
[550] This information was accessed July 5th 2011 from http://ofog.org/ but was subsequently removed.

The painting of the tank is a typical example of a provocative stunt with its message of "fuck you, this is our scene too, and now we control it temporarily". It is the devil-may-care attitude of the activists which makes it provocative, with the colour pink adding humorous incongruity. A pink tank is absurd since it is rendered useless when its camouflage colours are changed, not just to any colour, but pink – the most un-militaristic colour on the paint pallet, one that contradicts the macho associations of the military institution.

An international peace camp in Luleå in July 2011 has so far been the major event of the campaign. Under the title "War Starts Here – Let's Stop it Here" somewhere between 200 and 300 people participated. The reason for choosing Luleå was that it is close to Vidsel Test Range/NEAT, where both Swedish and foreign military practice and prepare for war. Ofog had held a peace camp in Luleå also in 2009 and 2010, but this was the biggest so far. In addition to international seminars covering everything from militarism & climate change to counter recruitment against military recruitment, Ofog had arranged one day of mass action on July 26th to mark NEAT pink. The action consisted of different steps with the possibility to participate in the marking without risking arrest, but many chose to enter the restricted area. The activities of the clowns that participated were described in Chapter 4. Ten international activists were arrested and detained at the local police station,[551] and more than 20 Swedish activists were arrested and later convicted and fined.

War Starts Here combined aspects of the absurd and provocative types of stunts. The colour pink is absurd because it is completely out of place: it does not fit in with the military. However, it is mainly a provocative type of action, the civil disobedience a

---

[551] Ofog, ""Släpp Ut Våra Vänner" – Fredsdemonstration Utanför Luleå Polisstation," http://ofog.org/pressmeddelanden/slapp-ut-vara-vanner-fredsdemonstration-utanfor-lulea-polisstation.

refusal to be intimidated by the threat of fines and a criminal record. Although not all civil disobedience is amusing, it is a refusal to accept the rationality of the prevailing ideas about right and wrong. In the case of War Starts Here, where the civil disobedience is combined with the absurd colour pink, some audience members smile when the military equipment is symbolically disempowered simply by changing its colour. Pink also has the advantage that it signalises openness and inclusiveness, carnival and creativity. It is difficult to present and frame 200 people dressed in pink as "dangerous", and for the activists who went further into NEAT in the days following the mass action, it also worked as a protection against accusations of espionage.

Britta's ladies gym against NEAT 2012

The year after the big international War Starts Here camp, Ofog was back in Luleå, but on a much smaller scale. About 20 people participated during a weekend in August and a smaller group continued the stay a bit longer to do civil disobedience actions while a military exercise was going on. Britta's gym against NEAT in downtown Luleå does not fit the definition of a humorous political stunt because there is no direct confrontation or blurring between the performers and audiences. However, it does have some absurd elements and is included here because I gathered a number of reactions from passers-by that document how difficult it is for activists to get their message across and are relevant for both humorous and non-humorous actions.

Brittas damgympa mot NEAT (Britta's ladies gym against NEAT) was a gym program announced to be suitable for everyone and took place in the main pedestrian area in Luleå during one of the busiest times of the week, Saturday afternoon. In the press release, Britta Fredh[552] as the initiator of the gym said:

I'm already active in Ofog, and felt that I wanted to do something creative against NEAT. What could be better than to gather and do a gym session together? In addition, we need to be fit in order to have the energy to fight for peace.[553]

The press release promised an interesting gym programme that would be suitable for everyone no matter seize, gender, and age. "The only demand is the will to do gym training for peace against NEAT."[554]

When I asked Jona, one of the initiators what the purpose of this gym was, the response was:

The purpose was to attack NEAT from a new direction. A gym session can be for or against anything, it is attention grabbing and people think it is funny. I feel more and more that it is important to generate positive emotions for people in order to gain acceptance and raise interest. The gym I had previously seen generated positive reactions. I think that people will remember a gym session against NEAT so much more than for example someone giving a speech and distributing flyers. That is not so attention grabbing, quite simply.[555]

Jona had done a similar event in Gothenburg when Sweden's right wing party *Sverigedemokraterne* held a meeting and in Stockholm in 2011. On these occasions she thought these gym

---

[552] The last name is spelled almost like the Swedish word for peace (fred) and pronounced the same way.
[553] Ofog, "Brittas Damgympa Mot Neat Har Premiär I Luleå," (press release 2012).
[554] Ofog, "Brittas Damgympa Mot Neat Har Premiär I Luleå."
[555] Personal communication with Jona December 3 2012.

sessions against racism and xenophobia had worked well and also gotten attention from the media beforehand.[556]

During the 45 minute gym session in Luleå, 10-15 women from Ofog participated. Others handed out flyers in the beginning, but soon ran out of flyers. While the gym session was going on, I made a little interview with some of the passers-by, asking what they had seen, what they thought about it, if they had noticed the banner that said *Britta's Ladies gym against NEAT*, if they knew what NEAT was, and if they had heard about the military exercise that would start the following Monday called *Nordic Air Meet*. The way the questions were phrased depended on how the conversation started, how people responded and if they knew about the military test area.

I had dressed in a way that did not make it apparent that I was part of Ofog or had anything to do with the gym and approached people that had looked at the gym for a few minutes. Some people did not want to talk, but most were willing to answer when I asked "I noticed that you are looking at the gym here. Do you mind if I ask you a few questions about it?" Altogether I talked to 15 people, six pairs and three individuals. Only four out of these 15 had heard about NEAT, and two of them only as a "yes, now that you say that it is Europe's largest military exercise place here in Norrbotton". The lively and colourful gym session with music generally caught people's attention. The weather was fine, and many people stopped to watch for a little while, but not the whole session. Even those who did not stop generally looked in the direction of the gym when walking past, so it was without doubt a useful way to catch attention, and the more movement the gym included the more

---

[556] Emma Löfgren, "Brittans Damgympa Dansar Mot Främlingsfientligheten," [Brittan's Ladies gym dance against xenophobia] *Dagens Nyheter*, December 8 2011.

people seemed to stop.[557] However, many did not notice the banner that made the connection to NEAT, and 11 out of 15 people that I talked to did not know what NEAT was. Consequently, people had no way of understanding that this was a protest against a military area. With the benefit of hindsight, it is possible to identify several ways that the message could have been emphasised: The participants could have been wearing something that said gym against NEAT, since people looked at the participants in the gym, not the banner next to them. It appeared to be a good atmosphere to hand out flyers in, so making sure to have enough flyers and people to hand them out would increase the possibility that passers-by understood what

Illustration 21. Ofog. Britta's Ladies gym against NEAT, main street in Luleå August 25, 2012. In the background some curious passers-by can be seen.

---

[557] The description of the reactions is based on my field notes August 25, 2012.

this was about even if they were not familiar with the abbreviation. However, the best thing is to make sure that you use terms that the people you reach out to associate with something. In Luleå, people are very well aware about the military activity in their area, although not how far it reaches and who gets the opportunity to practice there. But they refer to the name of the military airport, F21. Another opportunity for Britta and her friends would have been to refer to a more general concept, such as militarism like they had done in the other events that Jona mentioned in Gothenburg and Stockholm.

Svensk Vapenfadder – Swedish weapon sponsors

Svensk Vapenfadder means "Swedish weapon sponsors"[558], and is the name of a satiric not for profit association and a web page launched by Ofog activists on May 27, 2012. Under the heading "What is Svensk Vapenfadder", the campaign is explained this way:

> Svensk Vapenfadder is a not-for-profit association, started with the purpose of increasing the knowledge about Swedish arms export. We are religiously and politically independent, and united by our decision to change the negative attitude towards arms export found in the Swedish society.
>
> We believe that as a nation, we can and should be proud of the achievements of the Swedish conflict resolution indus-

---

[558] A more literal translation would be "weapon Godfather", since a 'fadder' is a Godfather or Godmother, the person who during a baptism promises to take responsibility for the child in case a child's parents die or are unable to take care of it. The same term is used by development agencies that facilitate individual sponsorships to children in poor countries. The Swedish term indicates an even closer relationship with the weapon than what is apparent in the English translation.

try. Swedish products for combat and surveillance are market leading both when it comes to efficiency and profit. Sweden exports most weapons in the world per capita. We think that is something to celebrate and as Swedes feel personally involved in.

As a weapon sponsor you become a sponsor of your very own weapon. You also become a member of the association Svensk Vapenfadder. For a modest sum you really make a difference, create public opinion and in addition you get a warm and personal relationship with your weapon that usually only the soldier in the field has.

As a weapon sponsor you will – no matter what weapon you personally have chosen – regularly receive reports about your weapon. Is it fully assembled? What conflict will it be shipped to? Has it contributed to any deadly shootings yet? In the case of deadly shootings we of course give an immediate update, something like that you should not go and wonder about!

We continuously work on expanding our offers, so that you easily can find a weapon that fits your personal style. There is a weapon for every taste!

Svensk Vapenfadder

Illustration 22. The logo of Svensk Vapenfadder.

341

The campaign slogan was "Swedish weapons – in war for you", and the webpage offered information about seven of the different types of weapons, weapon parts and dual purpose surveillance equipment that are produced in Sweden. One example is the Carl Gustaf granade launcher:

> Carl Gustaf, or granade launcher m/48 as it is also called, is a fairy-tale about success in Swedish arms export. The first model was launched already in 1948, but it is still going strong and has now been sold to more than 40 countries. Cambodia, Burma, Vietnam, India and Iraq, to mention some. But Carl Gustaf likes travelling and changing hands on the black weapon markets, and therefore it is an exceptionally exciting weapon to sponsor. If you chose a Carl Gustaf as your weapon, it might happen that you will be informed that it has contributed to deadly shootings not only in the country it was sold to, but in quite different places. It is especially popular for conflict resolution on the African continent. Carl Gustaf has been found during the civil wars in both Liberia and Somalia.

> Carl Gustaf is made by Saab in Sweden. The barrel is made in Eskilstuna, the system part and assembling in Karlskoga.

The webpage also had a list of many of the Swedish companies contributing to the arms industry, and a list of answers to frequently asked questions. People could choose between becoming a sponsor themselves and giving away a sponsorship to someone else by filling in a form asking for their name and their email address, and choose what weapon they wanted to sponsor. They would also be asked if they wanted to sponsor a child soldier in addition, and could pick the name of their weapon from a list of 13 more or less ridiculous names. Once the form had been submitted, it automatically generated an email to the email address that had been provided, congratulating this person with the sponsorship. When choosing a weapon, a price of the different sponsorships was given, but there was never any prompt to donate any money, and the page did not include an account number.

Under the heading "proud weapon sponsors", the page included a list of 11 politicians and civil servants closely linked with the arms industry, who was given a sponsorship as a present during the launch of the campaign. One example was this:

> Minister of trade Ewa Björling has a refreshingly minimalistic view of government intervention in Swedish arms deals with countries at war. She thinks that "ultimately it is the responsibility of the arms companies themselves in what market they choose to operate". Of course that does not exclude that the state can help when needed. Ewa Björling contributed to starting the front company supposed to make it possible for the Swedish state to build an arms factory in Saudi Arabia. She also tried, but sadly failed, to help the government owned company Svenska Rymdbolaget sell a surveillance system to Ghadaffi six months before he was brought down in Libya. For her zeal she is rewarded with a weapon sponsorship to nothing less than a JAS 39 Gripen.

All the information about both weapons and the VIP sponsors' statements was accurate and thoroughly researched.

The campaign was launched on May 27 2012 in two different ways: The VIP sponsors received a letter explaining that they had been chosen as VIP sponsors, including the text about their achievements published on the web page. We also had two stalls in Gothenburg and Stockholm, where Ofog activists in disguise recruited potential weapon sponsors in two central public spaces with many pedestrians. For the occasion we had produced a flyer telling about the campaign, brought along a little table where we offered coffee and displayed some of the descriptions about the VIP sponsors.

The activists in the two cities had chosen two different strategies in their approach towards the general public. In Stockholm they wanted to remain ambiguous, and not reveal that this was satire. In Gothenburg, the two of us had decided that we wanted to exaggerate our enthusiasm for the weapons so much that people by themselves would realise that this was satire.

One activist who participated in Stockholm wrote about his experiences:

> [I] encountered three people who expressed a positive attitude towards the weapon sponsor [campaign]. One of them was an officer. The other, a big middle aged man, did not say much about himself, but he had a lot of knowledge about the topic. He knew about different defence associations, and seemed to think that we did a good job. He asked a lot of curious questions. I tried to get his name and contact info, but did not succeed. He wanted to check out our organisation himself. He thought it was sad that the Swedish armed forces had received less and less money year after year if one accounts for inflation. He asked if we thought we would succeed in collecting enough money to really make a difference, it is a question of big sums. I said that we did not know yet. That we were still in an early phase and don't yet know what the result will look like, but that we of course hope to be able to collect a lot of money. He seemed a little suspicious about who we really were.[559]

The same person continues, now referring to himself in the third person:

> It was sad to notice that none of the people Paul talked to expressed criticism of what we tried to do. Can it be because many Swedes are scared of conflicts? Paul did not in any way encounter anyone who questioned if this was real

---

[559] Personal communication with Paul May 2012.

or if we were joking. It really did not look as if anybody saw through our satire.

Thomas, another person who participated during the launch in Stockholm, wrote

Most of the time it was unpleasant when people were extremely positive, but on one occasion it became really cool. A man with many years of experience from the armed forces and some arms companies swallowed the bait totally. He started talking about a new arms fair in Stockholm that he is the project manager of. Of course he agreed that the majority [of the population] has a way too negative image of weapons, and did not understand what stability it created. He went on for a few minutes before he went away with some concluding words about the possibilities for a future cooperation.

The two of us who were responsible for the launch in Gothenburg had chosen a different strategy, where we saw it as a goal to exaggerate so much that people by themselves would understand that this was ironic. But that was much more difficult than expected. I wrote about my own first encounter:

The very first person I talked to got very upset, and I did not manage to exaggerate the concept enough to make him understand that we were trying to satirise. He ended up leaving in anger, saying loud that this was "really sick" – something we could only agree with.

The rationale for making people grasp the irony was two-fold – our own well-being and what we felt comfortable with, and the idea to communicate anti-militaristic values and world views to people. When preparing, we identified three potential main scenarios, which I summed up before the actual launch:

The best for me will be to get people interested who are a bit sceptical at first, and then make them realise that this is satire, to make them feel smart and clever that they figured it out. The worst cases will be people who are genuinely interested and maybe become upset or angry if they realise that we are satirising about things they really believe is good. Then there might be really ignorant people who don't really understand, hopefully we can send them away with a leaflet and they will talk to someone who can figure it out.

Illustration 23. Ofog. The launch of Svensk Vapenfadder in Gothenburg. The coffee table with presentations of some of the VIP sponsors. Malin (right) in conversation with a curious passer-by and the author (in white jacket) trying to engage people in conversation.

During the two hours we spent in one of the most crowded pedestrian areas in Gothenburg, we became much better at this than I had been during my first encounter. My fellow recruiter, who called herself Malin for the occasion, perfected her performance. At the end of the day we had developed a routine which

346

we had not talked about in the planning. This idea was introduced by Jeanette, another Ofog activist, who was visiting us in order to take some photos and decided to contribute to our efforts. Jeanette started shouting like a street seller, quite loud, and with a monotone voice "Welcome to Svensk Vapenfadder, we have great offer today, become the sponsor of your very own weapon" and similar things. We noticed how it worked to grab attention, and became an opportunity for Malin and myself to approach those who suddenly started to look towards our table. Already the same day I noted how the irony became more obvious because of the incongruity between this type of communication, and the statements in what was said. When Jeanette had to leave, I followed up her style. My favorite line when a group of people approached was to say "Support the Swedish war industry". Then I would continue with various combinations of the following:

> Welcome to Svensk Vapenfadder. Become a sponsor today of your very own weapon produced in Sweden. This is your opportunity to support with your heart, not just with your wallet.

We established the routine that I would shout, and Malin would follow up. At first the shouting felt uncomfortable, but at the end of the day I wrote that "This shouting in the street I actually found rather liberating. Because it was so absurd that I found it impossible that anyone would think I was serious."

At the end of the day, I summed up the different scenarios Malin and I had encountered like this:

> Out like this, we encounter so many different people. Most don't want to talk at all. A few are curious by themselves when they see a stand and approach us. Some just want a cup of coffee, and the kids want the cookies. Some look at the stand or hear the shouting, and get curious and we can approach them. Some of them agree that the war industry is disgusting, and are relieved when they find out that it is

347

satire. Then they say that what we do is great and wish us good luck. Others like weapons and the war industry, and don't want to see the irony, or maybe don't want to admit it. One guy told me that he already had a weapon, and when I asked what kind it turned out to be a pistol from the Czech republic, and he started to show me his licence for it. I don't really think he understood the joke, although I told him we could offer something much bigger, like the JAS Gripen fighterplane. Some people never seem to get the irony. Hopefully they will take the leaflet, look at the webpage, or some friend will tell them they have been fooled. A lot of people just seem to live with information overload and don't want to hear or think or know.

In December 2012 in the week before Christmas, Jeanette contacted seven of the VIP sponsors. The opening was that now they had been sponsors for a while, Svensk Vapenfadder would like to ask if they could get a quote for the webpage. Jeanette only managed to get in contact with one person, the six others all had secretaries and did not return phone calls or emails. The politician Jeanette managed to reach directly did not want to have anything to do with Svensk Vapenfadder. After Jeanette had introduced herself and reminded the politician about the VIP sponsorship she received in May, the response was:

Politician: Alright, I don't take this very seriously probably...

Jeanette: What do you mean by that?

Politician: It was a rather unpleasant interference

Jeanette: How do you mean?

Politician: Well, I don't think I need to explain so much more I think. You know yourself what your purpose is, and I don't share the opinions you have... (hesitates) You're talking about that webpage, right...?

Jeanette: Yes, we have a webpage and an organisation.

> Politician: If we say it like this, I'm not interested in hav-
> ing contact with you this way, I think it is important with a
> good and straightforward discussion on good conditions
> when it comes to our export of defence materiel, and I
> didn't like this initiative, that is about what I have to say.[560]

It is possible to interpret the reactions of the politician in many
different ways. First of all it is rather remarkable that she knew
straight away what Jeanette was talking about in spite of the
almost seven months that had passed since she received the VIP
sponsorship from Svensk Vapenfadder. Although she expressed
some hesitation and asked if it was about the webpage, her first
response was not "what are you talking about?", but "Alright, I
don't take this very seriously probably…", straight away signaling
that she knew what it was all about and implying that she understood the irony. Then she proceeded to say that she disapproved
of the stunt and preferred a straightforward communication.

The six other politicians and civil servants who were contacted
only know themselves why they did not respond to Svensk
Vapenfadder. It is reasonable to assume that they realised they
were part of an ironic stunt and were wise enough to ignore it
since they were not put in a position where they were forced to
respond.

The idea of the weapon sponsor campaign was to my knowledge
first brought up at the workshop in Gothenburg in May 2011.
However, nobody wanted to carry it forward at that time, so it
remained unused during the summer. I mentioned the idea at the
next workshop in Malmö in September to see what that local
group thought about it. Also here there was agreement that it
was a good idea, but again nobody wanted to take responsibility
for it. During the national meeting, we set up a small working
group composed of people who wanted to explore the idea.
Although many creative ideas came up, such as actually sending

---

[560] The phone conversation was audio-recorded on December 14 2012.

phone messages to people, we decided to start slowly with a webpage.

After our first planning meeting, I wrote this about our expectations:

- Mentioning in different media, also mainstream
- Something that will be useful for the local groups
- Need to make sure we can keep track of number of sponsorships.[561]

After a skype conversation a few months later, I wrote this under the heading of what we wanted to communicate:

> It has to be interesting to read, and informative. Remove what is not funny and does not contribute information. We aim to touch people in the "crack" where they are wondering if this is serious or if someone is pulling their leg.[562]

Somewhere between 10 and 15 people were involved in the preparations and the launch. A small group of us had worked on it for quite a while. In addition, someone did the logo, another contributed with technical assistance for the web page and a third with proof reading. Others offered comments or participated as recruiters on the launch. A media spokesperson was ready on the phone, although she never got any calls. It was a typical example of Ofog's way of developing projects in collaboration.

At this point I had already written much about humour and the ambition of reaching the "crack" where the audience is uncertain if this is irony or "real" directly developed from ideas that had come up when I interviewed people. Thus, this is a good example of how data collection and interpretation cannot be

---

[561] Notes from planning meeting October 19 2011.
[562] Notes from Skype call January 3 2012.

considered totally separate in a participatory action research inspired project.

Svensk Vapenfadder never became the big campaign some of us had hoped it would. Some of the people who had been most engaged had other priorities after the launch and those who were interested in continuing only did a few attempts.

More than a year later the concept was used again during Almedalsveckan, a one week yearly political event on a Swedish island where politicians, civil society and media meet and discuss all sorts of political issues at small and big seminars. In 2013, Försvarsmakten and the weapon producer SAAB arranged a seminar about the JAS Gripen fighterplane at a place called "Defence Political Arena". Three people from Svensk Vapenfadder were ready to welcome the 60-70 participants with the phrase "Would you also like to have a more personal rela-tionship with JAS Gripen?" about 15 minutes before the seminar started. In a setting like this, people already had the arms indus-try in their mind.[563] Thomas, who was a Vapenfadder recruiter here as well had the experience that it was much easier to use the concept here than it had been a year before in Stockholm. For Louise, this was her first experience with being a Vapenfadder recruiter, and she remembers in particular a woman who was working for the defence political arena and was standing right next to them handing out her own leaflets. She came over to Louise to enquire what they were handing out, and Louise told her about how you could sponsor your own weapon. Louise tells that "She was very interested and said Vapenfadder sounded very good. While we were talking, she definitely thought it was for real and we swopped leaflets"[564] Louise did not know if she later read the leaflet and there were no one who came to talk to her after the seminar.

---

[563] Interviews with Thomas and Louise November 2013.
[564] Interview with Louise November 2013.

Because it took a while for the seminar to start, the Vapenfadder recruiters had time to observe the reactions of people who sat down to read the leaflet. Several people who appeared to come from Försvarsmakten and the armaments industry had responded positively when they were first approached by Vapenfadder, "yes they would like to have a more personal relation with the fighterplane", something which both Thomas and Louise observed. Louise only remembers one person who did not respond with a "yes" or "oh, that was nice". When the seminar started, the recruiters stayed and listened and observed people. Thomas' impression was that people's faces changed as they read the leaflet and it started to sink in that this could not be real. On the other hand, people from the peace movement and others who were critical of the JAS Gripen plans were first annoyed by Svensk Vapenfadder, but started to relax the more they read. Only a few people came to talk with Thomas after they had read the leaflet, and the Vapenfadder recruiters made sure to keep the mask and continue the play.[565]

Thomas had one conversation without being in the role as a recruiter that he remembered in particular. The man who approached Vapenfadder held a leading position at an arms factory. He told Thomas that they knew about Svensk Vapenfadder, and started to joke that they were hurt that none of their weapons were included in the leaflet and the webpage. However, as time passed he became annoyed and asked Vapenfadder to leave since they were interfering with someone else's event when they were distributing the leaflet, something he said was undemocratic.[566]

Thomas' impression was that the seminar at Almedalsveckan was a much better arena to use for the Vapenfadder concept than the launch on the street. Here they really managed to reach most of

565 Interview with Thomas November 2013.
566 Interview with Thomas November 2013.

352

the participants at the seminar and could observe them reading.[567] Nevertheless, it was not possible to evaluate what people thought about it.

The weapon sponsor campaign is a parody of the child sponsoring campaigns where people can sponsor a child and follow that particular child through its school years. However, the target here is not these child sponsorships, but the Swedish arms industry. It is an example of a supportive stunt, where the critique was disguised as an opportunity to show support for the arms industry. For those of us who participated, it created a steep learning curve about how to use irony in a way that the general public will understand it. We were very surprised by how hard this part was.

The launch of this supportive stunt differs from some of the other supportive stunts by not directly confronting the armaments industry. During the launch, Ofog did not try to invade a scene where major actors were present, but instead established a private scene among the general public. Because Ofog considered the general public the main audience in this action, it was no problem for the industry and the politicians exposed through the VIP sponsorships to ignore Svensk Vapenfadder. During Almedalsveckan the recruiters were a bit more confrontational, since they stood right outside the place where Försvarsmakten and SAAB were arranging a seminar. It is interesting to notice that the man from the arms company who approached one of the recruiters had heard about vapenfadder and knew straight away what it was, since the concept had been used only a few times more than a year before. Obviously it must have been a topic for conversation at some point. It also seems as if this man felt Vapenfadder was at least a little annoying, since he bothered to argue and called Ofog's presence undemocratic.

---

[567] Interview with Thomas November 2013.

The number of people from the general public Vapenfadder got in contact with was quite modest. Since the concept was only used a couple of times and it never went "viral" Vapenfadder shows a potential and a learning process, but it probably did not have much effect. The peak number of daily visitors to the webpage, 598 on the Monday after the launch was pretty good but not spectacular.

In preparing the launch, the aim had been to get some media coverage, and a press spokesperson was ready for calls on the phone. A few days before the launch a press release was sent out, and the morning after the action a new one. They did not result in any coverage. It is hard to judge if this is because the webpage was not convincing enough to look as the real thing, or if media decided not to cover it for other reasons. Nevertheless, this part of the stunt was a complete failure, documenting that not all humorous political stunts are covered by the mass media.

Speech bubbles at the Pride Parade

In August 2011, Ofog participated in the week long pride festival in Stockholm, organised by the gay community as a way to celebrate and show pride in their sexuality. Also present was the Swedish military, Försvarsmakten, represented by men and women who are openly homosexual in the military. Under a banner saying "Openness – part of our reality,"[568] Försvarsmakten had a stand used to promote the institution. This was a combination of the armed forces campaign slogan "Welcome to our reality" and the pride festival slogan of "openness".

Many Ofog activists are concerned with LBGTQ (Lesbian, Bisexual, Gay, Transgender, Queer) rights and themselves identify as homosexual or queer persons. They wanted to protest

---

[568] Ofog, "Ofog Visar Försvarsmaktens Verklighet I Prideparaden," http://www.ofog.org/nyheter/ofog-visar-f%C3%B6rsvarsmaktens-verklighet-i-prideparaden.

against the presence of Försvarsmakten in the parade, referring to the parade's code of conduct that the parade is nonviolent. In their feminist analysis, these activists in Ofog also think that being a feminist, one cannot at the same time endorse violent solutions to conflict.

Ofog activists therefore did an action to correct the image Försvarsmakten promotes of itself. 15 Ofog activists did a die-in with a banner saying "Your reality kills"in front of Försvarsmakten's stand. During the parade through Stockholm which is part of the festival, Ofog activists carried posters formed as speech bubbles in cartoons with different expressions referring to the "real reality" of working in the military. One bubble said "Here I walk to protect my human rights while my job is about abusing other's human rights", while others were "I'm just as good as killing as straight soldiers", "My job kills" "I think that some people's lives are worth more than others'" ,"Abusing other people's rights is part of my reality", "Försvarsmakten's reality = violence and repression" and "I think that Swedish children are worth more than Afghan children". These speech bubbles were carried next to the uniformed soldiers to make it look like their statements.

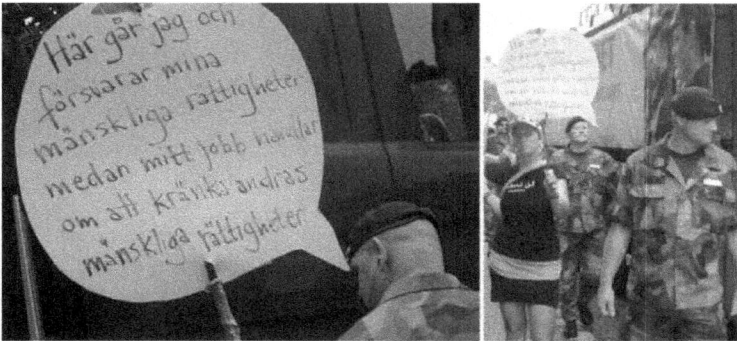

Illustration 24. Ofog. The text in both photos says: Here I walk to protect my human rights while my job is about abusing other's human rights.

Less than a month after the action, I made a phone interview with one of the participants, Sofia. She told me that they were about 10 people who all consider themselves part of the radical queer movement, and that it was all planned while they were at the festival when they saw Försvarsmakten's stall and realised they were there. The activists were not aiming at a lot of publicity, and did not send a press release before the action.

When they wrote the text for the different speech bubbles they wanted to focus on two things: That the military uses its participation in Pride for *pinkwashing* its image, and that its reality is not openness, but to kill and uphold injustice. Sofia used the term pinkwashing as a way of describing the armed forces' double standards. Apparent tolerance for LBGTQ persons creates positive associations at the same time as the discourse of militarism stands in stark contrast to radical LBGTQ values.[569] The participants in the action thought that being queer has to do with a lot more than policies about sexual identity. The group wanted to show that there is no consensus within the LBGTQ movement about the presence of Försvarsmakten in the parade. Therefore Sofia was also pleased to see that the action has led to internal debate within the LBGTQ movement.

While they prepared the speech bubbles, the activists did reflect that some of the statements were kind of harsh, but concluded

---

[569] The term pinkwashing is also used when the Israeli government uses its tolerance for LBGTQ persons to promote itself abroad to audiences that might be critical of the occupation of Palestine, see Sarah Schulman, "Israel and 'Pinkwashing'," *New York Times*, November 22 2011. The Breast Cancer fund which uses pink ribbons to create awareness about breast cancer writes: *"Pinkwasher: (pink'-wah-sher) noun. A company or organization that claims to care about breast cancer by promoting a pink ribbon product, but at the same time produces, manufactures and/or sells products that are linked to the disease."* Breast Cancer Action, "Before You Buy Pink," http://thinkbeforeyoupink.org/?page_id=13.

that they were all true. Looking back, Sofia comments that there was probably a difference between those that said "I" and those that said "my job". Although she does not say it explicitly, this is a reference to the nonviolence principle of distinguishing between a person and the role she performs.

Sofia explained that the action was not intended to be funny in the sense of making anyone laugh, and she is not certain what words are the best to describe what they aimed at doing, but thought humour was part of it, not laughter. She also saw it as a ridicule of the military's intention to use this as an opportunity to give a positive image of themselves, and that it can be funny when that is not possible for them. In this case, there is a difference between being there, where it was not humorous, and being part of an audience that hears about it later. While I have met people who do not consider this humorous at all, others, myself included, have smiled when they saw the photos from the parade. Thus, this is a clear illustration of how much perspective matters for causing amusement.

Returning to the model of humorous political stunts, this action is an example of a *corrective* stunt. Ofog presented an alternative version of how the soldiers speak about their job than what Försvarsmakten and the soldiers themselves would do. Ofog confronted their dominant discourse with a different perspective that aimed to dispute perceptions of what the reality of the armed forces is and should be. In contrast to many other corrective stunts, Ofog did not sneak onto a stage to display the correction, but did it openly in a way which could hardly be mistaken for being the soldiers' own statements. Through this direct confrontation it also has some similarities with a provocative stunt.

Ofog's speech bubble action generated many different types of reactions. During the parade itself, the individual soldiers did what they could to ignore it. Afterwards, a spokesperson for the soldiers, Michael "Totte" Ekdahl, chair of the association for homo-, bi and transpersons in Försvarsmakten (HoF) said they were going to report the activists to the police.[570] In an interview with a newspaper, and a subsequent opinion piece he wrote, he presented a very different perception of what was at stake than Sofia did. Without mentioning the critique of militarism, he said the individual soldiers felt hurt when opinions they did not have were attributed to them. This way, he moved the debate away from Ofog's intention of criticising an institution. Instead he contextualised the action as an attack on individual homosexual soldiers who had already encountered much prejudice. He wrote:

> It is very cynical to pick on the most vulnerable in all groups. The activists have made a conscious decision to achieve maximal pain for HoF's participants. This way, they have "kicked" our work for openness for LBGT-persons in FM [Försvarsmakten, the Swedish military] back as well as turned the Pride concept "openness" to suspiciousness.[571]

Similar comments were made in blogs and comments to the articles, for example this:

> And it is no problem to critisise the military in Sweden, but why have the bad taste to do it by picking on homosexuals and [transpersons] in this profession?[572]

Ekdahl was also suspicious of the motives of the Ofog activists. Instead of acknowledging this as a contribution to a debate about queer identity and militarism, he referred to their "conscious decision to achieve maximal pain." This kind of

---

[570] John Henzlert, "Soldater Kränkta under Prideparaden," [Soldiers offended during pride parade] *http://www.svd.se*, August 7 2011.
[571] Micael "Totte" Ekdahl, "Cyniskt Angrepp I Prideparaden," [cynical attack in the pride parade] *etc.se*, August 11 2011.
[572] Reader's comment to Ekdahl, "Cyniskt Angrepp I Prideparaden."

devaluation was also part of the comments: "Can one expect anything else. Left wing activists have never put democracy especially high on the agenda".[573]

Different bloggers and comments to blogs as well as the news report expressed much criticism of the action. The main line of argument was that it is offensive towards the individual soldiers. Only the soldiers themselves can tell if they felt personally hurt or not, but there was nothing in the speech bubbles that criticised the sexual identity of the soldiers. Instead, the bubbles offered a critique of the military and war and referred to the potential consequences of Swedish soldiers' participation in the war in Afghanistan. The soldiers were targets because they were soldiers, not because of their sexual identity. They were wearing their uniforms and carried a banner that promoted the training to become an officer in the armed forces. In a response to the debate article, Cattis Laska from Ofog wrote how she considered anti-militarist work an integrated part of the queer struggle. She finished with saying:

> Finally: War kills, LBGTQ-military personnel as well as civilians, and then it does not matter what sexual identity or gender identity the soldier who carries the deadly weapon or the officer that gives the order has.[574]

A year later, just before the next Stockholm Pride, Ofog's action from 2011 drew attention again. The action became part of a debate about who has the right to define "queer" and if the LBGTQ struggle should be limited to the rights of sexual minor-

---

[573] Reader's comment to Ekdahl, "Cyniskt Angrepp I Prideparaden."
[574] Cattis Laska, "Krigsmotstånd Central Del Av Queer Kamp," [War resistance central part of queer struggle] *etc.se*, August 18 2011.

ities or implies a much broader political focus that also can question capitalism and militarism.[575]

Under the heading "The whole parade became one long torment", one of the officers tells about how he experienced the episode. He filed a report to the police, but the prosecutor dismissed the case because he did not think the soldier had been the victim of any crime. However, in contrast to Ekdahl who wrote about the events the year before, this officer acknowledged Ofog's intentions to criticise militarism. When asked if he intended to participate in the parade again this year, he said:

> It will not destroy my intention and my commitment to show who I am. It is a little like an "antiprotest", throw dirt on me, but I walk anyway. Maybe because I know they have an agenda that is not about the LBGTQ-question but about the existence of the armed forces.[576]

In an interview with the same newspaper, Kristina Johansson from Ofog again emphasised why Ofog did this:

> For us it is obvious that Pride is political. If the armed forces are there it is political in a certain way. That is what we think you have to start talking about. That it is not just

---

[575] Peter Letmark, "Begreppet Queer Skapar Allt Större Oenighet," [The notion queer creates greater disagreements] *dn.se*, July 26 2012.
[576] Peter Letmark, "'Hela Paraden Blev En Enda Lång Pina'," ["The whole parade became one long torment"] *dn.se*, July 25 2012. The newspaper has added to the article that the person who was interviewed died a few days after the article was published. There have been many rumours about the cause of his death. Accusations have been made that Ofog's speech bobble action drove him to commit suicide. For instance this insinuation was made on January 28 2013 in a comment on Ofog's Facebook page.

a family party, that the questions are political in many different regards.[577]

Internally in Ofog, the action has also generated debate, both about tactics and about respect for individuals. To some people, this was simply too much of an exposure of individuals. Others that participated in the debate used a different type of argumentation: They did not object to exposing soldiers in uniforms this way, militarism is militarism no matter what sexual orientation the soldiers have. But from a strategic point of view they thought the action unwise, since it was too easy for opponents to reframe Ofog's intentions. They worried about the debate focusing on discrimination of LBGTQ persons instead of on militarism.

Sofia was not surprised to see that *Ekdahl* tried to frame this as an attack on individuals and their sexuality. When asked if she thought anything should have been done differently, her spontaneous reaction was "no". It was good that it generated debate within Ofog and the LBGTQ movement, and she is satisfied with the action.

Summing up on Ofog's public humour

The previous pages presented most of the outward directed humour that Ofog has engaged in while it has been active in Sweden, and revealed the diversity when it comes to the types of humorous political stunts that Ofog has initiated. Some of the stunts that have required most preparation have been supportive, such as Reality AB and Svensk Vapenfadder. The stunts that have challenged Försvarsmakten recruiting and brand building efforts have primarily been corrective, as the examples of adbusting and Ofog's speech bubbles in the pride parade illustrated. Many of the humorous political stunts that Ofog has performed have been provocative, and for example the speech bubbles in

---

[577] Dagens Nyheter, "Ofog Svarar: "Självklart Är Pride Politiskt"," [Ofog responds "Of course Pride is political"] *dn.se*, July 25 2012.

the pride parade were perceived as extremely provocative by the soldiers. Nevertheless, it is only the painting of the tank in Umeå which is a provocative stunt the way it is defined in the model. That Ofog has also used absurd stunts became clear from the clowning presented in the previous chapter. Thus the only type of stunt that Ofog has not experimented with is the naïve.

Returning to Berger's list of 45 humorous techniques, which is a useful way to understand what creates humorous incongruity, *irony* was the dominant technique in the two supportive stunts, Reality AB and Vapenfadder. They got their inspiration from making *parodies* of up-and-coming businesses and the child sponsoring organisations, but the real target was the discourse of militarism and arms production. However, in order for the irony to work the audiences were required to recognise the ways of communicating that were being parodied and simultaneously recognise the incongruity between the message and the way of communicating. One way for Ofog to make sure the audiences switched from the rational mode to the humorous mode was to use the technique of *exaggeration*. Another way of communicating the irony was by using modes of expression that did not fit with the message. For instance the street seller parody used in Vapenfadder was incompatible with the pretended aim to convince people to become weapon sponsors.

The technique of *absurdity* was the humorous ingredient in the War Starts Here actions at NEAT and the painting of the tank in Umeå. The corrective stunts with the speech bubbles and the adbusting of Försvarsmakten used parody, unmasking, ridicule and insults as their techniques.

Looking at the four elements of stage, actors, audiences and timing from the theatre metaphor reveals that Ofog has used many different stages – from the streets in Luleå, Stockholm and Göteborg with Reality AB, Svensk Vapenfadder and Britta's gym, to the tank in Umeå, the adverting boards and the Pride

Parade. Nevertheless, in spite of this diversity of stages, it is apparent that Ofog generally shies away from major stages and actors in its humorous political stunts. There were no parliaments or royal castles involved in Ofog's actions.

The main audience was the general public, preferably to be reached directly. This was the case with Reality AB, the ad-refinement, the ironic posters and flyers, Britta's ladies gym and Svensk Vappenfadder. The only actions which were exceptions were the speech bubble action at the pride parade and War Starts Here. Although the soldiers who were targeted at the pride parade cannot be considered main actors, they were representatives of the Swedish armed forces. Likewise, during War Starts Here the painting of the tank and the civil disobedience actions at NEAT also directly confronted these institutions and forced them to react. However, these two actions were also some of the cases included here that were the least obviously humorous.

Ofog has also had an ambition about obtaining coverage by the mass media in order to reach the general public, but has been far less successful with this than many of the other groups that use humorous political stunts.

Timing is a crucial factor for anyone aiming to enter major stages and confront important actors directly. Timing considerations become less troublesome when it comes to reaching out to the general public which meant that for instance Svensk Vapenfadder could work independently of what the arms industry did. The adbusting, on the other hand, only makes sense when it is seen in connecting with Försvarsmakten's ads.

After looking at Ofog's humorous political stunts in relation to the theoretical model presented earlier, the next section goes a step further and analyses what the consequences of this use of humour are, and what it means to the activists who engage in it.

363

Analysis: Humour in political activism

The previous section documented most of the outward directed humour that Ofog carried out in Sweden so far. This section continues the analysis about what this humour achieves in relations to people outside of Ofog and what it means to people within the network. It is based on written comments I collected in workshops about humour and on interviews with Ofog activists. The data reveal a very reflective attitude towards humour and contain many thoughtful responses that reflect the diverse attitudes and experiences of humour within the network.

Together the responses illustrate the diversity of all the stakeholders Ofog activists wish to reach out to. The four questions to the participants in the workshops were phrased like this: 1. What is the best example of a humorous nonviolent action that you know of? 2. What do you think can be achieved by using humour as a method in nonviolent actions? 3. How can humour influence the relations with the military, media, arms producers and police in nonviolent actions? 4. Can there be any problems with using humour as a method in nonviolent actions? The respondents focused on very different things, presumably what they were concerned about. Some focused on media, many on the police, a few on the workers at the arms factories and the military. In most of the written statements from the workshops there is no way of knowing if the comments reflect a personal observation of a concrete action, a speculation or a hope. What they document is the diversity of thinking about humour and its relations with challenging power, depending on the type of humour, its context and target.

In order to provide a structure, I present the material with the same headings as in chapter 4. However, I have divided "facilitating outreach and mobilisation" into two categories in order to acknowledge the difference between reaching out to mass media and the general population and consciously aiming to get more activists:

a) facilitating outreach
b) facilitating mobilisation
c) facilitating a culture of resistance
d) challenging power relations

After these four sections I round off with discussing two aspects of Ofog's use of humour that do not belong in any of these categories.

Facilitating outreach

Both activists and academics assume that creativity and humour contribute to reaching out to other people. Accounts of creative activist groups such as the Raging Grannies, Billionaires for Bush and CIRCA frequently report this.[578] Many of the examples from chapter 3 were also covered rather extensively by national mainstream mass media, for instance the Chaser's APEC stunt. However, the assumption about mass media appeal is so much taken for granted that no one has done a comparison between the attention given to humorous and non-humorous actions, so we do not know how big the effect is. Although this anecdotal evidence makes it reasonable to assume some effect, it would be interesting to look into the failed cases as well. With Svensk Vapenfadder Ofog tried to reach mass media with humour but was unsuccessful, and when other actions have received mass media coverage it has not been unproblematic.

It is not just in academic literature that the connection between humour/creativity and media coverage is assumed. The answers from the workshops with Ofog also reflect an expectation that humour can facilitate outreach to potentially new activists and

---

[578] Carole Roy, *The Raging Grannies: Wild Hats, Cheeky Songs, and Witty Actions for a Better World* (Montréal: Black Rose Books, 2004). pp. 1, 59-63; Bogad, "Carnivals against Capital." Day, *Satire and Dissent*: Chapter 5.

sympathetic passers-by as well as convince journalists that this is a story worth covering. This section is concerned with outreach to journalists and the general public, the next with reaching new activists.

In both workshops and interviews, many people mentioned that it is easier to reach the media if you do something humorous, and reaching out can be to both mass media and the general public. One person expressed this distinction in a written comment from a workshop:

> Mass media. Succeed in being portrayed as a creative movement. Avoid being portrayed as a destructive, lawless left leaning pack like the media otherwise maybe want to portray activists. General public: I think it is easier for an "ordinary person" to sympathise with civil disobedience actions if they are carried out in a humorous and clear and evidently non-aggressive way.[579]

Other respondents focused on how humour can catch attention and wake up people:

> Partly to make one's message more accessible to those who are "watching".[580]

> You reach new groups, that you in other cases can't reach. People who think politics etc. is dry and boring can be carried along with the help of humour.[581]

Along similar lines, someone suggested that humour can be a way to reach people in a different way:

> I think that you get out to more/*reach* to more. Humour tears down people's "protection walls" and it can be easier to accept/realise something you actually don't want. In ad-

---

[579] Written comment from workshop.
[580] Written comment from workshop.
[581] Written comment from workshop.

dition I think humour can demonstrate absurdity that can be difficult to realise because conventions and patterns in society are habits.[582]

The written comments were too short to discuss outreach in detail, but in the interviews a more nuanced picture appeared. Both Lena and Vera expressed the view that humour had not made it easier for Ofog to get media attention. As discussed in the previous chapter clowns can make good photos, for instance the image of the CIRCA clown Trixie that went around the world after the protests in Edinburgh. Nevertheless, Lena and Vera also said that in their experience, the media were more interested in the possibility that the clowns would break the law than in what the activists wanted to express with the clowning.

In Lisa's opinion it is very difficult to predict what will get attention. She sees the potential of humour, but was clear that humour is not the only possible option:

> Ofog is a quite small movement that attempts to highlight questions that no one really cares about. We need to pursue a way that is a little sensational. To get oneself arrested is one such way, and to be funny and dramatic is another very effective way. However, we could also be very serious; it is difficult to predict in advance what will gain a lot of attention.[583]

When I asked Vera what kind of response they obtained from media on the use of humour, she replied:

> We get the best response from media when we use humour, no doubt. The only thing that gets as much response is when we get arrested all of us, and that is a very laborious way to get media attention. I think it is easier to get media to write about the reason, the background to the action when you have used humour. They write just as much,

[582] Written comment from workshop.
[583] Interview September 2011.

they are just as susceptible to make an article as when you get arrested, but [when you get arrested] then they don't explain. In my experience it is more likely that you get some background when you have used humour.[584]

Here Vera brings in a crucial dimension in getting media attention: Although some might consider all coverage good coverage, she makes a distinction about the quality of the reports. In the quote above she said that she thought the quality was *best* when they used humour, and then commented on the *quantity* of the reports about civil disobedience. Straight after this quote, Vera continued to explain how media reports on civil disobedience actions have a tendency to focus on how many get arrested and where rather than why: for some reason these actions do not encourage journalists to reflect. Her conclusion is that a combination of civil disobedience and humour might be the best:

It works a little better if you have used humour, maybe in combination [with civil disobedience]. The best actions are often when we have something which is directed outwards, and someone who is arrested, then we get most attention from a purely media perspective. A little sad sometimes, and you don't want to play by their rules too much, but at the same time it is good to know what works and what does not work.[585]

Emma and Maria said more or less the same about the local press in their city. When they have arranged things like a candle lighting and one minute of silence for the victims of the weapons produced at the local arms factory, no media bothered to show up. But if someone announces that he or she will climb the fence in order to do a citizen inspection, they will be there. Maria expressed some of the same doubts as Vera about relying too much on the media:

---

[584] Interview September 2011.
[585] Interview September 2011.

It feels like a difficult balance, media would like you to do something spectacular (...) and they can always turn it around the way they want, so sometimes it feels best not to involve them. You never really know what happens.[586]

When asked if humour attracts people, Johanna answered:

Yes, I really think that it does. For instance when they painted pink hearts on tanks in Stockholm a couple of weeks ago [as part of the War Starts Here campaign]. As a response to a critical comment on Facebook someone had answered "but don't you see, it is hearts!" It is much easier for people to understand, as opposed to smashing [the tank] to pieces (...)It is more difficult to dismiss as a kind of ordinary vandalism or sabotage.[587]

Here Johanna considered painting hearts on a tank humorous, and explained why she thought it is much more difficult to dismiss this type of activity as vandalism.

Lena also gave a very sophisticated and rational explanation for why she thinks humour is an effective way of communication. When asked if something can be achieved by using humour which cannot be achieved otherwise, she spontaneously said yes. She elaborated that in a time where irony is used so much, it is almost necessary to use this way of communication. When people are presented with a sort of puzzle which they cannot solve straight away, it makes them feel smart, special and capable when they are able to figure it out within a reasonable time frame and are not tricked. Lena also thinks that the general public finds it difficult to take in all the pain and suffering in the world. If you just tell them about everything that is wrong, how Sweden contributes to war and how war starts here, most people just close their ears. So she explained that you have to take a *detour* in order for them to take it in, and humour and irony which they

---

[586] Interview September 2011.
[587] Interview June 2011.

have to crack and which make them feel smart can be one way of constructing this detour. A similar comment was made by Raging Granny Barbara Calvert Seifred in Roy's study. She said that

> Humour breaks down barriers... [and] eases the interactions. We're basically preaching in a way, but not in a preachy way... I think they're disarmed a little bit at first, then they understand the message and it's too late.588

She thought that the humour disarmed the audience, created a crack where the message could get in, and when the message was understood it was too late for that person to withdraw from the message. Roy also quoted Regina Barreca about humour's potential as an eye-opener:

> Humour can be a shortcut, an eye-opener... to get to the truth of the matter (...) When we can frame a difficult matter with humour, we can often reach someone who would otherwise withdraw.[589]

The comments resemble the logic behind the International Situationists and their notion of detournement. It also has similarities to the concept of appropriate incongruity. The humour that is likely to have this effect is the "intellectual" type based on techniques such as irony and wordplays. Examples of humour used by Ofog where Lena's "detour" would fit are Reality AB, Svensk Vapenfadder and the adbusting of Försvarsmakten's recruitment material.

---

[588] Roy, *The Raging Grannies: Wild Hats, Cheeky Songs, and Witty Actions for a Better World*: p. 60.
[589] Barreca 1996 quoted in Roy, *The Raging Grannies: Wild Hats, Cheeky Songs, and Witty Actions for a Better World*: p. 61.

Facilitating mobilisation

In much of the literature on humorous political activism presented in Chapter 1 it is assumed that humour makes it more attractive for new activists to be involved. One example is Shepard who has focused on all forms of play and not just humour. The potential for mobilisation is one of the conclusions of his work on playfulness in queer activism. Shepard writes: "When social actors organize in engaging, thoughtful ways, their work usually attracts followers. Through play, others are seduced to join."[590]

However, a closer look at the relationship between mobilisation and humour in Ofog reveals complexity: People get involved in Ofog from various starting points. Emma and Johanna for example knew someone who was already involved, others picked up a flyer or saw a poster about an action and decided to participate in it, or they had followed news on Ofog's email list. Maria mentioned that she was interested in the issues Ofog works with, and at first she was a bit put off by the humorous style which she had to get used to but now enjoys a lot. On the other hand someone else told me in an informal conversation that originally she was not especially concerned about militarism, but liked Ofog's style and inclusiveness. Lisa said that it was almost a coincidence that she became involved in Ofog and not another issue.

Many different factors are involved in determining if people get involved in political struggles, what level of engagement they have, if they maintain their commitment over long periods of time, leave activism altogether or return to it again later in life.[591]

---

[590] Shepard, *Queer Political Performance and Protest: Play, Pleasure and Social Movement*: p. 269.
[591] See for instance Catherine Corrigall-Brown, *Patterns of Protest: Trajectories of Participation in Social Movements* (Stanford, CA: Stanford University Press, 2012); James V. Downton and Paul Ernest Wehr, *The*

My own previous research had shown that humour might play a role in mobilisation of activists and supporters[592], so in all interviews I asked if people thought humour was important and if the use of humour would make more people interested in becoming involved in Ofog. I also wondered if humour helped present a clearer picture of what type of world it was that Ofog was working towards, a world with more warmth, carnival, humour and joy.

Lisa answered "absolutely" when asked if humour can be a way of getting more people involved in Ofog. It is one reason why she remained active in Ofog during a number of years. She agreed that humour can make it more clear what kind of world Ofog strives towards — to be easy-going, humorous and carnivalesque conveys a positive image of what it is that we want.[593] Johanna expressed a similar thought when she said "the world we want to see, we also have to try living."[594]

However, Lisa also thought humour has some disadvantages if activists focus too much on what they themselves think is funny and not on what is most effective. To her humour becomes meaningless if it is just funny for Ofog activists. In addition, Ofog risks being perceived as silly and losing trust. People will ask themselves how a "frivolous" group like this would be able

---

Persistent Activist: How Peace Commitment Develops and Survives (Boulder, CO: Westview Press, 1997); Bert Klandermans, "The Demand and Supply of Participation: Social-Psycological Correlates of Participation in Social Movements," in *The Blackwell Companion to Social Movements*, ed. David A. Snow, Sarah Anne Soule, and Hanspeter Kriesi (Malden, MA: Blackwell Pub., 2004); Mario Diani, "Networks and Participation," in *The Blackwell Companion to Social Movements*, ed. David A. Snow, Sarah Anne Soule, and Hanspeter Kriesi (Malden, MA: Blackwell Pub., 2004).
[592] Sørensen, "Humour as Nonviolent Resistance to Oppression."
[593] Interview September 2011.
[594] Interview June 2011.

to govern a society or be responsible for an economic policy. This said, Lisa did not think Ofog should take on this role: there are other groups for that. But according to her Ofog needs to think strategically about who is won over with humour, and who is scared away.[595]

Peter thought that humour and a light-hearted tone are important, and that Ofog has an image of being both serious and making spectacular actions. He considered humour important to the atmosphere in the group, otherwise people cannot keep going for a long time. Many organisations are very "weighted down with earnestness" as he said, and it can also be very aggressive.[596] Ofog is remarkably different and that is very important for Peter, otherwise he would not have remained in Ofog.

Gustav emphasised some of the same things as Peter, that humour is important for the people taking part, to find the energy to keep going. He definitely thought that Ofog's easy-going tone makes it easier for people to be involved in Ofog. Otherwise you are only able to take part for six months "and then you are totally hitting the wall," as he expressed it.[597] This "tone" also frames Ofog as innocent and harmless, showing that the activists are just human beings like anyone else.

Vera did not want to use the word "important" about humour, but she thought it is smart. She also agreed that humour makes Ofog attractive to some people, but it discourages others. In her city, there are people who do not want to be part of Ofog because they prefer to be dressed in black, be angry and look dangerous. But other people are drawn by the openness and the

---

[595] Interview September 2011.
[596] Interview September 2011.
[597] Interview September 2011.

positive style, and for Vera that optimistic and inclusive tone is an absolute necessity.[598]

In the next section about how humour influences activists themselves it becomes even more apparent how complex the relationship between humour and activism is.

Facilitating a culture of resistance

Facilitating a "culture of resistance" refers to humour's potential for sustaining and strengthening cultures that facilitate resistance. Chapter 1 introduced Scott's and Bayat's work about hidden transcripts and quiet encroachment. In Chapter 4 I noted how clowning for many activists is experienced as a personal libera-tion and how this type of activism provides new energy. It is perfectly possible to facilitate a culture of resistance without any use of humour, but previous research has suggested that it might help. Again this has also been confirmed by Shepard's work on play, although he does not use the term "culture of resistance":

> For many, play offers a life-affirming response to death and war. Here, play represents a counterbalance to disen-gagement; it is a way to stay engaged rather than fall into depression and personal alienation.[599]

That humour can help prevent burn-out and act as a counterbal-ance to the depressing issues of war and arms production was also confirmed by workshops and interviews with Ofog activists. Two workshop comments illustrate this.

> Laughter or happiness bubble in your stomach – and that is worth *so much* when you work with heavy issues. Happi-ness quite simple.[600]

---

[598] Interview September 2011.
[599] Shepard, *Queer Political Performance and Protest: Play, Pleasure and Social Movement*: p. 268.
[600] Written comment from workshop.

Feel better ourselves.[601]

Maria also stressed that for a network like Ofog concerned with such serious issues it is almost unavoidable to use humour because people need something that creates some distance from the topics. Otherwise she fears that activists may become very aggressive themselves in the end when they cannot find any energy.[602]

At the outset of the research project I expected to find a relatively clear distinction between humour which was directed outwards, and humour that was more internal. However, this distinction is not drawn automatically by activists themselves.

Sometimes humour is purely internal, as illustrated by an anecdote told during the workshop in May 2011. In connection with Ofog's participation in an action in Scotland, some people gave the police false names, which have an antimilitarist meaning in Swedish but made no sense to the English speaking police. One person was called Nei til Kärnvapen (No to Nuclear weapons), another Nedrusta Nå (Disarmament Now). These names then followed them in the prison, during police interrogations and DNA tests – much to the amusement of the activists.[603]

However, such a clearly internal type of humour is not very frequent. Many examples of humour which took place before 2011 intentionally had a "public" and visible side to them. But at the same time, they might have been difficult to grasp, and therefore ended up being more for the benefit of the activists themselves. An example of this is from Luleå 2010, where the participants in that year's summer camp and civil disobedience action were parodying the military recruitment ads "do you have what it takes to have an opinion?" It was the same ads that were

---

[601] Written comment from workshop.
[602] Interview September 2011.
[603] Episode told during workshop May 2011.

the target of the ad-refinements in Gothenburg mentioned previously. During the various actions, the activists carried speech bubbles saying things like "My brother thinks it sick to practice killing" and "my cousin does not think the military is good for democracy"[604], parodying the military ads.

Those who entered into the military test area were dressed as people from various professions which Ofog considered more useful for society than the military. They had statements attached to their clothing that said things like "My nurse does not think the USA should be able to practice bombing here," "My Librarian does not think that war will ever create peace" and "my carpenter does not think the USA should practice war in Norrbotten."[605]

However, although the satire was public, it mainly played an internal role. In Ofog's press releases about seven people entering the military area in a civil disobedience action, the way the activists are dressed is mentioned:

> Dressed as "people beneficial to society" – teacher, carpenter, cook, artist, nurse, librarian and farmer – they wanted to point towards alternatives to militarisation and specifically disturb the war preparations.[606]

---

[604] These statements (and many other examples using the same format) are visible in the photos from the action, available here: http://ofog.org/aktionsl%C3%A4ger-mot-usas-bomb%C3%B6vning-i-norrbotten accessed March 6 2012.
[605] These statements (and many other examples using the same format) are visible in the photos from the action, available here: http://ofog.org/aktionsl%C3%A4ger-mot-usas-bomb%C3%B6vning-i-norrbotten accessed March 6 2012.
[606] Ofog, "7 Personer Inne På Flygflottilj – Krig Kan Inte Få Förberedas Ostört! Pressmeddelande Från Nätverket Ofog, 29 Juli 2010," http://ofog.org/press/7-personer-inne-p%C3%A5-flygflottilj-

However, there is no reference to the parodies of the military ads, and the local news reports about the events did not mention it either.[607] This reflects that Ofog did not consider this humorous aspect of the action important in its relations to the media, and the observation above that the media primarily focus on the civil disobedience. Nevertheless, this does not mean that it did not play a role internally.

A similar example is from the camp in Karlskoga in 2007, close to the weapon producer Bofors the year before the clowns were successful in negotiating public space. At that time, the US TV Series *CSI* (Crime Scene Investigation) was very popular, so Ofog played on this theme and announced a crime scene investigation at Bofors where they suspected war crimes and crimes against humanity were taking place. The police tape to mark where the activists could not go contributed to the crime scene feeling.[608]

In 2009, NATO was carrying out an exercise in Norrbotten which it called "Loyal arrow". As a parody, Ofog named its protest camp and actions "Royal Error". Lisa explained how Ofog had done that on several occasions. When asked if other people though it was funny, she said:

> No, I'm not sure. It is something which can be quite difficult if you want to use humour. It easily becomes quite internal. We understand the joke and think it is funny ourselves, but no, of course it can be difficult for others to

---

%E2%80%93-krig-kan-inte-f%C3%A5-f%C3%B6rberedas-ost%C3%B6rt.

[607] I have not made a systematic search for local news reports, but Ofog has collected them on the webpage. Those from radio and TV are not accessible anymore, but some of the local newspapers are. I have read four of the longer news reports from various local newspapers, and none of them mentioned the professions beneficial to society or the parodies.

[608] Episode told during workshop May 2011.

understand (...) maybe it is just as much for our own sake, maybe it does not have to influence someone else.[609]

Royal Error was the same year that Reality AB was recruiting people to act as civilian casualties in the streets of Luleå. Another affinity group provided another example of this internal-external dynamic of humour. Emma was part of the group which acted as a support group for deserters. In a little leaflet, distributed to the soldiers the day before, the group invited all soldiers to participate:

> Welcome to support group conversation for deserters.
>
> Do you feel held back by the macho culture in the military and want to learn to show emotions? Is your integrity abused by orders from authoritarian officers? Do you want to lay down your arms? We invite you to participate in our five step programme where psychologists, social workers and life-coaches work closely for your re-integration into society. Friday June 12 we will be present outside F21 [the military airport] and receive both conscripts and professional soldiers. With coffee and cakes we create a nice atmosphere and through individual conversations and group exercises we work with issues of self-confidence, friendship and values. Spread the word at your regiment and together we can work for a world without war.[610]

Of course this should not be interpreted as a serious attempt of converting the soldiers, but through the exaggerations the action aimed at communicating different values. Instead of condemning the conscripts, it was an invitation to reflect on what it was that they were involved in. Emma explained how they had prepared a role play where some of the activists were soldiers and others

---

[609] Interview September 2011.
[610] Ofog, "Välkomna På Stödgruppssamtal För Desertörer," http://ofog.org/royal-errors-fredsaktivister-st%C3%B6r-natos-krigs%C3%B6vning.

were the counsellors. In front of the conscript soldiers on guard that day, they performed the role play. For instance they illustrated how to challenge your ideas about masculinity by practicing embracing your friend without slapping his back. They also provided alternatives to what the soldiers could do instead of guarding a military airport. An example was directed to the military police, who carry an armband with the letters MP. Instead of guarding the airport they could join the green party, which in Swedish is called Miljöpartiet and also uses the initials MP. After the performance the activists offered coffee to everyone, but as far as Emma remembers it was only the dialogue police who accepted the offer.

During the workshop in Gothenburg, the participants who first told me about this action generally thought that it went well, and that the soldiers had given the impression that they thought it was cool that something happened. However, one person mentioned that she did not want to participate herself because she thought it was targeting the conscript soldiers too much and not the military system. In our interview, Emma said she thought the action went well, but that she was not sure this had been the best way to convince the soldiers to desert. Nevertheless, when they left, the soldiers had given them the peace sign with their fingers.

I did not participate or observe this myself, but I suspect the achievements of this action were mainly internal. The participants presumably had a good time preparing and carrying it out, and managed to present their protest of the military exercises as a positive, dialogue oriented stunt rather than an angry and negative way of saying no. This way, it did have some of the characteristics of a supportive stunt. Nevertheless, as Lisa said as a general comment above, sometimes the impact on others is probably rather limited. The support group for deserters was not intended to reach the media, and although some of the soldiers might have had some reflections about their job, they did not appear to be the direct target either. Had that been the case, the activists had presumably chosen a method that involved less performance and more real dialogue. And in order to be successful that would probably have required a setting that was not so directly connected to a protest and civil disobedience action.

So far I have shown how humour can be a way to facilitate both outreach, mobilisation and a culture of resistance. Among Ofog activists is it common to consider humour important for their own well-being. Much of Ofog's humour is directed outwards, but several examples of humour that was public with all likelihood served a more internal function. In the next section humour's influence on the relations of power is the focus.

Challenging power relations through discursive guerrilla war

In Chapter 1 I discussed the complexities and limitations of understanding and analysing relations of power and what impact humour can or cannot have on these relations. Ofog's humorous political stunts illustrate the challenge of estimating what effect they have. The network's focus on the very broad and extremely powerful discourse of militarism makes it difficult to point towards any immediate results. Unlike some of the other groups who perform humorous political stunts, Ofog has a very broad agenda. Over the years, different parts of the network have worked on quite different issues – from the military test site Vidsel Test Range/NEAT to countering the armed forces' recruitment efforts and Swedish arms production. This diversity in focus and campaigns that seldom last more than a couple of years make it less likely for the network to be able to point towards a clear "success" regarding a clearly defined goal. That does not mean that Ofog's actions do not temporarily undermine relations of power, but it makes it much more difficult to identify a more permanent impact.

In the previous chapter it became clear how the clowns to a large degree focused on the immediate relations with police and military present during the actions. Most of Ofog's actions

380

described in this chapter challenge relations of power not at the level of interpersonal relations, but through attempts to destabilise dominant discourses. Reality AB challenged NATO's discourse of war as something connected to sophisticated technology and protection of human rights by reminding random passers-by in Luleå that war causes death and suffering and that civilians are most exposed. The corrected recruitment ads reminded viewers that one can "have what it takes" to have a political opinion without subscribing to the worldview Försvarsmakten communicates through its ads. Although the discussion afterwards got side-tracked, the speech bobble posters during the pride parade were also an attempt to weaken Försvarsmakten's discourse. Likewise, the ironic posters and flyers also interfere with various dominant militaristic discourses. All these humorous political stunts can thus be understood as "hit and run" attacks in this discursive guerrilla war. They might be short lived and temporary, but nevertheless they raise dissenting voices in the public sphere about what is true, right and just.

More knowledge about how these contributions to the discursive guerrilla war are received by various audiences would be an obvious topic for future research, since the data about how the general public perceives Ofog's humorous political stunts is limited. Above I included my observations about reactions to Svensk Vapenfadder and Britta's ladies' gym. The lack of media coverage also reveals that apart from the clowns' ability to make good photos, Ofog's use of humour has been of very limited interest to mass media. The information about how Ofog's actions are understood by people in positions of power is even more rudimentary. Apart from the one politician who did not like to be included in Svensk Vapenfadder, I cannot tell how these actions were perceived – if they were noticed at all – by politicians, arms producers and the authorities' representatives in the police and armed forces. However, Ofog activists have provided many comments on their perceptions of this interaction.

In the written comments from the workshops, there were many different answers to the two questions "What do you think can be achieved by using humour as a method in nonviolent actions?" And "How can humour influence the relations with the military, media, arms producers and police in nonviolent actions?" which dealt with humour's ability to challenge relations of power. What is most striking about the answers is the diversity. Those who commented on how humour affects relations of power wrote things like:

> To show the absurd in the system one protests against and resists. To reduce hostility between different sides in a conflict by doing something creative. (Just like it is good to have music in a demonstration and not just shout slogans.). To get each other to think creatively and therefore better find solutions.[611]

This person suggested that humour communicates less hostility, similar to the way the clowns in the previous chapter were communicating nonviolent values. This is supported by another person who suggested that:

> It is possible to make fun of and ridicule and resist what is terrible and horrible without being it yourself. By highlighting something from a "new" angle it can become so obvious how crazy power relations are that resistance can become beautiful and funny at the same time as it becomes more powerful.[612]

Someone else commented on the dilemma that humour might create for the police and military sent out to prevent or stop an action:

> In relation to military/police etc., make it more difficult for them to physically prevent the action. It is more difficult to

---

[611] Written comment from workshop.
[612] Written comment from workshop.

"brutally" stop someone you think is funny and sympathise with.[613]

The quote above can be an observation about a clowning action where the clowns succeeded in physically opening up space, but it might also be a comment on a different type of situation.

Another person, writing about actions against arms production, expressed hope that the employees at the factory would understand that the action was not directed against them, but the system they are part of:

> Think it can help clarify. For example, it makes workers at an arms factory [understand] that the action is not directed towards them but against the system.[614]

In the next quote, the person referred to humour's potential for creating uncertainty for people who are usually sure of themselves, in this way emphasising the common bond between all human beings no matter their role in society:

> I think a major point may be the uncertainty that humour can create in these meetings. All these actors hopefully need to think about and talk about such actions and then also talk about/think about the issue itself. Laughter is a good way to meet = disarming. We see we are humans.[615]

Finally, someone who wrote specifically about clowning expressed hope that the police would see the creativity and that it would make them reflect about their own organisation.

> On the occasions that I have participated in actions where there have been clowns present, the police have often interacted. I hope that they see that activists use creative

---

[613] Written comment from workshop.
[614] Written comment from workshop.
[615] Written comment from workshop.

methods for changing society, instead of violence. Make them reflect on their own organisation.[616]

The quotes reflect the wishes and hopes from people in a marginal anti-militarist network about what the use of humour achieves. Future research might reveal how it is perceived by people in positions of power and what meaning it has for them.

I separated the functions of humour into four different aspects of how it facilitates outreach, mobilisation, a culture of resistance and challenging relations of power. However, this categorisation is only for analytical purposes, because on the ground of political activism the four different aspects are closely linked together, and one humorous event might contribute to more than one aspect. Nevertheless, the four categories might be useful when navigating the complexities of humour. Although a particular event might not have sparked any reactions from people in positions of power, it was still a contribution in the discursive guerrilla war about what to consider true, right and just. Thus it can have reached out to many in the general public, or it can have contributed to a culture of resistance. The four different aspects make it easier to discuss exactly what a group can expect a particular humorous political stunt being planned to achieve, or evaluate its impact. It might also be a way to expand the repertoire if it turns out that a group has a tendency to focus on mobilisation, in spite of an outspoken goal of challenging an established power relation.

The two final sections treat two aspects of the use of humour that came up in the interviews and workshops but do not belong in any of the four categories above. The first issue is whether the distinction between the humorous and non-humorous actions is artificial and the second what the risks with humorous activism are.

---

[616] Written comment from workshop.

Artificial distinction between humorous and other creative actions

One thing that has become obvious during this research is that the distinction between humorous and other creative actions is rather artificial in the perspective of activists' lived experience. This is not something the informants tell explicitly, but it becomes clear from the stories people spontaneously start to tell. When I asked for examples about the use of humour, the first examples I was told were usually clearly humorous. However, several people continued with examples of actions which were creative and involved some kind of performance such as street theatre, but were not necessarily humorous.[617] For example, Ofog activists in Malmö made a street theatre of an auction of Swedish produced arms in the autumn of 2010. One person played the auctioneer, while others were playing the buyers from India, Pakistan and USA. The performance included a part where the Indian and Pakistani buyers kept overbidding each other. All the weapons came together with a civilian casualty who told how he or she had been bombed, shot or killed. This is not a humorous political stunt since there is no confrontation or blurred lines between audiences and performers, but it is obviously humorous. However, straight afterwards, the Malmö-Lund activists told about two other episodes, which were creative, thought provoking and drew attention, but were not humorous. One Christmas they hung toy automatic weapons in the public Christmas tree wrapped as gifts. Under the banner "Sweden sends hard gifts to the world's children again this year," they collected signatures against arms export from the general public. Another example was the "jump for peace" that they arranged in connection with a trial against activists who had done a citizen inspection at Aimpoint.

---

[617] Field note observation during interviews in Malmö, September 2011.

Humorous actions are different from other types of action. For analytical purposes, it makes sense to distinguish humorous from non-humorous actions. However, researchers should bear in mind that for many activists, this distinction between humour and other kinds of creative performance is more academic than experienced.

Risky humour

The final theme about humour and political activism from the interviews and workshops with Ofog activists is the potential risks with using humour. Here the findings from the field work are compared with the few existing reflections about risks in the literature on creative activism.

> 1. **The risk of being perceived as not serious about the issue**

Almost everyone I have asked about potential problems with using humour in activism responded that they see a risk of not being taken seriously. When asked about potential risks in the workshops, one person in a written comment expressed concern about being seen as unserious and self-centred:

> We can be seen as unserious. Childish, silly, without any-thing important, sensible, or important to say. Exhibitionistic: People have thought that we want to "be seen", without any more aims or thoughts than that.[618]

The risk of not being taken seriously expressed in this quote appears real enough: one must expect part of the audience to respond as if they believe that the pranksters are just out to have fun themselves.

In Day's analysis of Billionaires for Bush, she includes a quote from a woman who prefers "honest" and straightforward pro-

---

[618] Written comment from workshop.

test. Billionaires for Bush dressed as stereotypical rich characters and made an ironic performance in support of US president George Bush's economic policies benefitting the rich. After Bush left the White House, they have pursued the same issue. They are still Billionaires, but what they are for depends on the circumstances. The quote that Day refers to was broadcast in an interview on national radio when the Billionaires were present at a Bush fundraiser:

> I think they're making a mockery out of it and it's a joke, and it's pretty embarrassing. It's confusing to children and it's confusing to a couple of adults here as well. And I have more respect for the people over there who are saying what they happen to feel. They dress normally. They don't have to come in costume and have a gimmick.[619]

There is no way of knowing how representative this woman's views were, but they reflect the need for care. However, much more research is needed about how audiences perceive humorous political stunts before one can conclude that audiences prefer rational ways of communicating. Some audience members may prefer rationality because it is more familiar or easier to ignore.

Gustav is a Ofog activist who cautioned against too much humour. He emphasised that it is important to show that one understands the issue one works with:

> And then I don't always think it is good to use humour. Sometimes it is good to show that you are a serious person who has read a lot and do this because you really believe in it, and can argue your case as well.[620]

The issues of arms export and war that Ofog works with are probably some of the most controversial issues one can imagine.

---

[619] National Public Radio broadcast March 12, 2004, quoted in Day, *Satire and Dissent.* p. 181.
[620] Interview September 2011.

Humour about any sensitive issue like torture, hunger and people's loss of life and livelihood should of course be approached with care. There will probably always be people who consider black humour tasteless, but research about the use of humour in professions exposed to life and death indicates that black humour might be a way of coping with difficult issues.[621] Nevertheless, the most obscure and macabre might be best kept as internal jokes in order not to offend those who activists want to protect. However, it also depends on how the black humour is performed. Before I started this research project, I would have been doubtful about the possibility for creating humour around civilian casualties in war. Nevertheless I think Reality AB is a good example of black humour, and I have only met one person who openly disapproved of it.

All social movements considering using humorous political stunts need to take the risk of not being taken seriously into consideration. Fear of this consequence is probably the reason why humour is not used more, in spite of its potential benefits. Organisations and movements who have already established ways of communicating with their potential audiences based on rational arguments might simply find it too risky to experiment with humour. The *persistence of logical argument* is quite strong, even within a network like Ofog which is more willing to experiment with humour than most other organisations.

The interviews and workshops also revealed other potentially problematic issues:

2.   a risk of ridicule being experienced as abuse

---

[621] Ruth M. Strudwick, Stuart J. Mackay, and Stephen Hicks, "Cracking Up?," *Synergy* (2012); Wormer Katherine van and Mary Boes, "Humor in the Emergency Room: A Social Work Perspective," *Health & Social Work* 22, no. 2 (1997).

Another risk with humour is the potential ethical problem that ridicule might be experienced as abuse. If humorous intent can be reframed as abuse, a totally different discourse is in use than when something is considered to belong to the just-joking sphere.

Ofog's platform emphasises nonviolence and respect towards everyone, so Ofog activists can obviously get into trouble when an action involves ridicule or other expressions that might be interpreted as abuse. The speech bubble action at the Pride Parade is the most obvious example where the target explicitly said that they experienced this as abuse, and where also people within Ofog reacted. Although the activists who participated in the action wanted to expose the consequences of militarism and the presence of the soldiers in the pride parade, the soldiers who were targeted experienced it as an attack on them as individuals, raising the question of ethics.

In chapter 1 I presented Gantar's and Billig's thoughts about ethics and humour. If one insists on judging humour along ethical lines in spite of Gantar's conclusion that it is not possible, one point of departure that Gantar and Billig do not discuss is the position of those who initiate the humour. There is a huge difference between ridicule initiated by people in power aimed at a minority, and ridicule that comes from people in a subordinate position directed towards those more powerful. An example of the first was the so-called Muhammad cartoons published by *Jyllands-Posten* in 2005, where an established mainstream newspaper directed its satire towards a religious minority in Denmark. That is very different from humorous political stunts initiated by small activist groups and directed at powerful discourses and their representatives. When people in power try to use what Billig calls the "tease-spray" or the "just-joking spray", one can point out that they speak from a position of power and disapprove of their mockery, at the same time as one can approve of ridicule which kicks upwards.

However, although it is possible to make this distinction in principle, Ofog's speech bubbles at the pride parade illustrate some of the dilemmas. It was people in subordinate positions who ridiculed someone they saw as representatives of a powerful institution, but under the circumstances, the individual soldiers did not feel very powerful.

3. a risk of irony not being understood

In connection with the Vapenfadder campaign the participant observation made it very clear how problematic it can be to communicate with irony. No matter how exaggerated a group itself thinks it is, there is always a risk that people misunderstand the irony because the clues are not clear enough.

In Haugerud's article about the Billionaires for Bush, she writes that most passers-by who lingered for a little while realised that the performance was ironic. However, she also quotes two people who embody this risk that the irony might not be understood:

> 'Is it a joke? I can't figure out if it's a joke' said a woman encountering the Billionaires for the first time at their 2004 tax day event outside New York City's central post office. A male passer-by at the same event at first wondered: 'But are they for or against Bush?'[622]

That humour is not understood the way the initiators intended it to be seems especially to be a potential problem with the technique of irony where the literal meaning is different from the intended meaning. To understand irony requires what Hutcheon calls "discursive communities", where we share an understanding with others about what things mean. All humorous techniques can potentially be misunderstood just as rational communication can be, but the ambiguity of humour and especially irony means

---

[622] Haugerud, "Satire and Dissent in the Age of Billionaires," p. 154.

that the potential for misunderstandings is built into the fabric of this way of communicating. According to Hutcheon irony is not "just" the opposite of what is said or done, but something that "happens" in the tension between the people who initiate the irony, those who interpret it, the meaning which is stated as well as what is not stated.[623] Irony is based on the audience's moment of doubt about whether this is the actual meaning or not. For the prankster the more cues one gives, the "rougher" the irony is and more likely that many people will get it. On the other hand, if there are just a few cues, the irony gets better because of the ambiguity, but at the cost of the irony going over the head of more people.[624]

There are two potential sources for the misunderstandings. Sometimes the activists constructing humorous political stunts are just not skilled enough in designing irony. This can be because they are not able to exaggerate thoroughly or present the absurdity convincingly, which was probably the case for the Vapenfadder campaign. Nevertheless, it would also become a problem if political groups needed the skills of professional entertainers in order to be funny.[625]

The problem might also be that the irony is so sophisticated that it goes over the head of the intended audience. If it is based on references that the general public are not aware of they have no way of discovering the hidden meaning. Then the humorous political stunt risks becoming elitist, serving to show that "we are more clever than you", rather than engaging people in a debate

---

[623] Hutcheon, *Irony's Edge*: pp. 12-13.
[624] Hutcheon, *Irony's Edge*: p. 152.
[625] Day points towards this risk in Day, *Satire and Dissent*.

about a political issue.[626] And if an ironic message is taken literally, the result might be that stereotypes are reinforced.[627]

4. a risk of humour becoming too internal or an end in itself

If the goal is outwardly directed action and campaigning, and humour is one of the elements, it is important to consider beforehand how it will be understood and perceived by the intended audience. Generally it is more difficult to create actions that others will understand than what most activists assume, no matter if they are humorous or not. Activists would probably benefit from researching these issues by asking members of the potential audience what they think and evaluate their campaigns instead of relying on their personal assumptions and speculations. However, as described above there are also benefits to be gained from using humour internally when it comes to creating a culture of resistance, and as long as the internal humour does not obstruct the communication outwards it is hard to see any problems with internal humour.

5. the difficulty with combining the humorous and non-humorous

During its existence, Ofog has continuously combined humorous and non-humorous types of actions. Reality AB took place side by side and partly mixed with non-humorous street theatre, and the internal-external examples above illustrate the same overlaps. However, during the interviews one person in particular questioned if this was a good strategy. Lisa stressed that humour is important for her own commitment to Ofog, but she would like Ofog to be more cautious about mixing different

---

[626] Jacobs and Smith, "Romance, Irony, and Solidarity." p.74.
[627] Jacobs and Smith, "Romance, Irony, and Solidarity," p. 74; Day, *Satire and Dissent.*

approaches. We were talking about an idea for an ironic campaign that had come up during the workshop in Gothenburg but was never carried out. Lisa first emphasised that there has to be enough resources in the form of time and energy to do it properly, but then continued to talk about how mixing different strategies might be less efficient.

> .. there should be energy to do it properly (…) I did not think that we should do it this year [2011], because we already had a campaign with one concept, and it could become very confusing to have an ironic campaign and a serious campaign… and that was how it was when we did Reality AB, that it became a little double in a way, that at the same time we also had a non-ironic campaign, and maybe that is not very strategic, we ought to become better at choosing a focus. But in itself, [ironic campaigns] are a very good idea.[628]

Here Lisa reflected on what she considered the problems with mixing rational and humorous campaigns, comparing it to her memory of how reality AB worked. She continued:

> I think absolutely that [Reality AB] worked very well as it was, I think it would have worked even better if we had just gone for that, (…) maybe it became a little half done, that someone got the idea and that we did not do it 100%. But it is always like that.[629]

The problem that not everyone commits 100% to a certain idea is not something that is peculiar to humorous political stunts. Since it is only a minority of groups that primarily rely on humour in their communication, the majority of groups are likely to change between the humorous and the non-humorous. And as long as "seriousness" (= the rational) continues to be the norm, ideas for humorous campaigns will end up being a supplement to

---

[628] Interview September 2011.
[629] Interview September 2011.

the norm. Thus, the problem that Lisa is pointing out is unlikely to disappear unless groups dare to say that this time, we will try to let the humorous be the norm.

Lisa saw the potential that a humorous and non-humorous campaign about the same subject might appeal to and reach out to different audiences, and suggested that campaigns can run in parallel if it is not obvious that they originate from the same place.

> I think it can be difficult, but maybe it is possible to combine. It does not have to be very obvious that it is Ofog who does it, maybe Ofog runs a serious campaign, and then the ironic or upside down can just be there. It does not need to have any sender at all. Maybe we can reach different people that way. (...) It is difficult, because I really believe in the idea [of an ironic campaign], but I also believe in the idea of being serious (both laugh), (...) and I think that you have to choose, I really think you have to choose.[630]

In spite of Lisa's belief that ironic campaigns can be a useful tool, she still ended up stressing that she thinks it is important to choose and prefers that Ofog is cautious about mixing humorous and non-humorous approaches about the same issue.

Related to the issues that Lisa brought up is the problem with doing a humorous political stunt half-heartedly and mixing it with traditional protest. For activists who are used to "ordinary protest" it can be a challenge to leave all the usual symbols of protest behind, for instance when participating in a supportive stunt. However, the result of a mix might be that neither the supportive stunt nor the ordinary protest symbols come across. Instead the message one communicates is just confusing.

---

[630] Interview September 2011.

6. Satire risks making people disillusioned

The final potential problem with humour was not mentioned in workshops or interviews, but has appeared in the literature. Perhaps the most fundamental critique that has been directed against satire and irony is that they are cynical and make people disillusioned. They are good at criticising everything and everyone but do not present any alternatives.[631] However, this is a misreading of much satire and irony. Rebecca Higgie uses the Chaser team as an example of how one can make a distinction between cynicism and kynicism when discussing satire. Kynicism is a notion that comes from ancient Greek philosophy and Higgie says that "Kynicism is cynicism without the latter's nihilistic nature."[632] Whereas cynicism criticises without seeing any hope for change, "Kynicism also questions and doubts, but maintains that there is a better way of doing things".[633] Although the satire does not provide any alternatives to the prevailing political order, under the surface of the irony, a kynical approach finds that not all truth is said to be non-existent, just the particular truth of the prevailing order.[634] When it comes to the satire and irony in humorous political stunts, it is usually quite clear that the initiators are committed to improving and not just criticising. It is difficult to accuse the grassroots groups behind most of the stunts presented here of being cynical. The risk is much greater for professional comedians, though many of them have a direction in their social critique.

---

[631] For instance this is discussed in Jacobs and Smith, "Romance, Irony, and Solidarity."

[632] Rebecca Higgie, "Kynical Dogs and Cynical Masters: Contemporary Satire, Politics and Truth-Telling," *Humor: International Journal of Humor Research* 27, no. 2 (2014): p. 185.

[633] Higgie, "Kynical Dogs and Cynical Masters: Contemporary Satire, Politics and Truth-Telling," p. 185.

[634] Higgie, "Kynical Dogs and Cynical Masters: Contemporary Satire, Politics and Truth-Telling."

The potential risks with using humour that Ofog activists have identified vary a lot, but also have something in common. Fear that humour might offend, be misunderstood or lead to a group losing legitimacy are different reasons, but all result in a *persistence of logical argument* . However, an investigation into the potential problems also revealed that some of the potential problems might be due to general organisational and planning aspects. When evaluating a humorous political action and deciding if something similar should be repeated in the future, this might be worth taking into consideration.

The persistence of logical argument might also stem from the fact that subversive irony requires an intimate knowledge of dominant discourses – an intimacy that can also be considered complicity.[635] That is probably one reason why some political activists become uncomfortable when it comes to humour, including irony. To create irony is only possible if you know very well the language of what you want to ironise about. Hutcheon explains that there is an emotional element when it comes to producing and interpreting irony. Irony does not just say something about a certain topic; it also adds an emotion or an attitude towards it.[636] This emotional dimension might be problematic for activists concerned about being perceived as rational.

Conclusion

Activists in Ofog work with serious issues of war and war preparations, arms production and arms export. This chapter is not an attempt to document Ofog's whole history, but the part concerning the role of humour. Although a light-hearted tone, including humour, plays an important role in much of what Ofog does, it is far from the only thing. The majority of the civil disobedience actions are carried out with only hints of humour

---

[635] Hutcheon, *Irony's Edge*: p. 30.
[636] Hutcheon, *Irony's Edge*: p. 39.

and these hints are usually more for the benefit of the participants than directed outwards. In legal activities aimed at
awareness raising and opinion building, the use of humour takes
more space and has been used on numerous occasions as the
primary strategy, for example in Reality AB, Vapenfadder and
the satiric posters.

What is most striking with the humorous examples in this chapter is their diversity. As mentioned in Chapter 3, humour is so
diverse that it is almost impossible to make general statements
about the phenomenon. As Ofog activists have expressed in
interviews and written comments, they mean very different
things when they speak about humour. The people who have
participated in this research are just a small sample of a fairly
homogeneous group. They all have more or less the same background and political perspective. Nevertheless what they speak
about when they use the word humour is quite varied. Imagine
what it would have been like asking the same questions to a
group of people with highly varied cultural and political backgrounds.

This diversity makes it difficult to make generalisations about
using humour in a struggle, because the notion covers so many
different types of activities. In order for such a conversation to
be meaningful, it is necessary to examine specific humorous
actions and be clear about intended audiences.

Another finding from this chapter is that although the distinction between humorous and non-humorous actions is
meaningful for analytical purposes, it is not a difference which
makes much sense in the everyday life of activists. When people
are asked about humorous actions they usually start out telling
about humour, but it is not uncommon subsequently to switch
to actions that have other creative aspects. "On the ground" it
might make more sense to talk about to what degree methods
are creative, rather than humorous.

Complexity is also a key word when it comes to understanding the reactions to Ofog's humorous political stunts. The small inquiry I did during Britta's ladies gym against NEAT gave an idea about how difficult it can be to get the intended message across to the audiences. The reactions after the speech bubble action at the Pride Parade suggest some of the tactics that opponents may apply in order to devalue activists and reframe the discussion so it takes place on their home territory.

The functions of humour for Ofog activists were divided into facilitating outreach, mobilisation, a culture of resistance and challenging relations of power.

Facilitating outreach means reaching out to various audiences, but especially media and the general public. The findings in this chapter supported previous research in documenting how humour can be a good way to catch the attention of members of the general public otherwise not concerned about the issue. However, it is difficult to know if this attention leads to a change in opinion or behaviour. One Ofog activist suggested that ironic messages the audience can "crack" within a reasonable amount of time might make people feel smart and this way reach them at a deeper level. This would be an interesting topic for further research.

Many of the examples of humour presented in Chapter 3 were successful in reaching mass media with their humorous political stunts. This is not something Ofog has experienced, probably because most of the humorous political stunts have been directed more towards the general public than mass media. Since humour's appeal to mass media is so much taken for granted, little is known about how many other political groups have tried to reach media with humour but failed. It would also be interesting to compare what type of media coverage would result if the same amount of time and energy was spent on non-humorous activism but equally attention grabbing activities, such as civil disobedience.

Even though they mean such different things when they talk about humour, most of the people from Ofog I interviewed considered it an important factor in facilitating mobilisation. They said that it is an important reason why they joined, that they think it makes potential new activists interested in Ofog, and a reason why they stay committed. For a network working with such grave issues, humour is experienced almost as a necessity in order to prevent burnout.

Ofog is a network speaking from a marginalised position. Although many people in Sweden are highly critical of Sweden's arms export, Ofog is a very small network that is also marginalised within in the broader and more moderate peace movement that does not engage in civil disobedience. Some political groups decide to focus on a very narrow issue whereas others spread out their activities much broader. Ofog belongs to the last category, with attention going to arms production and military recruitment as well as military test sites. There are many reasons for this, but a consequence is that there are rarely any short term goals to reach, making it much more difficult to judge if a campaign has been successful and really challenged relations of power. It is difficult to see any changes in Swedish arms production, recruitment practices and use of test sites that can be attributed to Ofog activities. If one compares the resources that Ofog controls with those of the armed forces, FMV and the armament industry, it would be quite unrealistic to expect Ofog's humorous political stunts to create much permanent change, but Ofog provides a critical dissenting voice in a context where belief in military solutions to conflict dominates. Through the humorous political stunts, Ofog can be seen to wage a discursive guerrilla war where dominant discourses about NEAT/Vidsel Test Range, the job as a soldier and the results of Swedish arms production are challenged in many small ways. Although these challenges to dominant discourses are temporary, they do break the hegemony and at the same time give an impression of the *potential* that arises from this type of activism.

Ofog has used four of the five different types of humorous political stunts – the only type missing is the naïve stunt. The supportive, corrective and absurd stunts have been used in different forms, while the provocative has only been used when people in Umeå painted a whole tank pink.

Another conclusion is that one should not underestimate the power of the experience of challenging a major dominant discourse – and having fun at the same time. Although there is no sign that the discourse of militarism or the institutions that uphold it are about to be dismantled, all successful social movements had to start somewhere and appeared hopelessly naïve when they set out.

Finally, the chapter included a discussion about some of the risks with using humour. The most obvious risk, pointed out by almost everyone, is of audiences perceiving the presence of humour as a sign that the activists do not take the issues of war preparation and arms production seriously. This is a consequence of the widespread and taken for granted dichotomy between the "humorous" and the "serious", where the humorous cannot be serious at the same time. Speaking about "rational" or "non-humorous" types of actions as a contrast to the humorous avoids this problem. The other potential risks identified are of ridicule being experienced as abuse, irony being misunderstood, the humour becoming too internal, and the potential problems with mixing humorous and non-humorous methods in the same campaign. Although it was not brought up during the interviews and workshops, I also discussed the risk of satire being perceived as cynical.

Fear that humour might offend, be misunderstood or lead to a group losing legitimacy all result in a *persistence of logical argument*. Gantar suggested not caring about ethics when investigating laughter critically because it is an epistemological dead end. Nevertheless, activists performing humorous political stunts are operating in a world where ethics does matter, and are well advised to consider how their stunt is likely to be received also from this perspective. With ethics in mind they have a better chance of getting the political message across instead of spending their time defending their choice of method.

Nevertheless, when planning and evaluating a potential humorous action or campaign, it is worth keeping in mind that some of the problems that arise with an idea involving humour might be due to general organisational and planning challenges and not connected to the humour per se. For example it is a general problem for many groups that they pursue several ideas half-heartedly instead of committing 100% to one idea.

The next chapter is a case study of the strategies of another Scandinavian group working on anti-militarism. *Kampanjen Mot Verneplikt* (KMV), meaning *The Campaign Against Conscription*, worked under circumstances comparable to Ofog, but focused on one particular issue, total resistance to conscription.

Chapter 6: Kampanjen Mot Verneplikt – combining legal and spectacular actions

Introduction

How can you imprison a conscientious objector for 16 months without calling it a punishment? This was the central question for *Kampanjen Mot Verneplikt* (KMV), which means *The Campaign Against Conscription*. KMV was a Scandinavian campaign started in 1981 to work against conscription and support conscientious objectors who were imprisoned for their conviction. The case study focuses on the Norwegian conditions and the strategies used by the campaign to pressure the Norwegian government into changing the law. Although this is not the history of KMV, it includes many details about KMV's way of organising and working with both humorous and non-humorous activities. The purpose of this is to provide a coherent narrative about KMV and to show its similarities and differences with Ofog.

In the previous chapter Ofog activists' perceptions about the benefits and risks with using humour were discussed in relation to different audiences and functions related to outreach, mobilisation, a culture of resistance and challenging relations of power. Since nothing indicates otherwise, it is reasonable to assume that the KMV activists shared similar ideas about what humour could achieve. This chapter then takes the question of what role humour can play in challenging relations of power one step further and analyses how the humorous political stunts were integrated with three other non-humorous strategies.

The chapter begins with some background information about the campaign and the situation for the conscientious objectors. It continues by presenting four different strategies that KMV used in its struggle, the first and major one being 1. *to create a spectacle* around the court hearings and imprisonments. The group performed several humorous political stunts as part of this strategy which are especially relevant here. In addition, three other strategies were pursued: 2. Participants in KMV *used the court system* by filing charges against the state for violating their human rights, something that turned out to be essential for their success. 3. *Solidarity* work with other conscientious objectors around the world and 4. *Lobbying and participating in the public debate.* These different strategies are presented in some detail to make it possible to trace the use of humorous political stunts within a larger campaign. Because the legal strategy was decisive for KMV's success, this chapter does not have humour as its only focus.

The launch of KMV

KMV was launched in Halden in Norway on 28-29th of November 1981.[637] This was also the first time the name KMV was used publicly. KMV was a joint campaign involving Swedish and Norwegian activists, with some links to Denmark and Finland as well. The campaign was primarily concerned with the fate of the so-called total resisters who refused both military and substitute service, but also supported other conscientious objectors risking imprisonment. Some of the key Swedish and Norwegian activists knew each other from War Resisters' International and since they were so few in each country they decided to work closely together in a joint campaign.

Although many activities took place in Sweden and one person was very active in Finland, the major focus of KMV was the conditions in Norway. The language barrier was one reason it was difficult to get a bigger Finnish involvement and in Denmark the way the conscription system was organised meant there was very little interest in total resistance.

---

[637] The press releases from the founding meeting are dated late November.

403

In its main platform, a booklet published in 1981, KMV was introduced with an English name, ICR – Scandinavia. The booklet explained that the campaign had been underway in Scandinavia for more than two years, and that publishing the booklet was a step towards an active network. ICR was an abbreviation of *International Collective Resistance*, an international campaign for total resistance originating in 1974.

KMV's platform was a four page long pacifist-anarchist declaration. It refused both the military, direct and structural violence and enforcement of service to society, but spoke in favour of decentralised nonviolent resistance to violence and oppression.

Under the heading "Common anti-militarist understanding" the platform started:

> We look at ourselves as radical anti-militarists. Our resistance is not only directed against the military, but against any kind of violence. We strive towards the abolishment of all armies – both an army built on conscription and a recruited army. We dismiss conscription and all its consequences, especially the substitute service, the so-called civil service.[638]

The substitute service was described as an integrated part of the military system that can "never be in any fundamental opposition to the military service".[639]

The platform continued with the question of the development of modern weapons technology and linked the military system with patriarchy. It also noticed women's possibility for refusing to cooperate with the military system although they were not drafted. War preparations and militarism influence people's lives long before any service is demanded, and resistance should begin

---

[638] ICR Skandinavia, *Verneplikt: Statlig Tvangsarbeid.*
[639] ICR Skandinavia, *Verneplikt: Statlig Tvangsarbeid.*

"everywhere where there are psychological, political and economic preparations for war. Real peace work must imply a dismantling of society's violent structures".[640]

Under the heading "our goal" the platform described a society based on human rights and people's right to decide on issues related to their own life. It called for economic redistribution and decentralisation of big businesses, and stated that KMV would work towards building alternatives to show that another world is possible. "We see in nonviolent forms of action the only possible means of defence because it also includes the values it wants to defend, like openness, democratic decision making and so on."[641] Later in the text KMV emphasised the principal difference between a substitute service organised by the state and a completely volunteer and self-organised peace service.

The platform finished by noting KMV's international affiliations and the possibility of cooperating with other parts of the peace and environmental movements on issues where one worked in the same direction. It stated that KMV respected the work done by pacifist peace organisations that supported the substitute service, but that KMV saw "total resistance as the ultimate consequence of refusing to cooperate with the military system".[642]

---

[640] ICR Skandinavia, *Verneplikt: Statlig Tvangsarbeid*. A few women's names appear as participants in some of the major meetings and events which took place, almost all of them were partners of some of the men. The impression that the documents give is that the women mainly played supportive roles – making banners, doing the graphic design of posters etc. This division of labour is not unusual in places where only men are conscripted, but it means that the platform's association of militarism with patriarchy and the idea that women should actively refuse militarism although they were not drafted apparently did not result in a different practice within KMV.
[641] ICR Skandinavia, *Verneplikt: Statlig Tvangsarbeid*.
[642] ICR Skandinavia, *Verneplikt: Statlig Tvangsarbeid*.

With a few exceptions, the most active participants in KMV were men who were in the middle of their cases as total resisters or had recently finished them. As Ulf Norenius, one of the Swedish founders of KMV, answered when asked about why he became so involved in KMV: "You know, it creeps very close when you have to go to prison yourself, most people don't have to go to prison."[643]

Several of the founders of KMV had much experience from other anarchist, peace, radical law, solidarity and environmental groups which they were actively involved in parallel with the work in KMV. In Norway there was especially an overlap with Folkereisning Mot Krig (FMK) a pacifist organisation dating from 1937. Two of the Norwegian co-founders of KMV, Jørgen Johansen and Øyvind Solberg, explained how there was fierce discussion within FMK about whether one should accept the substitute service or not. The majority in FMK considered substitute service acceptable, while Johansen, Solberg and a few others did not and decided to form an independent group to work particularly on the issue of supporting total resisters and abolishing all conscription. According to Johansen, FMK's general assembly changed the organisation's position regarding total resistance several times. The total resisters in KMV remained active in FMK and the two groups worked closely together.[644]

KMV was a non-hierarchical group, deliberately organised as a campaign focusing on one particular issue. It was more of a loose network than a formal organisation. The highest authority in KMV was the *grand meeting*. Everyone could participate in these meetings which were held approximately two times a

---

[643] Interview with Ulf Norenius October 25, 2012.
[644] Personal communication October 9 2013.

year.[645] Between the grand meetings, the work was organised by individuals and local groups. During the 1980's the most consistent groups over time were in Oslo, Ise, and Gothenburg. Other local groups popped up and died out depending on where certain individuals lived and how involved they were in the campaign at that particular time.

Who were the total resisters?

In 1981, Norwegian conscientious objectors had to go through a thorough police interrogation and be accepted by the ministry of justice in order to be recognised. The substitute service was longer than for military service, presumably in order to make up for the fact that the conscientious objectors were not called up for repetition exercises like the military conscripts.[646] Neverthe-

---

[645] About half of them were organised in connection with another event. For instance, the first grand meeting after the founding meeting in Halden was held in June 1982 at Seltun gård outside of Bergen in Norway after a four day nonviolence training organised jointly by KMV and FMK. In June 1984 the meeting took place in connection with another meeting organised jointly between KMV and five other organisations. It was the 75 year commemoration at the grave of Rickard Almskoug, a Swedish conscientious objector who died in 1909 in prison in Västervik and was buried in Kalmar. The number of participants in the grand meetings is not always documented, but on one occasion only 9 people participated. (The names of all 9 participants in the grand meeting in Falun November 1-2 1986 are mentioned in the minutes, reproduced in newsletter 18). The grand meeting in August 1985 in Denmark in connection with a European march for nonviolence is described as "well visited" and had 24 participants. This number is listed in the minutes, the term "well visited" is used by the editors of the newsletter who also wrote that the grand meeting was successful in terms of making more contacts in Scandinavia and internationally. KMV, "Rundbrev 13," (Kampanjen Mot Verneplikt, September 1985).
[646] The term "repetition exercises" is a literal translation of the Swedish and Norwegian terminology for what in the US is called "army reserve

less, to the conscientious objectors it felt as if the duration of their service was a punishment for refusing to carry arms. Most conscientious objectors had no trouble explaining their strong pacifist conviction, objecting to participating in all wars and serving the substitute service. During the 1970's and early 1980's the number of applications for conscientious objector status was increasing.[647] The substitute service, which most conscientious objectors willingly accepted, was required to be "civilian in character and under civilian administration, without connection to military installations or activities."[648] The substitute service was mainly carried out within the areas of education, health care and cultural institutions. However, the small but diverse group of total resisters prevented the system from functioning smoothly since they refused both the military and substitute service.

In an article in one of KMV's newsletters, Øyvind Solberg gave a thorough description of nine groups that potentially could be called total resisters.[649] In relation to the way KMV focused its

---

training". In Sweden and Norway it was (and in Norway it still is) the term used for the training all conscripts who have finished basic military training were required to do for the rest of the time they were in the reserve, for most people until they were 45 years old. How long this repetition training was and how often the conscripts had to serve varied. NOU, "Nou 1979: 51 Verneplikt," (Oslo: Universitetsforlaget, 1979), pp. 29-30.

[647] Between 1979 and 1983 the numbers of recognised conscientious objectors per year varied between 1415 and 3034. Each year is not immediately comparable since not everyone received a decision the same year they applied. Justis- og politidepartementet [Department of Justice and Police], "St. Meld. Nr. 70 (1983-84) Om Verneplikt," (April 13 1984), p. 3.

[648] NOU, "Nou 1979: 51 Verneplikt."

[649] KMV, "Rundbrev 16," (Kampanjen Mot Verneplikt, February 1986), pp. 15-16.

work and prioritised its activities in Norway, three groups are of particular interest.

1. *Principled total resisters* who on principle refused all service to the state. Typically they were acknowledged as conscientious objectors because of their commitment to pacifism. When they were called up to serve their substitute service, they refused that as well. Next a court determined that the conditions were fulfilled for them to serve their service by force in an institution under the prison administration. This was regulated in §20 of the Norwegian law on conscientious objection from 1965. Since the time of the alternative service was 16 months, they should serve 16 months as well. They could either serve in a special place for total resisters, called camp Dillingøy, or spend 16 months in prison. Camp Dillingøy was an open institution and primarily established for the members of Jehovah's Witnesses, who agreed to serve there. The principled total resisters who were motivated by political arguments such as anarchism and refused to cooperate with the system in any way were transported to the prison by the police.

    The principled total resisters were not convicted of anything criminal, and the 16 months were not called a punishment. The time served was not entered into their criminal records, but apart from that there were no practical differences between their prison conditions and those of other prisoners. Solberg mentioned that some people refer to this group as the "true" total resisters, and it is principled total resistance which is the philosophy behind KMV's platform.[650]

---

[650] Øyvind Solberg, "Total Objectors," [total objectors] *Samvittighetsfanger i Norge*, not dated 1983; Øyvind Solberg, "Hvem Er Totalnektere," [Who to consider total resisters?] *KMV Rundbrev 16*, February 1986. Some cases are described in S.I.N, "Samvittighetsfanger

2. *Selective objectors*[651] were not pacifists, but applied to become conscientious objectors because they did not want to fight in wars under the present system. Generally they referred to Norway's membership in NATO or the existence of nuclear weapons. Since only pacifists who re- refused to participate in all wars could obtain the status of conscientious objector, the applications of the selective objectors were denied and they received their military call up orders. If they then refused, they were convicted to three months in prison. In a typical situation they would get a new call up order and refuse that as well. Sometimes they would be pardoned the second time, but the practice changed over time. The selective objectors were convicted of evading military orders and their time in prison was considered a regular punishment. In his article, Solberg mentioned that at least some of the selective objectors would also refuse the substitute service if they had had the opportunity. Even if they were not pacifists, they objected to the idea of people being obliged to have a duty to serve.[652]

I Norge - En Kommentar Til Stortingsmelding 70 - Om Verneplikt [Prisoners of Conscience in Norway - a Comment to Proposition 70 - About Conscription]," (1984).

[651] In Norwegian the term used was "situationsbestemte nektere" (Situation dependent objectors), but the term was debated and primarily used by those who objected to an expansion of the possibility to become a conscientious objector.

[652] Bo Nyborg Andersen and Terje Bjørnland, "Situationsbestemt Militærbekting," [Selective conscientious objection] *Samvittighetsfanger i Norge*, not dated 1983; Solberg, "Hvem Er Totalnektere." Some cases are described in S.I.N, "Samvittighetsfanger I Norge - En Kommentar Til Stortingsmelding 70 - Om Verneplikt [Prisoners of Conscience in Norway - a Comment to Proposition 70 - About Conscription]."

3. *Content dependent objectors* who were pacifists but refused the substitute service because it was not relevant and did not train them in a national defence based on nonviolence. By and large these objectors did part of their substitute service and then became total resisters during this process. They were sent to prison for the remaining time of the substitute service under the same conditions as the principled total resisters.[653]

These were the three main groups and their typical situation. However, the situation was frequently unpredictable and also changed during the time KMV was active. Also many other types of total resisters were active for shorter or longer periods of time or their cases were of interest to KMV. Usually the processes went on for many years, and it was not uncommon that people changed their positions during the time. For example, someone who was actually a principled total resister might declare himself a selective objector in order to get less time in prison.

In Sweden the situation was different. Principled total resisters were given a regular court case, charged with refusing to obey orders. During the campaign's existence, the length of the punishment was changed. Within KMV, many of the Swedish participants were so-called *late refusers*[654] who had done their military service but developed their conscientious objection later in life and refused to do the repetition exercises.[655]

KMV as an organisation was committed to principled total resistance, and not everyone who was spending time in jail for

<hr>

[653] Solberg, "Hvem Er Totalnektere." One case is described in S.I.N, "Samvittighetsfanger I Norge - En Kommentar Til Stortingsmelding 70 - Om Verneplikt [Prisoners of Conscience in Norway - a Comment to Proposition 70 - About Conscription]."
[654] The Swedish term is *eftervägrare*.
[655] Interview with Ulf Norenius October 25, 2012.

refusing military service felt comfortable in the group. This was one reason why an even more informal group was established in Norway, called *Samvittighetsfanger I Norge* (S.I.N) which means *Prisoners of Conscience in Norway*.[656] Another reason was that the concept of *prisoners of conscience* had other connotations which were more appropriate under some circumstances, e.g. when it came to cooperating with Amnesty International. Many of the most active activists in KMV were also heavily involved in S.I.N and changed their "hats" depending on the circumstances. S.I.N produced two issues of a newspaper and a report about conscientious objectors in prison as a reply to a government proposition on conscription.

Norway's way of treating the principled total resisters with 16 months in prison without calling it a punishment was unique in Europe. Officially the total resisters simply carried out their substitute service by force in an "institution under the administration of the prison administration". This contradiction – that what appeared as a punishment was called something else – became the core of the total resisters' spectacular protests and legal strategy, revolving around their court hearings and prison time and generating newspaper headlines like "Prison is not punishment."[657] The court hearings were not a real court case, since their only purpose was to establish the identity of the total resisters. They were not charged with anything criminal, but nevertheless, media frequently reported as if this was a serious criminal offence. This indicates that the Norwegian state had a hard time explaining its practice.

---

[656] The unusual way of abbreviating with full stops in between each capital letter was the group's own way of abbreviating its name.
[657] Sarpsborg Arbeiderblad, "16 Måneders Fengsel Er Ikke "Straff", Sier Myndighetene," [16 months in prison is not "punishment", says authorities] *Sarpsborg Arbeiderblad*, April 20 1982.

During the early 1980's the idea of total resistance became known in much wider circles, thanks to the young men's own efforts. Their visibility also made the number of total resisters grow. Between 1965 and 1984, eight people spent time in prison after being sentenced according to §20. At the end of 1984, 25 people had been convicted according to §20 and were waiting to go to prison.[658] In December 1985 this number had increased to more than 40, and KMV was in contact with 96 total resisters, estimating the real number to more than 100.[659]

The department of justice was responsible for all cases regarding conscientious objectors, and I had the opportunity to interview Jens Jensen[660] who represented the Norwegian state and the department of justice in questions regarding conscientious objection. The interview revealed that the representatives of the Norwegian state were unaware how closely the selective objectors and total resisters cooperated and how much the two groups felt they had in common. To the lawyers they appeared to be two very different types of cases because of the difference in legislation, but the people it concerned found a communality of interests because both groups spent time in prison for their convictions.

Jensen explained that he had forgotten about the issue of the total resisters serving their substitute service in prison until I reminded him about it when I contacted him for an interview. On the other hand, he had clear memories about the heated debates regarding the selective objectors. In the eyes of Jensen and his colleagues, the issue of total resisters was a minor one:

---

[658] Notis Øyvind Solberg, KMV, "Rundbrev 9," (Kampanjen Mot Verneplikt, November 1984), p. 4.

[659] KMV, "Rundbrev 16," p. 14.

[660] The informant wishes to remain anonymous, so this is a pseudonym.

> Those who did not want to perform substitute service for principled reasons, they were shrugged off, like okay, if they really want to make it so complicated for themselves, let them do that. (...) It was a small group that we [in the department of justice] didn't care much about.[661]

That the total resisters themselves and the Norwegian authorities had different views on the importance of the issue is no surprise. For most total resisters, refusing to perform substitute service was a decision that changed their lives. For the Norwegian authorities, they were a handful of people making life difficult for themselves and working on an obscure idea about abolishing military defence. Before, during and after KMV's campaign, the institution of conscription remained a cornerstone in Norwegian defence policy. However, although KMV was insignificant in the eyes of Jensen and he did not remember the change in their treatment, for KMV activists it was a major success they still talk about 25 years later.

After this introduction to KMV and the issues of total resistance and selective objection, the next section investigates the different ways KMV aimed to challenge the imprisonment of both groups.

KMV's strategy

As noted in the introduction, KMV's way of working can be divided into four major strategies which were pursued simultaneously: 1. To *create a spectacle* which was sometimes humorous 2. *Using the court system* when it seemed beneficial to KMV by filing charges against the state for violating the human rights of the total resisters. 3. *Solidarity* work with other conscientious objectors around the world and 4. *Lobbying and participating in the public debate*. I identified these four strategies by first making a chrono-

---

[661] Interview with Jens Jensen April 2013, adjusted in email correspondence June 26 2013.

logical list of all KMV activities mentioned in the newsletters. Looking at the outward directed activities and excluding internal meetings and meetings with other peace organisations, these four types of activities appeared to be distinct ways of working which have their own logic and goals. Taken together they contribute to facilitating outreach, mobilisation, a culture of resistance and challenging established relations of power. The first category of creating a spectacle also reflects the finding from chapter 5 that the distinction between humorous and other creative action is artificial and does not reflect activist experiences. Combined the two first strategies of creating a spectacle and using the court system were decisive in changing the legislation within a decade. These two strategies were the main outward directed activities of KMV, with the solidarity and lobbying playing only minor roles.

Creating a spectacle

Already at the founding meeting in Halden in 1981, KMV set the stage for the spectacles to come. Halden is a border town between Sweden and Norway and the town was symbolically chosen. The press was invited to Fredriksten Fortress, a 17th century fortress with a great stake in the past wars between Sweden and Norway.[662] A handful of participants in KMV burned their conscription books or call up orders and two speeches were held. The local newspaper carried a photo of six men setting fire to the military papers on the front page together with an article that quoted from KMV's platform.[663]

---

[662] King Karl XII, one of Sweden's so-called warrior-kings, died here in 1718. It is still under discussion if he was shot by a Norwegian bullet or by one of his own men.
[663] Halden Arbeiderblad, "De Brente Sine Vernepliktsbøker I Halden," [They burned their conscription books in Halden] *Halden Arbeiderblad*, not dated 1981.

415

Illustration 25. Jørgen Johansen's conscription book, burned at Fredriksten Festning, Halden, during the launch of KMV, November 1981.

Norenius explained how this and other burnings were part of a strategy of non-cooperation with the conscription system. When charged with refusing conscription[664] or a repetition exercise in Sweden, a number of people refused all cooperation with the court that was going to punish them. They did not show up in court voluntarily and made it as difficult as possible for the police to serve them the date of the trial. Some people refused to show up in court while most preferred to make the trial a political spectacle. When in prison, the non-cooperation could be to refuse to work or eat. Norenius himself refused to work, something which meant that he was sent to a high security prison.[665] The burnings of military documents as in Halden were part of this non-cooperation:

> [We really saw] the burning of the conscription books as a challenge towards the system, because it says in them that

---

[664] In Swedish the term is *groft lydnadsbrott*.
[665] In Swedish the term is *lukket anstalt*.

it is a document of value that you must take care of, that it is your duty to take care of it. And when we burned that and call up orders, then there is much more pressure in the protest [compared to other protests] (...). Then you challenge the state, take the initiative yourself [kind of say] "come on, press charges against me for this as well [if you dare]".[666]

None of the people I have interviewed had heard about anybody who was charged after burning the military documents, and they think the authorities were uncertain about how to handle the situation.[667] It became what is called a *dilemma action* where the state loses face no matter how it reacts.[668] They could let the young men get away with the burnings, thus giving them the opportunity to show their contempt publicly. Alternatively the authorities could press charges for the burnings, something which would give a group like KMV the chance for further publicity about the issue of conscription that they wanted to highlight. It added to the dilemma that most of these young men were well educated and otherwise relatively well adjusted in society. I will return to the subject of dilemma actions in Chapter 7.

Over the years, Norwegian participants in KMV tried in various ways to draw attention to their §20 court hearings, for example by bringing many supporters or by making the court hearing

---

[666] Interview with Ulf Norenius October 25, 2012. Burning call up orders has a long tradition in the US and was frequently done during the Vietnam War, but as far as Solberg and Johansen can remember they were also inspired by Gandhi's passport burnings in South Africa in the early 1900s to protest the discriminatory passes that all non-whites were required to carry.

[667] Interview with Ulf Norenius October 25, 2012, Jørgen Johansen and Øyvind Solberg January 31st 2013.

[668] Sørensen and Martin, "The Dilemma Action: Analysis of an Activist Technique."

itself into a spectacle. One of the first that is documented is that of Jørgen Johansen, another founder of KMV. Already in 1977 Johansen had been accepted as a conscientious objector and exempted from military service, but he also refused to carry out the substitute service. His §20 hearing was coming up in April 1982. Before this, he produced a poster which was displayed in public places. He invited everyone to come and watch this "drama in several acts arranged by the court and KMV".[669] According to Johansen the judge was very upset by the poster, claiming that it was provocative to call the court the organiser of a piece of theatre.[670] Already before the hearing, Johansen was interviewed by the local newspaper, and given the opportunity to explain several of the complicated details in this type of case – for instance how the state tried to define 16 months in prison as service to society and not a punishment.[671]

Usually these types of §20 cases did not take very long, but Johansen had called many witnesses, and two days were set aside by the court for the case. Johansen also spent a long time explaining his pacifist and anarchist convictions. Many people came to hear the case.[672] Johansen and his lawyer Øyvind Sol-

---

[669] Poster from Jørgen Johansen's personal archive. Apparently Johansen was inspired by a similar poster created by Ulf Norenius some years before.
[670] Personal communication.
[671] Erling Bakken, "Lokal Militærnekter "Annonserer" Egen Rettssak: - Enestående Å Måtte Sone for Overbevisning," [Local conscientious objector "announce" his own case: -Unique to serve time for conscience] Sarpsborg Arbeiderblad, April 6 1982; Sarpsborg Arbeiderblad, "Stor Interesse for Vernepliktsaken: Fullsatt Rettssal Og Mange Viktige Vitner," [Great interest in conscription case: Full court and many important witnesses] Sarpsborg Arbeiderblad, April 14 1982.
[672] The local newspaper reported that both Johansen and the judge carried in extra chairs, but that some people nevertheless had to follow the court proceedings sitting on the floor, a fact which was

berg argued that 16 months in prison cannot be considered anything else than a punishment, no matter what the official label is. They declared that by automatically sending someone to prison for 16 months, the state violated §96 of the Norwegian constitution which prohibits automatic punishment without a fair trial. Johansen and Solberg also remember one of the witnesses in particular. She held the most senior administrative position in the department of justice responsible for the conscientious objectors, and was asked to explain what type of court hearing this actually was. To Johansen and Solberg she appeared uncomfortable when she explained that it was not an ordinary criminal case or a civil case. Neither was it a special court. It was simply a meeting in the court room.[673]

The court did not agree with Solberg and Johansen's arguments, and Johansen's case ended with the court announcing that the conditions were fulfilled for him to serve his substitute service in an institution under the administration of the prison authorities. Nevertheless, the case was a huge success in terms of generating attention, both in the local area[674] and in one of the major national newspapers.[675] Several headlines included the obvious

---

documented by the accompanying photo. Sarpsborg Arbeiderblad, "Fullsatt Sal Da Rettssaken Mot Jørgen Johansen Tok Til I Dag," [The court was full when the case against Jørgen Johansen started today] *Sarpsborg Arbeiderblad*, April 19 1982.

[673] Interview with Jørgen Johansen and Øyvind Solberg January 31st 2013.

[674] The case was covered by the local newspapers in Sarpsborg, Halden and Fredrikstad, see for instance Ketil Strebel Pedersen, "Ise-Mann Må Avtjene Verneplikt I Fengsel?," [Man from Ise must serve conscription in prison?] *Fredrikstad Blad*, April 20 1982.

[675] Aftenposten, "Fengsel for Militærnektere Er Ikke Straff," [Prison for conscientious objectors is not punishment] *Aftenposten*, April 28 1982.

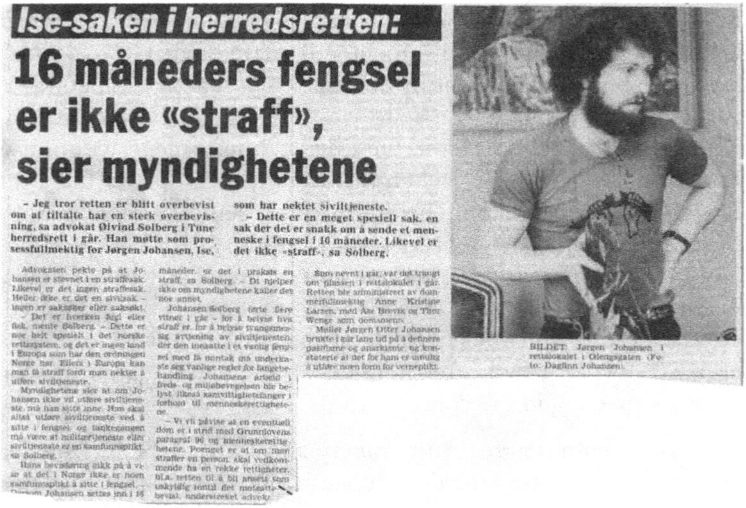

Ise-saken i herredsretten:

16 måneders fengsel er ikke «straff», sier myndighetene

– Jeg tror retten er blitt overbevist om at tiltalte har en sterk overbevisning, sa advokat Øivind Solberg i Tune herredsrett i går. Han møtte som prosessfullmektig for Jørgen Johansen, Ise, som har nektet siviltjeneste.

– Dette er en meget spesiell sak, en sak der det er snakk om å sende et menneske i fengsel i 16 måneder. Likevel er det ikke «straff», sa Solberg.

BILDET: Jørgen Johansen i rettslokalet i Olengsgaten. (Foto: Dagfinn Johansen)

Illustration 26. The local newspaper *Sarpsborg Arbeiderblad's* coverage of Johansen's case. The heading says "16 months in prison is not 'punishment', says authorities" *Sarpsborg Arbeiderblad*, April 20 1982.

contradiction "prison is not punishment",[676] a theme around which the subsequent legal processes revolved.

Johansen's court proceedings themselves had been very sober, and he and his lawyer and witnesses had tried to argue rationally why what was going on with the total resisters was wrong. In the spectacular actions to come this rational approach was replaced with attempts to expose the court as a farce, thus escalating with nonviolent means the tensions around the issue of total resistance.

---

[676] See for example Aftenposten, "Fengsel for Militærnektere Er Ikke Straff."; Sarpsborg Arbeiderblad, "16 Måneders Fengsel Er Ikke "Straff", Sier Myndighetene."

The first type of humorous political stunt that KMV engaged in was a so-called *jail-in*. On midsummer night in June 1983, 12 people managed to climb up on the prison wall of Oslo Kretsfengsel with ladders, and ten of them then jumped into the prison yard. Their demand was that either Johan Råum should be let out of prison, or they should all be locked up together with him. Since he was in prison because of his opinions and they all shared these views, the "visitors" argued that they ought to be imprisoned as well. Råum was a selective objector who had already served his first three months prison sentence, and was now serving the second. The prison authorities were not used to getting extra inmates and one can assume that the action must have been totally unexpected. The activists refused to leave and managed to have a meeting with the person in charge of the prison and Råum himself. They negotiated that a press conference should be held inside the prison before the ten activists were carried out by the police.

KMV called this a *rom-inn*, a literal translation of which would be an *escape-in*. The English term *jail-in*[677] does not really cover the meaning of trying to escape but doing it the wrong way, which is quite funny to those who speak Norwegian. After spending three to four hours at the police station they were all released. The story got considerable attention, for instance it was covered by the tabloid VG.[678] The newspapers reported that the prison authorities were not going to press charges, and that the action would have no legal consequences for the activists. One of the articles also mentioned that there was a nice and friendly atmosphere between the activists and the prison authorities, something

---

[677] Gene Sharp uses the term jail-in about various ways of seeking imprisonment, either to fill the jails, refuse to leave on bail or as in this case, seek imprisonment in solidarity with someone already imprisoned. Sharp, *The Politics of Nonviolent Action*: pp. 418-19.
[678] Erik H. Sønstelie and Bjørn Aslaksen, "Sett Oss I Fengsel," [Put us in prison] *VG*, June 24 1983.

De rømmer feil vei

«Løslat Johan Råum — ingen flere samvittighetsfanger!» Under dette slagordet stormet tolv medlemmer av en gruppe som kaller seg Norske samvittighetsfanger kretsfengslets murer. Fra utsiden. Ved hjelp av en medbragt stige brøt de seg raskt og effektivt inn i fengslet. Løslat Råum eller sett også oss i fengsel, var deres krav til myndighetene.

Det viste seg mye enklere å bryte seg inn i fengslet enn den motsatte veien. (Foto: Arne Ove Berge)

Gunnar Fortun

Det var klokka 11.00 den nøye planlagt aksjonen ble satt i verk. Ti personer hoppet ned i fengselsgården der fangene hadde luftepause. To ble sittende igjen oppe på muren og informerte tilskuerne som samlet seg om det som skjedde.

Tre og en halv time senere ble de alle lempet inn i politibiler og kjørt til politihuset på Grønland. Men før det skjedde hadde de både fått møte Johan Råum og fengselsledelsen. Det ble også tid til en pressekonferanse innenfor fengselsmurene.

Amnesty International

Johan Råum er den eneste nordmannen som står på Amnesty Internationals liste over samvittighetsfanger. Han sitter fengslet for andre gang for å ha nektet militærtjeneste. Han er såkalt situasjonsbetinget militærnekter. Det betyr at under andre forhold kan han tenke seg å avtjene verneplikten. Det han er uenig i er Norges deltakelse i NATO.

Den første dommen han fikk led på 90 dagers fengsel. Denne har han sonet. Dommen han nå soner lyder på 12 måneder, 3 av disse ble gjort ubetinget.

Flere aksjoner

— Dette er ikke siste gang en vi vil aksjonere for å rette søkelyset på samvittighetsfanger, sier representanter for aksjonistene. De har alle i likhet med Råum problemer med rettsvesenets i forhold til sin holdning til militærtjeneste eller siviltjeneste.

— Det er i dag bare to som anser fengslet for slike forhold. Men det er ca 150 som har fått slike dommer og som venter på å sone. Etter at Høyre kom til makta har det skjedd en kraftig skjerping av etterlettningen av dommene. Tidligere ble i ulle fall then andre dommen benådet, sier aksjonistene.

— Aksjonen er en flott støtte for meg og andre som rømmer i samme situasjon. Jeg håper at også jeg en gang får være med på lignende aksjoner til støtte for samvittighetsfanger, sier Johan Råum til Arbeiderbladet.

Ikke anmeldt

Etter tre-fire timer på politihuset ble de alle løslatt. Det vil ikke bli noen strafferaksjon mot de tolv fordi fengslet ikke ønsker å anmelde dem.

I det hele tatt var det en svært gemyttlig tone mellom fengselsledelsen og aksjonistene. Noe som ble poengtert av begge parter.

Politiet var av en eller annen grunn svært opptatt av å holde pressen på avstand. (Foto: Arne Ove Berge)

Illustration 27. *Arbeiderbladet's* coverage of the first jail-in June 24 1983. The heading says "They escape the wrong way".

which both sides pointed out.[679] However, in his own writings Johansen says that they were reported to the police for trespassing, but that the charges were later dropped because of "lack of evidence" as the official terminology goes.[680]

The masterminds behind the action were Knut Solberg and Øyvind Solberg who both had read and been inspired by Gene Sharp's 198 methods of nonviolent actions. After brainstorming about how to do the action, they asked if anybody else wanted to participate. Johansen was one of those who were eager, and the group organised the rope ladders and also practiced using them. Johansen and Solberg remember with great amusement that some of the KMV participants who stayed outside the wall hid the ladders, so when the police arrived they could not figure out how the KMV activists had managed to get up there. The police's own ladders were too short for them to reach the top of the prison wall and bring down those who were sitting there, something which added to the amusement. KMV had several activists who were experienced in working with the media, and

---

[679] Gunnar Fortun, "Rømning - Feil Vei," [Escaping - wrong way] *Arbeiderbladet*, June 24 1983.
[680] Persen and Johansen, *Den Nødvendige Ulydigheten* p.147. Several of the cases in connection with the actions done by the total resisters were "henlagt på grunn av bevisets stilling" as it is called in Norwegian. In Norwegian, a literal translation is not "lack of evidence", just that something is not right about the evidence. When the prosecutor dismisses a case for "lack of evidence", the accused cannot appeal this decision. The alternative decision for the prosecution, which would have been the correct thing to do in this case since there was plenty of evidence in the form of witnesses and written confessions, would have been to decide on a "waiver of prosecution" (påtaleunnlatelse). This is the term when the prosecutor still thinks the accused is guilty but do not expect to be able to win the case. In cases of "waiver of prosecution" the accused can demand to have a trial in order to clear his or her name. KMV would have enjoyed the possibility to appeal such a waiver of prosecution and the attention it would bring.

they had informed journalists whom they trusted that if they turned up at the prison at a certain time, something interesting was going to happen.[681] Officially the action was carried out by S.I.N, but judging from the KMV newsletter's references to the event, KMV felt very much responsible for it. The overlap between KMV and S.I.N is also confirmed by Johansen and Solberg.

A year later, a new jail-in was staged by S.I.N. This time it was for Rune Berg, another selective objector who was serving time.[682] A third jail-in was carried out on May 3 1987 in support of Bjørn Eggen who was on his second hunger strike. Four people jumped into the prison yard of Oslo Kretsfengsel and 8 others occupied the prison wall.[683] Eggen had completed his compulsory military service and four repeat exercises, but then became a principled total resister and was sent to prison for 143 days after his §20 hearing. Already in March 1987 he was taken to prison and went on a hunger strike. After 29 days his deteriorating health forced the prison authorities to bring him to hospi-hospital. Either a misunderstanding or a deliberate deception led Eggen to believe that he would be released and he started to eat again. When it turned out that he would instead be taken back to prison, he escaped from the hospital. During these months in 1987 Eggen's hunger strike, the jail-in and another support

---

[681] Interview with Jørgen Johansen and Øyvind Solberg January 31st 2013.

[682] On this occasion 8 people participated, but only 2 jumped into the prison yard. The newspapers found it especially interesting that one of the people who participated in the action was Johan Råum who had been the inmate who received unexpected visitors the year before. Stig Grimelid, "Ex-Fange Tilbake," [Ex-prisoner back] *VG*, August 28 1984; Esther Nordland, "Inntok Fengselsmurene," [Occupied the prison walls] *Arbeiderbladet*, August 28 1984.

[683] Aftenposten, "Aksjon På Fengselsmurer," [Action at prison walls] *Aftenposten*, May 4 1987.

action where 7 people locked themselves to a pillar outside of the government building in Oslo generated much media attention for the total resisters and KMV.[684] Solberg also remembers that KMV activists at some point organised a 24 hour vigil outside of the prison with torches, and that for several weeks there was a 24 hour presence outside of the government building in order to show support for Eggen.[685]

Hunger strikes were a way for the total resisters to bring attention to their cases once they were in prison, and several others before Eggen had been on hunger strikes and managed to get out using this method.[686]

---

[684] Newspaper coverage reprinted in KMV, "Rundbrev 18," (Kampanjen Mot Verneplikt, 1987); KMV, "Rundbrev 19," (Kampanjen Mot Verneplikt, June 1987). During this period there was another §20 hearing for a person who is not named in the coverage. His hearing ended with 5-6 members of the audience getting arrested when they refused to leave the court room. They had started to argue with the judge and then refused to leave. The incident became front page news in Aftenposten, one of Norway's largest and most influential newspapers. Olav Heltne, "Tiltalte Tok Bilde," [The accused took photo] *Aftenposten*, April 9 1987.

[685] Interview with Jørgen Johansen and Øyvind Solberg January 31st 2013.

[686] Fred Ove Reksten, a well-known musician, was a principled total resister who was sent to prison for 16 months in 1980. After a 20 day hunger strike he was released, but in July 1983 he was brought back to prison without any warning. Immediately he started a hunger and thirst strike, and after a few days he was released again. Annebrit Bertelsen, "Fred Ove Reksten Fri Igjen," [Fred Ove Reksten free again] *Klassekampen*, July 14 1983. The KMV newsletter says that he was called up for prison again in September 1984, but that he then moved to Sweden. KMV, "Rundbrev 8," (Kampanjen Mot Verneplikt, September 1984), p.9. During the second jail-in, Rune Berg had been on hunger strike for 25 days. When he reached the 40th day, his friends arranged an all-night vigil. After around 40 days of hunger strike, most people

KMV's second type of humorous political stunt took place on September 12 1983[687], a few months after the first jail-in in order to gain attention for the case of Øyvind Solberg. He was a lawyer by profession, an attorney for many of the total resisters and also one of the driving forces in KMV. Solberg did three months of his military service in the late 1960's after finishing law school, and says that he actually enjoyed the military training then. Because he had three children he obtained a postponement for the rest of his service, and he claims to have been a quite conservative law student. It was not until 1973-74 that he became radicalised and was drawn into anarchist and radical law circles. Only then did he start thinking seriously about militarism and conscription and realised that it was "completely hopeless" and that "I really can't be part of this".[688] When he was called up for a repetition exercise in the mid 1970's his pacifism had matured and he applied to become a conscientious objector. At that time he did not consider total resistance; that idea only started to form after he met other total resisters in FMK in 1979.

The conscription system moved slowly, and anyone who did not cooperate with the system could drag their cases out for years by ignoring letters and not showing up for the substitute service. Solberg's §20 hearing did not come up until 1983. Then he called his friend Jørgen Johansen and said "I would like you to be in

lose consciousness. KMV's newsletter reported that around 400 people participated in the vigil at some point during the night, with 200 at the same time. KMV, "Rundbrev 9," p.3. In 1985, a newspaper reported that Rune Berg was on hunger strike for 42 days. Berg had been sentenced to 95 days in prison, but since he ended his hunger strike after 42 days, I assume he was released because of the hunger strike. Terje Helsingeng, "Advokat Må I Fengsel," [Lawyer must go to prison] *VG*, September 12 1985.

[687] KMV, "Rettsal 8 Sprenges," (1983).

[688] Interview with Jørgen Johansen and Øyvind Solberg January 31st 2013.

court with me, I need your help". Johansen replied "Sure, I will come with you, but you are a lawyer, so you can defend yourself?" To Johansen's surprise, Solberg replied "No, no, I already have a defence lawyer, I would like to have you as the prosecutor!" At first Johansen thought that would not be possible to organise, but the real prosecutors seldom bothered to show up for the §20 hearings, because the result was not negotiable, always 16 months in prison. This was a fact that annoyed the activists in KMV a lot, and one of the reasons Solberg had the idea for this stunt. Johansen says "we were annoyed that the prosecutor did not show up in these cases, it all went so automatic that they did not *bother* to come". Solberg explains that "at the time, I had the idea that if you are going to do something, what if everything was turned upside down?" He had not heard about anyone who ever tried to do anything similar, but liked Monthy Python's humour and tried to apply a similar approach to political activism. Many people have a privately engaged lawyer, but Solberg is the only Norwegian who has ever had a privately engaged prosecutor.

Johansen borrowed a prosecutor robe and turned up in court, where he was sitting at the prosecutor's place when the judges turned up. There the judge asked "are you new here?", which Johansen could say yes to without lying. Johansen, who had long hair and a big beard, had done his best to tame it with hair pins and look respectable. Solberg had prepared a script for Johansen for the court proceedings, and because Solberg had himself worked as both a judge and a prosecutor after law school he knew which details to include in order to make the performance convincing. In court, nobody noticed that anything was wrong, and the proceedings went on for two hours. The whole event was filmed by KMV, and Johansen did indeed look very serious and convincing during the proceedings. Nevertheless, some of the things he said were rather outrageous. In his parody of the prosecutor, Johansen demanded that since Solberg was a lawyer, he ought to serve almost four times as long in prison as the

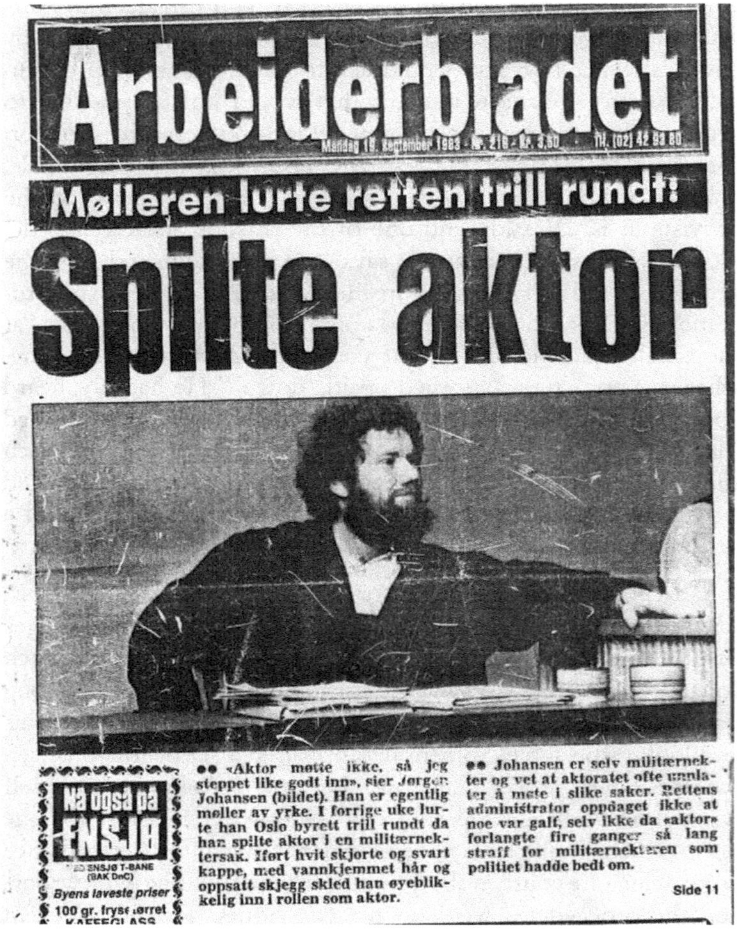

Arbeiderbladet

Mandag 19. September 1983

Mølleren lurte retten trill rundt!

Spilte aktor

Nå også på ENSJØ
ENSJØ T-BANE (BAK DnC)
Byens laveste priser
100 gr. fryse

●● «Aktor møtte ikke, så jeg steppet like godt inn», sier Jørgen Johansen (bildet). Han er egentlig møller av yrke. I forrige uke lurte han Oslo byrett trill rundt da han spilte aktor i en militærnektersak. Iført hvit skjorte og svart kappe, med vannkjemmet hår og oppsatt skjegg skled han øyeblikkelig inn i rollen som aktor.

●● Johansen er selv militærnekter og vet at aktoratet ofte unnlater å møte i slike saker. Rettens administrator oppdaget ikke at noe var galt, selv ikke da «aktor» forlangte fire ganger så lang straff for militærnekteren som politiet hadde bedt om.

Side 11

Illustration 28. *Arbeiderbladet's* front page after the prosecutor case became public. The heading says "Played prosecutor". *Arbeiderbladet*, September 19 1983.

police had initially demanded. Because Solberg had served part of his military service, he was facing 96 days under the administration of the prison authorities. Johansen demanded that he get 376 days.[689] Nevertheless, the judge did not notice anything wrong and it was KMV itself that told the press about the fake prosecutor.

At first, KMV was not sure what to do with the film, and it took almost a week before the story hit the media. But it exploded when part of KMV's film was shown as the major story of the 7pm news, *Dagsrevyen*. In 1983 Norway only had one TV channel called NRK, and "everyone" was watching that particular news broadcast.

The reporter introduced the two and a half minute story with "Last Monday Oslo byrett [Oslo court] was tricked by a fake prosecutor in a case about a conscientious objector."[690] In studio he continued with some of the facts in the case, and then part of the film was shown while Johansen was introduced. The speaker said about him that "he went to extremes and demanded a longer time in prison than what the police had asked for. He played his role so convincingly that the judge did not expose him." The voiceover added that the judge had told Dagsrevyen that the prosecutor did not say much, that there was little juridical argumentation and that was why he did not react. The broadcast then continued with an interview with Solberg in the studio. The interviewer asked the reason for showing up with a fake prosecutor, and Solberg replied: "The whole point was to show that the court system in these cases is a parody of a proper court system." Solberg explained the arrangement with the 16 months in prison and how the court really had no choice about how to rule. The journalist finished off with asking "you are

---

[689] Gunnar Fortun, "Spilte Aktor," [Played prosecutor] *Arbeiderbladet*, September 19 1983.
[690] NRK, "Fake Prosecutor in Dagsrevyen," (NRK, 1983).

yourself a lawyer. Is it not a violation of the court's dignity to do something like this?" Solberg got the last word with his reply "In my opinion it is the court that has violated my dignity when I'm dragged in front of a court which is such a parody."[691]

When the deception was revealed, both Johansen and the judge were interviewed by several of the national Norwegian newspapers. The judge is quoted for saying

> I was shocked when I heard what had happened. All my colleagues have reacted strongly and want Oslo byrett [Oslo court] to take action. I will report the case to the police and the department of justice.[692]

When asked by the journalist whether he had any suspicions, the judge said: "No, usually this is routine cases. 'The prosecutor' gave a plausible explanation for showing up, something the police usually don't do in these cases." The newspaper finished the article paraphrasing the judge: "he [the judge] admits that 'the prosecutor' seemed convincing when he in a trustworthy way argued that Solberg's time in prison should be expanded compared to the police demand."[693]

---

[691] In Norwegian the interviewer asked "Er det ikke at krænke rettens værdighet å gjøre noe slik? " and Solberg replied "Jeg oplever det heller slik at retten krænker min værdighet når jeg blir drat inn for en domstol som er en parodi. "

[692] Tormod Haugstad, "Her Blir Dommeren Lurt Av Falsk Aktor," [Here the judge is fooled by fake prosecutor] *Dagbladet*, September 20 1983.

[693] Haugstad, "Her Blir Dommeren Lurt Av Falsk Aktor." In Norway the prosecutor is a representative from the police. Unlike in many other countries, the police and prosecution are not two different institutions. In a different newspaper, the judge was asked if he really didn't notice that "the prosecutor" was not authentic. The answer is: "No, the case was quite short, and 'the prosecutor' did not say much during the case. At least not anything that caused any suspicion." In the same article,

For KMV, it was all about the possibility to show what a farce the court cases were. Solberg expressed it directly in the interview in NRK – they considered the court a parody of a proper court system and wanted to expose that. In a newspaper article, Solberg and Johansen were also quoted as saying that they hoped a case would be raised against them. Johansen said:

> We hope there will be a case against us, so that we can show what happens to us conscientious objectors. I take responsibility for what I have done and I'm prepared to be punished for it. Most likely I will demand to get the law's harshest punishment.[694]

The point about demanding the harshest punishment was a Gandhi-inspired approach designed to show that he really was prepared to take responsibility for his actions. At first, Johansen and Solberg had their hopes fulfilled. The court filed a report to the police against both of them as well as Solberg's lawyer Wulfberg.[695]

In his report of the event, judge Alfsen described the proceedings differently from what Johansen and Solberg remember. Alfsen thought that Johansen did not say much, and that there was nothing unusual in what he said:

> At the start of the court procedure on September 12 a person dressed in a black lawyer robe appeared and let the recording clerk understand that after the police had been

---

the general secretary of the Norwegian lawyer association was also interviewed. He was quoted for saying that "I think it is arrogant of the prosecution to consider a case straightforward, and therefore fail to appear. The prosecution has itself to blame in this case." Gunnar Fortun, "Rettsvesenet Kan Takke Seg Selv," [The judicial system has itself to blame] *Arbeiderbladet*, September 20 1983.
[694] Fortun, "Rettsvesenet Kan Takke Seg Selv."
[695] Aftenposten, "Falsk Aktor Og Impliserte Politianmeldt," [False prosecutor and implicated reported to the police] *Aftenposten*, September 21 1983.

informed that a defence lawyer would participate (what usually does not happen in this kind of cases), they had decided to participate as well. The person sat down at the prosecutor's usual place. Because of the information the person had given, the recording clerk wrote "public prosecutor Jørgen Johansen" on the piece of paper with the names of those who appear in court at the table of the court (...) Jørgen Johansen de facto performed as the prosecutor in the case. He did not engage in any legal argumentation against the relative substantial pleas made by Solberg and lawyer Wulfsberg, since he "was not prepared for this".[696]

Alfsen wrote that Johansen, Solberg and Wulfberg had violated several paragraphs in the criminal code and courts act[697] for "unauthorised exercise of official authority" or assisting in this, and they had shown contempt for the court. Alfsen's superior used this report to report Johansen, Solberg and Wulfberg to the police the day after the deception was first revealed in newspapers and on national TV.[698]

Solberg came close to losing his right to practice as a lawyer, but got away with a "serious warning" from the department of justice because he assisted Johansen in impersonating the prosecutor.[699] However, even the highest placed civil servant in the

---

[696] Terje Alfsen, "Report," (1983).
[697] In Norwegian names for these laws are "straffeloven" and "domstolloven".
[698] Conrad Clementsen, "Anmeldelse," (1983).
[699] KMV, "Rundbrev 6," (Kampanjen Mot Verneplikt, May 1984), p. 6. Solberg told in the interview with me that several years later while he was in court regarding a different case, he was approached by the judge after the proceedings. The judge remembered the case of the fake prosecutor well and it turned out that he had been working in the department of justice at the time. He had been on the committee that decided what the reaction against Solberg should be. He said it had been very close for Solberg, but according to the now-judge, he had

department of justice, Departementsråd Leif Eldring, could see the comic side of the case according to the well-respected newspaper *Aftenposten*.[700]

The legal proceedings against all three were dismissed for lack of evidence, although both Johansen and Solberg requested that they be tried in court. Both argued that it was in their interest to be tried, Solberg because he had no possibility of appealing the warning he had received[701], and Johansen because of the "harassment" he had been met with in the mass media.[702] However, none of them heard back from the police. The main reason they would have liked to have a trial was of course the possibility of generating more publicity about the total resisters.[703]

In Johansen's and Solberg's opinion, most people that heard about this stunt really liked it and thought it was good fun. They have only heard one person being sceptical about it – a FMK member who thought the deception was not in the spirit of

---

more or less saved Solberg because he had been so amused by the incident. Johansen and Solberg are not sure what happened to Solberg's lawyer Wulfsberg, but think that he received a warning as well.
Interview with Jørgen Johansen and Øyvind Solberg January 31st 2013.
[700] Aftenposten, "Falsk Aktor Og Impliserte Politianmeldt."
[701] Øyvind Solberg, "Sak Nr. 55156/83," (1984).
[702] Jørgen Johansen, "Sak Nr. 55156/83," (1984).
[703] Solberg's §20 hearing was rescheduled for February 29 1984. To avoid a repetition, the court and the real prosecutor locked themselves in for 10 minutes before the court was opened for Solberg and his lawyer. Again there was quite a lot of press coverage, and some of it got the facts wrong. They wrote that Solberg had been the accused in the court in Oslo and convicted to 96 days in prison. Several of them had to print corrections explaining that Solberg had not been accused of anything illegal and was not convicted and sentenced to prison; the court had only ruled that the conditions for him to serve his substitute service in an institution under the prison administration had been met. Newspaper articles not dated, but photocopied in KMV, "Rundbrev 6," p. 8.

Gandhian nonviolence because deceiving the court betrayed the principle of honesty.

Meanwhile, different kinds of spectacular dramas in the courts continued. On November 16 1983, Knut Solberg, another principled total resister (not related with Øyvind Solberg) had his court case in Oslo. He started out with three demands to the judges: 1. The judges had to be willing to make an independent decision in this case. 2. The judges had to promise to follow their conscience, and not just rule according to the laws. 3. The judges also had to promise to take Solberg's conscience into consideration so that they together could make an ethical ruling in the case. The main judge dismissed these demands straight away, which made Knut Solberg state that he considered this response very arrogant, and that he did not have any confidence in the court. He and the audience then proceeded with the court hearing, while the judges and the prosecutor left "for a break". After a while they came back with the police, and declared that everyone in the audience was expelled. Both the audience and Knut Solberg left voluntarily in order to finish their version of the protocol somewhere else, while the hearing inside finished without Solberg being present.[704]

In May 1984, the principled total resister Harald Eraker set fire to his conscription book during his court hearing with these words:

> This is not a real court case. Neither they nor I have any kind of influence on what happens. I will be given 16 months in prison anyway, and for me there is no purpose in

---

[704] Gunnar Fortun, "'Overtok' Hele Rettssaken," ['Took over' the whole court] *Arbeiderbladet*, November 17 1983.

testifying. Therefore I will not cooperate any more in this case.[705]

Five other activists were in the court to support Eraker. They carried a banner saying "stop the court parody. Remove §20". The action was covered by a national Norwegian newspaper and the report included a big photo of the burning of the conscription book, the activists and the banner. Eraker was interviewed at length about his conscientious objection and the newspaper article also included a quote about how he considered the courts a parody:

> This is not a court case. I will be told that I'm going to prison for 16 months, but I could have received that in a letter. Instead they dress this in a legal frame. The only thing the judge has to do is to establish that I'm Harald Eraker and that I refuse substitute service.[706]

The article also showed that the total resisters now had established a reputation and were known to the press. The journalist wrote that the events in court "are the latest in a number of actions in connection with court cases against conscientious objectors".[707]

Numerous other actions were carried out in connection with the §20 court cases. The activities are only mentioned briefly in KMV documents, but show a steady flow of efforts to expose the parodies of the §20 hearings and in other ways bring attention to the total resisters. On October 24, 1986 Dag Olav

---

[705] Kirsten Offerdal, "Brann Vernepliktsboka Si I Rettssalen [Burned His Conscription Book in Court]," *Vårt Land*, May 11 1984.
[706] Offerdal, "Brann Vernepliktsboka Si I Rettssalen [Burned His Conscription Book in Court]."
[707] Offerdal, "Brann Vernepliktsboka Si I Rettssalen [Burned His Conscription Book in Court]."

Majken Jul Sørensen

Sivertsen burned his conscription book in Oslo byrett.[708] Jan Otto Nilsen made a funeral for §20 out of his hearing when he tore the page with the paragraph out of the law book, burned it inside the court and later tried to bury it on the lawn outside of the Norwegian government building. However, the guards came running and he did not manage to actually get §20 in the ground.[709] On November 20 1986 total resister Morten Rønning and the audience showed up for his §20 hearing dressed as clowns under the motto "§20 is a parody". The event is described in the newsletter:

> And parody it became! The clowns came up with so much silliness and antics that the police were called and the clowns expelled. The conclusion was that you don't get more fun than what you make yourself. Wonder who will be the next judge who voluntarily takes a total resister case?[710]

Solberg also remembers a clowning episode, but is not sure if it was the same or another event where Morten Rønning was using a red clown nose. Every time someone said "§20", Rønning would stand up, grab the red nose on his face and move the nose to and from his face while he in a mocking, high pitched voice repeated "§20, §20, §20". Solberg noticed how the two lay judges were struggling to prevent themselves from smiling, while the main judge looked gravely at Solberg and said "do you have anything to do with this, lawyer Solberg?"

---

[708] Arbeiderbladet, "Brant Opp Vernepliktboka," [Burned Conscription Book] *Arbeiderbladet*, October 25 1986.
[709] Interview with Jørgen Johansen and Øyvind Solberg January 31st 2013. The written documentation does not reveal exactly which day this took place, but sometime during the summer or autumn of 1986. The event is mentioned in the minutes of the grand meeting in Falun, November 1-2 1986, printed in KMV, "Rundbrev 18," p. 4.
[710] KMV, "Rundbrev 18," p. 10.

Other occasions than the court hearings were also used to create a spectacle. During a parliamentary hearing about conscription in Norway in 1985 some total resisters came to listen to the debate dressed in prison uniforms. The two or three times resisters were referred to in the debate they stood up.[711]

In 1988 KMV produced a poster with the heading "Wanted". It showed 24 smiling young men and the time they were going to spend in prison for their conscientious objection. The text underneath the photos said:

> Here are 24 of the almost 200 conscientious objectors who are going to prison in Norway. Six of them have been summoned to prison, but have evaded. They are considered dangerous because they are expected to resist with nonviolent means. They are all supporters of nonviolence and freedom of conscience, and work for a nonviolent alternative to the military defence. It is important that they are arrested and sent to prison before such ideas are spread. Possible information about the wanted should be given to the department of justice or to the nearest police authority.[712]

December 1 is recognised as international day for prisoners for peace, and for some years KMV in Norway marked this by

---

[711] The event is described in the minutes of the grand meeting held in Denmark, August 3 1985. The minutes are included in KMV, "Rundbrev 13," p. 3.

[712] The poster is reprinted in KMV, "Rundbrev 27," (Kampanjen Mot Verneplikt, November 1988). With much smaller print it said that KMV had produced the poster and explained: "[The poster] can give the impression that the authorities have begun to search for the conscientious objectors publicly. That is not true: The authorities will rather not say anything publicly about imprisonment of conscientious objectors. It is a bit too difficult to explain why Norway still imprisons conscientious objectors at the same time as it supports freedom of conscience."

Illustration 29. KMV poster from 1988. Under the heading "Wanted" it shows 24 men and the time they were going to spend in prison for their conscientious objection.

inviting people to burn their conscription books in front of the parliament. The event in 1989 was documented in the newsletter. Next to two banners saying "The parliament is arming, we disarm" and "conscription books to be burned here" they kept a fire going. Solberg remembers that they had made sure in advance that someone who still had a conscription book would turn up and burn it. But out of the blue, people they did not know at all just came by, threw their conscription books in the fire and left without a word.[713] One report of the event said that the conscription books with their plastic cover gave a thick, black smoke,[714] while another newspaper reported that 20 people followed the encouragement to burn their conscription books and that the people who did that were all reported to the police.[715] Solberg never heard that anyone was actually prosecuted for burning his conscription book[716], so it might well be another case which was dismissed for "lack of evidence".

To sum up on KMV's spectacular events, they included the humorous political stunts with the fake prosecutor, the jail-ins and the clowning. In addition, conscription book burnings and the funeral procession in court were spectacular and attention grabbing, but not humorous. Looking at the number of events, this strategy appears to have been KMV's preferred choice, something which was also confirmed in the interviews. In the analysis below I investigate what role the humorous political

---

[713] Interview with Jørgen Johansen and Øyvind Solberg January 31st 2013.

[714] The article is reprinted in KMV, "Rundbrev 30," (Kampanjen Mot Verneplikt, February 1990), p.13., but it does not say which newspaper it is.

[715] Gunn Gravdal, "Vernepliktsbøker Brent," [Conscription books burned] *Aftenposten*, December 2 1989.

[716] Interview with Jørgen Johansen and Øyvind Solberg January 31st 2013.

stunts played for KMV's success in changing Norway's law on conscientious objection.

The Norwegian authorities responded to the strategy of creating a spectacle in numerous ways, but the design of the actions meant that it seldom was possible to ignore the total resisters completely. Frequently the police were brought in to arrest the total resisters and/or their supporters and remove them from the court room or the prison walls. At other times the police only became involved after the event when charges were pressed against the total resisters, for instance with regard to the fake prosecutor.

Jensen remembers that in the department of justice he and his colleagues were aware that "[the total resisters] made quite some noise" as he spontaneously called it, and he remembers the case with the fake prosecutor. When asked what he thought about it he said: "Nothing else than that we had a quite relaxed attitude to it. What was problematic were [the selective objectors] who were not exempted from military service."[717]

There is no reason to doubt Jensen regarding the department of justice's position when it came to the spectacular events. Although they were responsible for the conscientious objectors' cases, it was the courts and prison authorities who were first in line when KMV took action. It would have been very interesting to have data about the reactions from both the juridical and lay judges who witnessed all these actions, but unfortunately such an investigation would be very difficult to carry out after so many years. However, even if the department of justice did not have to deal directly with the spectacular actions, the situation was different when it came to KMV's legal strategy of suing the Norwegian state.

---

[717] Interview with Jens Jensen April 2013.

Using the courts

In parallel with the spectacular actions which exposed the court hearings as a farce, KMV attempted to use the court system to expose the state rationally as well. However, contrary to many other organisations that pursue a legal strategy, KMV did not see this as the only possible course of action, and the legal strategy was combined with a successful media strategy.

Norenius from Sweden was the first of the total resisters from KMV to apply to the European Commission of Human Rights at the Council of Europe. He was one of the late refusers who had done his military service. When he was called up in 1963, he decided to do his 10 months with an open mind, but when I interviewed him he said that "if I wasn't an anti-militarist before, I became one". The first time he was called up for his repetition exercise he received a postponement because he was studying, but when it was time for the second repetition he refused to participate. According to the practice of the time he was convicted to one month in prison for this "severe refusal to accept orders".[718] The next time he refused his repetition exercise he was first convicted to two months in prison, but when he appealed the higher court lowered it to one month again. Because he refused to work while in prison he was sent to a high security prison, something he referred to as "the university of life".[719]

After being denied the opportunity to have his case heard by the Supreme Court in Sweden, Norenius complained to the European Commission of Human Rights. His argument was that his total resistance was treated differently than that of the Jehovah's Witnesses because they were automatically exempted from both compulsory military service and substitute service in Sweden.[720]

---

[718] In Swedish the term is *grovt lydnadsbrott*.
[719] Interview with Ulf Norenius October 25, 2012.
[720] This was not the case in Norway where members of Jehovah's Witnesses had to serve 16 month in an institution under the

Illustration 30. The text in this drawing says "pacifist" for the prisoner to the right. Underneath it says "You are imprisoned for murder, and I for refusing to kill". Norenius referred to this cartoon and said "And this was true in Sweden in 1984, I was doing time together with murderers". The origin of the drawing is unknown.[721]

He considered it discrimination when those who were basing their total resistance on religious grounds received a different treatment compared to him and others with political motivations whose total resistance led to fines and a prison sentence.[722] Not surprisingly for Norenius, his case was dismissed by the commis-

---

administration of the prison authorities, something they accepted to do in a special camp called Camp Dillingøy.

[721] The drawing was popular within KMV and included as an illustration in several places, for instance the poster that Johansen made before his court hearing.

[722] An extract of the decision of the commission is reprinted in KMV, "Rundbrev 11," (Kampanjen Mot Verneplikt, April 1985), pp. 5-8.

sion. The explanation for the dismissal was that membership in Jehovah's Witnesses was convincing evidence that someone held strong religious believes preventing him from performing any compulsory service. According to the commission no similar evidence could be found in other cases, and the Swedish state's need for conscripts was reason enough to convict non-religious total resisters to prison.[723]

When I asked how KMV decided which cases to take to court, the driving force seems to have been individual persistence rather than a collective decision about which case would have a chance. Norenius said that "here it is oneself who chooses. It was not the campaign as such [that decided], it was more about someone who wanted to try." However, once someone decided to go ahead it appears to have been self-evident that he would receive the support of the campaign.

While Norenius' case regarding the Swedish conditions was still under consideration, Johansen took his case to the same European Commission of Human Rights at the Council of Europe with a different argumentation and referring to Norwegian conditions. Johansen's original court hearing had happened in April 1982. After that, he appealed to the Supreme Court in Norway, but the case was dismissed in November the same year. Johansen had still not been summoned to camp Dillingøy, but on May 4 1983 applied to the European Commission of Human Rights to consider his case a violation of several articles of the European Convention on Human Rights.[724] In May 1984 the

---

[723] The commission wrote: "It is understandable therefore, if national authorities are restrictive in exempting total resisters from any kind of service, the purpose being to avoid the risk that individuals who simply wish to escape service could do so by pretending to have objections of conscience against compulsory service in general." KMV, "Rundbrev 11," p. 7.
[724] European Commission of Human Rights, "Decision of the Commission as to the Admissibility Application No. 10600/83 by

commission decided to ask the Norwegian state for a written explanation, but only regarding article 5.[725] This article of the Convention about "Right to liberty and security" states in §1 that:

> Everyone has the right to liberty and security of person. No one shall be deprived of his liberty save in the following cases and in accordance with a procedure prescribed by law:
>
> (...)
>
> (b) the lawful arrest or detention of a person for non-compliance with the lawful order of a court or in order to secure the fulfilment of any obligation prescribed by law;[726]

Johansen and his lawyer Øyvind Solberg argued that there must be a limitation to this, and that "the effect of the present Norwegian law is that a certain group of men must be imprisoned for sixteen months".[727]

Johansen's case at the European Commission of Human Rights was first mentioned in a national Norwegian newspaper June 24 1984, when the commission asked the Norwegian state to give a

---

Jørgen Johansen against Norway," in *10600/83* (Strasbourg1985). The "European Convention on Human Rights" is the short version of the name. The full name is "Convention for the Protection of Human Rights and Fundamental Freedoms"

[725] European Commission of Human Rights, "Decision of the Commission as to the Admissibility Application No. 10600/83 by Jørgen Johansen against Norway."

[726] Council of Europe, "European Convention on Human Rights," 1950.

[727] European Commission of Human Rights, "Decision of the Commission as to the Admissibility Application No. 10600/83 by Jørgen Johansen against Norway."

written explanation about its practice.[728] It became a rather big case on March 9, 1985, when it became known that the commission had asked the Norwegian state to appear before the commission in order to explain its practice[729], and the Norwegian state immediately stopped imprisonment of the principled total resisters while the case was pending.[730] Only one other case against the Norwegian state had ever been considered for admission by the commission, so this was an important case that officials took very seriously.[731]

That the case was important for the Norwegian state was confirmed by Jensen. When asked if the case was embarrassing for Norway, he said:

> Not embarrassing, no, not to go there, but of course quite a lot of prestige was at stake when you are dragged to the European Commission of Human Rights. If the commission had found that Norway's praxis was contrary to international law, then of course it would have been problematic. (...) There is no doubt that from the state's side, quite a lot of effort was invested in the case (...) when the case was taken to Strasbourg and [the commission] accepted to take it, it was time to start working.[732]

---

[728] Erling Rimehaug, "Militærnektersak Til Topps," [Conscientious objector case to the top] *Vårt Land*, June 27 1984.

[729] Articles from Aftenposten and VG reprinted in KMV, "Rundbrev 11," p.13-14.

[730] The decision is mentioned on the front page of KMV, "Rundbrev 11." and refers to a letter from the prime minister's secretary of information. The first to benefit from this was Bjørn Bremnes, who had been summoned to the prison on April 9 1985. In Ocober 1986, one and a half years later, Bjørn Bremnes had still not been taken to prison. Alf Bjarne Johnsen, "Fengsel for Totalnekter?," [Prision for total resister?] *VG*, March 16 1985. KMV, "Rundbrev 17," (Kampanjen Mot Verneplikt, October 1986), p. 22.

[731] Johnsen, "Fengsel for Totalnekter?."

[732] Interview with Jens Jensen April 2013.

Although Jensen did not agree that it was embarrassing for the government, he left no doubt that the case was important for the Norwegian state in terms of prestige and the time spent on it.

The actual meeting took place on October 14 1985. Since the Norwegian state was sending five representatives, Johansen and Solberg decided to bring two other lawyers with them. For the local newspaper in the town where Johansen had had his first court hearing in 1982, *Sarpsborg Arbeiderblad*, this was such a major event that it decided to send a journalist to Strasbourg to cover the case. In an interview a few days before the hearing, Solberg showed great optimism about the prospects for the case to succeed. Johansen expressed his ambivalence towards the court system and probably spoke for many in KMV when he said:

> - I cannot escape the feeling that this is more a game about paragraphs than a question of justice, says Jørgen Johansen in a comment. – After all, it is 21 European governments that finance the commission and [they] presumably wish to safeguard the states' interests. Personally I make a clear distinction between law and justice, but hope that this case is such a clear breach of the Convention on Human Rights that it is unavoidable to get a fair judgement. As an anarchist it is fun to get permission to negotiate with the state. That has probably never happened before either for anarchists or for peace movements. At least the state has been forced to the table to talk, says Jørgen Johansen.[733]

However, the optimistic quotes in the newspapers are with all likelihood part of involving media in the spectacle. In the minutes of the KMV grand meeting held on January 1st 1985, it says "Jørgen Johansen has little hope of winning in the European Council which he calls just as corrupt as the Norwegian court

---

[733] Kjell Eriksson, "Regner Med Seier I Strasbourg," [Expect victory in Strasbourg] *Sarpsborg Arbeiderblad*, not dated 1985.

system"[734]. It seems fair to assume that the minutes present a more honest attitude than what Johansen told the journalist.

The newspaper that quoted Johansen's ambivalence about the commission's ability to make a fair judgement also states that: "The Norwegian state also obviously considers the case very serious. The delegation has now been expanded from five to six participants." It continues to list the names of the highly ranked civil servants from the ministry of justice and the ministry of foreign affairs.[735]

The Commission of Human Rights spent 5 hours deliberating the case, but in the end it was considered inadmissible. Solberg was terribly disappointed, although he had not expected to win, he had been fairly certain that at least it would be considered by the commission. The announcement that the case was inadmissible was given straight after the deliberations, but it took some months before the explanation for the decision was released. In this period all that was public was that Johansen's complaint had been dismissed, but no one knew why.[736]

---

[734] The minutes are reprinted in KMV, "Rundbrev 10," (Kampanjen Mot Verneplikt, January 1985).

[735] Eriksson, "Regner Med Seier I Strasbourg."

[736] Two newspapers reported some rumours about the decision: *VG*, a national tabloid, carried an interview with the Norwegian permanent member of the Commission of Human Rights. He said that most cases like this are dismissed much earlier: "This is not an obvious case, therefore it led to a lot of discussions". The newspaper continued that according to its information, "several representatives showed great understanding for the Norwegian conscientious objector." The article is not dated but reprinted in KMV, "Rundbrev 14," (Kampanjen Mot Verneplikt, [Extra] November 1985), p. 6. The reporter from *Sarpsborg Arbeiderblad* wrote that the five hour discussion was exceptionally long, and might indicate that the commission was divided. He continued that the secretariat that prepared the cases for the commission considered

When the decision from the commission was released in December 1985, it became clear that the commission had accepted the arguments of the Norwegian state. The time Johansen would spend in prison could not be considered a punishment since he would be released if he changed his mind and decided to perform the substitute service.

> The commission considers that there is a difference in the character of the detention in the applicant's case as compared with detention after conviction. The applicant may at any time be released, provided that he changes his attitude. This fact may be of little interest to the applicant, but it distinguishes his detention from normal incarceration following a criminal conviction.[737]

Around 8-10 principled total resisters who had had their court hearings were now facing 16 months in prison. In spite of the defeat in Strasbourg, KMV decided to continue pursuing the path of the courts. Already in 1982, KMV had raised a case against the state, claiming that the imprisonment of the principled total resisters was a breach with the Norwegian Constitu-Constitution's article 96 which prohibits punishments without a judgement.[738] This case was dismissed by the court because no individual total resister was named, and the court could not make a judgement just because an organisation thought it was unconstitutional.[739]

---

this "sensational". The article is not dated but reprinted in KMV, "Rundbrev 14," p. 6.

[737] European Commission of Human Rights, "Decision of the Commission as to the Admissibility Application No. 10600/83 by Jørgen Johansen against Norway," p. 23.

[738] Aftenposten, "Vernepliktsnektere Til Sak Mot Staten," [Draft refusers file charges aginst the State] *Aftenposten*, January 9 1982.

[739] Interview with Jørgen Johansen and Øyvind Solberg January 31st 2013.

In May 1986, two of the people who had been summoned to prison decided to pursue this path again and filed charges against the Norwegian state at the court in Oslo. Bjørn Bremnes and Tom Nilsen claimed that the state was violating article 96 of the Constitution. While the case was under consideration, the department of justice decided that no principled total resisters should be imprisoned.[740]

Because of the ruling in Strasbourg, Solberg knew what line of argument the representatives of the Norwegian state were most likely to pursue. He decided to sharpen his argumentation around the issue of the "choice" that the state claimed the total resisters had to change their mind and perform the substitute service. Solberg remembers that he made a comparison with the way the Nazis in Germany had told members of Jehovah's Witnesses that they could just change their faith, and then they would not be required to go to the concentration camps.[741] KMV also called Nils Christie, a famous Norwegian professor of criminology, as one of their witnesses. He testified that although the total resisters were not technically punished according to the Norwegian state, in reality their time in prison resembled that of other prisoners in all respects. And in the Norwegian criminal law, you had to have committed quite serious crimes in order to be sentenced to 16 months imprisonment. Compared to many other places, Norway had (and still has) a rather liberal prison policy.

Oslo court decided on the case January 12-13 1987, and did not find any violation of the constitution. The conclusion was the same as in Strasbourg; the total resisters would be released as soon as they changed their minds.[742] KMV appealed the deci-

---

[740] KMV, "Rundbrev 17," p. 3.
[741] Interview with Jørgen Johansen and Øyvind Solberg January 31st 2013.
[742] KMV, "Rundbrev 18," p. 2.

sion, and it took another two years before the case was heard in January 1989 in Eidsivating Lagmannsrett.[743] The court had seven judges – three of them had a law degree and four of them were lay judges with no judicial background. Six of the seven judges agreed with the earlier ruling, but one of the lay judges dissented, something which according to Solberg was very important.

KMV activists lost in all the cases where they tried to challenge the Swedish and Norwegian states with legal means. That the courts uphold the status quo in cases like this is no surprise. Many social movements that have tried to battle states and big business with legal means discover that the court system is geared towards protecting those with money and power rather than being an institution where "justice prevails".[744]

However, in spite of losing the legal battle, KMV in Norway was still successful in using the cases to generate attention. Below it will become apparent how big a role these cases played in changing the law. Not only did they stall the imprisonment while they were pending, they also drew the civil servants' attention to the problems with the law.

Solidarity

In addition to the two main strategies of creating a spectacle around their cases and using the courts to challenge the state, KMV's activities also reflected other ways of working. One of them was solidarity with conscientious objectors and especially total resisters in other parts of the world as well as within Scan-

---

[743] KMV, "Rundbrev 30," p.14.
[744] See for instance Brian Martin's work on the problems with using official channels, including the courts in Martin, *Justice Ignited: The Dynamics of Backfire*. Another source is Thane Rosenbaum, *The Myth of Moral Justice: Why Our Legal System Fails to Do What's Right*, 1st ed. (New York: HarperCollins, 2004).

dinavia. KMV activists advised other potential total resisters about the consequences of different types of refusal. In some periods this was organised as a service with special phone numbers and people on duty to receive calls[745], at other times it was more sporadic.

Several times it was also suggested to establish a symbolic "refugee camp" in Sweden for Norwegian total resisters. It was discussed during the grand meeting in June 1982, where two different strategies were suggested: a permanent "refugee camp" as a community, or a tent camp during the summer of 1983. Norenius and his partner offered their house as a place for such a community,[746] and their letter also outlined the logic which must have been discussed during the June 1982 meeting. They wrote:

> At the meeting at Seletun, Bergen, last summer we discussed the possibilities for opening a "refugee camp" in Sweden for Norwegian total resisters. Admittedly, total resistance is a crime both in Norway and in Sweden, and there exists an extradition treaty between the two countries. However, the point is that the Norwegian total resisters have not been convicted, and hence ought not to be extradited.[747]

KMV was assuming that the fact that the total resisters in Norway were not convicted in a regular trial, but "just" serving their

---

[745] See for instance the front page of KMV, "Rundbrev 6." And KMV, "Rundbrev 13," p.12.

[746] Letter from Berit Nilsson and Ulf Norenius to participants in KMV, not dated. The letter refers to the meeting in Seltun in June 1982, and was written before the follwing summer. From Jørgen Johansen's personal archive.

[747] Letter from Berit Nilsson and Ulf Norenius to participants in KMV, not dated. The letter refers to the meeting in Seltun in June 1982, and was written before the following summer. From Jørgen Johansen's personal archive.

substitute service in an institution under the administration of the prison authorities, would prevent the authorities from using the regular extradition system between the two countries. Apparently no one took up the offer from Norenius and his partner, as the plans for a permanent refugee camp never went ahead.[748] When interviewed, Norenius reflected on the limitation of letting the Norwegian resisters stay with friends in Sweden on an individual basis.

> It's an idea, but it costs quite a lot in terms of resources. Of course you could let these young Norwegian men come to Sweden and stay with friends and they would also be able to work and so, but then you don't get this refugee camp effect, it does not become a political question. It becomes support of an individual and that is good, but the issue [of conscription] you don't get anywhere with.[749]

Here it becomes apparent that even when it came to solidarity work, KMV was still thinking in terms of using the refugee camp to generate publicity and making a spectacle around the total resisters.

In July 1983 it was announced to have a symbolic tent camp in Krokstrand on the Swedish west coast, close to the border. A Norwegian journalist who visited reported that 16 Norwegian total resisters participated, but in spite of the newspaper's refer-

---

[748] The idea of a permanent place is mentioned again in December 1985 when a group of people had plans about a nonviolence centre in Örebro, and in the minutes from the grand meeting in Falun November 1986 but apparently never carried out. Minutes of the grand meeting in Falun, November 1-2 1986, printed in KMV, "Rundbrev 18," p. 4.
[749] Interview with Ulf Norenius October 25, 2012.

ence to these "sensational plans"[750], the camp did not have any political significance for KMV.

Another type of solidarity work was with conscientious objectors and especially total resisters in other parts of the world. The KMV newsletter frequently had updates about new and ongoing cases and legal developments in countries such as West Germany, Poland, South Africa, Greece, France and Spain. This type of solidarity also went the other way. When Norenius refused to perform his repetition exercise he received several letters of sympathy. During the court procedure the judge read several letters out loud; one came from Argentina and demanded that Norenius be acquitted. The support appeared to have meant much to Norenius: the letter from Argentina was something he mentioned spontaneously when talking about his own case.

On a few occasions, the KMV newsletter reported on actions in sympathy with the Norwegian principled total resisters. In August 1985, in connection with a march for nonviolence in Denmark, some actions were carried out to show sympathy with total resisters. The group considered the conditions for conscientious objectors worst in Spain, France and Norway, and wanted to occupy their embassies in Copenhagen.[751] At the Norwegian embassy, some protesters climbed up with a banner outside, while others found their way to an entryway which they blocked. They were careful to let through people who wanted to apply for a visa or other services, but not the staff.

Norenius who participated at the Norwegian embassy thinks that somewhere between 10 and 15 people took part. He remembers

---

[750] John Johansen, "'Flyktningeleir' I Sverige," ['Refugee camp' in Sweden] *Fredrikstad Blad*, July 8 1983.
[751] The French embassy was so heavily guarded that they never managed to get inside and instead made a human carpet outside to block it. The Spanish embassy was held for an hour before the police attacked and beat up some of the occupiers.

it as a fun and successful nonviolent direct action. "It all went really well, and there was never any expression of hatred or heated atmosphere." To him, it was an example of how nonviolence changed how others perceived the situation. The first sign of the police they saw were two or four policemen in their short sleeved summer uniforms and characteristic police caps. They sat down and chatted with the occupiers while they waited for backup. When the backup arrived they could all hear the sirens from a distance, and out poured the police in full riot gear with helmets, shields and machineguns, lining up in a row. When the person in charge had been briefed about the situation, he gave an order, and all the police went to change into what Norenius called "almost civilian cloth" – the short sleeved shirts and usual caps. Norenius was the designated negotiator, since he knew the Norwegian case quite well. The demand for all three occupations was "Freedom for all conscientious objectors", and at the Norwegian embassy they demanded to talk to the ambassador. In an article about the event that Norenius wrote for a Swedish newspaper, he said that they managed to have a "real political debate" with the employees at the embassy. Altogether the Norwegian embassy was occupied for two hours and twenty minutes before all the occupiers were carried out to a police bus. When they were released from police custody one by one during the evening, the cheers and celebrations outside of the police house increased. As far as Norenius remembers they got a lot of positive media coverage of the event.[752]

Another international solidarity action took place in October the same year. When Johansen's case was up for consideration in Strasbourg, Spanish total resisters held a demonstration outside the Norwegian Embassy in Madrid. The newsletter also reprint-

---

[752] Interview with Ulf Norenius October 25, 2012 and Ulf Norenius, "När Fredsaktivisterna Utvisades," [When the peace activists were expelled] *Arbetaren*, August 23 1985.

ed articles in French and Flemish about the situation for the Norwegian total resisters.[753]

Such solidarity actions were with all likelihood reported home to Oslo by the embassies, but it is difficult to know if they had any impact, since they are not referred to in the department of justice's suggestion to change the law on conscientious objection. However, it helped the Norwegian total resisters feel that they were not alone and not forgotten.

KMV also sought solidarity from Amnesty International, but the relationship was ambivalent. Amnesty International works for respect for human rights and amnesty for political prisoners, and until 1979 it recognised the total resisters as prisoners of conscience.[754] Then the organisation made it clear that it accepted conscription and it was only the selective objectors who declared that they were willing to perform the substitute service but not granted the status of conscientious objector that were considered prisoners of conscience by Amnesty International.

In 1986 selective objector Ulf Alstad was recognised as a prisoner of conscience by Amnesty International when he was serving his second prison sentence. This recognition was reported in *Aftenposten*, one of the major Norwegian newspapers.[755] A group of people from KMV and S.I.N did a solidarity action outside of the department of justice while Alstad was in prison. They climbed into a couple of trees with a banner saying "Amnesty demands: Set Ulf Alstad free". In addition they requested to talk to the minister of justice. That demand was not heard but they were promised that if they climbed down and cleaned up after themselves they could meet with the minister's Secretary of State

---

[753] KMV, "Rundbrev 18," p. 3.
[754] Bjørnar Berg, "Samvittighetsfanger I Norge," [prisoners of conscience in Norway?] *Dagbladet*, November 26 1996.
[755] Aftenposten, "Godtatt Som Samvittighetsfange," [Accepted as prisoner of conscience] *Aftenposten*, February 12 1986.

the next day, something they accepted. However, Amnesty International did not like the way KMV and S.I.N had used its name. In a subsequent meeting with Amnesty's section in Norway, KMV agreed not to use slogans at future events which could be misinterpreted as if Amnesty International was the organiser.[756]

Amnesty International had (and still has) a very high standing in Norwegian society, and when Norway ended up on Amnesty's list of countries that violate human rights because of its treatment of the selective objectors, it became news. For instance, in 1987 it was covered by a national Norwegian newspaper that Lars Aasen, a selective objector, had been adopted as a prisoner of conscience by local Amnesty groups in the Netherlands, Austria and Great Britain.[757] Johansen and Solberg explained that when the selective objectors had been accepted as prisoners of conscience they were "playing in a completely different league", that generated media attention because of Amnesty's status, and then the spectacular actions became superfluous.

This view is also confirmed by Jensen who remembers that the total resisters were not a concern at the department of justice, just something they had to "manage". The selective objectors who were adopted by Amnesty, on the other hand, were a totally different matter:

> What were a little touchy were those who were adopted by Amnesty as prisoners of conscience. That Norway ended up on Amnesty's list of countries that had prisoners of conscience was troublesome in itself. That was a little sen-

---

[756] The action and the meeting with Amnesty International is described in the minutes of the grand meeting in Oslo, March 8 1986, reprinted in KMV, "Rundbrev 17."

[757] NTB, "Norsk Militærnekter Adoptert," [Norwegian conscientious objector adopted] *Arbeiderbladet*, November 25 1987.

sitive, but apart from that group [of selective objectors], everything about the conscientious objectors was something that just had to be managed.[758]

KMV frequently pointed out what they considered Norwegian politicians' double standards – that when Amnesty International criticised other countries that was something good, but when the organisation pointed towards flaws in Norway's way of treating its conscientious objectors it was something different. A short but amusing example of this is when Øyvind Solberg met and talked with the Norwegian King about the subject "Amnesty International and prisoners of conscience in Norway". In an article titled "Meeting with the boss", Solberg wrote:

> The King has several times encouraged people to support Amnesty International. This can seem uncontroversial, also various [Norwegian] governments have given their support to Amnesty's struggle for human rights. The problem is that Amnesty thinks that Norwegian authorities violate human rights by imprisoning conscientious objectors. Does the King support Amnesty's demand to release Norwegian prisoners of conscience? The King did not want to tell. He would rather not talk about the subject at all, except that he thought it would be very few conscientious objectors who were imprisoned. Therefore we talked about something else, like abortion for instance.[759]

However, KMV's relationship with Amnesty International remained ambivalent since Amnesty International did not accept the Norwegian principled total resisters as prisoners of conscience during the 1980's. Over the years KMV lobbied for a change in Amnesty's position and participated in some of their meetings in the hope of getting Amnesty to take a stand against the treatment of the total resisters. They did get support from

---

[758] Interview with Jens Jensen April 2013.
[759] Øyvind Solberg, "Møte Med Sjefen," [Meeting with the Boss.] *Basta* 1(1990).

some people within Amnesty, but nevertheless the lobbying remained unsuccessful.[760]

KMV spent quite some time on solidarity work with conscientious objectors in prison, and also received some support from abroad. There is a considerable overlap between KMV's and S.I.N's solidarity work and the spectacular actions. The jail-ins for instance can be understood as a show of solidarity, although they were primarily constructed to create a spectacle. Had they only been intended as an act of solidarity, KMV would not have called journalists in advance.

Lobbying and participating in the public debate

The documents that KMV produced give an impression of a group showing surprisingly little interest in direct lobbying of decision makers compared to many other campaigns and organisations. KMV did write open letters and met with politicians and representatives from the authorities, but this activity has not left many traces. Compared to the attention given to other types of activities, these meetings mainly appear to be mentioned as side remarks hidden among the more important business of creating a spectacle around the court hearings and imprisonment. For instance, all I have been able to find regarding the meeting with the Secretary of State in 1986 mentioned above in connection with Alstad's case is this:

> During 'the conversation' the next day we did not get many concessions or promises about change, but we presented our view and also got some information about the government's plans and attitudes after the Strasbourg case.[761]

---

[760] Interview with Jørgen Johansen and Øyvind Solberg January 31st 2013.
[761] The meeting with the Secretary of state is mentioned in the minutes of the grand meeting in Oslo, March 8 1986, reprinted in KMV, "Rundbrev 17," p. 8.

One can wonder why the "government's plans and attitudes" did not deserve more attention. I suspect that the reason the KMV newsletters reflect so little interest in lobbying efforts is that the meetings were experienced as insignificant. The minutes of a grand meeting in 1985 describe how KMV representatives met with three different political blocs (the liberal-conservatives, the social democrats and the socialists) before the parliamentary debate about the conscription system in Norway. In the minutes it says that "None of the political parties wanted any change in the law, that was the conclusion of the meetings".[762]

However, attitudes towards lobbying differed from person to person, and especially Solberg was an eager participant in the public debate. He wrote a considerable number of open letters and letters to the editors of numerous newspapers where he argued rationally for KMV's ideas and a better treatment of the total resisters. One of the open letters also reflect KMV's playful attitude. In 1983, KMV together with five other organisations wrote to the King, suggesting a change to the traditional speech on New Year's Eve. Usually the King used the opportunity to send a greeting to the country's armed forces at home and abroad. Reminding the King that not everyone serves their service in the armed forces, they suggested that he send the greeting to "everyone serving conscription, whether it is in the armed forces, in civilian service or in our prisons".[763]

There is not much to sum up regarding KMV's lobbying activities. They were almost non-existent compared to the attempt to create a spectacle and the use of legal procedures against the Norwegian state. Below it will also be apparent that the law was

---

[762] The meetings are referred to in the minutes of the grand meeting held in Denmark, August 3 1985. The minutes are included in KMV, "Rundbrev 13," p. 2.

[763] The suggestion was printed in a Norwegian newspaper (unknown which). The article is reprinted in KMV, "Rundbrev 5," (Kampanjen Mot Verneplikt, February 1984), p. 8.

not changed because of initiatives from the politicians, but because the legal strategy in the courts prompted the civil servants in the department of justice to look for a less controversial treatment of the total resisters.

The legal procedures that changed the law

In June 1990, the parliament changed the legislation that had made it possible to serve the substitute service in an institution under the administration of the prison authorities, and the new law took effect on January 1 1991.[764] At the same time, the criteria for being accepted as a conscientious objector were also slightly revised, making it possible for those who objected because of the existence of weapons of mass destruction to be recognised as conscientious objectors as well, but through a different bill. The activities of KMV and S.I.N described above were decisive in bringing about this change. However, the process of discussing and deciding on official reports and white papers in order to change laws can be long and winding. In this case some of the processes were exceptionally long and exceeded the decade that KMV existed as an active campaign. Tracing the changes is complicated by the fact that the issues of total resistance and selective objection were two very different issues when it came to the laws that regulated them.

In 1974 the Norwegian government decided to appoint a committee whose task was to write a Norwegian Official Report on conscription.[765] The reason the committee was appointed was

---

[764] Lovdata, "Lov 1965-03-19 Nr 03: Lov Om Fritaking for Militærtjeneste Av Overbevisningsgrunner [Militærnekterloven]," http://lovdata.no/all/hl-19650319-003.html.
[765] This is called a *Norsk Offentlig Utredning (NOU)* in Norwegian. For translation of Norwegian terms regarding parliamentary procedures into English I have relied on the parliament's own explanations.

the rise in the number of both conscientious objectors and selective objectors. One of the questions the report was to discuss was the criteria for exemption from military service. The committee did not present its findings until 1979, and in spite of the report's more than 350 pages, the question of total resistance is barely touched. Only the camps where Jehovah's Witnesses agreed to serve their substitute service after their §20 hearings were mentioned. The people who refused this and were sent to serve "under the administration of the prison authorities" were indeed very few before 1979, but it is noticeable that they were not mentioned at all.

This official report meant that the parliamentarians in the justice committee required a white paper[766], which was presented by the department of justice in 1984, 10 years after the first committee was constituted.[767] The white paper discussed the criteria for exemption from military service and how the selective objectors were treated. But this report devoted no attention to the issue of total resistance, in spite of the fact that KMV had made this a public issue by then.

The justice committee in the parliament was dominated by representatives from the Liberal-Christian government coalition parties. Not surprisingly, the committee was divided when it came to the question of expanding the criteria for being exempted from military service. The majority was satisfied with the present order and did not intend to make it possible for more young men to have their reasons for applying for conscientious objector status accepted.[768] After a decade of report writing and

Stortinget, "Parliamentary Procedure," http://stortinget.no/en/In-English/About-the-Storting/Parliamentary-procedure/.
[766] *Stortingsmelding* in Norwegian.
[767] Justis- og politidepartementet [Department of Justice and Police], "St. Meld. Nr. 70 (1983-84) Om Verneplikt."
[768] Justiskomiteen, "Innst. S. Nr. 111. Innstilling Fra Justiskomiteen Om Verneplikt (St. Meld. Nr. 70 for 1983-84)," (February 1 1985).

debate the political constellations had changed so much that changes that appeared obvious in 1974 were no longer acceptable.

However, when the justice committee's suggestion was presented in parliament, it was followed by a heated debate that brought up many issues, especially concerning the selective objectors. Those who wanted a change were repeatedly accused of eroding the idea of conscription and Norway's *defence will*.[769] Nevertheless, the debate in parliament revealed that there was still a strong opposition to the present law and that the Christian party was about to change its position. From the debate it is quite obvious that those politicians in favour of a change were especially concerned about the criticism from Amnesty International. One parliamentarian even considered it "shameful" for Norway.[770] Another parliamentarian mentioned that he expected the protests from young men who were denied the status of conscientious objector to increase in "numbers and intensity".[771] Although the white paper did not discuss the total resisters, their existence was also mentioned in the debate by parliamentarians who wanted to remove the possibility to serve the substitute service in prison.[772] Since this praxis was not mentioned in the document itself, the only explanation for the references to total

---

[769] Forhandlinger, "Forhandlinger I Stortinget Nr. 192. Sak Nr. 3. Innstilling Fra Justiskomiteen Om Verneplikt. (Innst. S. Nr. 111, Jf. St. Meld. Nr. 70 for 1983-84)," (March 12 1985), pp. 2836, 52, 56.

[770] Forhandlinger, "Forhandlinger I Stortinget Nr. 192. Sak Nr. 3. Innstilling Fra Justiskomiteen Om Verneplikt. (Innst. S. Nr. 111, Jf. St. Meld. Nr. 70 for 1983-84)," pp. 2832, 44, 47.

[771] Forhandlinger, "Forhandlinger I Stortinget Nr. 192. Sak Nr. 3. Innstilling Fra Justiskomiteen Om Verneplikt. (Innst. S. Nr. 111, Jf. St. Meld. Nr. 70 for 1983-84)," p. 2853.

[772] Forhandlinger, "Forhandlinger I Stortinget Nr. 192. Sak Nr. 3. Innstilling Fra Justiskomiteen Om Verneplikt. (Innst. S. Nr. 111, Jf. St. Meld. Nr. 70 for 1983-84)," pp. 2838, 41.

resistance are the total resisters' own efforts to place their treatment on the agenda.

When Jensen recalled the events from this time, it was obvious that the question of selective objection were a much more challenging issue for the department of justice than the total resisters. He repeatedly referred to the total resisters as a minor issue that the department had to "manage", and compared the sensitivity of the issue to the selective objectors like this:

> When it came to how infected the question was, the issue of selective objection was an extremely sensitive political question, in comparison to the management of the total resisters (...). [The total resisters] were more or less a footnote in comparison.[773]

The law changes that were passed in 1990 concerned both §1 which regulated who could be considered a conscientious objector and thus mainly affected the selective objectors, and §§19 and 20, which concerned the treatment of the total resisters. Below I will discuss these two processes separately.

Changing §1

Regarding §1, parliamentarians from the socialist party were for several years a driving force for expanding the right to conscientious objection. They wanted many of those who were considered selective objectors and convicted to prison sentences to be recognised as conscientious objectors. According to the representatives of the socialist party, there had for several years been a parliamentarian majority in favour of expanding this right, but the government was on purpose delaying proposals for change.[774]

Already on August 5 1986, Kjellbjørg Lunde as a member of parliament proposed that the parliament should order the gov-

---

[773] Interview with Jens Jensen April 2013
[774] Stortinget, *Spørretime [Question Time]*, 1987-88, November 2 1988.

ernment to suggest a law change that would expand the right to conscientious objection. The committee of justice decided against this[775], and instead parliament on November 19 1986 sent the case to the government for "investigation and pro-nouncement".[776] The government took a long time to investigate this, and on November 2 1988, an upset Kjellbjørg Lunde took the opportunity during question time in parliament to ask about the case. When the minister replied that the working group was about to finish its work, Lunde reminded the parliament that it was two years ago since the case was sent to the government for "investigation", and a year since the minister was supposed to present the findings. "When the minister of justice cannot give a reply a year after the case was supposed to have been presented, I consider it pure delaying tactics."[777]

---

[775] Justiskomiteen, "Innst. S. Nr. 17. Innstilling Fra Justiskomiteen Vedrørende Forslag Fra Stortingsrepresentant Kjellbjørg Lunde Datert 5. August 1986 Om Utvidelse Av Adgangen Til Å Nekte Militærtjeneste På Et Alvorlig Overbevisningsgrunnlag.," (October 30 1986).

[776] Forhandlinger, "Forhandlinger I Stortinget Nr. 53. Sak Nr. 5. Innstilling Fra Justiskomiteen Vedrørende Forslag Fra Stortingsrepresentant Kjellbjørg Lunde Datert 5. August 1986 Om Utvidelse Av Adgangen Til Å Nekte Militærtjeneste På Et Alvorlig Overbevisningsgrunnlag (Innst. S. Nr. 17, Jf. Document Br. 8:1)." (November 19 1986).

[777] *Spørretime [Question Time]*, p.488. Before this the Socialist Party had already had to inquire about the investigation. On March 11 1987, during question time in parliament, when the members of parliament can ask questions to the government, another member of parliament asked the minister of Justice how the case was proceeding. The minister answered that she expected the government to present its conclusion in the second parliament session in 1987. Stortinget, *Spørretime [Question Time]*, 1986-87, March 11 1987, p. 2535.

The debates about a changed legislation revealed that this was a highly sensitive issue that many were concerned about. The discussion was not just about the conscience of the limited number of young men who applied to become conscientious objectors, but about the risk of weakening the military defence. The changes that were finally passed in 1990 made it possible for some of the selective resisters to become conscientious objectors. Those who refused to serve because of Norway's membership in NATO would not experience any changes, but those who referred to the existence of nuclear arms or other weapons of mass destruction could now become conscientious objectors.

Changing §§19 and 20

Total resisters serving their substitute service in an institution under the prison administration were regulated by §§19 and 20. Regarding these changes the process was different, and the parliamentarians much less involved. The initiative to change these paragraphs came from the department of justice, and was first mentioned in a proposition to the parliament that suggested a new bill, *ot. prp. nr 39*, in February 1989. Because of various delays, the proposal was not discussed by the parliament's justice committee until June 1990[778] and finally passed later the same month.[779]

---

[778] Justiskomiteen, "Innst O. Nr. 75. Innstilling Fra Justiskomiteen Om Lov Om Endringer I Lov 19 Mars 1965 Nr 3 Om Fritaking for Militærtjeneste Av Overbevisningsgrunner Og Militær Straffelov 22 Mai 1902 Nr 13," (June 8 1990).
[779] Forhandlinger, "Forhandlinger I Odelstinget Nr. 28. Sak Nr. 7.Innstilling Fra Justiskomiteen Om Lov Om Endringer I Lov Av 19. Mars 1965 Nr 3 Om Fritaking for Militærtjeneste Av Overbevisningsgrunner Og Militær Straffelov Av 22. Mai 1902 Nr 13. (Innst O. Nr. 75, Jf Ot.Prp. Nr 35)," (June 11 1990). There were several reasons for the delay. There was not enough time to consider the proposed changes in the 1988-89 parliamentarian session. An identical

The suggested change regarding §§19 and 20 was one suggestion among several others regarding changes to the law on conscientious objection.[780] In the proposition to the parliament called ot. prp. 35 it appeared as if the debate that KMV had initiated about their treatment being unconstitutional and a violation of their human rights was the main reason why the department suggested these changes. The department referred to this criticism and Johansens's case in Strasbourg, but concluded that since KMV activists lost both in Strasbourg and the case against the Norwegian state, the parliament was not obliged to change the law.[781] The suggested law change was introduced in a peculiar way:

> Even if it must be assumed that the arrangement [with serving substitute service in prison] is not contrary to In-

---

proposal was presented again in September 1989 as ot. prp. nr 10 for the 1989-90 session. Again the paper was not discussed, this time because there was a change in the government (for reasons that had nothing to do with the total resisters). In March 1990 the proposal was included in ot. prp. 35. Justis- og politidepartementet [Department of Justice and Police], "Ot Prp Nr 35 (1989-1990) Om Lov Om Endringer I Lov 19 Mars 1965 Nr 3 Om Fritaking for Militærtjeneste Av Overbevisningsgrunner Og Militær Straffelov 22 Mai 1902 Nr 13," ed. Justis- og politidepartementet [Department of Justice and Police] (March 2 1990). The department of justice described the situation of the total resisters the same way in all these three proposals.

[780] Justis- og politidepartementet [Department of Justice and Police], "Ot Prp Nr 35 (1989-1990) Om Lov Om Endringer I Lov 19 Mars 1965 Nr 3 Om Fritaking for Militærtjeneste Av Overbevisningsgrunner Og Militær Straffelov 22 Mai 1902 Nr 13."

[781] Ot. prp. 35 did not mention that there was a dissenting vote in Eidsivating Lagmansrett when the appeal case was heard, in spite of the fact that dissenting votes are usually considered important when laws are changed.

ternational law or the Constitution, it is a question whether the present arrangement is appropriate.[782]

The word "appropriate"[783] is a bit peculiar because it does not really say anything. Did it mean that the lawyers at the department of justice was aware that they had the law on their side, but themselves found it odd to keep people in prison for 16 months without calling it a punishment? Or did it mean that they were aware that KMV were likely to keep making trouble? Or could it be a reference to the solidarity actions that had been carried out at Norwegian embassies in Denmark and Spain?

Since Jensen did not remember the issue of total resistance and details about the law change any more, he only commented generally about how the lawyers in the department of justice thought at this time:

> This is how it is when you start to approach a grey zone, even if you are not crossing the borderline. If there are other solutions which mean that you stay clear of being near the borderline, then you rather withdraw and find other solutions.

With this general statement Jensen meant that even if the Norwegian authorities had the possibility to continue the "prison without punishment" practice, it was considered near a grey zone since there was so much controversy about it. Because another solution was available, the regular trial that KMV demanded, proposing this change was a withdrawal from the grey zone. One reason Jensen was certain that the case in Strasbourg played an important role for changing §§19 and 20 is the closeness in time.

---

[782] Justis- og politidepartementet [Department of Justice and Police], "Ot Prp Nr 35 (1989-1990) Om Lov Om Endringer I Lov 19 Mars 1965 Nr 3 Om Fritaking for Militærtjeneste Av Overbevisningsgrunner Og Militær Straffelov 22 Mai 1902 Nr 13," p. 5.
[783] The original Norwegian text uses the word *hensiktsmessig*.

Although a couple of years passed, he saw this as the only possible explanation for the change, and law changes always take time.

> It is obvious that [the case in Strasbourg] brought the question on the agenda. So if it was the same type of question, then I think you can say quite clearly that there is a connection, I don't think there is any doubt about that.[784]

The argument used in the report for abolishing the possibility to serve the substitute service in prison reflected what KMV had said for years. It did not seem fair that the selective objectors were convicted to an unconditional prison sentence of two times 3-4 months in a regular trial, while those who served the substitute service spent at least twice as long in prison. The department of justice acknowledged that:

> While it can be adduced that compulsory service [in prison] is not completely comparable with serving a prison sentence, the reality for those concerned is comparatively modest when disregarding the economic circumstances.[785]

From a judicial perspective it is notable that this suggestion from the department of justice was passed without much comment or discussion. The legislative work preceding the conscientious objection law of 1965, *Ot prp 42*, explicitly said that "punishment ought not to be used as a reaction towards conscripts who refuse substitute service on principled reasons."[786] That is, no person refusing substitute service because of his conviction should be

---

[784] Interview with Jens Jensen April 2013.

[785] Justis- og politidepartementet [Department of Justice and Police], "Ot Prp Nr 35 (1989-1990) Om Lov Om Endringer I Lov 19 Mars 1965 Nr 3 Om Fritaking for Militærtjeneste Av Overbevisningsgrunner Og Militær Straffelov 22 Mai 1902 Nr 13," p. 6.

[786] Ot prp 42 quoted in Justis- og politidepartementet [Department of Justice and Police], "Ot Prp Nr 35 (1989-1990) Om Lov Om Endringer I Lov 19 Mars 1965 Nr 3 Om Fritaking for Militærtjeneste Av Overbevisningsgrunner Og Militær Straffelov 22 Mai 1902 Nr 13," p. 4.

punished. In light of the fact that previous lawmakers explicitly had declared that total resistance should not be punished, it was quite drastic to turn it into a crime in 1990. The lack of debate is a clear indication that most people probably had considered the 16 months in prison a punishment in spite of the official terminology. There did not seem to be any reason to discuss the principles when the result of the change was a considerably shorter time in prison.

Jensen explained that the law did not operate in a vacuum, but followed trends and developments in society. So although he agreed that it was a big principle change to go from no punishment to convicting people to time in prison, "legislation adapts to the situations and questions that appear"[787]. I asked Jensen if it was unusual that a law change was suggested by the department of justice, but he said that:

> It was not an exceptional way of doing it. In cases when problems and questions press their way forward without any commissions having written a word about it, it is done this way. So I wouldn't say it was extraordinary. It is when things start to get troublesome for the government and they see that here there might be reason to make a change that they present a report and this is probably what happened here.[788]

A united justice committee supported the suggestion from the department of justice regarding the changes to §§19 and 20 with the remark that the practice of serving substitute service in prison was "unfortunate on principle" and continued "Even if forced service in prison is not imprisonment, the difference in reality is small for the person concerned."[789]

---

[787] Interview with Jens Jensen April 2013.
[788] Interview with Jens Jensen April 2013.
[789] Justiskomiteen, "Innst O. Nr. 75. Innstilling Fra Justiskomiteen Om Lov Om Endringer I Lov 19 Mars 1965 Nr 3 Om Fritaking for

There was only a very short debate in parliament preceding the decision to change the law. However, although no parliamentarians were involved in suggesting the changes, two of them referred to the end of the practice with substitute service in prison as the most important part of the revision.[790]

Analysis: The role of humour within a campaign

From silence to spectacle

Traditionally conscientious objection to military service is considered an individual moral choice that each conscript has to make on his or her own. However, just as laws do not operate in a vacuum but reflect changes in society, so do individuals' conscience develop influenced by inspiration and debate from their surroundings.

The Norwegian state was uncomfortable with the whole issue of imprisonment of conscientious objectors, something which is obvious from the interview with Jensen, the official reports and white papers, and the debates in parliament. For a country like Norway that claimed to be a defender of human rights, it was

---

Militærtjeneste Av Overbevisningsgrunner Og Militær Straffelov 22 Mai 1902 Nr 13," p. 3.

[790] Olav Akselsen from the social democratic party said that "The current arrangement with forced placement in prison after an administrative decision is unfortunate on principle according to the view of [the social democratic party]." Lisbeth Holand from the socialist party added that "I think the most positive is that the arrangement with forced service in prison will be abolished. Forhandlinger, "Forhandlinger I Odelstinget Nr. 28. Sak Nr. 7.Innstilling Fra Justiskomiteen Om Lov Om Endringer I Lov Av 19. Mars 1965 Nr 3 Om Fritaking for Militærtjeneste Av Overbevisningsgrunner Og Militær Straffelov Av 22. Mai 1902 Nr 13. (Innst O. Nr. 75, Jf Ot.Prp. Nr 35)." pp. 405-406

problematic to be accused of violating the rights of the conscientious objectors. That authorities preferred to keep the issue quiet can be illustrated by an anecdote that Norenius told. Although this happened in Sweden it is still an illustration of the preference for silence. Many years after his imprisonment for refusing a repetition exercise Norenius received a new call up order. This time it was not for the regular armed forces, but for what is called *civil defence*, a part of the Swedish *total defence* strategy. Norenius wrote to them that he was going to refuse the exercise and reminded them of a case back in the 1950's where a Swedish woman called Barbro Alving had refused to participate in civil defence. The case was famous since she was a well esteemed writer and journalist known by her pen name Bang and served a one month prison sentence for her refusal.[791] Norenius wrote that "if you really want to, I'm prepared to take this fight, but otherwise you can have your call up order back".[792] After that he has never heard from the military authorities again, and his interpretation is that they prefer to keep it as quiet as possible around the total resisters.

Until the beginning of the 1980's total resistance was almost non-existent in Norway, and to the Norwegian state this was desirable. The state's representatives preferred to deal with the young men on an individual basis and when necessary send them to prison without any publicity. KMV was a very small political group, but managed to move the issue of total resistance from the arena of personal, individual choices to a collective challenge, making "noise" on the way as Jensen called it. In less than a decade total resistance was on the agenda as never before. Their situation was discussed in parliament, debated in major newspa-

---

[791] Majken Jul Sørensen, "Swedish Women's Civil Defence Refusal 1935-1956," in *Women Conscientious Objectors - an Anthology*, ed. Ellen Elster and Majken Jul Sørensen (London: War Resisters' International, 2010).
[792] Interview with Ulf Norenius October 25, 2012.

pers and parliamentarians questioned by journalists about their opinion on the issue. Court hearings were turned into a theatre stage and the Norwegian state had to defend its practice in front of the European Commission of Human Rights, an issue it took so seriously that no total resisters were imprisoned while the case was pending.

Total resistance went from being a possibility that most young men had probably never even considered, to a viable option chosen by more than 100. Although this is a very small number compared to all those who went into military service and the substitute service during the same period, it is still a dramatic increase when the choice involved such far reaching consequences.

Each individual total resister was probably aware that the more their numbers increased, the greater the chance that they together would provide enough pressure to change the legislation. Most of the Norwegian total resisters involved in KMV never went to prison for total resistance, including both Johansen and Solberg. Nevertheless, there were no guarantees, especially not for the first ones. All they knew was that 16 months in prison was a real possibility and that only hunger strikes had made it possible for other conscientious objectors in prison to get out.

Johansen felt that he had no choice: cooperating with the military system by performing the substitute service was never an option for him.[793] Nevertheless, it is reasonable to assume that most people would consider this a difficult choice, and a considerable number most likely had second thoughts. To most potential total resisters, no matter how politically important they considered their refusal to cooperate with the military system, it would have been fairly easy to justify both to themselves and to

---

[793] Personal communication April 5 2013.

others the less dramatic choice of complying with the substitute service.[794]

One challenge with making conscientious objection into a collective issue was that refusing conscription was (and still is) framed as an individual moral choice rather than a social phenomenon. This was reflected by KMV's ambivalent attitude towards the legal system. On one hand, many KMV participants tried to cooperate as little with the courts as possible, seeing them as the extended arm of the military system. On the other hand, the §20 court hearings were one of the best opportunities to generate publicity about the fate of the total resisters. KMV participants frequently used their court hearings for all they were worth, for instance when Johansen impersonated the prosecutor during Solberg's hearing, when Eraker burned his conscription book in court or when Nilsen made a funeral procession and tried to bury §20. In spite of the ambivalence, KMV participants also tried to give the state some of its own medicine when they raised cases against the Swedish and Norwegian states for violating their human rights.

The total resisters did have a very good case in Norway, which made it more likely that they would succeed. No matter what one thinks about conscription, it violates logic to send someone to prison and not call it a punishment. In all other European countries with conscription and the right to conscientious objection, total resistance was considered a crime and the total resisters convicted in an ordinary trial. It was also obvious that

[794] Norenius, for instance, told about a conscientious objector from Greece whom he met at a conference in Denmark, who had just been released after serving an eight year prison sentence and was about to go back for a second term of eight years. Reflecting on how it is an individual choice how far you are ready to take the non-cooperation, Norenius spontaneously commented: "I would probably have attempted to avoid eight years in a Greek prison if I was [him and] in Denmark, but he was going back."

the time - 16 months - was out of proportion both with sentences for ordinary crimes and selective objection in Norway as well
as the punishment for total resistance in Sweden.

The result of the campaign is an indication that the principled
total resisters had a much better case than the selective objectors.
The cases of the principled total resisters and the selective
objectors appeared to have equal weight in the actions that KMV
and S.I.N carried out. Nevertheless, the new law that went into
force in 1991 changed the conditions for the principled total
resisters dramatically, while the circumstances for the selective
objectors changed only slightly. It turned out to be easier to
gather a parliamentary majority for the total resisters than for the
selective objectors. This happened in spite of the fact that both
Amnesty International and the parliamentarians from the socialist party were much more concerned with the selective objectors
than the total resisters. Although it carried some weight in the
debate that Norway was on Amnesty's list of countries violating
human rights, this argument was not heavy enough when the
debate turned to the risk of Norway losing its "defence will".

In the end, the department of justice had no problem convincing
a united parliament that the contradiction "prison is not punishment" was not "appropriate". A reason for the success on the
issue of total resistance was probably also that the resisters now
actually would be punished, something that can be framed as a
more "conservative" line. On the contrary, the change regarding
the selective objectors suggested by the socialist party could only
result in fewer punishments and more conscientious objectors.

Johansen is convinced that when they started the campaign,
most people did not have a clue that total resistance was even a
possibility, and most of the politicians, bureaucrats and judges
did not fully understand what legislation Norway had and what
they contributed to enforce. Johansen thinks that the facts only
started to dawn on the elite after several years of spectacular

actions, lobbying and the hearing in Strasbourg. He considered it "an erroneous law that very few people understood and no one could [actually] defend." Johansen is certain that the Strasbourg case was an eye-opener, and that the civil servants who had participated went home knowing that they had to change the legislation. This view is supported by the fact that the initiative to change the law came from the department of justice itself and by the quotes from Jensen above.

KMV's success in Norway is quite impressive when taking into account the limited resources that were available to the network. As late as March 1985, when the NOU about conscription was discussed in parliament, only a few politicians mentioned the total resisters during the parliamentary debate.[795] When KMV met with them in advance, no one was prepared to propose a law change.[796] Just 4 years later the department of justice proposed a change which was accepted unanimously by parliament.

Most parliamentarians have probably forgotten about KMV long ago – even Jensen who was working on issues of conscientious objection regularly only had vague memories about this group of total resisters. Should they remember, the politicians would probably hesitate to admit that KMV was decisive for their change of mind. Nevertheless, it is difficult to see any other factors than the total resisters' own effort, creativity and persistence. Johansen said "there is no other explanation than our actions"[797], and Jensen was certain that the case in Strasbourg played a decisive role.

---

[795] Forhandlinger, "Forhandlinger I Stortinget Nr. 192. Sak Nr. 3. Innstilling Fra Justiskomiteen Om Verneplikt. (Innst. S. Nr. 111, Jf. St. Meld. Nr. 70 for 1983-84)."
[796] KMV, "Rundbrev 13," p. 2.
[797] Interview with Jørgen Johansen and Øyvind Solberg January 31st 2013.

Looking at the timing of the change it is even possible to assume that two factors were more important than others. Early in 1985 the Strasbourg case had not yet received much attention in Norway; this only happened later that year. It therefore seems reasonable to give that case much credit for the sudden change in attitude. Secondly there are the numbers: At the end of 1984, 25 men had had their §20 hearing and were waiting to go to prison.[798] In December 1985 this number had increased to more than 40, and KMV wrote in its newsletter that the campaign was in contact with 96 total resisters.[799] The department of justice did not know about all these because they had not yet had their §20 hearings, but the 40 existed in the system. It is not clear if the department of justice was aware of the increase. Since Jensen's memories of the whole issue of total resistance were so vague, he did not remember anything about the numbers. The department of justice did not keep a record of the number of total resisters, since they were considered to be serving their substitute service just like the other conscientious objectors. Neither was the increase mentioned in ot. prp. 35. On the other hand it seems unlikely that such a dramatic increase in numbers should go unnoticed and not be part of the reason the department of justice suggested abolishing the arrangement with serving substitute service in prison.

If the court cases against the Norwegian state and the numbers of total resisters played such an important role, did it mean that the spectacular actions had been superfluous, and that Johansen's case in Strasbourg alone could have changed the law? That we will never know, but that seems unlikely too. The two strategies of creating a spectacle and using the courts went hand in hand, and it is reasonable to assume that the numbers grew because of all the attention that the total resisters received for all

---

[798] Notis Øyvind Solberg, KMV, "Rundbrev 9," p. 4.
[799] KMV, "Rundbrev 16," p. 14.

of their actions, spectacular as well as "sober". Further research such as interviews with a number of the total resisters who joined KMV during these years might clarify how they heard about KMV and what convinced them to become total resisters themselves. However, it is just as reliable to draw from findings from the case study with Ofog and my previous research on Otpor. That a creative and spectacular style of protest, including humour, is likely to attract more people became clear when the themes of outreach, mobilisation and a culture of resistance were discussed in Chapter 4 and 5.[800]

The role of the humorous political stunts

The humorous political stunts that KMV activists performed were a vital part of their strategy. The stunts were an unpredictable obstruction of the state's intention of carrying out the court procedures in an orderly fashion, and they were a way to get attention. The stunts were part of the discursive guerrilla war about what is true and just concerning total resistance.

KMV used two types of humorous political stunts which in two distinct ways positioned KMV as a critic of Norwegian authorities' discourse about total resisters. In both of these stunts, it was the dominant discourse of military service as the norm which was under attack as well as the option of accepting the substitute service as a valid alternative. To KMV the substitute service was something the representatives of the dominant discourse had adopted as a way to appear more tolerant and inclusive while still upholding the military service as the norm.

The prosecutor impersonation was a supportive humorous political stunt, and included all the characteristics of this type of stunt described in chapter 3. Instead of a conventional and rational protest, it was framed as a support and encouragement

---

[800] It is also supported by my earlier research. Sørensen, "Humor as a Serious Strategy of Nonviolent Resistance to Oppression."

to the Norwegian authorities' position on total resistance. Johansen made the court into a parody when he appeared overenthusiastic in his role and suggested that Solberg should be sentenced three times as long as the law demanded. It was an invasion of the authorities' own stage, right in front of their eyes. Although it is not an important stage for national politics like the parliament, it was an absolutely crucial stage for legitimising the treatment of the principled total resisters and dressing their imprisonment in a legal frame. It is difficult to imagine a more appropriate scene to invade when the intention was to disrupt the Norwegian state's routines regarding the total resisters.

At this point in time, KMV was not a well-known group. They did not have any celebrities to promote their cases, they were rather few and had very limited resources. In this particular case, Johansen's performance and improvisations skills turned out to be so convincing that the usual actors on the stage did not even realise that their usual performance had been turned into a play of politics. To the larger audience, the Norwegian public, the stunt served to expose the reality of the total resisters' cases. Each person who heard or read about this stunt made his or her individual interpretation of its meaning, but in the newspaper coverage the stunt was presented according to the taste of KMV. They framed it as astonishing that a fake prosecutor could demand an imprisonment so much longer than what the law prescribed without anybody noticing. To the authorities it must have been rather discomforting to have their practice on an issue they preferred to keep out of the public eye exposed this way. According to Johansen and Solberg, the case is unique in the history of Norwegian judicial practice. According to their friends and colleagues, it is still something that lawyers and judges talk about, and a friend of Johansen who is an attorney has called this "the most hilarious thing I have heard in many, many years".[801]

The jail-ins were provocative humorous political stunts. In this type of stunt there is no attempt to disguise behind irony and double meanings that this is a protest as in the other types of humorous political stunts. The humour derived from playful twists to the provocation, in this case by someone unexpectedly making their way into the prison instead of the conventional goal of escaping. Just as in the prosecutor case, KMV invaded a stage which was central for their struggle, the prison walls. Again this was not a major national scene, but just as the court room it was loaded with symbolism. If the usual actors in the court room – the judges, prosecutor and their assistants – were unprepared for a fake prosecutor, the prison authorities were probably even more unaccustomed to citizens clamouring to get in. Afterwards, a dilemma arose for the prison authorities and prosecutor: Charge the intruders with trespassing or pretend that nothing happened? According to Johansen the case was "dismissed for lack of evidence" in spite of a written confession, the same thing which happened in the prosecutor case. KMV interpreted this to mean that the authorities did not want any further publicity about the incident. When it came to the audience of the Norwegian population, again KMV managed to reach them through mass media. Once they had access to the media, the stunt spoke for itself. However, it was a type of stunt which depended on surprise, and could only work this way a limited number of times – after a while, it would not be newsworthy any more.

The central aspect in both the jail-ins and the prosecutor case was how KMV positioned itself in relation to the dominant discourses of crime and punishment. The fake prosecutor did

---

[801] Interview with Jørgen Johansen and Øyvind Solberg January 31st 2013.

not argue against sending Solberg to prison, but instead was very supportive of the legal practice and demanded that the total resister receive a longer sentence. In the jail-ins there was no disguise, but an open provocation when they demanded that either the prisoner of conscience be set free, or they should all be imprisoned with him. In the case of the prosecutor, it was an attempt to expose the absurdity in sending someone to prison without calling it punishment. The jail-in served to expose and ridicule the practice of sending conscientious objectors to prison.

Reflecting on what they did at the time, Johansen said that

> It was not always a clear political message that we sent out, it was about showing them the finger, doing things that were totally unexpected. After a while we wanted to get attention from the media, we were so annoyed with not being heard. [Usually] we only got small letters to the editor in the newspapers, and then we soon realised that spectacular actions made it easier to get through to the media."[802]

Johansen's reference to "show them the finger" indicates that the provocation was important to KMV. He elaborated on the statement that it was not a clear political message by explaining that the actions themselves did not show why they did them. Although they brought banners for the jail-ins, someone who just heard about someone jumping into the prison would not understand the connection to conscientious objection without an explanation.[803] Likewise, a story about a fake prosecutor tells that

---

[802] Interview with Jørgen Johansen and Øyvind Solberg January 31st 2013.

[803] To illustrate this point, Johansen told about someone in his family who knew someone who happened to be doing time in the prison when the first jail-in took place. According to this person, the inmates in the prison had no idea what the drama was all about until they read about it in the newspaper the next day.

the court system can be fooled but the listener needs much more information in order to understand the context of total resistance. Johansen might have a point here, but the scenes that KMV's chose to invade were central in their struggle and what they wanted to change about their situation. In the prosecutor case they snuck in behind the backs of the authorities, in the jail-in they openly captured the prison walls. In both cases the boldness and devil-may-care attitude of it causes admiring smiles and the absurdity invited people to ask themselves, "why would anyone voluntarily climb into the prison? How come that no one notices a fake prosecutor?" In the jail-in case the amusement increased for passers-by who could wonder "what should be the punishment for this provocation – prison as the activists had demanded?"

These humorous political stunts were an integrated part of KMV's strategy, but they were only part of it and their contribution to the success cannot be understood in isolation from the other strategies. The spectacles around the imprisoned conscientious objectors were not just created with humour, but with actions involving non-humorous conscription book burnings, hunger strikes and a funeral for §20. In the previous chapter I indicated how the distinction between humorous actions and other types of creative activism can be seen as artificial and does not reflect the lived experience of many activists. When it comes to KMV this is evident from the fact that the humorous political stunts they performed can best be analysed as part of a strategy that aimed to create a spectacle, humorous as well as non-humorous.

KMV and the courts

KMV had an ambivalent attitude towards the judicial system. On the one hand, the legal system was used to convict the selective objectors to prison and send the total resisters to serve their substitute service "in an institution under the administration of the prison authorities". As anarchists, most of the participants in

KMV had a very negative attitude towards the state and therefore also its legal system. Johansen expressed this explicitly when he doubted that he had a chance with the commission in Strasbourg. On the other hand, KMV activists did what they could to use the legal system to their advantage, by suing the Norwegian state.

Little has been written about how social movements interact with the legal system. Gustafsson and Vinthagen make an international review in their article "Rättens rörelser och rörelsernas rätt"[804] and provide a framework for investigating KMV's interactions with the legal system. Gustafsson and Vinthagen's aim is to move the discussion about social movements' experiences with the law away from dichotomous understandings. In earlier writings about the subject there has been a tendency to see the law either as the extended arm of the state that movements cannot influence (legal pessimism) or an overly optimistic view about the legal system's contribution to social change (legal optimism).[805]

Thomas Mathiesen suggest a third approach in his book "Retten i samfunnet"[806] He calls this a *critical* approach in between the two extremes that "leads to a very careful and thoughtful use of legal strategies".[807] Mathiesen focuses on what lawyers can do to promote the interests of "weak" groups; his critical approach does not include what activists without formal law qualifications

[804] Håkan Gustafsson and Stellan Vinthagen, "Rättens Rörelser Och Rörelsernas Rätt [the Law's Movements and the Movements' Law]," [The law's movements and the movements' law.] *Tidsskrift for Rettsvitenskap* 123, no. 4-5 (2010).
[805] Gustafsson and Vinthagen, "Rättens Rörelser Och Rörelsernas Rätt [the Law's Movements and the Movements' Law]," p. 642.
[806] Thomas Mathiesen, *Retten I Samfunnet: En Innføring I Rettssosiologi*, 6. ed. (Oslo: Pax, 2011).
[807] Mathiesen, *Retten I Samfunnet: En Innføring I Rettssosiologi*: p. 196.

can do. He proposes five different legal strategies, but emphasises that the list is not exhaustive. The most obvious is to *bring concrete cases to court*, but Mathiesen warns about the risk of the whole question the weak party wants to raise becoming *legalised*. By this he means that the judicial process and its rules count more than the issue itself. Probably the biggest problem with legalisation is the risk that if one loses in court, the case is closed in public. There is no doubt that Mathiesen raises an important point, but this was not so relevant for KMV. Even though Johansen, Bremnes and Nilsen lost their cases, KMV was prepared to continue its campaign with different actions. This might be because of most KMV participants' anarchistic worldview. Although Solberg had some expectation that they could win legally, most activists presumably expected the Norwegian state to win. So although it might have looked as if the case was now closed, KMV all the time had new plans, and the department of justice started to work for a law change in spite of the legal victories.

Most people in KMV viewed Johansen, Bremnes and Nilsen's cases in a way that resembles Mathiesen's next legal strategy, that lawyers *use the court as an arena*. The court becomes a political platform without letting the judicial form and the prospects of winning or losing dominate. Mathiesen refers to Jaques Vergés' notion *breaking process*[808] where the parties do not have the same values and do not agree on the rules. When it comes to KMV, many of the §20 hearings were such a use of arena/breaking process where the court was used as a platform to express disapproval and lack of respect for the court, for instance by burning the conscription book and symbolically bury §20.

Mathiesen's last three legal strategies concern lawyers working systematically with cases, work in movements or the practice of jurisprudential work. That Solberg was a lawyer by profession

[808] Mathiesen, *Retten I Samfunnet: En Innføring I Rettssosiologi*: p. 209.

gave the campaign an opportunity to navigate the judicial system without making some of the obvious blunders that organisations without such knowledge might have made. It is probably also a contributing aspect to the fact that KMV never let the issue of total resistance become legalised in spite of the amount of time spent on legal cases.

Similarity to Mathiesen, Gustafsson and Vinthagen also present a model between the legal optimistic and legal pessimistic. But where Mathiesen is concerned with the role of lawyers in the legal strategies, Gustafsson and Vinthagen are interested in the relation between the law and social movements in a broader sense that also includes how organisations and citizens can use the law to their advantage. They suggest five strategies that social movements have at their disposal in their attempts to influence the law. 1. Social movements can "compensate for implementation of existing laws". 2. They can try to reform the law on the system's terms. 3. They can "challenge existing law" by breaking the law. Even more far reaching is 4. To create new law and 5. To "undermine existing law by resisting and subverting the power-relations that uphold the law".[809]

The case study of KMV shows how the group used two or three out of these five categories in its work in Norway. The number depends on how one understands Gustafsson and Vinthagen's fifth category of undermining the law.

First of all KMV tried to use the method of *reforming* the law through its lobbying activities, vigils outside of the prison and the hunger strikes. These are methods mentioned by Gusafsson and Vinthagen.[810] The two authors do not consider the possibil-

---

[809] Gustafsson and Vinthagen, "Rättens Rörelser Och Rörelsernas Rätt [the Law's Movements and the Movements' Law]," p. 684.
[810] Gustafsson and Vinthagen, "Rättens Rörelser Och Rörelsernas Rätt [the Law's Movements and the Movements' Law]," p. 686.

ity of using the court procedures themselves to reform the law, but both Johansen's complaint to Strasbourg as well as Bremnes' and Nilsen's case against the Norwegian state are examples of trying to reform the law by using the existing system to the extent possible. Even if KMV in these cases followed the rules of the established system, one can also understand their activities around the reform work as a method for gaining media attention, something they considered necessary in order to create change. This way the experiences from KMV show how reform work in court and the struggle for media attention can complement each other. It is interesting that even if KMV lost according to the system in all court levels, the law change that they finally won was also on the system's terms.

Secondly, KMV *challenged* the law during the court cases and imprisonment of the selective objectors and the total resisters. The humorous political stunts with the jail-ins as well as other spectacular actions with burning conscription books, burying §20 and playing a clown in court all violated existing laws and norms. Gustafsson and Vinthagen point towards this strategy's potential to bring attention from mass media[811], something which also happened after many of these challenges, in particular the first jail-in.

It is not so easy to place KMV's action with the fake prosecutor in Gustafsson and Vinthagen's typology. It is possible to interpret the fake prosecutor as another example of challenging the law, but the action can also be understood as an example of *undermining* the law. Gustafsson and Vinthagen mention strikes, boycotts and sabotage as examples of this legal strategy[812], and at first glance a single fake prosecutor does not have the potential

---

[811] Gustafsson and Vinthagen, "Rättens Rörelser Och Rörelsernas Rätt [the Law's Movements and the Movements' Law]," p. 686.
[812] Gustafsson and Vinthagen, "Rättens Rörelser Och Rörelsernas Rätt [the Law's Movements and the Movements' Law]," p. 688.

to exert the force that they describe in this category. On the other hand, they characterise the category as "One attempt to practically prevent and at the same time convince others that the legal activity must stop for political/ethical reasons".[813] Gustaffson and Vinthagen do not provide examples of this unusual method where the undermining of the law actually takes place within the court room itself. Nevertheless it is perfectly possible to interpret the fake prosecutor as a direct undermining of the law within the court room. Because of this parody of a prosecutor Solberg could not be considered to fulfil the conditions in §20 after the deliberations this day: the case had to be heard again later with a real prosecutor present. The presence of the fake prosecutor thoroughly sabotaged the court hearing, although only temporarily. The stunt was a concrete prevention of the smooth functioning of the law and intended to convince others that the law should be changed, just like Gustaffson and Vinthagen characterise undermining in their typology.

To sum up the relationship between KMV and the courts, the group was successful in bringing about a law change, but it was not the court cases against the state that directly led to this. Rather the legal strategy worked indirectly through the attention the issue of total resistance generated.

The role of other factors

KMVs ability to reach mainstream media both with its spectacular actions and the legal strategy is with all likelihood part of the reason for its success in changing §§19 and 20. Without this attention there would probably not have been such a dramatic increase in the number of total resisters, and there would not have been any "noise" to make the department of justice reflect on the existence of the total resisters. Over the years, KMV

---

[813] Gustafsson and Vinthagen, "Rättens Rörelser Och Rörelsernas Rätt [the Law's Movements and the Movements' Law]," p. 688.

activists and supporters created several front page stories, numerous news reports in print media, a steady stream of letters to the editors and the fake prosecutor even hit the 7pm TV news. However, it is important to notice that the coverage of the jail-in and fake prosecutor stunts were not as extensive as Johansen imagined. A systematic search of a large number of Norwegian newspapers revealed that the cases were indeed reported in some newspapers, but it was far from the "all" that Johansen implied in the interview.[814]

From the data here, it is not possible to say much about the effects of the two strategies of solidarity and lobbying. They seem to have played a minor role for KMV when it came to time

---

[814] I am basing this judgement on a wide search for KMV in seven selected mainstream regional and national newspapers for the period 1980-1989 (*Aftenposten, Adresseavisen, Hamar Arbeiderblad, Klassekampen, Morgenbladet, Nationen, Nordlys* and *Stavanger Aftenblad*). These newspapers can be searched electronically at the National Library in Oslo. For these wide searches I used the search words "Kampanjen mot verneplikt", "siviltjeneste i fengsel" (substitute service in prison) and "nektet siviltjeneste" (refused substitute service). In the same newspapers I also searched specifically for the first jail-in and the fake prosecutor case, narrowing the search period to June 24-27 1983 and September 20-21 1983, but with the broad search words "fengsel" (prison) and "aktor" (prosecutor). For *Nordlys* and *Stavanger Aftenblad* I did a manual search for the same dates using the microfilms as well. I also searched manually through the microfilms of six other national and regional newspapers (*Arbeiderbladet, Dagbladet, VG, Finmarksposten, Fædrelandsvennen, Bergens Tidende*) for the same time periods. Although many KMV actions were covered and some of them extensively by some newspapers, it was far from all newspapers that reported about the first jail-in and the fake prosecutor. For instance, the searches did not reveal any coverage at all in *Adresseavisen, Hamar Arbeiderblad, Morgenbladet, Finmarksposten, Fædrelandsvennen, Bergens Tidende* and *Nationen. Nordlys, Stavanger Aftenblad* and *Klassekampen* only had short reports.

and effort, and they do not seem to have had any impact on changing the law. However, it would have been extremely unusual to have a political campaign that did not try to explain its goals through lobbying and participating in the public debate.

Even if the solidarity did not have a direct effect on the outcome, it can have contributed to sustaining a culture of resistance in KMV. The emphasis that Norenius put on the support letter he received from Argentina is an indication of this. The importance of solidarity work would be an interesting topic for further research, but since many activists spent time on solidarity activities, it seems appropriate to draw attention to the fact that solidarity work did not seem to have much relevance in this case. Even the occupation of the embassy in Denmark that Norenius described as a successful nonviolent action in terms of dialogue with the employees at the embassy and maintaining nonviolent discipline did not leave any traces in the legislative work for the law change. That does not mean that it was not noticed, but at least it did not make its way into the official documents.

Had the idea with a permanent refugee camp at the Swedish side of the border been carried out, it would probably have been its spectacularity that could have contributed to success rather than the solidarity it was a sign of.

Another important factor for KMV's success was the smooth functioning of the network. The men who were most active got along well both as activists and as friends, and managed to create a very supportive an open atmosphere that encouraged creative actions. Johansen was proud that

> Everyone who did something, they got a pat on the shoulder, *yes!* [Someone would say] 'I saw you did this, I saw you wrote that article or organised that meeting.' We supported each other, it was a very positive atmosphere, there

wasn't any trouble or fighting within the group, it was [like a] *party!*, (…) a constant party."[815]

Solberg agreed with this positive description, and added that "and if anybody disagreed about something, that was okay." Johansen continued: "I can't remember any political disagreements within KMV, like there were in other groups I have been part of. (…) It was just supportive reactions."[816]

Although KMV fizzled out in the early 1990's without reaching the goal of abolishing conscription, it was probably the success regarding §20 that was the main reason. Had the Norwegian authorities continued to send total resisters to prison to serve their substitute service, the resistance would have continued. KMV was prepared to go further and try new ways. The group even warned the department of justice that more was to come during a meeting on April 21, 1986.[817]

---

[815] Interview with Jørgen Johansen and Øyvind Solberg January 31st 2013.

[816] Interview with Jørgen Johansen and Øyvind Solberg January 31st 2013.

[817] KMV, "Rundbrev 17," p.14. One of these new ways was outlined by Solberg in a letter to Johansen. Although it was never turned into reality, this new strategy which Solberg labelled a "dilemma action" shows that KMV was certainly not running out of ideas: "If we look at those who have previously been in prison for forced service [of their substitute service], no one has ever asked to be released [because he changed his opinion regarding serving the substitute service]. The difference is that they all the time had the *possibility*. But what if one uses the possibility and is released [?] Since no one has tried this, there is no established procedure. One can imagine two possibilities: Either the person will be summoned to Dillingøy in order to be given a new place of service. Or the person will immediately be transported to Dillingøy upon the release. In the last case, the person can walk out straight away, since it is an open camp. In the first case, the person can just not show up. The only reaction to this is a new summon and maybe transport to prison. Then the same can be repeated. For this, it

The decision to change the law in Norway was made in June 1990. This timing with the fall of the Berlin wall in 1989 and the end of the cold war raises the question of whether this structural factor might have played a role. Although it is a relevant question, there is nothing in the data to support this connection and it appears to be a coincidence. The changes to both §§1, 19 and 20 had been on the way for years. The department of justice argued in favour of a changes to §§19 and 20 already in February 1989, at a time when Norwegian authorities had no reason to believe the Berlin wall was about to fall. The wording of the

---

is again possible to imagine two possibilities. The authorities will let the person walk out of prison as often as he wants to. One day in prison, and then a few days or months in liberty before a new transport to the prison. The disadvantage with this it that it will take many years to serve all the 16 months. Another disadvantage is the situation of the prison. People who come and go will lead to unrest and administrative problems. The most likely is therefore that the authorities after a while will say stop and refuse to release the person even if he declares that he is willing to perform "normal" substitute service. The disadvantage with this is that the authorities lose their main argument of claiming that substitute service in prison is not punishment. Assuming that this argument is decisive for the assessment of punishment versus not punishment another disadvantage arises: The inmate can by his own way of acting decide if the detention is punishment or not!" The quote is from a letter from Solberg to Johansen. The letter is not dated, but it refers to the fact that Bjørn Bremnes has been summoned to prison on May 5, and that Øyvind will sue the state on Bremnes' behalf, so it must have been written around March or April 1986. The letter is in Johansen's personal archive. No KMV activist ever had to try this strategy in practice, but it is obvious what a dilemma it would have created for the Norwegian authorities. It is also documentation that KMV was not running out of creative ideas about how to challenge the Norwegian authorities.

revised bill did not change during the almost 1½ years that passed before the decision to change the law was made.[818]

Dissolving KMV

The victory of the revised law in Norway meant that the air went out of KMV and it gradually dissolved. It appears that some of the most energetic individuals had already started to spend their time on other political questions and movements before the law was passed without new people taking over. Norenius thinks that an important reason was that many of the most active people became fathers during these years, and it was demanding to have young children and continue this type of political activism. Thus, what in social movement literature is called their *biographical availability* diminished.[819] When the Norwegian state again started to imprison total resisters as a punishment after a regular trial, the most active people had moved on to other issues without being replaced. Another reason Norenius identified was the general tendency of people leaving one movement or organisation for other challenges. Solberg said that "it just fizzled out", and Johansen commented that "no one was sent to prison, there was nothing to make a fuss about, few court hearings, pause in the imprisonments."

KMV continued to have some activity during the early 1990's and a magazine called Basta was produced at irregular intervals between 1990 and 1994. According to Solberg, one of the important campaigns during these years was to encourage people to opt out of the conscription system, but it never really took off. When the first of the total resisters convicted according to the

---

[818] Justis- og politidepartementet [Department of Justice and Police], "Ot Prp Nr 35 (1989-1990) Om Lov Om Endringer I Lov 19 Mars 1965 Nr 3 Om Fritaking for Militærtjeneste Av Overbevisningsgrunner Og Militær Straffelov 22 Mai 1902 Nr 13."
[819] Corrigall-Brown, *Patterns of Protest: Trajectories of Participation in Social Movements*: pp. 20-23.

new legislation went to prison in 1994 there was some more activity and new newsletters before it fizzled out again.[820] A web page called KMV still exists but was last updated in 1998.[821]

The impact of KMV

Ajangiz has argued that in order to understand the changes in the length of military service and the abolition of conscription in many European countries during the 1990s the role of social forces, including the number of conscientious objectors cannot be ignored.[822] He considers Spain the most obvious example where a strong movement of total resisters compelled the decision to abolish conscription in 1996 with effect from 2001. Compared to KMV, the Spanish movement was very strong. Between 1988 and 1999 more than 20,000 people in the state of Spain spent time in prison in the struggle against conscription.

Apart from the situation in Spain and a Swedish investigation[823] there does not exist any literature in English or the Scandinavian languages about total resistance and its influence on politics and law.

Although KMV failed in its attempt to abolish conscription altogether, the changes to §§19 and 20, which meant that the arrangement with substitute service in prison was abolished, was a major victory for the group. Their decade long struggle had

---

[820] KMV, "Utopi Eller Apati: Rundbrev for Kampanjen Mot Verneplikt " (Nr. 1 Vinter 1994), p. 2.

[821] KMV, http://www.arbeidskollektivet.no/kmv/.

[822] Rafael Ajangiz, "The European Farewell to Conscription?," in *The Comparative Study of Conscription in the Armed Forces*, ed. Lars Mjøset and Stephen van Holde, *Comparative Social Research* (Emerald Group Publishing, 2002).

[823] Janne Flyghed, "Konsten Att Disciplinera En Opposition," [The art of disciplining an opposition.] *Retfærd, Nordisk Juridisk Tidskrift* 12, no. 2 (1989).

also had practical consequences for the men who had declared total resistance. While the legal cases in Strasbourg and against the Norwegian state were pending, no total resisters were taken to prison. Solberg is proud that up to a hundred people who had had their §20 hearings in reality got an amnesty. Although such an amnesty was never officially declared, they just fell through the cracks in the system.

Johansen and Solberg also think that KMV had other effects that had not been goals of theirs, but nevertheless the result. During the years that KMV was active, it became easier to become a conscientious objector based on a pacifist conviction. Although there was no change in the law, they noticed that in practice it became easier to be accepted in the police interrogation. So although KMV did not work on the rights of the conscientious objectors performing substitute service (they had their own organisation), Johansen and Solberg believe that KMV influenced their situation. In Norway there does not exist any study to document this claim, but the tendency to adjust the treatment of all the conscientious objectors based on the number of total resisters has been clearly documented in Sweden.[824] It is a divide and rule tactic the state can use to separate the moderate antimilitarists (who accept the substitute service) from the more radical total resisters.

According to Johansen and Solberg, KMV was also part of a process of radicalisation of the whole peace movement that happened in the 1980's in both Sweden and Norway. A relatively small number of people, including Johansen, Norenius and Solberg, were driving forces in this process. Creative and confronting ideas were being reinforced by an encouraging and supportive activist environment. For instance, FMK's magazine *Ikkevold* exposed secret NATO bases in Norway in 1983. In addition to being secret, the bases were also prepared to receive

---

[824] Flyghed, "Konsten Att Disciplinera En Opposition."

nuclear weapons in spite of Norway's official position of refusing nuclear arms on its territory in peace time. The editorial
committee of *Ikkevold* was accused of espionage and the case
went all the way to the Supreme Court before the members of
the committee were found not guilty. In Sweden a train that
carried Haubits cannons to be exported to India was stopped in
1987 in a civil disobedience action and the whole Swedish arms
export industry scrutinised. The military air facility in Rygge in
Norway was temporarily closed down in 1983-84 in some of
Norway's biggest civil disobedience actions opposing military
activity. It would be an interesting area for further investigation
to see if Johansen and Solberg are right in believing that KMV
was important for this radicalization process.

Conclusion

The purpose of this case study has been to show how KMV's
use of humour worked as part of a strategy within a larger campaign, and to the extent possible establish which effect the
humour had compared to other factors.

Through the actions that were carried out and those that only
remained ideas KMV demonstrated much creativity as well as a
good understanding of what aspects of the treatment of the total
resisters made the Norwegian authorities most vulnerable. At the
time it called itself a *campaign*, with the terminology of today it
would probably have been called a *network*. Its way of organising
has a striking similarity with Ofog, except that the transnational
character made KMV rather exceptional for its time.

Both total resistance and selective objection were a response to
the system of conscription, which meant that the Norwegian
state was the initiator of this "engagement". However, from
1981 it was not just the young men who were forced to respond
to call up orders from the state and make up their mind about
their position – the state also had to respond to numerous
initiatives from KMV and S.I.N. that went way beyond an

individual refusal. By 1985 the number of total resisters in Norway had grown considerably.

The case study identified four different strategies that KMV pursued:

1.   Spectacular actions took place primarily in the courts and prisons. They aimed to expose the court hearings as a farce and draw attention to both total resisters and selective objectors serving time in prison, no matter if this was labelled punishment or substitute service. KMV used two types of humorous political stunts – the provocative jail-ins and the supportive fake prosecutor. Looking back with the benefit of hindsight, Johansen was not satisfied with the fact that these two types of humorous political stunts did not speak for themselves about the issue of total resistance and conscientious objection. Nevertheless the scenes of prison walls and court rooms stand out as highly relevant for the changes KMV demanded. There are many humorous political stunts where one could be much more critical about why a particular scene was chosen for a certain message.

2.   The challenges the state seemed to take most seriously were the use of the courts against the Norwegian state. Johansen complained to the European Commission of Human Rights at the Council of Europe that the Norwegian state was violating the European Convention on Human Rights when he was forced to serve the substitute service in prison while the state refused to call it a punishment. The state naturally enough found it necessary to defend itself and spent many resources on this. Although the informant from the Norwegian state insisted that being dragged to the court was not an embarrassment as long as the state won, it still turned out to be a decisive factor for the law change that eventually took place.

The case in Norway where Bremnes and Nilsen filled charges against the state for violating the constitution was another important case. Although KMV activists lost both these cases in court, they demonstrated that there was a grey zone which the state decided to withdraw from, something which was confirmed without doubt from the same informant. The legal strategy was combined with a media strategy, thus showing even this type of legal battle's potential for contributing to the spectacle.

3. Solidarity activities with other total resisters around the world probably meant much to individuals. It was a welcome support when groups in other countries carried out actions in solidarity with KMV, for instance at the Norwegian embassies in Denmark and Spain. However, there is no data to tell if this was something the Norwegian authorities registered or cared about.

4. Some individuals within KMV, especially Solberg, wrote many letters to the editors about total resistance, and this way participated in the public debate. KMV also had meetings with political parties and tried to lobby for their case, but compared to how many political groups operate, KMV as a campaign showed surprisingly little interest in this part of its work.

The four strategies demonstrate how humour can successfully be used as part of a larger campaign. In the analysis of the case I showed that humour was an effective way to draw attention to an issue that concerned only very few people. The stunts' media appeal indicates that KMV were able to reach out to many more people than those who felt the imprisonment on their own body. The humour was with all likelihood a contributing factor to the dramatic increase in the number of total resisters. However, there is no doubt that humorous political stunts did not do this alone – they were an integrated part of a strategy where the legal cases probably influenced the Norwegian authorities more directly. In just four years the situation changed from absolutely no parliamentarian interest in the fate of the total resisters to a unanimous "yes" for the law change suggested by the civil servants.

KMV and Ofog resemble each other in many ways, especially when it comes to the radical anti-militarist ideology and the way of organising. However, there are also some notable differences. Whereas KMV was focusing on the issues of selective objectors and total resisters in prison, and only that, Ofog is concerned about a much broader range of issues. One reason KMV could claim such a major victory after a decade of organising was that it was so committed to this particular issue. It helped KMV that the Norwegian legislation violated simple logic when it claimed that prison was not punishment. Nevertheless the issue of total resistance was so radical and something that concerned so few people that it is difficult to see the law change as anything else than a major achievement for such a small group.

The interview with Jensen who represented the Norwegian state and the department of justice in questions regarding conscientious objection provided much insight about the processes that were taking place on the other side of the table. Although the information concerned this particular case it also illustrates some consequences that might be interesting to many social movements as more general observations.

First of all the alliance that the total resisters and the selective objectors had formed made no sense to those on the other side. Where Solberg and Johansen saw a natural connection because both groups were serving time in prison for their refusal to cooperate with the military system, Jensen saw two completely different groups with little in common.

The case also revealed that contact with politicians is not necessarily the key to changing laws. For the selective objectors, representatives from the socialist party were important for pushing their case forward. However, the proposal for a revision of the relevant paragraphs concerning total resistance came from the civil servants in the department of justice.

KMV grew out of the so-called youth rebellion of the late 1960's, which did not really manifest itself in Scandinavia until the 1970's. The spread of the idea of total resistance based on combining anarchism and pacifism was part of the political radicalisation of the late 1970's. Two of the three key people I interviewed from KMV had actually performed regular military service, and it was the repetition exercises that got them involved in total resistance.

Although a major part of KMV's work regarding the situation in Norway is described and analysed here this is not the history of KMV. A thorough history would require more focus on the work done in Sweden and the network-like informal way of organising which characterised KMV and set it apart from many other organisations. This said, I hope the case study has provided enough details to give more than a taste of how KMV organised, strategised and developed ideas.

Chapter 7: Humorous political stunts and relations of power

Introduction

The first three chapters presented the relevant literature on political humour, nonviolence and power, the methodological considerations behind the thesis and the definition and model of humorous political stunts. Chapters 4-6 analysed the data from the two case studies about Ofog and KMV. This chapter discusses the potential and limitations of the humorous political stunt's engagement with relations of power. I will return to findings presented earlier and discuss them in relation to each other.

In Chapter 1 I discussed different understandings and definitions of power and resistance and the implications for research on humour. I quoted some humour scholars that persistently claim that humour cannot change political circumstances and is merely a vent for frustration. A similar discussion has been taking place within performance studies about the efficacy of the carnivalesque in protest. Such ideas reflect an old-fashioned *realpolitik* perspective on power and seem to miss the point that most humorous political stunts are aiming to make.

Below I problematise the arguments from both humour studies and performance studies in relation to my findings and a perspective on power and resistance which takes Foucault, Scott and Bayat into consideration. After a brief discussion of the problems with how to measure impact, I look at humorous political stunts' potential impact on facilitating outreach and mobilisation, a culture of resistance and challenging relations of power from this perspective. Afterwards the chapter revisits the model of five types of humorous political stunts and the theatre metaphor, before proceeding to Vinthagen's theory of nonviolent action and its four dimensions – dialogue facilitation, power breaking, utopian enactment and normative regulation. Here I investigate how different types of humorous political stunts strengthen or weaken the various elements. It appears that humorous political stunts work especially on the power breaking dimension, under some circumstances can contribute to dialogue facilitation, and that some types of stunts are good examples of temporary utopian enactments.

How to evaluate the impact of humorous political stunts?

Social relations are complex, and all social science struggles with the question of how to "prove" causal relationships. Knowing that there will seldom be a conclusive answer, approaching the subject requires clarity about what one considers an effect under particular circumstances, and how much effect is required in order to have achieved change.

Humorous political stunts are one type of method that activists can use, alongside many options for rational communication. In most cases, the same people who carry out humorous political stunts also engage in non-humorous, rational activism as the work of for instance Ofog, KMV, Otpor and Netwerk Vlaanderen show. A few groups or individuals have specialised in humorous political stunts, like the Yes Men and Mark Thomas, but nevertheless they are still part of larger movements fighting for similar goals about social justice.

Day in her writing about ironic activism points out that the activists are aware that the stunts in themselves will not be able to convert committed conservatives.[825] However, groups that perform humorous political stunts are parts of larger trends that may or may not be considered successful social movements a hundred years from now. Over time, some social movements

---

[825] Day, *Satire and Dissent*: pp. 182-83.

without doubt shape society and contribute to change regarding small and big issues.

To date most experiments with humorous political stunts have been rather small scale. The week long Santa action is one of the most extensive examples when it comes to the number of participants and time. But the culmination in the shopping centres did not involve more than 50 people during one afternoon. What would have happened if the humorous political stunts had been carried out on a larger scale? How would it affect those in powerful positions if they had involved ten times as many people, and occurred ten times as frequently? The answers to these questions of course involve speculation or counter-factual history writing, but asking the questions assumes that the potential of humour might only just have been touched.

Imagine an army of Santas handing out presents in every single shop in Copenhagen before Christmas, not just two places. Imagine Reality AB actually bringing hundreds or even thousands of victims of "collateral damage" to a NATO exercise: how would Swedish authorities have reacted then? Imagine Ofog's ad corrections being present on every ad, not just a few. And not just on one occasion, but every single time the military advertises in order to recruit new soldiers.

Some pranksters aim to change particular circumstances, and if the goal is limited, it is possible to see if they succeed or not. At one level KMV had a very bold goal, to abolish conscription, but the group also had a much more limited objective, to change the law that gave many of its members 16 months in prison. Although they did not succeed in ending conscription, they were very successful in changing the law and reducing their time in prison considerably.

Ofog is a group operating with a much more diffuse goal, a peaceful world. Those who are active do not expect to win this battle in their lifetime, but at least they can look themselves in the mirror and say that they tried. The institutions that a group like Ofog is up against have almost unlimited resources. The Swedish armed forces control an annual budget of 40 billion Swedish crowns, spend 1 billion of this on advertising, and are one of the biggest employers in Sweden.[826] Ofog is a network of volunteers. Of course a few humorous political stunts will not dismantle Swedish militarism, but neither will a similar level of action using rational arguments and non-humorous political activism.

Although the potential of humour should not be dismissed because no immediate result can be documented in terms of law or policy changes, one should be careful not to fall in the trap of viewing everything that activists do as a success. Even if activists themselves consider a certain activity important and meaningful, it might look different through the eyes of an observer. Of course activists need to justify to themselves why they do what they do, and it is extremely painful to reach the conclusion that "what we did was badly planned, carried out half-heartedly and did not have any impact". The case study of Ofog showed how the Ofog activists did not evaluate their actions in relation to the goal of dismantling militarism. Probably because "militarism" is so diffuse, it is difficult to know when one has had any influence. Instead Ofog activists focused on the relations immediately observable, such as reactions from police and civilian passers-by. Likewise it can be difficult for a researcher supportive of a certain struggle to conclude that actions taken by friends did not seem to reach their goals at all.

Schriver and Nudd have suggested looking at performative protests as a continuum rather than as a dichotomous suc-

---

826 Försvarsmakten, "Om Försvarsmakten "
http://www.forsvarsmakten.se/sv/Om-Forsvarsmakten/.

cess/failure.[827] They base this idea on a Foucaudian power analysis which recognises that even when what one opposes looks like a monolithic force it still has multiple sources.[828] Their continuum is a major step forward from perceiving success/failure as either/or, but it is still far from catching the complexities of humorous political stunts and their effects on various audiences. To mention just one example, it is perfectly possible to be successful when it comes to mobilising new activists, but an utter failure in changing a policy.

However, a more nuanced view of success and failure should not neglect the fact that many political activists have much to learn when it comes to evaluating their own actions. Seldom is it made explicit what the criteria for success are, and there is a strong tendency to view one's own actions in a positive light. This might be natural in order to make one's own actions meaningful, but such an approach is not necessarily effective in bringing about change.

In Chapter 4, several activists emphasised the positive relations clowns could develop with the police. However, although such good relationships can be one aspect of a successful nonviolent action, it would be strange if good relations became the main goal. The risk of being side tracked from the activists' core issues of militarism, neo-liberalism and social justice is a general problem and not something peculiar to humorous activism. A non-humorous example from Chapter 6 about KMV can illustrate this. The occupation of the Norwegian embassy in Denmark in support of the total resisters was described by one of the participants as a very successful nonviolent action. However, what he implicitly treated as criteria for success were the friendly atmos-

---

[827] Schriver and Nudd, "Mickee Faust Club's Performative Protest Events," p. 203.

[828] Schriver and Nudd, "Mickee Faust Club's Performative Protest Events," p. 207.

phere, the maintenance of nonviolent discipline and the action going according to plan. These are all meaningful aspects of nonviolent actions, but to me one very important success criterion ought to be the impact on Norwegian authorities, something which was not mentioned. The same problem was apparent in several of Ofog's actions. When clowning, success was measured in the relationship with the police – not the influence on the arms producer Bofors or those responsible for running the Vidsel Test Range.

Impact on outreach and mobilisation

One way to evaluate the impact of humorous political stunts is to investigate whether they influence outreach and mobilisation, a culture of resistance or relations of power. When it comes to outreach, it is obvious that humorous political stunts can sometimes open the door to mainstream mass media for small activist groups. A quote from a US prankster sums up this aspect of the relationship between the media and humorous political stunts:

> The media can never deny coverage to a good spectacle. No matter how ridiculous, absurd, insane or illogical something is, if it achieves a certain identity as a spectacle, the media has to deal with it. They have no choice.[829]

Although this process might not always be as automatic as it is assumed by this prankster and it is not unheard of that media remain silent about major spectacles, some of the people who perform humorous political stunts are tremendously successful in generating media attention for their stunts. I have not compared the media coverage of conventional protest systematically with humorous protest, but most activists who have tried to gain access to the media will agree that the coverage Solvognen and KMV obtained for the army of Santas, the jail-ins and the fake prosecutor were out of proportion to the coverage given to

[829] Harold, *Ourspace*: p. 86.

conventional demonstrations or public awareness raising meetings. Netwerk Vlaanderen's ACE bank that invested in oil, weapons and child labour, the dropping of the teddy bears over Belarus, and Voina's giant penis on the bridge in St. Petersburg are other examples of humorous political stunts covered internationally by mainstream media. Likewise with the Chaser's APEC stunt where they entered the security area with an entry pass with the word "joke" across it.

Although Ofog activists had the impression that civil disobedience actions might generate more coverage than humorous actions, at least one person experienced that the quality of the reports was much better when they used humour. However, a humorous political stunt is not in itself enough to gain media attention, and it remains a challenge to obtain coverage that communicates the message and not just the method. When the Yes Men's corrective stunt about compensation to the victims of the Bhopal catastrophe from Dow Chemicals appeared on the BBC, it was due to a mistake by the BBC. Although the Yes Men are very skilful it seems unlikely a group can rely on such luck when planning, and the BBC invitation was a scenario the Yes Men had not counted on.

In previous chapters I distinguished between humorous political stunts' ability to facilitate outreach and mobilisation. Facilitating mobilisation requires outreach to a certain part of the population that one expects to be sympathetic to the cause and willing to join the carnival themselves. Existing literature points towards humour's potential for facilitating mobilisation. The case study of Ofog confirmed this potential and regarding KMV humour probably played a role in increasing the number of total resisters.

Impact on cultures of resistance

When I started this research project my main interest was the pranksters' interaction with the opponent, but along the way it became more and more difficult to maintain this distinction between the impact on those outside the movement and those

505

inside since they influence each other. The case study on Ofog explored this internal-external dynamic where humour might happen in public, but mainly be for the benefit of the activists themselves.

It might appear to outsiders as if social movement organisers are "wasting their time" when they frequently preach to the converted through humorous political stunts. However, things that appear meaningless to the outsider might contribute significantly to higher morale and energy within the movement, which in turn have the potential to lead to more energy to spend on other types of activism. This aspect of social movement organising I have referred to as building and sustaining *cultures of resistance*.

In an article called "Anger, Irony, and Protest: Confronting the Issue of Efficacy, Again" Chvasta positions activist academic Benjamin Shepard, who has used much creative protest in gay and anti-war activism, against political scientist Robert Weissberg. According to Chvasta, Shepard thinks that the carnivalesque does not work anymore, and Weissberg thinks that it has never worked and is actually counterproductive. Chvasta herself thinks that the carnivalesque has to be combined with lobbying.[830]

According to Chvasta, Weissberg thinks that only institutionalised efforts of lobbying can bring about change. The carnivalesque is ineffective and potentially harmful because it takes too much focus and energy. However, what Weissberg considers effective lobbying, some activists would probably call a lame co-optation where activism has its teeth extracted so they can no longer bite the system. In Chapter 1 I presented a number of authors who have written about tactical carnival and the

---

[830] Marcyrose Chvasta, "Anger, Irony, and Protest: Confronting the Issue of Efficacy, Again," *Text and Performance Quarterly* 26, no. 1 (2006): p. 12.

carnivalesque and found that the reasons for using creativity are seldom purely concerned with achieving immediate political goals, but about making activism and political campaigning sustainable.[831] But how is it exactly that preaching to those who are already converted contributes to sustaining a culture of resistance? Day discusses this in a chapter about irony in activism.[832] She quotes Jonathan Gray for saying that there is a reason why religious preachers do preach to the converted every week. Reminders and reinforcement are important, and religious leaders are aware of this. Day herself adds that "affirmation and reinforcement fulfil an integral community-building function, which is a crucial component of nurturing a political movement."[833] Humour can be one aspect in this community building.

The energy which is available to activists is not a fixed amount, and participating in activities one considers fun and meaningful is likely to create *more* energy and motivation to continue. People who feel that others value their contributions, have close friends within the movement, think activism is enjoyable and believe their contribution will make a difference are much more likely to stay in activism and dedicate more time and effort to it. A good atmosphere contributes to creating a community, and having a good laugh together can be one way to make it more bearable to concern oneself with the apparently never ending uphill battles against for instance war, dictatorships, poverty and climate change.

---

[831] Bogad, "Carnivals against Capital."; Bogad, "Tactical Carnival."; Sombutpoonsiri, "The Use of Humour as a Vehicle for Nonviolent Struggle."; Shepard, Bogad, and Duncombe, "Performing Vs. The Insurmountable."

[832] Day, *Satire and Dissent*.

[833] Day, *Satire and Dissent*: p. 146.

Impact on challenging relations of power

There are numerous ways to approach the issue of how humorous political stunts challenge established relations of power. Later in the chapter I return to Vinthagen's theory of nonviolent action for the purpose. Here I suggest four other elements that both researchers and activists can evaluate.

1. Discursive guerrilla war

Most organisers of humorous political stunts are well aware that their challenges are not "real" resistance as the concept is understood in the old-fashioned *realpolitik* approach to power. Instead humorous political stunts can be understood as engagements in the *discursive guerrilla war* over what is true, right and just in the domains that the activists are concerned about. The previous chapters discussed how especially the corrective stunts presenting alternatives can be such guerrilla attacks.

One of the ways that power is challenged in humorous political stunts is when different dominant discourses are played out against each other. These different discourses usually exist side by side governing different domains, but can be brought together and contrasted with each other. For example, in western societies, discourses of profit, human rights and gift giving are all dominant discourses regarding a desirable life. When a humorous political stunt manages to rub some of these discourses against each other, an interesting dynamic arises when one dominant discourse is used to criticise another. This was the case when the Santas in Copenhagen positioned the naïve and generous gift-giving Santa against discourses about theft and private property. In Belarus the discourse of human rights was used to challenge the discourse of respect for national sovereignty and air space. This way of playing dominant discourses against each other is not unique to humour, but one reason that humour arises for some audiences is that they spot the incompatibility and incongruity among discourses. However, this is probably also a reason why other people are not amused at all – they see one of the discourses as being much more important under the circumstances (profit, sovereignty) and thus no appropriate incongruity arises for them.

2.   How do others respond to humorous political stunts?

Another way to investigate how humour has engaged with relations of power is to look at responses to it. The different examples have documented some of the many types of reactions, and how important it is for a social movement to be able to read what is going on. Sometimes those who are being challenged can ignore the attempt to undermine them. For instance, NATO did not get into trouble for ignoring Reality AB. At other times no reaction might stem from the fact that no one suspects that a prank is taking place, such as when the Yes Men spoke at the textile conference in Finland. But frequently humorous political stunts are met with sanctions from authorities: elves, Santas and clowns are handcuffed and taken to prison.

Several authors writing generally about humour have made the observation that it can be difficult to find an adequate response to a humorous attack.[834] Both Palmer and Speier have indicated that the best response is probably to come up with an even better witticism.[835] However, everyone who has found them-selves the victim of someone's joke knows how difficult it can be to find a witty retort on the spot. None of the defenders of the dominant discourses under attack in the examples presented here have tried to respond this way in public.

---

[834] Palmer, *Taking Humour Seriously*: p. 169. Speier, "Wit and Politics: An Essay on Power and Laughter," p. 1386. Sørensen, "Humor as a Serious Strategy of Nonviolent Resistance to Oppression."
[835] Palmer, *Taking Humour Seriously*: p. 169. Speier, "Wit and Politics: An Essay on Power and Laughter," p. 1386.

Reactions to social movements' campaigns and actions are complex processes, potentially involving a large number of people in different positions. It is pointless to try to understand reactions isolated from the whole interaction, but focusing on responses reveals diversity and a number of nuances that reach far beyond the common sense categories of support or repression.

Most humorous political stunts differ from conventional protest because of the pretence that the instigators are not protesting. The disruption through pretence opens up possibilities for transformation rather than opposition. For many humorous political stunts it is natural to use a vocabulary of confrontation, opponent etc. The activists who initiate the stunts frequently see a clear division line between themselves and those they consider powerful. On the other hand, the use of humour means that it is much more difficult for representatives of the dominant discourse to frame these actions as ordinary protest, although they frequently try. Since non-protesting protesters cannot easily be categorised with other protesters, the show is interrupted in a different way. On the surface, the fan club was not protesting Howard's politics, they were celebrating him. The Polish TV walkers did not strike or march in a demonstration, they just took their TVs for a walk at a certain time. Ofog's company Reality AB did not demonstrate when the NATO exercise took place, they just helped improve it. The Yes Men did not disrupt WTO meetings, they just clarified the institution's message. None of them fit into the ordinary play called "dominant discourse tolerates protest".

3.   Does humour speak to a common humanity?

In Chapter 4 I demonstrated how clowns can show what another world can look like at the same time as they often aim to speak to a shared humanity that transcends roles of activists and police officers. Even when they are annoying, nonviolent rebel clowns to some degree appeal to the shared experience of what it means to be human. However, I also pointed out that the relations are fragile, and if the clowning is not experienced as sincere the possibility will collapse.

In *Redeeming Laughter: The Comic Dimension of Human Experience*, Peter Berger writes that the ability to perceive something as comic is a unique human feature. To him, humor is an intrusion into the non-humorous paramount reality that dominates most people's everyday existence. The idea of "intrusion" becomes a striking expression for describing the humorous political stunts. It is both an intrusion into authorities' and conventional non-humorous protesters' paramount reality. Berger uses the term transcendence to describe this intrusion:

> ...the comic transcends the reality of ordinary everyday existence; it posits, however temporarily, a different reality in which the assumptions and rules of ordinary life are suspended.[836]

Berger does not discuss whether this transcendence can also take place when someone does something they intend to be humorous, but that the butt of the joke or part of the audience does not perceive it as funny at all. What happens then? Does the transcendence still work with the police officers who do not want to play along with the clowns? Can the transcendence only take place for those who agree that this was humorous? As mentioned in Chapter 1, Palmer has emphasised how humor is fragile and easily can fail. Accepting something as humorous is not straightforward and self-evident; it is a struggle over what meaning to attribute to what is said or done, and depends on the context. Humorous intent is not enough for humor to succeed.

---

[836] Berger, *Redeeming Laughter.* p. 205. Berger refers to this as "transcendence in a lower key", and uses "transcendence in a higher key" to describe a religious experience of the comic in the human condition that is not relevant here.

The butt of the joke or prank does not have to agree that something is funny, but either the audience agrees that an event was humorous, or there is something special about the occasion which a given culture considers humorous.[837] The butts of the pranks may not consider them funny at all, but nevertheless at some level it is possible to interpret the pranks as an appeal to our common humanity, no matter if this is done consciously by the pranksters or not. When Berger discusses the comic and its intrusion into the paramount reality he does not address these issues.

In my opinion, humorous political stunts have a potential for transforming relations of power because they highlight the contradictions and weaknesses of the dominant discourse, using a format that is recognisable as humorous also for those who are the butt of the joke. The comic is an intrusion into our paramount reality and temporarily suspends the world as we know it. Even when the "victims" are not amused, the presence of the comic still communicates to everyone involved that we are all humans in spite of our different roles in society. However, this is another topic for further research.

Humorous political stunts call for a lexicon of disruption, challenge, transformation and transcendence, rather than "opposition", because the choice of humour as a method is in itself much more inclusive and transformative than oppositional. This vocabulary reflects a Foucauldian understanding of power formations and dominant discourses, and can be found in academic fields such as queer theory and performativity studies which directly draw on Foucault as well as queer activism that has inspired other political movements to create a more playful

---

[837] Palmer, *Taking Humour Seriously*.

atmosphere.[838] However, a similar vocabulary can also be found in fields like peace studies and postcolonial resistance studies where Foucault has a less prominent place, but where resistance and opposition nevertheless are understood as multifaceted and relational.[839]

By applying the metaphor of theatre and pointing out the elements of pretence in the stunts, these investigations into the humorous political stunt have shown how current (political) reality is temporarily forced aside to reveal a glimpse of other potential (political) realities.

4. Dilemma actions

The fourth and final way I suggest to approach the subject of humour and relations of power in this section is through the concept of *dilemma actions*. In nonviolent action theory, a dilemma action is constructed so the target has to make a choice between two or more responses, each of which has significant negative aspects for them. The responses are not readily comparable and this is the nub of the dilemma. In a typical dilemma action involving nonviolent action, the opponent can either let the activists proceed to achieve their immediate goals or use force to stop them with the risk of adverse publicity.[840]

---

[838] Steven Epstein, "A Queer Encounter: Sociology and the Study of Sexuality," *Sociological Theory* 12, no. 2 (1994); Steven Seidman, "Queering Sociology, Sociologizing Queer Theory: An Introduction," *Sociological Theory* 12, no. 2 (1994); Shepard, *Queer Political Performance and Protest: Play, Pleasure and Social Movement.*

[839] Johan Galtung, *Transcend and Transform: An Introduction to Conflict Work* (London: Pluto Press in association with TRANSCEND, 2004); David Jefferess, *Postcolonial Resistance: Culture, Liberation and Transformation* (Toronto: University of Toronto Press, 2008); Vinthagen, *Ickevåldsaktion.*

[840] Sørensen and Martin, "The Dilemma Action: Analysis of an Activist Technique." George Lakey was the first to identify this dynamic in the

Dilemma actions do not have to be humorous but many humorous political stunts are dilemma actions. In both the Polish examples, the communist Polish regime was caught in a dilemma. If they continued to let people take their TVs for a walk, dissent could continue. But as soon as they made something innocent illegal, they made fools of themselves. Likewise with the happenings of Orange Alternative – police arresting elves who had not uttered a word of protest risked becoming a target of further ridicule. The Chaser's APEC stunt is also an example of a dilemma action. The Australian authorities and the world leaders could either laugh or be outraged. If they laughed, they implicitly admitted that their security arrangements were ridiculous. When they prosecuted the comedy team, they made themselves vulnerable to accusations of lacking a sense of humour.

Dilemma actions, humorous as well as non-humorous, undermine relations of power when those apparently in a subordinate position can use creativity and surprise to catch the more powerful off balance and place them in situations where no response appears quite right.

To sum up this section about how to evaluate the impact of humorous political stunts, it is first and foremost important to be clear about exactly what impact one is aiming to measure. Humorous political stunts can have an influence on many different levels, to do with their potential for outreach and mobilisation, creating and sustaining cultures of resistance as well as challenging relations of power. Next I briefly revisit my model of humorous political stunts before I approach the subject of

---

nonviolence literature, although he called it a "dilemma demonstration". George Lakey, *Powerful Peacemaking: A Strategy for a Living Revolution* (Philadelphia, PA: New Society Publishers, 1987 [1973]).

impact by combining my model and Vinthagen's theory of nonviolent action.

The model of humorous political stunts revisited

In previous chapters I introduced numerous humorous political stunts and analysed them according to my model presented in chapter 3. The model divides the stunts according to their way of relating to dominant discourses' logic and claims to truth.

Supportive stunts pretend to help or celebrate people in positions of power or their dominant discourse, with irony and exaggeration used to reveal that the support is in fact not sincere at all. An example of a supportive stunt was Ofog's company Reality AB which was a tool for engaging the general public in a different discussion about war when the "recruiters" were searching for people for a summer job as civilian victims of "collateral damage" during a NATO exercise in Sweden.

Corrective stunts share some similarities with the supportive stunts in the way that they at first glance look as if they are the real thing. However, a closer look reveals that the identity of a powerful institution or person has been "borrowed" in order to present a corrected version of its message. It is not a fake message, but an honest representation of the aspect of the discourse that those in powerful positions prefer to keep quiet about. The Yes Men's stunts where they impersonated representatives of the World Trade Organisation and the company Dow Chemicals are some of the most famous examples of these types of corrections. However, many others have used similar techniques for instance Ofog when the group added text to the Swedish armed forces recruitment ads in an attempt to make passers-by reflect on the messages.

Those who perform naïve stunts take a very different approach and pretend that they are not aware that what they do can be interpreted as dissent, for example by hiding their message behind something innocent and normal. However, they can also do like Solvognen did before Christmas in Copenhagen and take on a naïve and innocent role like Santa, and perform the ordinary duties of this role figure, like giving gifts away.

Absurd stunts do not directly relate to the dominant discourses at all. Instead they use absurdity to maintain a distance from all claims to truth, like the clowns in Chapter 4. The Polish Orange Alternative also staged absurd happenings in the late 1980s when Poland was under communist rule. There was no obvious expression of dissent in the silliness and the authorities had difficulties finding an adequate response to the pranks when they presented no obvious threats or political content.

Finally there are the provocative stunts. They challenge the dominant discourses and their representatives head on without "hiding" behind irony, impersonations or innocence. Instead they add an incongruous element which causes audiences to smile. When KMV staged their jail-ins they were very confrontational about the issue of imprisoned conscientious objectors, but by jumping into the prison yard instead of a more conventional escape over the walls many people had to laugh. It further added to the amusement that it became rather difficult to punish them for trespassing since they had themselves demanded to be imprisoned together with their friend.

In order to further analyse the dynamics of interaction in each stunt, the metaphor of play was used to illustrate the complexities of each stunt and the differences between them depending on the *stage, actors, audience* and *timing*. The metaphor serve as a way to illustrate how easy the dynamic of the interaction can be changed depending on each of these four different dimensions. The challengers can intensify or make their challenge less dangerous with just a little change in one aspect. The metaphor is also an attempt to illuminate the dynamics of the interaction involved in the stunts. The challengers can seldom determine the

outcome alone, exactly what happens also depends on the responses from the established players and the audiences.

1.   The examples have illustrated some of the diversity in
humorous political stunts when it comes to the type of *stage* the
pranksters enter and the way they do it. In Australia, John Howard Ladies' Auxiliary Fan Club went for a major stage, targeting
Howard in the midst of an election campaign, while Ofog and
the Polish TV-walkers preferred the more accessible stage of the
streets. In some stunts the stage was openly "invaded" right in
the face of the audience and the other actors, like in KMV's jail-
ins, while the Yes Men snuck in using disguise and were not even
recognised as challengers until after the stunt was over. The stage
can be virtual, or it can be a physical place.

2.   *Actors* in this theatre also vary tremendously – from the
Prime Minster in the Australian case, to less known actors in the
others. The challengers can be few in numbers – the Yes Men
were just two individuals with much help - or they can be many,
as the Polish TV-walkers. However, there seems to be a tendency that humorous political stunts are initiated by small groups of
tightly knit challengers – something which is not strange when
considering the need for planning and scripting. In all the stunts
I have looked at, the highest number of challengers found is the
100 Santas that came to Copenhagen just before Christmas in
1974.[841]

One reason is probably that performing a humorous political
stunt requires more skills and dedication than signing a petition
or participating in a demonstration. However, this creates a
potential risk of humorous political stunts being an elite endeav-
our for those who can afford to spend much time on preparing
for political activism.

Nonviolent activists have numerous audiences in mind when
they design their actions. Some are just desperate and want to do

---

[841] Rasmussen, *Solvognen: Fortællinger Fra Vores Ungdom.*

something. Others carefully calculate how they think their opponent will react, and plan to achieve a certain reaction from particular stakeholders. Sometimes activists are not so concerned about the reaction from the opponent or there is no particular opponent such as in the Santa actions, but want to reach out to the general public or attract more activists. Many actions are successful and achieve their aims, but sometimes things do not go as planned.

3. Who are the *audiences* for the stunt, and how do audience members react? Do the challengers treat the audiences as part of the play, as in the Reality AB, or is the play most successful with an audience that will later watch a movie of it, as in the case of the Yes Men? Throughout the thesis I have talked about humour's ability to facilitate outreach to media and passers-by and mobilisation of new participants. One of the features of a humorous political stunt is that audience expectations are challenged. People watching the show on the political scene usually have perceptions about what is going on and what they are going to hear from different institutions and organisations. The challengers manage to turn these expectations upside down when a lecturer or a prosecutor says something outrageous and turns out to be someone else.

The way different audiences interpret humorous political stunts is probably the most crucial factor highlighted by the theatre metaphor. It does not matter what message the challengers had in mind if it is interpreted differently. How different audiences interpret a show is also what is most difficult to discover. Even when asked directly about their personal opinions, there is no guarantee that audience members speak their minds and not what they think others wish to hear.

4. The *timing* of the stunt is sometimes crucial for the development of the stunt, at other times less important. When activists are concerned with meeting the general public it might

not appear to matter so much exactly when the stunt is staged. However, as the experience from Ofog's Vapenfadder showed, timing the stunt in a way so the audience is already thinking about the topic might help get the intended message across. In stunts such as those carried out by John Howard Ladies' Auxiliary Fan Club and the Chaser's ridicule of APEC security, a successful event depends on timing it with the presence of the other actors required to be on the scene to play their roles. Turning up a day too early or too late will ruin the stunt.

Considering each of the four aspects of the theatre metaphor – stage, actors, audience and timing – can give an indication of the criteria for a successful stunt, and how to increase the pressure if the stunt did not generate the expected reaction. Above I indicated numbers and frequency as two ways to increase the potential of a humorous political stunt; these four aspects are other ways of thinking along the same lines. Imagine how much more attention KMV would have received if those jumping into the prison and demanding to be locked up had been more prominent actors – say the prime minister, the bishop or their children. If Ofog had been a little bolder, they could have taken their victims of "collateral damage" to a stage where it would have been difficult to ignore them, the NATO exercise itself, something which would also have given the stunt a different audience. If Netwerk Vlaanderen had timed their search for landmines with an important meeting at the bank, it might also potentially have increased the visibility of the stunt.

Writing about politics in terms of theatre does not mean that challengers that interrupt the show are just "playing" and not serious about the issue concerned. Using this metaphor is a way to take a step back and create an analytical distance. It is also a reflection of the fact that all social interaction can be thought of as a "performance", and that both the representatives of the dominant discourses and the challengers play their part in this interaction.

The phenomenon I have termed humorous political stunts differs from other types of political humour by being done in public, and its confrontational attitude. The chapter on clowning revealed that this particular sub-category of an absurd stunt through the use of play and otherness can communicate nonviolent values and appeal to a mutual recognition of the human in the other. Well done clowning might transcend differences between different groups (like police and protesters), even when those who are the butt of the joke are ridiculed for their signs of importance and authority, as long as they have just a little critical self-distance.

The two case studies documented how humour can be one way of reaching out to more people, and how it can make activism more sustainable. The KMV chapter also illustrated how humour can work together with other strategies and be successful in achieving a limited goal. A single stunt cannot be expected to achieve all this by itself, but together they point towards the potential inherent in humour.

It is the way the organisers of the humorous political stunts set out to challenge dominant discourses and taken for granted assumptions that should be analytically distinguished from non-humorous forms of protest. In addition to the appeal to our common humanity, the dilemmas they create for their opponents differ because they have not accepted the usual role of "protester" in the political game, but pretend that something else is going on.

Humour and Vinthagen's four dimensions of nonviolent action

In chapter 1 I introduced Vinthagen's theory of nonviolent action and its four dimensions of dialogue facilitation, power breaking, utopian enactment and normative regulation. Taking the insights provided by the model of humorous political stunts and the metaphor of play into consideration, how does the use of humour in nonviolent action influence the rationality of each of these four dimensions? In what way does it help or hinder the logic of the nonviolent action?

1. Dialogue facilitation

In his concept of dialogue facilitation, Vinthagen combines Gandhi's *satyagraha* with Jürgen Habermas' thoughts on the *ideal speech situation*. In the ideal speech situation, the participants mean what they say and they treat each other's statements with mutual trust. The communication is undisturbed by power relations, and there is time enough to hear all people's opinions and explore what they mean. Everyone with a stake in the issue under consideration participates on equal terms and all have access to relevant information. Rational arguments are allowed to rule and the best argument wins, not the person who is in a position to force her opinion on someone else or best at manipulating. Finally, everyone is ready to change their point of view based on convincing arguments by someone else. The ideal speech situation is an utopia that can never occur in practice, but that should not prevent people from striving for it. Another aspect to consider when evaluating the effect of humour is who the activists are aiming to have a dialogue with.

However, there are some problematic aspects with the ideal speech situation that can be highlighted from the perspective of humour. Sammy Basu has shown how the distrust in the ambiguity of humour is a shortcoming in Habermas' ideal speech situation, since humour is a way for both the strong and the weak to find more "room to manoeuvre".[842] My findings about humorous political stunts support Basu's perspective, because even when they are ambivalent, humorous political stunts usually remain dialogue oriented, both towards those who represent a

---

[842] Sammy Basu, "Dialogic Ethics and the Virtue of Humor," *Journal of Political Philosophy* 7, no. 4 (1999): p. 396.

dominant discourse and other audiences. Although Basu does not elaborate on how exactly humour can overcome the differences, he considers it social *glue* that serves to incline one towards empathy with others.[843] This inclusive humour "cultivates the pleasurable recognition of our mutual absurdities with the Other".[844] Sombutpoonsiri found that the multiple voices that can exist side by side in carnival foster an atmosphere of dialogue despite the existence of prejudices and antagonism. A joyful atmosphere has the posibility of transforming hostility between demonstrators and authorities and contributing to maintaining nonviolent discipline.[845] My analysis of the humorous political stunts showed that they almost always are communicating with multiple audiences. Compared to violent resistance, humorous nonviolent actions appear to signal more openness because of their playful attitude. This is especially obvious in carnivalesque protests of naïve Santas, absurd clowns and pink carnivals, but also other types of stunts can frequently be understood as dialogue oriented if the alternative had been more disruptive forms of protest. Some activists also find it easier to communicate with others when they are playing a role and can leave their usual shy self at home.

However, for those watching the clowns and the Santas the message might be unclear, something which risks distorting the communication. The risk of being misinterpreted when using humour is probably higher than with rational communication. The people behind the actions are with all likelihood perfectly aware of the possibilities for the discussion to side-track, but consider the attention they get for an issue important enough to run the risk. Audiences might be suspicious of the communica-

---

[843] Basu, "Dialogic Ethics and the Virtue of Humor," p. 394.
[844] Email correspondence with Sammy Basu July 31 2012.
[845] Sombutpoonsiri, "The Use of Humour as a Vehicle for Nonviolent Struggle," p. 289.

tive intentions when it is not obvious to them what the message is or it is loaded with possibilities for multiple interpretations as in the absurd stunts.

In supportive and corrective stunts, the messages are more obvious, but audiences used to rational communication might prefer honest, unambiguous communication that does not require them to figure out what the intentions are. In addition, part of the audience might become uncomfortable if it is not clear who is responsible for what information, as when the Yes Men impersonated a Dow spokesperson on BBC. It is necessary to bear in mind that no form of action is likely to satisfy all audiences. Just as some people feel constrained or uneasy by Habermas' demand for rationality, others are lost without it. However, no matter how the audiences interpret humorous political stunts the pranks almost always provide "material" for conversation. It is both a way to strengthen the dialogue among the grassroots and provoke those in power positions to at least pay some attention.

When evaluating the limitations and possibilities of the dialogue element in nonviolent actions, one should not compare it only with rational communication in the ideal speech situation. On the other side of the spectrum stands the choice of violent resistance or sabotage, such as taking up a gun, burning cars or smashing windows. Compared to that even the most ambiguous and confrontational humorous political stunts are considerably more dialogue oriented, also in the sense of Habermas' ideal speech situation.

In cases where the nonviolent activists are especially concerned with appearing willing to engage in dialogue, for instance if they aim to convert the opponent to their cause, it is probably wise to shy away from humour and especially ridicule. Activists who have no problem "loving their enemy" and who can always present a friendly and non-threatening face probably benefit from rational communication since ambiguous humorous messages are likely to create more confusion than clarity.

However, for activists who are angry and frustrated, the ambiguity of humour might facilitate dialogue compared to violent actions and aggressive shouting. From the perspective of the tradition of nonviolence, Voina's painting of the big penis on the bridge in St. Petersburg as a "fuck you" to the secret police was more dialogue oriented than smashing their windows, especially towards audiences who see or hear about it. On the other hand, painting the penis is less dialogue oriented than sitting down and having a rational conversation about what one thinks is wrong with the secret police. This is not to say that smashing windows and setting cars on fire is not communicative in the sense of sending a clear message of frustration and contempt, but it is even further from Habermas' ideal speech situation of respectful dialogue than the painting on the bridge. To the secret police, it might not make much of a difference, and it is even possible that the painting would anger them more than a broken window. However, to the general public the painting sends signals of clever provocateurs rather than an angry mob out of control. In the study and practice of nonviolence one emphasises that how audiences perceive and interpret an action matters as much as the intentions and facts about what happens.[846] Thus, both the traditions of nonviolence discourage anything that can be considered vandalism, the principled tradition because vandalism and sabotage are perceived as morally wrong, and the pragmatic tradition because of the way such actions are perceived by others.

However, dialogue is just one element of the nonviolent action, Vinthagen has also identified three other dimensions.

---

[846] I am grateful to Håkan Thörn for a conversation that helped me clarify this point about communication and dialogue.

2.   Power breaking

However much nonviolent activists strive towards dialogue with representatives of what they oppose and object to, the possibility for dialogue is heavily influenced by the existing power relations. The ideal speech situation requires that everyone involved in the conversation are striving towards the utopia; it is not something that can be done by just one party. The problem is that those who benefit from the status quo seldom find much reason to engage in dialogue until they are forced to do so. They resist this dialogue on equal terms with all possible means, including devaluing the activists as persons and their motives, reframing what the action is about and using all official and unofficial sanctions at their disposal. The most obvious aspect of a nonviolent action is the attempt to break these existing relations of power by pressuring those who refuse to engage into interaction.

With a Foucaudian understanding of power, people can never be outside the relations of power that they want to challenge, but have to act from within. Sombutpoonsiri's thesis about the Serbian group Otpor emphasised humour's excorporation potential, where parody and satire can be used to resist power from within the existing culture.

Many of the humorous political stunts aim to challenge and transform the power relations. Usually this remains a temporary symbolic power breaking, when those in power are ridiculed, humiliated and shown not to be so powerful and almighty as they first appeared. This is most obvious in the provocative stunts, as when Studio Total violated Belarusian airspace to drop teddy bears supporting human rights or Voina painted the penis on the bridge in St. Petersburg. Actions like these shout "see, they are not that almighty anyway". In some of the naïve stunts, such as the innocent advertising for sausages on the butcher's van door in Denmark, the provocation is less direct and a bit more intellectually sophisticated.

However short and symbolic, the humorous political stunts can be powerful contributions in what I call the *discursive guerrilla war* that the activists are waging. If Foucault is right that the main source of disciplining a society is through discourse, then a key role of resistance is to combat dominant discourses. Viewed from this perspective, humorous political stunts have much to contribute in this battle about what is true, just and right and what meaning to attribute to events and actions.

Corrective stunts are the avant-garde of the discursive guerrilla war. It is not just a stage which is occupied: they also include a clever message or a suggestion for an alternative cause of action. When the Yes Men impersonated representatives of Dow and the WTO, they showed that BBC and conference organisers could be fooled, but that was a side effect. The main point was to establish a stage for presenting an alternative way of acting for Dow and the WTO. Even if they probably did not expect these institutions to listen, they succeeded in showing audiences that alternative ways of behaving were actually a possibility.

At other times, humorous political stunts break the power of those representing dominant discourses when they force a theme on the public agenda. Mark Thomas broke Indonesian government representatives' silence about human right violations when his supportive stunt tricked them into admitting to human rights violations while being filmed. Likewise, when Netwerk Vlaanderen created ACE bank that relied on investments in controversial industries such as oil, weapons and child labour it drew attention to a subject which all the major banks would have preferred to keep silent about. Total objectors from KMV had little possibility to draw attention to their fate via traditional channels of communication, but when they staged stunts like the jail-in and the false prosecutor, media coverage enabled others to know about their situation which the Norwegian state was mainly silent about. When the representatives of the Norwegian state then responded, a sort of dialogue had been started. Although it was still far from the utopia in the ideal speech situation, it was a move away from total silence.

Controlling language and symbols is an important aspect of upholding a dominant discourse. The possibility to name and label the world can be just as important for hegemony as physical control through the threat of violence. A consequence of this understanding is that one should not underestimate the threat to the dominance that arises from undermining symbols and language. Well done supportive and corrective humorous political stunts skilfully twist and play with words and images and bring in new associations. Ofog's weapon sponsors, ad corrections and Reality AB are examples of this parody and ridicule of the language of power. When the Swedish armed forces through their recruitment ads tried to define military solutions as the only solutions for anyone who "had what it takes to have an opinion", Ofog used their own symbols and language to suggest alternatives from peace activists who were not afraid to have a different opinion.

Social movements have their own hierarchies and systems of power. Although many political groups are aware of this and consciously work to counter inequalities through their decision making practices and ways of organising their work, they will probably always be there. Humorous political stunts, especially absurd ones, can also be a way to point towards a movement's own power structures and aim to transform them. Clowns cannot only create uncertainty among representatives of the authorities, but also among activists of the "old school" who are most comfortable with rational arguments.

3. Utopian enactment

According to Vinthagen, it is not just the existing power relations that stand in the way of an ideal speech situation. Communication about sensitive issues, such as political struggles, is also highly influenced by emotions. Emotions were long a neglected research area when it came to social movements, but

527

now many texts have documented how feelings of anger and grief are central for the moral shocks and outrage that are strong driving forces for many activists.[847] Nepstad and Smith argue that it is inaccurate to see emotions and rationality as opposites:

> We need to cease viewing emotions and rationality as dichotomous. Moral outrage is a logical reaction to the torture, disappearances, and assassinations of innocent civilians and to the lies disseminated by a government to cover its role as an accomplice to these atrocities.[848]

Nepstad and Smith consider moral outrage a rational response to accounts of torture and killing of civilians, thus it does not make sense to claim that emotions and logic can and should be separated from each other.

However, in the context of nonviolent action, negative emotions like anger and longing for revenge towards those responsible for wrongdoing and injustice may block activists' thinking about constructive solutions and a future peaceful co-existence. The aspect of the nonviolent action which carries an utopian enactment can present a more constructive element. This does not contradict anger as an emotional kick-starter for activism, but is a supplement when it comes to thinking about the future. Utopi-

---

[847] See for instance James M. Jasper, *The Art of Moral Protest: Culture, Biography, and Creativity in Social Movements* (Chicago: University of Chicago Press, 1997). Other sources are the contributions in Jeff Goodwin, James M. Jasper, and Francesca Polletta, eds., *Passionate Politics: Emotions and Social Movements* (Chicago: University of Chicago Press, 2001). Chvasta, "Anger, Irony, and Protest: Confronting the Issue of Efficacy, Again."

[848] Sharon Erickson Nepstad and Christian Smith, "The Social Structure of Moral Outrage in Recruitment to the U.S. Central America Peace Movement," in *Passionate Politics: Emotions and Social Movements*, ed. Jeff Goodwin, James M. Jasper, and Francesca Polletta (Chicago: University of Chicago Press, 2001).

an enactments demonstrate that alternatives to the prevailing order are possible here and now, however fleeting and temporary. With this enactment, nonviolent action suggests alternative ways of structuring society.

As discussed in chapter 1, the definition of humour includes an emotional aspect. This indicates that the humorous mode speaks to an emotional side of people that might not be reached the same way when we operate in the non-humorous mode. This makes humorous political stunts a good starting point for investigating emotional aspects of nonviolent activism. Sombutpoonsiri's thesis with its concept of the carnivalesque as well as Bogad et al.'s idea about tactical carnival also point towards this side of humour.

Humorous political stunts speak to the imagination, thinking out of the box, encouraging audiences to look at reality from a new perspective. This is an aspect where they differ from many conventional expressions of protest. Thinking about the future is not limited to the usual way of "doing politics", but instead an encouragement to "play politics". Orange Alternative showed with their happenings that the grey everyday life of communist Poland could easily be turned into a carnival, thus hinting at other possible ways of living in the future. Also the army of Santas which used the naïve Santa figure to communicate values of generosity and solidarity concretely enacted how the world could be different. Similarly, all the other figures speaking to fantasy and imagination emphasise that the organisers value diversity and creativity. In addition, absurd stunts are a way of illuminating the absurdity of various situations.

When it comes to the corrective stunts, they can be much more concrete and specific than the naïve and absurd about what alternatives they suggest. The logic of the absurd requires the clowns and elves to remain ambiguous about what the future could look like, but corrective stunts do not have this limitation. For instance, the Yes Men showed how the WTO could close itself down, and that Dow indeed had a possibility for apologising and compensating the victims of the Bhopal catastrophe.

However, there is a limitation with using humour to present these alternatives. Especially when it comes to the carnivalesque, some observers might associate the playful frame with irresponsibility and not consider it "serious" enough. This is less of a risk in the corrective stunts, but here the "dishonesty" might in some people's eyes disqualify the expression of dissent from seriousness. It might also become more difficult to reach out to potential allies and new activists who find it a challenge to let go of their anger and don't feel at home in an environment that they see as too silly.

4. Normative regulation

The fourth and final aspect of nonviolent action that Vinthagen identified he called normative regulation, which points towards the struggle for making nonviolence the norm, the normal, and violence the abnormal. For Gandhi and his followers this involved living by the principles of nonviolence in all aspects of life, something they translated into service to society. The challenge was not just to fight injustice, but also to build alternatives in parallel. In western societies, this aspect of nonviolence is rather neglected, although some communities that practice both resistance and construction can be found. The most widespread aspect of attempted normative regulation can be found in trainings before nonviolent actions where the participants practice how to remain nonviolent in spite of provocations.

Almost all the humorous political stunts contribute to the normative regulation aspect of a nonviolent action because of the inherent playful attitude that speaks to our common humanity. This is especially obvious with the same stunts that contribute to utopian enactments. Many accounts describe how clowns and a carnivalesque atmosphere deescalate tensions and make the atmosphere less hostile, especially in cases where protesters are directly confronting a massive police presence and there is a considerable risk of violent clashes. It does not even have to be all protesters who are playing these roles: the mere presence of some in the frontline appears to make the situation less tense. However, as pointed out by some informants, individual police might be provoked and the ambiguity of the clown role that teases and ridicules does allow for many possible interpretations of intentions. Humour which is perceived as aggressive might make an opponent insecure about how true the nonviolent intentions are. Judging whether humour is appropriate in the situation is similar to the dilemma when it comes to dialogue facilitation: In cases where protesters have no problem maintaining their nonviolent discipline and remaining calm and dignified without abusing their opponent, the ambiguity of humour makes the nonviolent intention and norm less obvious. However, when this is not the case and there is a risk of the nonviolent protest turning aggressive, using humour and the carnivalesque to maintain nonviolent discipline is much preferable, although it remains ambiguous.

Although humour at some level contributes to this normative regulation, the stunts presented here are temporary interventions and usually their main purpose is a short breaking of established relations of power. They are miles away from the Gandhian constructive programs and the contribution to the normative regulation is very superficial compared to the ideal. However, as Vinthagen points out when presenting his theory, the normative regulation aspect is generally neglected in the western world where most of my examples of humorous political stunts come from.

This discussion about humour's relation to Vinthagen's theory of nonviolence and its four dimensions has revealed that humour can contribute to the goals of a nonviolent action, but also that some aspects of some types of humorous political stunts might be problematic because of the ambiguity of humour. While humour can help emphasise one of the aspects of nonviolence, at the same time it might become problematic when it comes to others. Table 3 schematically sums up some of these relationships. However, to make it even more complex, it is also im-important to take into consideration which audiences or actors the activists are aiming to influence in what way. To take some examples: The main strength of KMV's jail-ins and fake prosecutor actions were that they broke the power of Norwegian authorities, although only for a short while. They also had a dialogue oriented element towards the general public who were not aware of the situation of the total resisters. On the other hand the deception with the fake prosecutor and the provocation in the jail-ins did not facilitate dialogue with Norwegian authorities. There is an ever-present tension between the elements of dialogue facilitation and power breaking in a world of unequal power relations. Neither were these two actions in themselves utopian enactments since they did not "speak" about the alternatives KMV sought. Like all the other humorous political stunts the contribution to the normative regulation is only superficial because of the temporary nature of the stunts.

In other stunts, other aspects appear most clearly. Mark Thomas broke the power of Indonesian government officials when he tricked them into talking about their human rights abuses on camera under the disguise that he would teach them how to improve their relations to the media. This was not oriented towards dialogue with the Indonesian government. However, revealing what the government representatives had said was an utopian enactment of a world where representatives of a government do not lie to the public.

That a single action or stunt is not able to be the ideal when it comes to all the four aspects is not a problem unique to humorous political stunts. Nonviolent activists encounter the same

Dimension	Dialogue facilitation	Power breaking	Utopian enactment	Normative regulation
How do humorous political stunts potentially weaken nonviolent action?	Ambiguity about who is behind a stunt and what the organisers actually mean might make the dialogue more difficult. The deceptions in some stunts can be interpreted as dishonesty that weakens the dialogue.	Silliness can be interpreted as if the activists are not serious about the issue. Especially the naïve and absurd stunts run this risk.	Ridicule and humiliation can be counterproductive when it comes to the utopian enactment.	Humour perceived as aggressive might cast doubt on how deep the commitment to nonviolence is.
How do humorous political stunts potentially strengthen nonviolent action?	All types of humorous political stunts can be interpreted as dialogue oriented. Play is communicative, especially compared to violence and hostility. Corrective stunts communicate a suggestion for an alternative cause of action. Many activists experience a personal liberation when taking on a role. Stunts frequently provide material for conversation. Also those who disagree talk about them.	All humorous political stunts temporarily break the hegemony of powerful dominant discourses. Humorous political stunts contribute to *discursive guerrilla war*, challenging dominant perceptions about what is true and just. Absurd stunts can break power within the activists' own group.	Many stunts give positive and constructive images of an alternative and more just future with room for tolerance and diversity. Corrective stunts clearly point towards an alternative.	The playful attitude of humorous political stunts speaks to a shared humanity.

533

Table 3. (previous page) The relationships between Vinthagen's four dimensions of nonviolence and humorous political stunts.

contradictions between the different dimensions of an action when they engage in non-humorous action planning. This issue is something for both activists and academic researchers to consider further. There is no "solution" to this problem, and no perfect humorous political stunt exists. Judging what is most appropriate will always be a question about which aspect of a nonviolent action one considers most important in the circumstances.

Conclusion

Humorous political stunts have an ability to appeal to the imagination, to people's desire for spectacle and drama. They create a tension between the said, the unsaid, the skills and the attention of both the initiator of the irony and its interpreters. Political activists who undertake stunts like these see a possibility to destabilise established relations of power when communication becomes even more complex than usual. This is not to say that irony is automatically at the service of those with less power, but those already in power have much less interest in modes of communicating based on an unpredictable ambiguity with an uncertain outcome. However, this ambiguity and built-in tension can be a way for activists to reach out, mobilise, contribute to creating a culture of resistance, and challenge established relations of power.

Looking at the data on humorous political stunts from the perspective of Vinthagen's four dimensions of nonviolent action revealed that most stunts' biggest contribution is to temporarily and symbolically break the power of dominant discourses. By engaging in this discursive guerrilla warfare, humorous political stunts show the potential of a different future. A single humorous political stunt is unlikely to achieve much, but as part of bigger campaigns and movements stunts provide attention-grabbing dissenting voices that speak from a different position than conventional forms of protest.

In addition to their power breaking potential, some humorous political stunts are also oriented towards dialogue facilitation, although they are far from Habermas' ideal speech situation which is based on logic and reason. Activists who find it unproblematic to remain dignified and calm are probably better off with non-humorous forms of communication if the dialogue element of nonviolent action is what counts most for them. However, if the alternative to a humorous political stunt is displaying anger and smashing windows, even the most provocative humorous political stunt is more dialogue oriented. Although the target might not experience it as dialogue oriented, other audiences are more likely to see a smart provocateur with a message rather than frustration out of control. In most nonviolent actions there is a built-in tension between the dialogue-facilitating and the power-breaking elements. Dialogue without power breaking is unlikely to move the powerful to change that matters. On the other hand, power breaking without dialogue becomes a way of polarising political differences and cementing established points of view rather than searching for ways to create change together in the Gandhian spirit of holding on to one's truth while approaching Truth.

Corrective and absurd humorous political stunts also contribute to the utopian enactment element of the nonviolent action when they display a tolerance for diversity or temporarily enact alternative courses of action for powerful institutions. At one level all the humorous political stunts are contributing to the normative regulation aspect of a nonviolent action since they question the discourse that violence is normal. On another level, because they are only a temporary power breaking, they are very far from Gandhi's idea of the constructive programme on which Vinthagen based this notion.

535

Conclusion

Introduction

This conclusion sums up the thesis' major findings as well as the theoretical implications for research on humour and nonviolence. In addition, I will briefly discuss the practical implications the findings might have for social movements working for peace and social justice.

Humour, power and nonviolent resistance

Nonviolent resistance has been practised for centuries and studied within academia for decades, but understandings of the dynamics of nonviolent action are still rudimentary. Since nonviolence has been neglected and violent resistance glorified to such a degree, there is much history to recover and contemporary practice to document in order to provide reliable analysis of what impact nonviolent action can have on relations of power. When it comes to studying the use of humorous methods as part of a nonviolent campaign, hardly any research has been done previously.

In humour research it has long been debated if humour can be a form of resistance, or if it is merely a vent for frustration. However, framing humour's subversive potential as a question of either/or is a simplification of complex processes. Some political humour is probably meaningless in the context of struggles for social and political change. Nevertheless, jumping straight from this to the conclusion that humour cannot make a difference or even that it is counterproductive seems rather premature. Authors such as Foucault, Scott and Bayat have investigated the subtle workings of power and resistance in ways that take into consideration that neither power nor resistance can be considered one dimensional. Humour researchers who are sceptical about humour's ability to play a role in resistance do not appear to take these authors' work on power into consideration. Instead they speak generally about resistance as if it is something that is either openly declared and will lead to violent revolution, or totally absent. This study demonstrates why such an approach is inadequate. In order to investigate how humour can sometimes be resistance it is necessary to use a more sophisticated language on what humour is as well as a nuanced power theory which can reflect the dynamic interaction between all the actors involved.

Although there has been little systematic inquiry into the relationship between humour and nonviolence, what has been done shows that the interesting question is not if a single instance of humour can change relations, which is of course unreasonable to expect, but rather

> *What role* can humour play in facilitating resistance to dominant discourses and powerful institutions and people?

This has been the guiding question for my research.

Both in academic research and everyday language it is common to speak about humour as if it is one "thing", thereby allowing all humour to be judged and evaluated from the same perspective. This is probably also a reason why a number of humour scholars have insisted that humour cannot have an effect on resistance. Based on one type of data (often jokes) they make overly broad generalisations about all humour. The only thing all humour has in common is that it includes an incongruity that causes at least part of the audience to be amused. Apart from this very basic characteristic, humour is extremely diverse. Humour is a way of communicating and is not inherently positive or negative. Just like any other form of communication it can be used to make people happy or to cause them intended or unintended harm. Some humour will reinforce the status quo, whereas other humour encourages rebellion, and some may even have mixed effects.

537

Humour can be expressed through a wide range of techniques such as irony, exaggeration, parody and impersonations through different media including jokes, cartoons, theatre, music and graffiti. This complexity means that participants in social movements discussing the pros and cons of humour in general terms might actually be discussing very different things without realising it. If they want to discuss if humour can be used as an appropriate method it is probably wiser to talk about the possible benefits and potential risks of a specific action. Likewise, academics interested in understanding humour must also specify exactly what type of humour in what context they are interested in.

Another problem with both academic and everyday language is labelling the opposite of humour "serious". This implicitly assumes that something cannot be humorous and serious at the same time. Since a lot of political humour is both, it is better to call the opposite of humour "rational" or "non-humorous". This is not to say that those who use humour are not rational, but that their method of communication instead is based on contradictions and ambiguity which distort usual forms of rational communication.

Humorous political stunts and the power of nonviolence

In order to investigate what role humour can play in facilitating resistance to dominant discourses I have focused on one particular form of humorous action and performance that I call *humorous political stunts*. I chose the term "stunt" because it is not so clearly associated with one particular activist or academic tradition as other possibilities such as "action", "hoax", "performance" or "prank". I have defined a humorous political stunt as a performance/action carried out in public which attempts to undermine a dominant discourse. It is either so confrontational that it cannot be ignored or involves a deception that blurs the line between performers and audiences. It includes or comments on a political incongruity in a way that is perceived as amusing by at least some people who did not initiate it.

However, even within this particular form of humorous political activism there is a huge diversity in the way it is practised. I have identified five distinct ways for those who perform humorous political stunts to position themselves in relation to dominant discourses and people in positions of power.

Supportive stunts use irony, parody and exaggeration to disguise their critique. Instead of being openly critical, they pretend that they support and celebrate their target or want to protect it from harm. The targets will know that they are being watched, and the audiences are presented with an image of the target's vulnerable sides.

Corrective stunts aim to transcend the inequality in power by presenting an alternative version of "the truth". They temporarily "steal" the identity of the institutions and companies they are aiming to unmask. From this disguise, they present a more honest representation of who the target really is. The correction can for instance be an exaggeration that exposes greed and selfishness, or it might just be the facts in language that everyone can understand. The Yes Men have made this type of "identity correction" an art form under the slogan "sometimes it takes a lie to expose the truth"[849], but many others have used similar tactics.

Naïve stunts bring the unequal relations of power to everyone's attention by tackling the opponent from behind an apparent naiveté. What is actually critique is camouflaged as coincidences or a normal activity. While the supportive and corrective stunts often exaggerate and overemphasise what those in positions of

---

[849] Front cover of Bichlbaum and Bonanno, "The Yes Men Fix the World."

539

power say, people who carry out naive stunts pretend that they are not aware that they have challenged any power.

Absurd stunts rely on total silliness and absurdity. From this position, the activists are ridiculing everything and everyone claiming to know the one and only truth – be it governments, institutions, or people within their own movement who take themselves a bit too seriously. The absurd action shares some similarities with the naive regarding the apparent naiveté of the activists, but whereas the participants in the naive stunt appear not to understand, the absurd pranksters refuse to acknowledge that any truth exists.

Provocative stunts do not pretend anything like the four other strategies. They are an openly declared challenge to claims to status and power. They include an element that part of the audience considers amusing, for instance when they manage to expose shortcomings and present the "almighty" as humans with flaws. The pranksters do not deny the unequal relations of power, as in absurd stunts, or present any alternatives like the supportive or corrective actions do: they simply appear not to care about the consequences of their actions.

This typology of humorous political stunts takes some of the complexity of the phenomenon into consideration. What happens in an absurd stunt is so different from what happens in the supportive and corrective that one cannot evaluate and analyse them as if they are the same. They have the incongruity in common, but when it comes to how they temporarily destabilise relations of power they are very different – both in the way they position themselves in relation to dominant discourses and the responses they generate. People exposed to political humour react in many different ways, of course, depending on whether they are passive bystanders, an audience getting involved, police ordered out to intervene or the target of ridicule and humiliation.

In addition, reactions depend on the context, the message and the medium used.

Another method to approach the diversity of humorous political stunts I have developed is to apply the *theatre metaphor*. Since all political activity can be understood as a form of theatre where the actors enact a drama, the metaphor can be a way to catch other elements of the diversity. Analysing the stunts from the perspective of the *stage, actors, audiences* and *timing* can provide insight for both activists and academics. For researchers it is a way of analysing the relational and dynamic aspects of the stunts. One can ask who initiates the stunts and who involuntarily becomes an actor in the play of politics? Where do the stunts take place, and who are the audiences? How do the different audiences respond, and how is the whole affair timed? For academics, these questions might provide new insights, but the four elements can also be a way for activists to consider how to make a humorous political stunt more effective. If an action has not had the desired effect, changing some elements might in-crease the pressure on governments, appeal more to media or challenge dominant discourses more effectively. If it is difficult to get close to certain main actors like prime ministers, maybe the effect can increase if one attempts to capture another stage or considers changing the timing.

Vinthagen's theory of nonviolent action has identified four central dimensions which he has termed dialogue facilitation, power breaking, utopian enactment and normative regulation. Looking at humorous political stunts through this framework reveals some of the ways that humour can contribute to the goal of the nonviolent action, but also indicates situations where humour might be counterproductive.

When it comes to Vinthagen's first dimension of dialogue facili-tation, humorous political stunts are more dialogue oriented than resistance that involves smashing windows and setting cars on fire, at least when looking from the tradition of nonviolence and considering other audiences than the target. On the other hand, one can imagine forms of communication that are more dialogue oriented than a humorous political stunt, since the ambiguity of humour can distort communication when it is not clear what the message is or who is behind it. In addition, ridicule might hurt in a way that hinders dialogue, and campaigns that rely on ambiguity, double meanings, and incongruity might be perceived as unpredictable. Targeted governments and companies might not experience it as worthwhile to have a rational dialogue. Although humour can contribute to presenting a friendly face to outsiders, target companies and institutions might become more cautious in their attempt to engage in a dialogue with humorous activists.

If one is interested in humorous political stunts' ability to challenge relations of power, Vinthagen's second dimension of a nonviolent action, power breaking, is perhaps the most interesting. A single humorous political stunt can usually not be expected to have more than a temporary and symbolic effect, but all resistance has to start from somewhere. A humorous strategy can be built around a series of stunts. If one agrees with Foucault and believes control of discourses to be one of the most important aspects of domination in a society, then it also follows that attacks on the core of these discourses are an important method of resistance. I have introduced the term *discursive guerrilla warfare* to indicate how humorous political stunts can be "hit and run" attacks on such dominant discourses. Many of the stunts are not just suggesting small adjustments or moderate reform of the current world order, but have attacked essential aspects of dominant discourses like neo-liberalism, consumerism and militarism.

The naïve and absurd stunts have demonstrated a particular ability to contribute to the part of a nonviolent action expressing the third and fourth dimension of Vinthagen's theory, the utopian enactment and normative regulation. The naïve and absurd Santas, clowns and elves speak to people's imagination, popular myths and folklore as well as childhood memories. Although this is also temporary, these figures are one way of illustrating what a different world order valuing spontaneity, creativity and imagination could look like.

The case studies about Ofog and KMV

The ways researchers gather information influence the type of answers they can provide. No knowledge is neutral and research that does not explicitly attempt to speak from the perspective of those in subordinate positions will almost inevitably benefit most those with status and privilege and further cement established relations of power. My research project was explicitly developed to investigate humour from the perspective of nonviolent activists in order to see how humour can be used as part of a struggle for a more just and peaceful world. Inspired by the values behind participatory action research and feminist standpoint theory I developed a case study strategy to investigate two detailed case studies using a triangulation of methods.

Ofog is a Swedish anti-militarist network working against Swedish arms production and the militarisation of society. Together with the network I investigated how humour can be used as part of a strategy to challenge militarism. I used participant observation, carried out interviews and initiated workshops to investigate humour together with Ofog. This case study primarily investigates what meaning humour has for the activists who engage in it and how they perceive its effect. It also documents some of the "messy" processes of day to day activism and how difficult it can be to make priorities about what activity to pursue next. The research did not generate as much change over time as I had anticipated. Although I never imagined predicting the course of events, I had expected to witness an increase in the use of humour, an even more reflexive attitude and strategic planning that included more humour. Although this lack of development probably says more about me than about other participants in Ofog, it is also a testimony to what I have called the *persistence of logical argument.* Even within a network that is very interested in using humour and where activists have an open mind when it comes to experimenting with new types of actions, there is still a tendency to believe that rational discourse will be more effective.

2½ years of participant observation and interviews with people in Ofog about events that took place before I became involved made it possible to document Ofog's extensive use of humour. Four out of the five different types of humorous political stunts have been carried out by Ofog activists. Radical clowning, a particular version of the absurd stunt where people dress in a mixture of military uniforms and clowning attributes, was one of the forms of humour that had been used most frequently within the network. For activists in Ofog, it is considered a way to challenge and ridicule police and military in uniforms. This form of activism is found in many parts of the western world where it is part of the traditions of tactical carnival and playful protest.

On several occasions Ofog has engaged in supportive and corrective stunts. A supportive stunt that has become part of Ofog's humorous baggage was when people from the network invented the company Reality AB, that was going to "help" NATO during an exercise in the north of Sweden by recruiting civilians to play dead and traumatised victims of "collateral damage". The one provocative stunt that Ofog has carried out was when a whole tank was painted pink as part of a campaign to mark out the places where war starts.

I analysed humour's role in facilitating resistance from four different perspectives. First of all, humour is perceived as a good way to facilitate outreach to media and passers-by. One person I interviewed suggested that because understanding humour requires an intellectual detour, it reaches them at a different level. Since activists have the impression that many people meet conventional non-humorous protest with a preformed opinion about what the activists are going to say and how they themselves are going to respond, it is difficult to reach them. The detour that is required to reconcile and grasp the incongruity creates a crack where you might be able to catch people off guard. However, when it comes to media the situation is not straightforward. Although many groups have successfully reached out to mass media through a humorous political stunt, Ofog has not had the same experience.

Secondly, many activists consider humour a good way to mobilise new activists, and several Ofog activists mentioned the network's use of humour as something they found attractive. However, to know more precisely how effective humour is for mobilisation would require a different study where one observes if an increase in the use of humour is followed by more people joining in. Alternatively it is possible to interview newcomers about their perceptions about what motivated them to become involved.

Thirdly, when it comes to facilitating a culture of resistance, it is possible to say something more conclusive. For many Ofog activists, clowning and other types of humour can be a personal liberation and a way to make activism more sustainable and prevent burn-out. Contrary to some perceptions, energy for activism is not a zero-sum game where time and energy spent on one thing automatically mean less time and energy for other activities. Instead some of the humorous actions are felt to create a good atmosphere and new energy within the network, which in turn can be used on non-humorous activities. The feeling of contributing to resistance might become self-reinforcing.

Fourth and finally, the data in the case study on Ofog reveal the activists' wishes and hopes about how humour will challenge relations of power. Since Ofog is working on such broad issues, it is not possible to point towards a "victory". It would be naïve to expect a network of volunteers like Ofog to dismantle Swedish arms production or export with a few humorous political stunts. Nevertheless, even if this is a small network, one should

545

not underestimate the power of dissenting voices. All resistance to dominant discourses has to start from somewhere, and Ofog activists can be considered combatants in the discursive guerrilla war that attempts to undermine the dominant discourse of militarism in Sweden. However, one should be careful not to jump from this conclusion to seeing success when it is not justified. Some humorous political stunts are probably not very effective if they do not reach any audiences, or if the messages are not communicated clearly because of lack of skills or unforeseen circumstances.

Investigating the meaning of humour also revealed that the distinction between humour and other types of creative activism might make sense from an analytical perspective, but it does not reflect the lived experience of all political activists. Interviewing people about "humour" provided many examples of creative activism that did not necessarily include the appropriate incongruity which is central to the definition of humour. Likewise, the idea that there would be a clear distinction between "internal" humour and humour which was directed outwards to communicate with media, the general public, potential new activists as well as the target of an action also turned out to be naïve. Although some humour was clearly internal or directed outwards, the case study of Ofog also provided examples of humour which was visible to outsiders, but nevertheless appeared mainly to be for the benefit of the activists themselves.

Kampanjen Mot Verneplikt (KMV) was a Scandinavian campaign active in the 1980's in support of total resisters who refused both military and substitute service. This case study focused on the campaign's work in Norway where the primary goal was to change the law that sent the total resisters to prison for 16 months without calling it a punishment. I found that KMV pursued four different strategies in this work. Firstly, the campaign developed a strategy of creating a spectacle around the court hearings and imprisonments of the total resisters and selective objectors. Part of the spectacle was two types of humorous political stunts – a provocative stunt where the activists jumped the prison walls, not to escape, but as a jail-in where they demanded that either their friend be released, or that they go to prison with him since they shared his opinions. KMV activists were also behind a supportive stunt where one activist showed up in court as the prosecutor when another activist was having his court hearing that would send him to jail for total resistance. In spite of the exaggerations, the parody of the prosecutor was so convincing that the judge did not notice anything wrong, something which subsequently generated much media attention.

KMV's other strategy was to use the legal system against the Norwegian state. One activist filed a complaint with the European Commission of Human Rights at the Council of Europe, and two others made a court case against the Norwegian state for violating the constitution when they were sent to prison without a proper trial. KMV participants lost both these cases, but nevertheless they generated so much attention that in 1989 the civil servants in the department of justice proposed a law change in accordance with what KMV found acceptable. In 1985 there had been no interest among the parliamentarians in the fate of total resisters, but a few years later the department of justice's proposed change of the relevant paragraphs was accepted unanimously by the parliament.

Thirdly, KMV also engaged in solidarity activities with other total resisters and as a fourth strategy some individuals were very active in writing letters to the editor and other lobbying activities. However, in this particular case these last two strategies do not seem to have had much effect on the law change although they meant a lot to some individuals.

The case study of KMV showed in detail how various humorous and non-humorous aspects of a campaign can complement each other. Humour has the potential to play an important role within a campaign that combines humorous as well as non-humorous

547

elements. Here it was the ability to generate attention from media and interest from potential new total resisters that seemed to be decisive. Although the department of justice did not keep track of the numbers of total resisters, KMV's list of contacts grew and an increasing number of young men decided to become total resisters during the 1980's.

When I was looking for cases that would be rich in information about humour it was not a sampling criterion that the political activists in the case studies were concerned about the same or similar themes. As it turned out, both Ofog and KMV are/were radical anti-militarists organised like networks that work as marginalised groups within a democratic setting. Although it is not possible to make strong conclusions based on just two case studies, it is striking that both of these marginal groups organised in network structures found it useful to use humour. It might be worth exploring further if small and marginalised organisations see humour as an opportunity to gain attention, while larger organisations do not see the need or fear the risks associated with humour. Even if the persistence of logical argument could be found in Ofog, it might be even more pronounced in formal organisations where all activities need to be approved at the top of the organisation.

In spite of the similarities, there are also major differences between Ofog and KMV. An obvious one is the separation in time, so while Ofog is still an active network, KMV has dissolved. However, the most significant difference is that KMV worked on a campaign with one particular aim in mind, while Ofog's focus is much broader. It might seem like an obvious finding, but the two case studies confirm that it appears to be easier for a group that keeps a narrow focus to get direct results. KMV did have a good case because of the obvious contradiction in sending someone to prison for 16 months without calling it a punishment, but it probably helped that they remained focused on this particular issue.

The risks and limitations with humorous political stunts

The case studies have shown that using humorous political stunts has many potential benefits for social movements that aim at facilitating outreach and mobilisation, a culture of resistance and challenging established relations of power. However, this should not make activists and academics blind to the risks and limitations. Using humour includes a risk of not being taken seriously and a risk of the humour becoming too internal. Trying to combine the humorous and the non-humorous might also become a challenge.

Many of the humorous political stunts included here were extremely successful in generating media attention. However, Ofog has not had the same experience so one should not assume that humorous political stunts are a guaranteed path to the front pages. Since the stunts that become most known are often spread via mass media, there is an inevitable selection bias in the stunts included here. We know little about all the attempts made that never reach the media because of issues like unfortunate timing, bad planning or journalists' hesitations to cover it. To uncover all the attempts that never succeeded would require ethnographic research comparable to what I did with Ofog.

All social movements with political messages face the problem that some people do not understand their message, but the risk seems to increase when humour is involved. The Yes Men tried on many occasions to make absurd statements without getting any response. Irony in particular can be a tricky technique since it based on saying one thing, but meaning something entirely different. Although other humorous techniques as well as rational communication sometimes result in confusion or bewilderment, ironic statements risk being mistaken for the real opinion. On some occasions when people in Ofog were experimenting with irony to confront militarism, their statements were understood literally as support for arms manufacturers and NATO. In such situations it is not unusual to blame the audiences for being stupid, but as Hutcheon has written, irony requires a discursive community which had not been created on these occasions and might be more difficult to establish than we think. Activists engaging in ironic communication must be careful not to create ironic distance and hierarchies between those who "get it" and those who do not.

Humorous political stunts provide an opportunity for social movements to be creative in search of new ways to challenge dominant discourses. Many people might find an outlet for their creativity and talents that otherwise has little value among fellow activists. However, this constant changing and shifting is demanding. If the stunts are not re-invented, they lose their energy, so a certain stunt can only be repeated a limited number of times in a certain context. In addition, humorous political stunts predominantly seem to be carried out by small tightly knit groups who spend a lot of time preparing their stunts. Some people might consider this a potential problem that results in elitism, since not everyone can afford to spend so much time on activism. Although it has not been a problem in my case studies, there is also a potential trap in humour becoming an end in itself. Because humour generates good feelings for the activists themselves they need to evaluate if humour is a self-indulgence that is no longer considered one potential method in a struggle, but creates an ironic distance to the subject.

Using humour, and especially ridicule, can also be discussed from an ethical perspective. What is experienced as humour by the initiators and part of the audience might look entirely different to the butt of the ridicule. Gantar found an epistemological dead end regarding this question and concluded that it is impossible to judge humour from an ethical perspective. Nevertheless, political activists are likely to be judged from this perspective anyway and ought to take it into consideration when planning.

I have suggested that if one insists on judging humorous political stunts along ethical lines, an important place to start is the position of those who use humour and ridicule. There ought to be a major difference between ridicule initiated by those in positions of power that kick down, and ridicule initiated by marginalised political activists kicking upwards.

However, although this can be a good starting point for an ethical judgement, two examples from the case studies illustrate some of the dilemmas that will inevitably arise. Although Ofog and KMV wanted to challenge the discourse of militarism and those on top of the hierarchies, the individuals they encountered did not always feel very powerful. On one occasion a group of openly homosexual soldiers from the Swedish armed forces participated in the Pride Parade in Stockholm. Next to them a group of Ofog activists walked with speech bubbles made out of cardboard with statements that was supposed to look as if they were the soldiers' statements. Although the text was related to war, the death of civilians, and Sweden's military presence in Afghanistan the individual soldiers experienced it as an attack on their sexuality since it took place during the parade.

Likewise, the judge in the case where KMV turned up with a fake prosecutor was quoted in a newspaper for saying "I was shocked when I heard what had happened" and he made his superior file a report to the police.[850] He did not explicitly say that he felt abused, but it is not unreasonable to assume that at least some people would have felt that way under similar circumstances. KMV was targeting the court system, not an individual, in order to expose the system as a farce. Nevertheless this judge, just as the soldiers in the Pride Parade, became the direct victim, raising the question of whether Ofog and KMV behaved unethi-

---

[850] Haugstad, "Her Blir Dommeren Lurt Av Falsk Aktor."

cally. In both cases it was people in subordinate positions who ridiculed those they saw as representatives of powerful institutions – the court system and the military. Nevertheless, those who initiate a stunt cannot dictate the emotional responses of others.

Further research in the field

As mentioned in the introduction, this study has generated more questions than answers, something which is often the case when researching an area where little or nothing was known previously. Much research about humour's role in nonviolent resistance remains to be done. For starters, it would be interesting to see if the typology of humorous political stunts applies worldwide, namely whether it is possible to classify examples from other cultures according to the same five types that I have used here. And is the use of this type of humorous political activism really spreading globally and increasing in frequency as some authors have indicated? A related task is to continue the theoretical exploration of the borders of humorous political stunts.

Equally interesting would be more research on the reactions to humorous political stunts. I have focused on the meaning humour has for the activists, but other studies could do more to uncover what others think about it. A whole range of thrilling questions remain unanswered: Is it really true that humorous political stunts are better at getting media attention, or is this assumption a reflection of a selection bias when one is forced to analyse stunts already described in the literature or known from mass media? What can be observed about a target's reaction when they are confronted with a humorous political stunt, and what do they themselves think about it? Do they experience it as dialogue oriented, or does the ambiguity of humour distort the communication? How do other audiences, such as potential new activists and the general public, respond? Can the detour demanded by humour really find or create cracks and reach people at a deeper level? Does the ambiguity of humour make it easier to communicate complex messages, or does humour increase the risk of side-tracking so the focus ends up on the method and the spectacle rather than the message that the activists want to communicate?

In order to investigate social movements' humorous political stunts, it is a requirement that the groups' histories are documented. For both my case studies it was necessary to document their activities in order to provide context for their use of humour. The world over, there are numerous small networks whose histories need to be written.

The main data for this research was from two Scandinavian case studies, but a few of the other examples as well as earlier research has documented that humour can play an important role also under authoritarian circumstances, for instance in reducing fear. Researchers with access to this type of data can bring important insights to the study of nonviolent resistance that can also have practical implications.

Theoretically my research has relied primarily on the theory of nonviolent action. It has only touched the surface when it comes to perspectives from performance studies and social movement theories. There are whole bodies of literature with insights about street performance and emotions within social movements that might be interesting for future studies.[851]

One finding from the study was that from the perspective of activists, the distinction between humour and other types of creative and spectacular activism appears rather artificial. Research on the effect of all kinds of creative activism could

---

[851] A starting point for such an inquiry could be to look at humorous political stunts from the perspective of Richard Schechner's holistic view on play, performance, ritual and politics presented in: Richard Schechner, *The Future of Ritual: Writings on Culture and Performance* (London: Routledge, 1993).

investigate differences between humorous activism and other types of creative activism.

Finally there is the question of the choice of methodology for researching nonviolence and social movements. Researchers with access to money and research time have a tremendous responsibility to use such resources wisely. It is important to choose topics and questions that are not just interesting for the researcher herself and will benefit her career, but also make a difference for people struggling for peace and justice. Much inspiration can be drawn from participatory action research and intervention research for activists and academics aiming at bridging the gap between these two worlds. There is a huge potential for systematic comparative "experiments" about nonviolence in general and humorous political stunts in particular. One line of experiments would be to compare the consequences of using humorous and non-humorous methods about the same political issue. Another type of intervention/action research would be to work together with activists in order to make "bigger" humorous political stunts in terms of frequency and number of participants. My research has pointed out some of the potential with humorous political stunts, but it has documented only the tip of the iceberg of what is achievable through this type of action.

References

Ackerman, Peter, and Jack DuVall. *A Force More Powerful: A Century of Nonviolent Conflict*. New York: St. Martin's Press, 2000.

Ackerman, Peter, and Christopher Kruegler. Strategic Nonviolent Conflict: The Dynamics of People Power in the Twentieth Century. Westport, CT: Praeger, 1994.

Aftenposten. "Aksjon På Fengselsmurer." [Action at prison walls] *Aftenposten*, May 4 1987.

Aftenposten. "Falsk Aktor Og Impliserte Politianmeldt." [False prosecutor and implicated reported to the police] *Aftenposten*, September 21 1983, 4.

Aftenposten. "Fengsel for Militærnektere Er Ikke Straff." [Prison for conscientious objectors is not punishment] *Aftenposten*, April 28 1982.

Aftenposten. "Godtatt Som Samvittighetsfange." [Accepted as prisoner of conscience] *Aftenposten*, February 12 1986.

Aftenposten. "Vernepliktsnektere Til Sak Mot Staten." [Draft refusers file charges aginst the State] *Aftenposten*, January 9 1982.

Ajangiz, Rafael. "The European Farewell to Conscription?". In *The Comparative Study of Conscription in the Armed Forces*, edited by Lars Mjøset and Stephen van Holde, 307-33: Emerald Group Publishing, 2002.

Alfsen, Terje. "Report." Report to Alfsen's superior, September 20 1983.

Andersen, Bo Nyborg, and Terje Bjørnland. "Situationsbestemt Militærbekting." [Selective conscientious objection] *Samvittighetsfanger i Norge*, not dated 1983.

Anonymous. "Burmese Humour." Accessed March 22 2011 from http://www.freezarganar.org/Burmese-humour.asp.

Anonymous. *C.I.R.C.A G8 Road Blockade* youtube.com, 2005. Accessed October 27 2013 from http://www.youtube.com/watch?v=MX0aQU9x0Z4

Anonymous. *Circa Recruitment Video* youtube.com, not dated. Accessed October 27 2013 from http://www.youtube.com/watch?v=t_jS3Wh8g6s

Anonymous. *Clandestine Insurgent Rebel Clown Army in Rostock 2007.* youtube.com, 2007. Accessed October 27 2013 from http://www.youtube.com/watch?v=3h1CH0Vchv8

Anonymous. *The Clown Army, Christiania 2005* youtube.com, 2005. Accessed October 27 2013 from http://www.youtube.com/watch?v=l5NmhJLAO1w

Anonymous. *Clownplay with Policeman @ G8* youtube.com, 2005. Accessed October 27 2013 from http://www.youtube.com/watch?v=YrwxqOTI0zI

Anonymous. *G20 Toronto Protests Send in the Clowns* youtube.com, not dated. Accessed October 27 2013 from http://www.youtube.com/watch?v=EMSJiUpeWso

Anonymous. *Glasgow Section of Clandestine Insurgent Rebel Clown Army* youtube.com, not dated. Accessed October 27 2013 from http://www.youtube.com/watch?v=xqgcBblriBQ

Anonymous. *Rebel Clown Army at Faslane 08/07/2012* youtube.com, 2012. Accessed October 27 2013 from http://www.youtube.com/watch?v=aB7AMrnKFbM

Anonymous. *Rebel Clown Army Cologne* youtube.com, not dated. Accessed October 27 2013 from http://www.youtube.com/watch?v=iK9ZPVL4xU8

Anonymous. *You Can Not Give an Anarchist Clown Directions (Especially While Wearing Riot Gear)* youtube.com, 2013. Accessed October 27 2013 from http://www.youtube.com/watch?v=p5Geje_W6sQ

Arbeiderbladet. "Brant Opp Vernepliktboka." [Burned Conscription Book] *Arbeiderbladet*, October 25 1986.

Bakhtin, M. M. *Rabelais and His World*. Translated by Helene Iswolsky. Bloomington, IN: Indiana University Press, 1984 [1965].

Bakken, Erling. "Lokal Militærnekter "Annonserer" Egen Rettssak: - Enestående Å Måtte Sone for Overbevisning." [Local conscientious objector "announce" his own case: -Unique to serve time for conscience] *Sarpsborg Arbeiderblad*, April 6 1982.

Banksy. *Wall and Piece*. London: Century, 2006.

Barash, David P. *Approaches to Peace: A Reader in Peace Studies*. 2nd ed. New York: Oxford University Press, 2010.

Barker, Colin. "The Making of Solidarity at the Lenin Shipyard in Gdansk." Chap. 10 In *Passionate Politics: Emotions and Social Movements*, edited by Jeff Goodwin, James M. Jasper and Francesca Polletta, 175-94. Chicago: University of Chicago Press, 2001.

Basu, Sammy. "Dialogic Ethics and the Virtue of Humor." *Journal of Political Philosophy* 7, no. 4 (1999): 378-403.

Bayat, Asef. *Life as Politics: How Ordinary People Change the Middle East*. Stanford, CA: Stanford University Press, 2010.

Becker, Howard S. "The Epistemology of Qualitative Research." Chap. 13 In *Contemporary Field Research: Perspectives and Formulations*, edited by Robert M. Emerson, 317-30. Prospect Heights, IL: Waveland Press, 2001.

Belarusian Human Rights House. "Two Belarusians Detained on Charges of "Teddy Bear Drop"." *humanrightshouse.org*, July 23 2012. Accessed August 13, 2012 from http://humanrightshouse.org/Articles/18403.html

Benton, Gregor. "The Origins of the Political Joke." Chap. 2 In *Humour in Society: Resistance and Control*, edited by Chris Powell and George E. C. Paton, 33-55. New York: St. Martin's Press, 1988.

Berg, Bjørnar. "Samvittighetsfanger I Norge." [prisoners of conscience in Norway?] *Dagbladet*, November 26 1996, 36.

Berger, Arthur Asa. *An Anatomy of Humor*. New Brunswick, NJ: Transaction, 1993.

Berger, Arthur Asa. *Blind Men and Elephants: Perspectives on Humor*. New Brunswick, NJ: Transaction, 1995.

Berger, Peter L. Redeeming Laughter: The Comic Dimension of Human Experience. New York: Walter de Gruyter, 1997.

Berlingske Tidende. "Bedrevidende Julenisser." [Know-all Santas] *Berlingske Tidende*, December 24 1974, 6.

Bertelsen, Annebrit. "Fred Ove Reksten Fri Igjen." [Fred Ove Reksten free again] *Klassekampen*, July 14 1983.

Bibby, Paul. "Chaser Comics Say APEC Stunt Went Too Far." *The Age (Melbourne)*, September 12 2007. Accessed March 30 2011 from http://www.theage.com.au/news/tv--radio/chaser-comics-say-apec-stunt-went-too-far/2007/09/11/1189276725655.html

Bichlbaum, Andy, and Mike Bonanno. "The Yes Men Fix the World." Docudramafilms, 2009.

Bichlbaum, Andy, Mike Bonanno, and Bob Spunkmeyer. *The Yes Men: The True Story of the End of the World Trade Organization*. New York: Disinformation, 2004.

Billig, Michael. Laughter and Ridicule: Towards a Social Critique of Laughter. London: Sage, 2005.

Blee, Kathleen, and Amy McDowell. "Social Movement Audiences." *Sociological Forum* 27, no. 1 (2012): 1-20.

Bleiker, Roland. *Popular Dissent, Human Agency, and Global Politics*. Cambridge: Cambridge University Press, 2000.

Bogad, L. M. "Carnivals against Capital: Radical Clowning and the Global Justice Movement." *Social Identities* 16, no. 4 (2010): 537-57.

Bogad, L. M. Electoral Guerrilla Theatre: Radical Ridicule and Social Movements. New York: Routledge, 2005.

Bogad, L. M. "A Place for Protest: The Billionaires for Bush Interrupt the Hegemonologue." Chap. 14 In *Performance and Place*, edited by Leslie and Helen Paris Hill, 170-79. London: Palgrave Macmillan, 2006.

Bogad, L. M. "Tactical Carnival: Social Movements, Demonstrations, and Dialogical Performance." In *A Boal Companion: Dialogues on Theatre and Cultural Politics*, edited by Jan Cohen-Cruz and Mady Schutzman, 46-58. New York: Routledge, 2006.

Boulding, Elise. *Cultures of Peace: The Hidden Side of History*. 1st ed. Syracuse, NY: Syracuse University Press, 2000.

Boyd, Andrew, and Dave Oswald Mitchell. *Beautiful Trouble: A Toolbox for Revolution*. New York: OR Books, 2012.

Braithwaite, David. "Chaser Bust 'Proves Security Success'." *The Age (Melbourne)*, September 6 2007 Accessed September 3 2013 from http://www.theage.com.au/news/national/chaser-duo-held-over-apec-stunt/2007/09/06/1188783379922.html

Branagan, Marty. "The Last Laugh: Humour in Community Activism." *Community Development Journal* 42, no. 4 (2007): 470-81.

Breast Cancer Action. "Before You Buy Pink." Accessed September 12 2013 from http://thinkbeforeyoupink.org/?page_id=13.

Brissenden, Michael. "7:30 Report - Australian Broadcasting Corportion - Campaign Focuses on Rates Fallout." Sydney: Australian Broadcasting Corporation, November 8 2007.

Brown, Leslie, and Susan Strega, eds. *Research as Resistance: Critical, Indigenous and Anti-Oppressive Approaches*. Toronto: Canadian Scholars' Press, 2005.

Bruner, M. Lane. "Carnivalesque Protest and the Humorless State." *Text and Performance Quarterly* 25, no. 2 (2005): 136-55.

Burcharth, Martin. "Krampetrekning Før Valget." [Dying twitch before election] *Klassekampen*, October 30 2010, 26-27.

Carlbom, Mats. "Vitryssland Utvisar Sveriges Ambassadör." [Belarus expels Sweden's ambassador] *dn.se*, August 3 2012. Accessed August 4 2012 from http://www.dn.se/nyheter/sverige/vitryssland-utvisar-sveriges-ambassador

Carlsen, Jon Bang. "Dejlig Er Den Himmel Blå [Beautiful Is the Blue Sky]." 45 min: C&C productions Aps, 1975.

Carter, April. People Power and Political Change: Key Issues and Concepts. Abingdon, UK: Routledge, 2012.

Case, Charles E., and Cameron D. Lippard. "Humorous Assaults on Patriarchal Ideology." *Sociological Inquiry* 79, no. 2 (2009): 240-55.

Chambers, Robert. Participatory Workshops: A Sourcebook of 21 Sets of Ideas and Activities. London: Earthscan, 2002.

Chambers, Robert. *Revolutions in Development Inquiry*. London: Earthscan, 2008.

Charmaz, Kathy. "Grounded Theory." Chap. 15 In *Contemporary Field Research: Perspectives and Formulations*, edited by Robert M. Emerson, 335-52. Prospect Heights, IL: Waveland Press, 2001.

Chenoweth, Erica, and Maria J. Stephan. *Why Civil Resistance Works: The Strategic Logic of Nonviolent Conflict*. New York: Columbia University Press, 2011.

Chvasta, Marcyrose. "Anger, Irony, and Protest: Confronting the Issue of Efficacy, Again." *Text and Performance Quarterly* 26, no. 1 (2006): 5-16.

CIRCA. "Clandestine Insurgent Rebel Clown Army " Accessed August 2 2006 from http://www.clownarmy.org/.

Clark, Howard, ed. People Power: Unarmed Resistance and Global Solidarity. London: Pluto Press, 2009.

560

Clementsen, Conrad. "Anmeldelse." Letter from Conrad Clemetsen to Oslo politikammer, September 30 1983.

Cohen-Cruz, Jan, and Mady Schutzman. *A Boal Companion: Dialogues on Theatre and Cultural Politics*. New York: Routledge, 2006.

Condren, Conal. "Between Social Constraint and the Public Sphere: On Misreading Early-Modern Political Satire." *Contemporary Political Theory* 1 (2002): 79-101.

Condren, Conal. "Satire and Definition." *Humor: International Journal of Humor Research* 25, no. 4 (2012): 375-99.

Corrigall-Brown, Catherine. *Patterns of Protest: Trajectories of Participation in Social Movements*. Stanford, CA: Stanford University Press, 2012.

Coser, Rose Laub. "Laughter among Colleagues." Psychiatry: Journal of the Biology and the Pathology of Interpersonal Relations 23, no. 1 (1960): 81-95.

Council of Europe. "European Convention on Human Rights." 1950. Accessed October 2 2012 from http://www.echr.coe.int/NR/rdonlyres/D5CC24A7-DC13-4318-B457-5C9014916D7A/0/CONVENTION_ENG_WEB.pdf

Coy, Patrick G. "Shared Risks and Research Dilemmas on a Peace Brigades International Team in Sri Lanka." *Journal of Contemporary Ethnography* 30, no. 5 (2001): 575-606.

Crawshaw, Steve, and John Jackson. Small Acts of Resistance: How Courage, Tenacity, and Ingenuity Can Change the World. New York: Union Square Press, 2010.

Critchley, Simon. *On Humour*. London: Routledge, 2002.

Dagens Nyheter. "Ofog Svarar: "Självklart Är Pride Politiskt"." [Ofog responds "Of course Pride is political"] *dn.se*, July 25 2012. Accessed August 13 2012 from http://www.dn.se/insidan/insidan-hem/ofog-svarar-sjalvklart-ar-pride-politiskt

Davies, Christie. "Humour and Protest: Jokes under Communism." *International Review of Social History* 52, no. S15 (2007): 291-305.

Davies, Christie. *Jokes and Their Relation to Society*. Berlin: Mouton de Gruyter, 1998.

Davis, Murray S. *What's So Funny?: The Comic Conception of Culture and Society*. Chigaco: University of Chicago Press, 1993.

Day, Amber. Satire and Dissent: Interventions in Contemporary Political Debate. Bloomington, IN: Indiana University Press, 2011.

Debord, Guy. *Society of the Spectacle*. Detroit: Black & Red, 1970.

Dentith, Simon. *Bakhtinian Thought: An Introductory Reader*. London: Routledge, 1995.

Diani, Mario. "Networks and Participation." Chap. 15 In *The Blackwell Companion to Social Movements*, edited by David A. Snow, Sarah Anne Soule and Hanspeter Kriesi, 339-59. Malden, MA: Blackwell Pub., 2004.

Dickins, Jim. "APEC Security to Cost $24m a Day " *http://www.news.com.au*, June 3 2007. Accessed September 3 2013 from http://www.news.com.au/national/apec-security-to-cost-24m-a-day/story-e6frfkvr-1111113665331

Divinski, Randy, Amy Hubbard, J. Richard Kendrick, and Jane Noll. "Social Change as Applied Social Science." *Peace & Change* 19, no. 1 (1994): 3-24.

Dowler, Lorraine. "The Four Square Laundry: Participant Observation in a War Zone." *Geographical Review* 91, no. 1/2 (2001): 414-22.

Downe, Pamela J. "Laughing When It Hurts: Humor and Violence in the Lives of Costa Rican Prostitutes." *Women's Studies International Forum* 22, no. 1 (1999): 63-78.

4444444444

Downton, James V., and Paul Ernest Wehr. *The Persistent Activist: How Peace Commitment Develops and Survives*. Boulder, CO: Westview Press, 1997.

Dudden, Arthur Power. "The Record of Political Humor." *American Quarterly* 37, no. 1 (1985): 50-70.

Dunbar, Norah E. Banas John A. Rodriguez DarielaLiu Shr-JieAbra Gordon. "Humor Use in Power-Differentiated Interactions." *Humor: International Journal of Humor Research* 25, no. 4 (2012): 469-89.

Duncombe, Stephen. Dream: Re-Imagining Progressive Politics in an Age of Fantasy. New York: New Press, 2007.

Duree, Ashley. "Greed at the New York Stock Exchange and the Levitation of the Pentagon: Early Protest Theatre by Abbie Hoffman and Jerry Rubin." *Voces Novae: Chapman University Historical Review* 1, no. 1 (2009): 51-72.

Ekdahl, Micael "Totte". "Cyniskt Angrepp I Prideparaden." [cynical attack in the pride parade] *etc.se*, August 11 2011. Accessed September 2 2011 from http://www.etc.se/nyhet/cyniskt-angrepp-i-prideparaden

Ekstra Bladet. "De Røde Julemænd " [The red Santas] *Ekstra Bladet*, December 24 1974, 2.

Emerson, Robert M. *Contemporary Field Research: Perspectives and Formulations*. 2nd ed. Prospect Heights, IL: Waveland Press, 2001.

Encyclopædia Britannica Online. "Irony." 2012.

Epstein, Steven. "A Queer Encounter: Sociology and the Study of Sexuality." *Sociological Theory* 12, no. 2 (1994): 188-202.

Eriksson, Kjell. "Regner Med Seier I Strasbourg." [Expect victory in Strasbourg] *Sarpsborg Arbeiderblad*, not dated 1985.

Euronews. "Swedish Activists Behind Belarus Teddy Bear Stunt." *euronews.com*, August 2 2012. Accessed August 7 2012 from http://www.euronews.com/2012/08/02/swedish-activists-behind-belarus-teddy-bear-stunt/

European Commission of Human Rights. "Decision of the Commission as to the Admissibility Application No. 10600/83 by Jørgen Johansen against Norway." In *10600/83*. Strasbourg, 1985.

Fletcher, John. "Of Minutemen and Rebel Clown Armies: Reconsidering Transformative Citizenship." *Text and Performance Quarterly* 29, no. 3 (2009): 222-38.

Flyghed, Janne. "Konsten Att Disciplinera En Opposition." *Retfærd, Nordisk Juridisk Tidskrift* 12, no. 2 (1989): 18-34.

FMV. "Europe's Largest Overland Test Area." Accessed January 2 2013 from http://www.vidseltestrange.com/europe%E2%80%99s-largest.

Fo, Dario. *Plays*. 2 vols London: Methuen Drama, 1997.

Forhandlinger. "Forhandlinger I Odelstinget Nr. 28. Sak Nr. 7.Innstilling Fra Justiskomiteen Om Lov Om Endringer I Lov Av 19. Mars 1965 Nr 3 Om Fritaking for Militærtjeneste Av Overbevisningsgrunner Og Militær Straffelov Av 22. Mai 1902 Nr 13. (Innst O. Nr. 75, Jf Ot.Prp. Nr 35)." June 11 1990.

Forhandlinger. "Forhandlinger I Stortinget Nr. 53. Sak Nr. 5. Innstilling Fra Justiskomiteen Vedrørende Forslag Fra Stortingsrepresentant Kjellbjørg Lunde Datert 5. August 1986 Om Utvidelse Av Adgangen Til Å Nekte Militærtjeneste På Et Alvorlig Overbevisningsgrunnlag (Innst. S. Nr. 17, Jf. Document Br. 8:1).", November 19 1986.

Forhandlinger. "Forhandlinger I Stortinget Nr. 192. Sak Nr. 3. Innstilling Fra Justiskomiteen Om Verneplikt. (Innst. S. Nr. 111, Jf. St. Meld. Nr. 70 for 1983-84)." March 12 1985.

Fortun, Gunnar. "'Overtok' Hele Rettssaken." ['Took over' the whole court] *Arbeiderbladet*, November 17 1983.

Fortun, Gunnar. "Rettsvesenet Kan Takke Seg Selv." [The judicial system has itself to blame] *Arbeiderbladet*, September 20 1983.

Fortun, Gunnar. "Rømning - Feil Vei." [Escaping - wrong way] *Arbeiderbladet*, June 24 1983.

Fortun, Gunnar. "Spilte Aktor." [Played prosecutor] *Arbeiderbladet*, September 19 1983, 1 and 11.

Foucault, Michel. "Disciplinary Power and Subjection." Chap. 11 In *Power*, edited by Steven Lukes, 229-52. New York: New York University Press, 1976.

Foucault, Michel. "The Subject and Power." *Critical Inquiry* 8, no. 4 (1982): 777-95.

Frampton, Caelie, Gary Kinsman, A.K. Thompson, and Kate Tilleczek, eds. *Sociology for Changing the World: Social Movements/Social Research*. Black Point: Fernwood, 2006.

Francis, Linda E. "Laughter, the Best Mediation: Humor as Emotion Management in Interaction." *Symbolic Interaction* 17, no. 2 (1994): 147-63.

Fraser, Mark W., and Maeda J. Galinsky. "Steps in Intervention Research: Designing and Developing Social Programs." *Research on Social Work Practice* 20, no. 5 (2010): 459-66.

Fuller, Abigail A. "Toward an Emancipatory Methodology for Peace Research." *Peace & Change* 17, no. 3 (1992): 286.

Försvarsmakten. "Om Försvarsmakten " Accessed July 13 2013 from http://www.forsvarsmakten.se/sv/Om-Forsvarsmakten/.

Galperina, Marina. "Why Russian Art Group Voina 'Dicked' a St. Petersburg Bridge." Accessed April 19 2011 from http://animalnewyork.com/2010/06/why-russian-art-group-voina-dicked-a-st-petersburg-bridge/.

Galtung, Johan. Peace by Peaceful Means: Peace and Conflict, Development and Civilization. London Sage Publications, 1996.

Galtung, Johan. *Transcend and Transform: An Introduction to Conflict Work*. London: Pluto Press in association with TRANSCEND, 2004.

Galtung, Johan. "Violence, Peace, and Peace Research." *Journal of Peace Research* 6, no. 3 (1969): 167-91.

Galtung, Johan, and Arne Næss. *Gandhis Politiske Etikk*. 3. utg. ed. Oslo: Pax, 1994.

Gandhi. *The Collected Works of Mahatma Gandhi*. 6th rev. ed. 100 vols New Delhi: Publications Division, Ministry of Information and Broadcasting, Govt. of India, 2000.

Gandhi, Mohandas Karamchand. *All Men Are Brothers*. 1st Indian ed. Ahmedabad: Navajivan Publishing House, 1960.

Gandhi, Mohandas Karamchand. *The Story of My Experiments with Truth*. Ahmedabad: Navajivan Publishing House, 1927.

Gantar, Jure. *The Pleasure of Fools: Essays in the Ethics of Laughter*. London: McGill-Queen's University Press, 2005.

Gianas, Tom, and Michael Moore. "The Awful Truth." UK Channel 4, April 25 1999.

Gilbert, Joanne R. *Performing Marginality: Humor, Gender, and Cultural Critique*. Detroit: Wayne State University Press, 2004.

Gilbey, Ryan. "Jokers to the Left, Jokers to the Right." http://www.theguardian.com, July 17 2009. Accessed September 6 2013 from http://www.theguardian.com/film/2009/jul/17/prank-movies-bruno-sacha-baron-cohen

Gilligan, Andrew. "Indonesians Admit Torture in TV 'Sting' " *Sunday Telegraph* January 17 1999. Accessed May 5 2012 from http://www.etan.org/et/1999/january/15-21/19abri.htm

Goffman, Erving. *The Presentation of Self in Everyday Life*. Garden City, NY: Doubleday, 1959.

Goodwin, Jeff, James M. Jasper, and Francesca Polletta, eds. *Passionate Politics: Emotions and Social Movements*. Chicago: University of Chicago Press, 2001.

Gravdal, Gunn. "Vernepliktsbøker Brent." [Conscription books burned] *Aftenposten*, December 2 1989.

Gray, Stephen. "The Mustache Brothers." *thanassiscambanis.com*, not dated. Accessed March 29 2011 from http://thanassiscambanis.com/sipa/?p=39

Grimelid, Stig. "Ex-Fange Tilbake." [Ex-prisoner back] *VG*, August 28 1984.

Gruner, Charles R. *The Game of Humor: A Comprehensive Theory of Why We Laugh*. New Brunswick, NJ: Transaction Publishers, 1997.

Gustafsson, Håkan, and Stellan Vinthagen. "Rättens Rörelser Och Rörelsernas Rätt [the Law's Movements and the Movements' Law]." *Tidsskrift for Rettsvitenskap* 123, no. 4-5 (2010): 637-93.

Halden Arbeiderblad. "De Brente Sine Vernepliktsbøker I Halden." [They burned their conscription books in Halden] *Halden Arbeiderblad*, not dated 1981.

Hariman, Robert. "Political Parody and Public Culture." *Quarterly Journal of Speech* 94, no. 3 (2008): 247-72.

Harold, Christine. *Ourspace: Resisting the Corporate Control of Culture*. Minneapolis, MN: University of Minnesota Press, 2007.

Harrebye, Silas. "Cracks: Creative Activism – Priming Pump for the Political Imagination or a New Compromising Form of Democratic Participation Balancing between Critique, Cooperation, and Cooptation on the Margins of the Repertoire of Contention?" PhD Thesis, Roskilde University, 2012.

Hart, Marjolein C. 't , and Dennis Bos, eds. *Humour and Social Protest*. Cambridge: University of Cambridge Press, 2007.

Hašek, Jaroslav. The Good Soldier Švejk and His Fortunes in the World War. New York: Crowell, 1974.

Hattenstone, Simon. "Joking Aside." *The Guardian*, July 1 2006. Accessed May 21 2012 from http://www.guardian.co.uk/stage/2006/jul/01/comedy.shopping

Haugerud, Angelique. *No Billionaire Left Behind: Satirical Activism in America*. Stanford, CA: Stanford University Press, 2013.

Haugerud, Angelique. "Satire and Dissent in the Age of Billionaires." *Social Research* 79, no. 1 (2012): 145-68.

Haugstad, Tormod. "Her Blir Dommeren Lurt Av Falsk Aktor." [Here the judge is fooled by fake prosecutor] *Dagbladet*, September 20 1983.

Helmy, Mohamed M., and S. Frerichs. "Stripping the Boss: The Powerful Role of Humor in the Egyptian Revolution 2011." *Integrative Psychological & Behavioral Science* 47, no. 4 (2013): 450-81.

Helsingeng, Terje. "Advokat Må I Fengsel." [Lawyer must go to prison] *VG*, September 12 1985.

Heltne, Olav. "Tiltalte Tok Bilde." [The accused took photo] *Aftenposten*, April 9 1987, 1 and 4.

Henriksen, Birger. "Svensker Teddy-Bombet Hviterussland " [Swede teddy-bombed Belarus] www.TV2.no, August 2 2012. Accessed August 3 2012 from http://www.tv2.no/nyheter/utenriks/svensker-teddybombet-hviterussland-3843398.html

Henzlert, John. "Soldater Kränkta under Prideparaden." [Soldiers offended during pride parade] http://www.svd.se, August 7 2011. Accessed August 7 2011 from http://www.svd.se/nyheter/inrikes/soldater-krankta-under-prideparaden_6373850.svd

Higgie, Rebecca. "Kynical Dogs and Cynical Masters: Contemporary Satire, Politics and Truth-Telling." *Humor: International Journal of Humor Research* 27, no. 2 (2014): 183-201.

Hiller, Harry H. "Humor and Hostility: A Neglected Aspect of Social Movement Analysis." *Qualitative Sociology* 6, no. 3 (1983): 255.

Hmielowski, Jay D., R. Lance Holbert, and Jayeon Lee. "Predicting the Consumption of Political TV Satire: Affinity for Political Humor, the Daily Show, and the Colbert Report." *Communication Monographs* 78, no. 1 (2011): 96-114.

Holmbäck, Christopher, and Urban Hamid. "Framtidens Svenska Militärer Rekryteras Tidigt." *Re:public*, 2012, 10-19.

Hong, Nathaniel. "Mow 'Em All Down Grandma: The 'Weapon' of Humor in Two Danish World War II Occupation Scrapbooks." *Humor: International Journal of Humor Research* 23, no. 1 (2010): 27-64.

Hutcheon, Linda. Irony's Edge: The Theory and Politics of Irony. London: Routledge, 1995.

ICR Skandinavia. *Verneplikt: Statlig Tvangsarbeid: Et Hefte Fra ICR - Skandinavia* [Conscription: state forced labour: A booklet from ICR - Scandinavia]. Bergen: FMK, 1981.

Independent Institute of Socio-Economic and Political Studies. "Teddy-Bear Landing – How the Belarusians Evaluated It." Independent Institute of Socio-Economic and Political Studies, 2012.

Jacobs, Ronald N., and Philip Smith. "Romance, Irony, and Solidarity." *Sociological Theory* 15, no. 1 (1997): 60-80.

Jasper, James M. The Art of Moral Protest: Culture, Biography, and Creativity in Social Movements. Chicago: University of Chicago Press, 1997.

Jefferess, David. *Postcolonial Resistance: Culture, Liberation and Transformation*. Toronto: University of Toronto Press, 2008.

Jennings, Leonie E., and Anne P. Graham. "Exposing Discourses through Action Research." Chap. 10 In *New Directions in Action Research*, edited by Ortrun Zuber-Skerritt, 165-81. London: Falmer Press, 1996.

Johansen, John. "'Flyktningeleir' I Sverige." ['Refugee camp' in Sweden] *Fredrikstad Blad*, July 8 1983.

Johansen, Jørgen. "Humor as a Political Force, or How to Open the Eyes of Ordinary People in Social Democratic Countries." *Philosophy and Social Action* 17, no. 3-4 (1991): 23-27.

Johansen, Jørgen. "Sak Nr. 55156/83." Letter to Oslo politikammer, November 9 1984.

Johansson, Anna. "Skratt, Humor Och Karnevalistisk Praktik Bland Nicaraguanska Kvinnor: Om Genus, Makt Och Motstånd." Chap. 7 In *Motstånd*, edited by Mona Lilja and Stellan Vinthagen, 197-218. Malmö: Liber, 2009.

Johansson, Anna, and Stellan Vinthagen. "Dimensions of Everyday Resistance: An Analytical Framework." *Critical Sociology* (2014, in press).

Johnsen, Alf Bjarne. "Fengsel for Totalnekter?" [Prision for total resister?] *VG*, March 16 1985.

Jorgensen, Aage. "Touring the 1970's with the Solvognen in Denmark." *The Drama Review: TDR* 26, no. 3 (1982): 15-28.

Jorgensen, Danny L. Participant Observation: A Methodology for Human Studies. London: Sage, 1989.

Justis- og politidepartementet [Department of Justice and Police]. "Ot Prp Nr 35 (1989-1990) Om Lov Om Endringer I Lov 19 Mars 1965 Nr 3 Om Fritaking for Militærtjeneste Av Overbevisningsgrunner Og Militær Straffelov 22 Mai 1902 Nr 13." edited by Justis- og politidepartementet [Department of Justice and Police], 1-10, March 2 1990.

Justis- og politidepartementet [Department of Justice and Police]. "St. Meld. Nr. 70 (1983-84) Om Verneplikt." April 13 1984.

Justiskomiteen. "Innst O. Nr. 75. Innstilling Fra Justiskomiteen Om Lov Om Endringer I Lov 19 Mars 1965 Nr 3 Om Fritaking for Militærtjeneste Av Overbevisningsgrunner Og Militær Straffelov 22 Mai 1902 Nr 13." June 8 1990.

Justiskomiteen. "Innst. S. Nr. 17. Innstilling Fra Justiskomiteen Vedrørende Forslag Fra Stortingsrepresentant Kjellbjørg Lunde Datert 5. August 1986 Om Utvidelse Av Adgangen Til Å Nekte Militærtjeneste På Et Alvorlig Overbevisningsgrunnlag.", October 30 1986.

Justiskomiteen. "Innst. S. Nr. 111. Innstilling Fra Justiskomiteen Om Verneplikt (St. Meld. Nr. 70 for 1983-84)." February 1 1985.

Kanaana, Sharif. "Humor of the Palestinian 'Intifada'." *Journal of Folklore Research* 27 no. 3 (1990): 231-40.

Kanonudvalget. "Julemandshæren [the Santa Claus Army]." Det danske kulturministerium,Accessed June 18 2012 from http://kulturkanon.kum.dk/scenekunst/julemandshaeren/Begrunde lse_Julemandshaeren/.

Katherine van, Wormer, and Mary Boes. "Humor in the Emergency Room: A Social Work Perspective." *Health & Social Work* 22, no. 2 (1997): 87-92.

Kenney, Padraic. *A Carnival of Revolution - Central Europe 1989*. Princeton, NJ: Princeton University Press, 2002.

Kessel, Martina, and Patrick Merziger. *The Politics of Humour: Laughter, Inclusion, and Exclusion in the Twentieth Century*. Toronto: University of Toronto Press, 2012.

Kirby, Sandra L., Lorraine Greaves, and Colleen Reid. *Experience Research Social Change: Methods Beyond the Mainstream*. 2nd ed. Toronto: University of Toronto Press, 2010.

Klandermans, Bert. "The Demand and Supply of Participation: Social-Psycological Correlates of Participation in Social Movements." Chap. 16 In *The Blackwell Companion to Social Movements*, edited by David A. Snow, Sarah Anne Soule and Hanspeter Kriesi, 360-79. Malden, MA: Blackwell Pub., 2004.

Klandermans, Bert, and Suzanne Staggenborg. *Methods of Social Movement Research*. Minneapolis, MN: University of Minnesota Press, 2002.

Klein, Naomi. *No Logo: No Space, No Choice, No Jobs*. London: Flamingo, 2001.

Klepto, Kolonel. "Making War with Love: The Clandestine Insurgent Rebel Clown Army." *City* 8, no. 3 (2004): 403-11.

KMV. Accessed November 3 2012 from http://www.arbeidskollektivet.no/kmv/.

KMV. "Rettsal 8 Sprenges." poster from KMV, September 12 1983.

KMV. "Rundbrev 5." Kampanjen Mot Verneplikt, February 1984.

KMV. "Rundbrev 6." Kampanjen Mot Verneplikt, May 1984.

KMV. "Rundbrev 8." Kampanjen Mot Verneplikt, September 1984.

KMV. "Rundbrev 9." Kampanjen Mot Verneplikt, November 1984.

KMV. "Rundbrev 10." Kampanjen Mot Verneplikt, January 1985.

KMV. "Rundbrev 11." Kampanjen Mot Verneplikt, April 1985.

KMV. "Rundbrev 13." Kampanjen Mot Verneplikt, September 1985.

KMV. "Rundbrev 14." Kampanjen Mot Verneplikt, [Extra] November 1985.

KMV. "Rundbrev 16." Kampanjen Mot Verneplikt, February 1986.

KMV. "Rundbrev 17." Kampanjen Mot Verneplikt, October 1986.

KMV. "Rundbrev 18." Kampanjen Mot Verneplikt, 1987.

KMV. "Rundbrev 19." Kampanjen Mot Verneplikt, June 1987.

KMV. "Rundbrev 27." Kampanjen Mot Verneplikt, November 1988.

KMV. "Rundbrev 30." Kampanjen Mot Verneplikt, February 1990.

KMV. "Utopi Eller Apati: Rundbrev for Kampanjen Mot Verneplikt ", Vinter 1994 Nr. 1 Vinter 1994.

Krause, Adam. *The Revolution Will Be Hilarious*. Porsgrunn, Norway: New Compass Press, 2013.

Kulkarni, Kavita. "Billionaires for Bush: Parody as Political Intervention." Accessed July 21 2012 from http://hemi.nyu.edu/journal/1_1/kulkarni.html.

Kupchinsky, Oleg. "Toys for Democracy: In a Siberian City, Activists Find a Creative Way to Protest " *rferl.org*, January 16 2012. Accessed August 7 2012 from http://www.rferl.org/content/toys_for_democracy_siberia/244536 88.html

Lakey, George. *Powerful Peacemaking: A Strategy for a Living Revolution*. Philadelphia, PA: New Society Publishers, 1987 [1973].

Larsen, Egon. Wit as a Weapon: The Political Joke in History. London: F. Muller, 1980.

Laska, Cattis. "Krigsmotstånd Central Del Av Queer Kamp." [War resistance central part of queer struggle] *etc.se*, August 18 2011. Accessed September 2 2011 from http://www.etc.se/debatt/krigsmotst%C3%A5nd-central-del-av-queer-kamp

Lasn, Kalle. *Culture Jam: The Uncooling of America*. 1st ed. New York: Eagle Brook, 1999.

Letmark, Peter. "Begreppet Queer Skapar Allt Större Oenighet." [The notion queer creates greater disagreements] *dn.se*, July 26 2012. Accessed August 13 2012 from http://www.dn.se/insidan/insidan-hem/begreppet-queer-skapar-allt-storre-oenighet

Letmark, Peter. ""Hela Paraden Blev En Enda Lång Pina"." ["The whole parade became one long torment"] *dn.se*, July 25 2012. Accessed August 13 2012 from http://www.dn.se/insidan/insidan-hem/hela-paraden-blev-en-enda-lang-pina

Lewin, Kurt. "Action Research and Minority Problems." *Journal of Social Issues* 2, no. 4 (1946): 34-46.

Lien Huong, Nghiem. "Jokes in a Garment Workshop in Hanoi: How Does Humour Foster the Perception of Community in Social

Movements?". *International Review of Social History* 52, no. S15 (2007): 209-23.

lip. "Sol(Hverv)Vognen." [Untranslatable wordplay] *Information*, December 24 1974, 1.

Lovdata. "Lov 1965-03-19 Nr 03: Lov Om Fritaking for Militærtjeneste Av Overbevisningsgrunner [Militærnekterloven]." Accessed December 10 2012 from http://lovdata.no/all/hl-19650319-003.html.

Lukes, Steven. *Power: A Radical View*. London: Macmillan, 1974.

Lundberg, Anna. "Queering Laughter in the Stockholm Pride Parade." *International Review of Social History* 52, no. S15 (2007): 169-87.

Löfgren, Emma. "Brittans Damgympa Dansar Mot Främlingsfientligheten." [Brittan's Ladies gym dance against xenophobia] *Dagens Nyheter*, December 8 2011. Accessed December 5 2012 from http://www.dn.se/sthlm/brittans-damgympa-dansar-mot-framlingsfientligheten

Maceri, Domenico. "Dario Fo: Jester of the Working Class." *World Literature Today* 72, no. 1 (1998): 9-15.

MacLeod, Jason. *Civil Resistance in West Papua*. Brisbane: University of Queensland Press, 2015, in press.

MacLeod, Jason. "Civil Resistance in West Papua (Perlawanan Tanpa Kekerasan Di Tanah Papua)." PhD thesis, The University of Queensland, 2012.

Marcuse, Herbert. "Repressive Tolerance." In *A Critique of Pure Tolerance*, edited by Robert Paul Wolff, Barrington Moore and Herbert Marcuse, 95-137. Boston: Beacon Press, 1969.

Martin, Brian. "Gene Sharp's Theory of Power." *Journal of Peace Research* 26, no. 2 (1989): 213-22.

Martin, Brian. *Justice Ignited: The Dynamics of Backfire*. Lanham, MD: Rowman & Littlefield, 2007.

Martin, Brian. "Researching Nonviolent Action: Past Themes and Future Possibilities." *Peace & Change* 30, no. 2 (2005): 247-70.

Martin, Lauren L. "Bombs, Bodies, and Biopolitics: Securitizing the Subject at the Airport Security Checkpoint." *Social & Cultural Geography* 11, no. 1 (2010): 17-34.

Martin, Rod A. *The Psychology of Humor: An Integrative Approach*. Burlington, MA: Elsevier Academic Press, 2007.

Mathiesen, Thomas. Retten I Samfunnet: En Innføring I Rettssosiologi. 6. ed. Oslo: Pax, 2011.

McGuinness, Kate. "Gene Sharp's Theory of Power: A Feminist Critique of Consent." *Journal of Peace Research* 30, no. 1 (1993): 101-15.

McIntyre, Alice. *Participatory Action Research*. Los Angeles: Sage Publications, 2008.

McIntyre, Iain. How to Make Trouble and Influence People: Pranks, Hoaxes, Graffiti & Political Mischief-Making from across Australia. Melbourne: Breakdown Press, 2009.

McTaggart, Robin. "Issues for Participatory Action Researchers." Chap. 13 In *New Directions in Action Research*, edited by Ortrun Zuber-Skerritt, 243-55. London: Falmer Press, 1996.

Mersal, Iman. "Revolutionary Humor." *Globalizations* 8, no. 5 (2011): 669-74.

Merziger, Patrick. "Humour in Nazi Germany: Resistance and Propaganda? The Popular Desire for an All-Embracing Laughter." *International Review of Social History* 52, no. S15 (2007): 275-90.

Meyer, John C. "Humor as a Double-Edged Sword: Four Functions of Humor in Communication." *Communication Theory* 10, no. 3 (2000): 310-31.

Misztal, Bronislaw. "Between the State and Solidarity: One Movement, Two Interpretations - the Orange Alternative Movement in Poland." *British Journal of Sociology* 43, no. 1 (1992): 55-78.

Mulkay, Michael J. On Humour: Its Nature and Its Place in Modern Society. Cambridge: Polity Press, 1988.

Nepstad, Sharon Erickson. *Nonviolent Revolutions: Civil Resistance in the Late 20th Century.* Oxford: Oxford University Press, 2011.

Nepstad, Sharon Erickson. *Religion and War Resistance in the Plowshares Movement.* New York: Cambridge University Press, 2008.

Nepstad, Sharon Erickson, and Christian Smith. "The Social Structure of Moral Outrage in Recruitment to the U.S. Central America Peace Movement." Chap. 9 In *Passionate Politics: Emotions and Social Movements,* edited by Jeff Goodwin, James M. Jasper and Francesca Polletta, 158-74. Chicago: University of Chicago Press, 2001.

Netwerk Vlaanderen. "Demining Action 18/10/2005." 2005.

Netwerk Vlaanderen. "Demining Team Begins Its Work at AXA." Netwerk Vlaanderen Accessed 12 October 2011 from http://www.netwerkvlaanderen.be/en/index.php?option=com_con tent&task=view&id=47&Itemid=268.

Nilsen, Don L. F. "The Social Functions of Political Humor." *Journal of Popular Culture* 24, no. 3 (1990): 35-47.

Nordland, Esther. "Inntok Fengselsmurene." [Occupied the prison walls] *Arbeiderbladet*, August 28 1984.

Norenius, Ulf. "När Fredsaktivisterna Utvisades." [When the peace activists were expelled] *Arbetaren*, August 23 1985.

Notes from Nowhere. We Are Everywhere: The Irresistible Rise of Global Anticapitalism. London: Verso, 2003.

NOU. "Nou 1979: 51 Verneplikt." Oslo: Universitetsforlaget, 1979.

NRK. "Fake Prosecutor in Dagsrevyen." NRK, September 19, 19:00 1983.

NTB. "Norsk Militærnekter Adoptert." [Norwegian conscientious objector adopted] *Arbeiderbladet*, November 25 1987.

Obrdlik, Antonin J. "'Gallows Humor'- a Sociological Phenomenon." *The American Journal of Sociology* 47, no. 5 (1942): 709-16.

Offerdal, Kirsten. "Brann Vernepliktsboka Si I Rettssalen [Burned His Conscription Book in Court]." *Vårt Land*, May 11 1984.

Ofog. "7 Personer Inne På Flygflottilj – Krig Kan Inte Få Förberedas Ostört! Pressmeddelande Från Nätverket Ofog, 29 Juli 2010." Accessed March 6 2012 from http://ofog.org/press/7-personer-inne-p%C3%A5-flygflottilj-%E2%80%93-krig-kan-inte-f%C3%A5-f%C3%B6rberedas-ost%C3%B6rt.

Ofog. "Aktioner." Accessed September 6 2013 from http://ofog.org/avrusta/aktioner.

Ofog. "Brittas Damgympa Mot Neat Har Premiär I Luleå." press release August 25 2012.

Ofog. "Civil Olydnad." Accessed January 10 2012 from http://ofog.org/civil-olydnad.

Ofog. "English." Accessed January 10 2012 from http://ofog.org/english.

Ofog. "Försvarsmakten Rädda För Clownarmén I Göteborg." Accessed July 30 2013 from http://ofog.org/nyheter/forsvarsmakten-radda-for-clownarmen-i-goteborg.

Ofog. "Ofog Visar Försvarsmaktens Verklighet I Prideparaden." Accessed August 7 2011 from http://www.ofog.org/nyheter/ofog-visar-f%C3%B6rsvarsmaktens-verklighet-i-prideparaden.

Ofog. "Ofogs Plattform." Accessed January 2 2012 from http://ofog.org/ofogs-plattform.

Ofog. "Rosa Stridsvagn - Pepp Inför Sommarens Massaktion!" Accessed April 20 2011 from http://ofog.org/pressmeddelanden/rosa-stridsvagn-pepp-infor-sommarens-massaktion.

Ofog. ""Släpp Ut Våra Vänner" – Fredsdemonstration Utanför Luleå Polisstation." Accessed September 12 2013 from http://ofog.org/pressmeddelanden/slapp-ut-vara-vanner-fredsdemonstration-utanfor-lulea-polisstation.

Ofog. "Stadsvandring I Krigsföretagens Och Fredsinitiativens Stockholm." Accessed September 6 2013 from http://ofog.org/nyheter/stadsvandring-i-krigsforetagens-och-fredsinitiativens-stockholm.

Ofog. "Vi Har Vad Som Krävs För Att Ha En Åsikt!" Accessed August 15 2011 from http://ofog.org/nyheter/vi-har-vad-som-kr%C3%A4vs-f%C3%B6r-att-ha-en-%C3%A5sikt

Ofog. "Välkomna På Stödgruppssamtal För Desertörer." Accessed March 6 2012 from http://ofog.org/royal-errors-fredsaktivister-st%C3%B6r-natos-krigs%C3%B6vning.

Olesen, Thomas. "The Funny Side of Globalization: Humour and Humanity in Zapatista Framing." *International Review of Social History* 52, no. S15 (2007): 21-34.

Oring, Elliott. *Engaging Humor*. Urbana, IL: University of Illinois Press, 2003.

Otchet, Amy. "Mark Thomas: Method and Madness of a TV Comic." *The UNESCO Courier*, 1999, 46-50.

Palmer, Jerry. *Taking Humour Seriously*. London: Routledge, 1994.

Pandiri, Ananda M. *A Comprehensive, Annotated Bibliography on Mahatma Gandhi*. Ahmedabad: Navajivan Publishing House, 2002.

Patton, Michael Quinn. *Qualitative Research and Evaluation Methods*. 3 ed. Thousand Oaks, CA: Sage Publications, 2002.

Peacock, Louise. *Serious Play: Modern Clown Performance*. Bristol: Intellect Books, 2009.

Peczak, Mirosław, and Anna Krajewska-Wieczorek. "The Orange Ones, the Street, and the Background." *Performing Arts Journal* 13, no. 2 (1991): 50-55.

Pedersen, Ketil Strebel. "Ise-Mann Må Avtjene Verneplikt I Fengsel?" [Man from Ise must serve conscription in prison?] *Fredrikstad Blad*, April 20 1982.

Persen, Åsne Berre, and Jørgen Johansen. *Den Nødvendige Ulydigheten* [the Necessary Civil Disobedience]. Oslo: FMK, 1998.

Pi-Sunyer, Oriol. "Political Humor in a Dictatorial State: The Case of Spain." *Ethnohistory* 24, no. 2 (1977): 179-90.

Potts, Karen, and Leslie Brown. "Becoming an Anti-Oppressive Researcher." Chap. 10 In *Research as Resistance: Critical, Indigenous and Anti-Oppressive Approaches*, edited by Leslie Brown and Susan Strega, 255-86. Toronto, ON: Canadian Scholars' Press, 2005.

Rasmussen, Nina. *Solvognen: Fortællinger Fra Vores Ungdom* [The Sun Chariot: Tales From our Youth]. Copenhagen: Rosinante, 2002.

Rawls, John. "Definition and Justification of Civil Disobedience." Chap. 6 In *Civil Disobedience in Focus*, edited by Hugo Adam Bedau, 103-21. London: Routledge, 1991.

RFE/RL. "Belarusian 'Toy Protest' Inmate Goes on Hunger Strike " *rferl.org*, February 22 2012. Accessed August 7 2012 from http://www.rferl.org/content/belarusian_activist_jailed_over_toy_protest/24492383.html

RFE/RL. "'Police Detain Stuffed Animals' in Minsk Toy Protest " *rferl.org*, February 10 2012. Accessed August 7, 2012 from http://www.rferl.org/content/belarus_activists_hold_toy_protest/24480210.html

RFSL. "Ockupationen Av Socialstyrelsen 1979 [the Occupation of the the National Board of Health and Welfare 1979]." Accessed March 15 2012 from http://www.rfsl.se/?p=987.

Ricketson, Matthew. "Chaser Ratings Rocket on APEC Antics." *The Age (Melbourne)*, September 13 2007. http://www.theage.com.au/articles/2007/09/13/1189276851780.html

Rimehaug, Erling. "Militærnektersak Til Topps." [Conscientious objector case to the top] *Vårt Land*, June 27 1984.

Roberts, Adam, and Timothy Garton Ash, eds. Civil Resistance and Power Politics: The Experience of Non-Violent Action from Gandhi to the Present. Oxford: Oxford University Press, 2009.

Rodrigues, Suzana B., and David L. Collinson. "'Having Fun'? Humour as Resistance in Brazil." *Organization Studies* 16, no. 5 (1995): 739-68.

Romanienko, Lisiunia A. "Antagonism, Absurdity, and the Avant-Garde: Dismantling Soviet Oppression through the Use of Theatrical Devices by Poland's Solidarity Movement." *International Review of Social History* 52, no. S15 (2007): 133-51.

Romanos, Eduardo. "The Strategic Use of Humor in the Spanish 15m Movement." In *Crisis and Social Mobilization in Contemporary Spain: The 15m Movement*, edited by B. Tejerina and I. Perugorría. Farnham: Ashgate, 2015, in press.

Rose, Alexander. "When Politics Is a Laughing Matter." *Policy Review*, no. January (2002): 59-71.

Rosenbaum, Thane. The Myth of Moral Justice: Why Our Legal System Fails to Do What's Right. 1st ed. New York: HarperCollins, 2004.

Routledge, Paul. "Sensuous Solidarities: Emotion, Politics and Performance in the Clandestine Insurgent Rebel Clown Army." *Antipode* 44, no. 2 (2012): 428-52.

Routledge, Poul. "Toward a Relational Ethics of Struggle: Embodiment, Affinity, and Affect." Chap. 8 In *Contemporary Anarchist Studies: An Introductory Anthology of Anarchy in the Academy*, edited by Randall Amster, Abraham DeLeon, Luis A. Fernandez, Anthony J. Nocella and Deric Shannon, 82-92. New York: Routledge, 2009.

Roy, Carole. "The Irreverent Raging Grannies: Humour as Protest." *Canadian Woman Studies* 25, no. 3/4 (2006): 141-48.

Roy, Carole. The Raging Grannies: Wild Hats, Cheeky Songs, and Witty Actions for a Better World. Montréal: Black Rose Books, 2004.

Roy, Carole. "When Wisdom Speaks Sparks Fly: Raging Grannies Perform Humor as Protest." *Women's Studies Quarterly* 35, no. 3/4 (2007): 150-64.

Rutman, Deb, Carol Hubberstey, April Barlow, and Erinn Brown. "Supporting Young People's Transition from Care: Reflections on Doing Participatory Action Research with Youth from Care." Chap. 6 In *Research as Resistance: Critical, Indigenous and Anti-Oppressive Approaches*, edited by Leslie Brown and Susan Strega, 153-79. Toronto, ON: Canadian Scholars' Press, 2005.

S.I.N. "Samvittighetsfanger I Norge - En Kommentar Til Stortingsmelding 70 - Om Verneplikt [Prisoners of Conscience in Norway - a Comment to Proposition 70 - About Conscription]." November 1984.

Sarpsborg Arbeiderblad. "16 Måneders Fengsel Er Ikke "Straff", Sier Myndighetene." [16 months in prison is not "punishment", says authorities] *Sarpsborg Arbeiderblad*, April 20 1982.

Sarpsborg Arbeiderblad. "Fullsatt Sal Da Rettssaken Mot Jørgen Johansen Tok Til I Dag." [The court was full when the case against Jørgen Johansen started today] *Sarpsborg Arbeiderblad*, April 19 1982.

Sarpsborg Arbeiderblad. "Stor Interesse for Vernepliktsaken: Fullsatt Rettssal Og Mange Viktige Vitner." [Great interest in conscription case: Full court and many important witnesses] *Sarpsborg Arbeiderblad*, April 14 1982.

Sayre, J. "The Use of Aberrant Medical Humor by Psychiatric Unit Staff." *Issues in Mental Health Nursing* 22, no. 7 (2001): 669-89.

Schechner, Richard. The Future of Ritual: Writings on Culture and Performance. London: Routledge, 1993.

Schechter, Joel. *Satiric Impersonations: From Aristophanes to the Guerrilla Girls*. Carbondale, IL: Southern Illinois University Press, 1994.

Schilling, Robert F. "Developing Intervention Research Programs in Social Work." *Social Work Research* 21, no. 3 (1997): 173-80.

Schock, Kurt. "Nonviolent Action and Its Misconceptions: Insights for Social Scientists." *PS: Political Science & Politics* 36, no. 4 (2003): 705-12.

Schock, Kurt. *Unarmed Insurrections: People Power Movements in Nondemocracies*. Minneapolis, MN: University of Minnesota Press, 2005.

Schriver, Kristina, and Donna Marie Nudd. "Mickee Faust Club's Performative Protest Events." *Text and Performance Quarterly* 22, no. 3 (2002): 196-216.

Schulman, Alex. "Och Vad Håller Sveriges Försvarsmakt På Med." [And what is Försvarsmakten doing?] *Aftonbladet*, January 27 2013. Accessed September 11 2013 from http://www.aftonbladet.se/nyheter/kolumnister/alexschulman/article16136491.ab

Schulman, Sarah. "Israel and 'Pinkwashing'." *New York Times*, November 22 2011. Accessed September 12 2013 from http://www.nytimes.com/2011/11/23/opinion/pinkwashing-and-israels-use-of-gays-as-a-messaging-tool.html?_r=3&

Scott, James C. *Domination and the Arts of Resistance: Hidden Transcripts*. New Haven, CT: Yale University Press, 1990.

Scuderi, Antonio. "Unmasking the Holy Jester Dario Fo." *Theatre Journal* 55, no. 2 (2003): 275-90.

Seidman, Steven. "Queer-ing Sociology, Sociologizing Queer Theory: An Introduction." *Sociological Theory* 12, no. 2 (1994): 166-77.

Semelin, Jacques. Unarmed against Hitler: Civilian Resistance in Europe, 1939-1943. Westport, CT: Praeger, 1993.

Sharp, Gene. *The Politics of Nonviolent Action*. Boston: Porter Sargent, 1973.

Sharp, Gene. Sharp's Dictionary of Power and Struggle: Language of Civil Resistance in Conflicts. New York: Oxford University Press, 2012.

Sharp, Gene. Waging Nonviolent Struggle, 20th Century Practice and 21th Century Potential. Boston: Porter Sargent, 2005.

Shepard, Ben. "The Use of Joyfulness as a Community Organizing Strategy." *Peace & Change* 30, no. 4 (2005): 435-68.

Shepard, Benjamin, L.M. Bogad, and Stephen Duncombe. "Performing vs. the Insurmountable: Theatrics, Activism, and Social Movements." *Liminalities: A Journal of Performance Studies* 4, no. 3 (2008): 1-30.

Shepard, Benjamin Heim. Queer Political Performance and Protest: Play, Pleasure and Social Movement. New York: Routledge, 2010.

Simon, Eli. *The Art of Clowning: More Paths to Your Inner Clown*. 2nd ed. New York: Palgrave Macmillan, 2012.

Smith, George W. "Political Activist as Ethnographer." In *Sociology for Changing the World: Social Movements/Social Research*, edited by Caelie Frampton, Gary Kinsman, A.K. Thompson and Kate Tilleczek, 44-69. Black Point: Fernwood, [1990] 2006.

Snow, David A., and Danny Trom. "The Case Study and the Study of Social Movements." In *Methods of Social Movement Research*, edited by Bert Klandermans and Suzanne Staggenborg, 146-72. Minneapolis, MN: University of Minnesota Press, 2002.

Solberg, Øyvind. "Hvem Er Totalnektere." [Who to consider total resisters?] *KMV Rundbrev 16*, February 1986.

Solberg, Øyvind. "Møte Med Sjefen." *Basta* 1 (1990): 12-13.

Solberg, Øyvind. "Sak Nr. 55156/83." Letter to Oslo politikammer, November 5 1984.

Solberg, Øyvind. "Total Objectors." [total objectors] *Samvittighetsfanger i Norge*, not dated 1983.

Solvognen. "Solvognens Julemandshær (Synopsis Og Invitation)." 1974.

Sombutpoonsiri, Janjira. "The Use of Humour as a Vehicle for Nonviolent Struggle: Serbia's 1996-7 Protests and the *Otpor* (Resistance) Movement." PhD Thesis, La Trobe University, 2012.

Somekh, Bridget. *Action Research: A Methodology for Change and Development*. Maidenhead: Open University Press, 2006.

Speier, Hans. "Wit and Politics: An Essay on Power and Laughter." *American Journal of Sociology* 103, no. 5 (1998): 1352-401.

Stortinget. *Spørretime [Question Time]*, 1987-88, November 2 1988.

Stortinget. *Spørretime [Question Time]*, 1986-87, March 11 1987.

Stiehm, Judith. "Nonviolence Is Two." *Sociological Inquiry* 38, no. 1 (1968): 23-29.

Stokker, Kathleen. *Folklore Fights the Nazis: Humor in Occupied Norway, 1940-1945*. Madison, WI: University of Wisconsin Press, 1997.

Stokker, Kathleen. "Quisling Humor in Hitler's Norway: Its Wartime Function and Postwar Legacy." *Humor* 14, no. 4 (2001): 339-57.

Stortinget. "Parliamentary Procedure." Accessed October 9 2013 from http://stortinget.no/en/In-English/About-the-Storting/Parliamentary-procedure/.

Stringer, Ernest T. *Action Research*. 3rd ed. Los Angeles: Sage Publications, 2007.

Strudwick, Ruth M., Stuart J. Mackay, and Stephen Hicks. "Cracking Up?". *Synergy* (2012): 4-7.

Studio Total. "Why We Did It." Accessed August 8 2012 from http://www.studiototal.se/teddybears/why-we-did-it.html.

Sturdee, Nick. "Don't Raise the Bridge: Voina, Russia's Art Terrorists." *The Guardian*, 12 April 2011. Accessed December 17 2011 from http://www.guardian.co.uk/artanddesign/2011/apr/12/voina-art-terrorism?INTCMP=SRCH

"Suomalaiset Brysselissä: 19 Pidätetty, Odottelemme Epätietoisuudessa." *iltalehti.fi*, April 1 2012. Accessed April 2 2012 from http://www.iltalehti.fi/ulkomaat/2012040115400832_ul.shtml

Szego, Julie. "Four Play First Thing in the Morning: That's Some Fan Club." *The Age*, November 2 2007, 8. Accessed June 1 2012 from http://go.galegroup.com/ps/i.do?id=GALE%7CA280757832&v=2.1&u=uow&it=r&p=AONE&sw=w

Sønstelie, Erik H., and Bjørn Aslaksen. "Sett Oss I Fengsel." [Put us in prison] *VG*, June 24 1983, 8.

Sørensen, Majken Jul. "Humor as a Serious Strategy of Nonviolent Resistance to Oppression." *Peace & Change* 33, no. 2 (2008): 167-90.

Sørensen, Majken Jul. "Humorous Political Stunts: Speaking "Truth" to Power?". *European Journal of Humour Research* 1, no. 2 (2013): 69-83.

Sørensen, Majken Jul. "Humour as Nonviolent Resistance to Oppression." MA Thesis, Coventry University, 2006.

Sørensen, Majken Jul. "Swedish Women's Civil Defence Refusal 1935-1956." In *Women Conscientious Objectors - an Anthology*, edited by Ellen Elster and Majken Jul Sørensen, 33-37. London: War Resisters' International, 2010.

Sørensen, Majken Jul, and Brian Martin. "The Dilemma Action: Analysis of an Activist Technique." *Peace & Change* 39 no. 1 (2014): 73-100.

Tang, Lijun, and Syamantak Bhattacharya. "Power and Resistance: A Case Study of Satire on the Internet." *Sociological Research Online* 16, no. 2 (2011).

Taylor, Phil, and Peter Bain. "'Subterranean Worksick Blues': Humour as Subversion in Two Call Centres." *Organization Studies* 24, no. 9 (2003): 1487-509.

Tellesen, Hilary Beth. "Alternative Subterfuge: Pranking Rhetoric in Shopdropping and Identity Correction." MA Thesis, California State University, 2009.

Teune, Simon. "Humour as a Guerrilla Tactic: The West German Student Movement's Mockery of the Establishment." *International Review of Social History* 52, no. SupplementS15 (2007): 115-32.

The Laboratory of Insurrectionary Imagination. "The Laboratory of Insurrectionary Imagination." Accessed August 28 2013 from http://labofii.net/.

The Santas from the theatre group Solvognen. "Solvognen: Derfor Malede Vi Byen I Folkets Farve." [Solvognen: The reason we painted the city in the colour of the people] *B.T.*, December 23 1974.

The Space Hijackers. "The Space Hijackers " Accessed August 28 2013 from http://www.spacehijackers.org/html/history.html.

Thomas, Mark. *As Used on the Famous Nelson Mandela*. London: Ebury, 2007.

Thompson, Nato, Gregory Sholette, Joseph Thompson, Nicholas Mirzoeff, C. Ondine Chavoya, Arjen Noordeman, and Massachusetts Museum of Contemporary Art. *The Interventionists: Users' Manual for the Creative Disruption of Everyday Life*. North Adams, MA: MASS MoCA, 2004.

Thorne, Barrie. "Political Activist as Participant Observer: Conflicts of Commitment in a Study of the Draft Resistance Movement of the 1960's." *Symbolic Interaction* 2, no. 1 (1979): 73-88.

Tilly, Charles. *Popular Contention in Great Britain, 1758-1834*. Cambridge, MA: Harvard University Press, 1995.

Tsakona, Villy, and Diana Elena Popa. "Humour in Politics and the Politics of Humour: An Introduction." In *Studies in Political Humour: In between Political Critique and Public Entertainment*, edited by Villy Tsakona and Diana Elena Popa, 1-30. Amsterdam: John Benjamins, 2011.

Tsakona, Villy, and Diana Elena Popa. Studies in Political Humour: In between Political Critique and Public Entertainment. Amsterdam: John Benjamins, 2011.

Tucker, Kenneth H. Workers of the World, Enjoy! Aesthetic Politics from Revolutionary Syndicalism to the Global Justice Movement. Philadelphia, PA: Temple University Press, 2010.

Vacarro, Jeanne. "Give Me an F: Radical Cheerleading and Feminist Performance." Accessed July 21 2012 from http://hemi.nyu.edu/journal/1_1/cheerleaders.html.

Webb, Graham. "Becoming Critical of Action Research for Development." Chap. 9 In *New Directions in Action Research*, edited by Ortrun Zuber-Skerritt, 137-61. London: Falmer Press, 1996.

Weber, Thomas. "'The Marchers Simply Walked Forward until Struck Down': Nonviolent Suffering and Conversion." *Peace & Change* 18, no. 3 (1993): 267-89.

Weiskopf, Richard, and Stephan Laske. "Emancipatory Action Research: A Critical Alternative to Personnel Development or a New

Way of Patronising People." Chap. 8 In *New Directions in Action Research*, edited by Ortrun Zuber-Skerritt, 121-36. London: Falmer Press, 1996.

Weitz, Eric. "Failure as Success: On Clowns and Laughing Bodies." *Performance Research* 17, no. 1 (2012): 79-87.

Wettergren, Åsa. "Fun and Laughter: Culture Jamming and the Emotional Regime of Late Capitalism." *Social Movement Studies* 8, no. 1 (2009): 1-0.

Vinthagen, Stellan. *Ickevåldsaktion: En Social Praktik Av Motstånd Och Konstruktion* [Nonviolent Action: A Social Practice of Resistance and Construction]. Göteborg: Institutionen för freds- och utvecklingsforskning (PADRIGU) Göteborgs universitet, 2005. PhD thesis.

Vinthagen, Stellan. *A Theory of Nonviolent Action: How Civil Resistance Works*. London: ZED Books, 2014, in press.

Vos, Pieter De. *The Ace-Bank Hoax*. 2006. Accessed June 4 2012 from http://vimeo.com/10899863

Wright, John. Why Is That So Funny? A Practical Exploration of Physical Comedy. London: Nick Hern Books, 2006.

Wright, Steve. Home Sweet Home: Banksy's Bristol: The Unofficial Guide. Bristol: Tangent, 2009.

Zelizer, Craig. "Laughing Our Way to Peace or War: Humour and Peacebuilding." *Journal of Conflictology* 1, no. 2 (2010).

Zijderveld, Anton C. Reality in a Looking-Glass: Rationality through an Analysis of Traditional Folly. London: Routledge & Kegan Paul, 1982.

Zuber-Skerritt, Ortrun. "Emanicipatory Action Research for Organisational Change and Management Development." Chap. 6 In *New Directions in Action Research*, edited by Ortrun Zuber-Skerritt, 83-105. London: Falmer Press, 1996.

Zuber-Skerritt, Ortrun. *New Directions in Action Research.* London: Falmer Press, 1996.

Zunes, Stephen, Lester R. Kurtz, and Sarah Beth Asher. *Nonviolent Social Movements: A Geographical Perspective.* Malden, MA: Blackwell, 1999.